KB055007

주한미군지위협정(SOFA)

재무 · 상무 · 교통 분과위원회 2

주한미군지위협정(SOFA)

재무 · 상무 · 교통 분과위원회 2

한국학술정보

| 머리말

미국은 오래전부터 우리나라 외교에 있어서 가장 긴밀하고 실질적인 우호 · 협력관계를 맺어 온 나라다. 6 · 25전쟁 정전 협정이 체결된 후 북한의 재침을 막기 위한 대책으로서 1953년 11월 한미 상호방위조약이 체결되었다. 이는 미군이 한국에 주둔하는 법적 근거였고, 그렇게 주둔하게 된 미군의 시설, 구역, 사업, 용역, 출입국, 통관과 관세, 재판권 등 포괄적인 법적 지위를 규정하는 것이 바로 주한미군지위협정(SOFA)이다. 그러나 이와 관련한 협상은 계속된 난항을 겪으며 한미 상호방위조약이 체결로부터 10년이 훌쩍 넘은 1967년이 돼서야 정식 발효에 이를 수 있었다. 그럼에도 당시 미군 범죄에 대한 한국의 재판권은 심한 제약을 받았으며, 1980년대 후반 민주화 운동과 함께 미군 범죄 문제가 사회적 이슈로 떠오르자 협정을 개정해야 한다는 목소리가 커지게 되었다. 이에 1991년 2월 주한미군지위협정 1차 개정이 진행되었고, 이후에도 여러 사건이 발생하며 2001년 4월 2차 개정이 진행되어 현재에 이르고 있다.

본 총서는 외교부에서 작성하여 최근 공개한 주한미군지위협정(SOFA) 관련 자료를 담고 있다. 1953년 한미 상호방위조약 체결 이후부터 1967년 발효가 이뤄지기까지의 자료와 더불어, 이후 한미 합동위원회을 비롯해 민 · 형사재판권, 시설, 노무, 교통 등 각 분과위원회의 회의록과 운영 자료, 한국인 고용인 문제와 관련한 자료, 기타 관련 분쟁 자료 등을 포함해 총 42권으로 구성되었다. 전체 분량은 약 2만 2천여 쪽에 이른다.

2024년 3월

한국학술정보(주)

| 일러두기

· 본 총서에 실린 자료는 2022년 4월과 2023년 4월에 각각 공개한 외교문서 4,827권, 76만 여 쪽 가운데 일부를 발췌한 것이다.

· 각 권의 제목과 순서는 공개된 원본을 최대한 반영하였으나, 주제에 따라 일부는 적절히 변경하였다.

· 원본 자료는 A4 판형에 맞게 축소하거나 원본 비율을 유지한 채 A4 페이지 안에 삽입하였다. 또한 현재 시점에선 공개되지 않아 '공란'이란 표기만 있는 페이지 역시 그대로 실었다.

· 외교부가 공개한 문서 각 권의 첫 페이지에는 '정리 보존 문서 목록'이란 이름으로 기록물 종류, 일자, 명칭, 간단한 내용 등의 정보가 수록되어 있으며, 이를 기준으로 0001번부터 번호가 매겨져 있다. 이는 삭제하지 않고 총서에 그대로 수록하였다.

· 보고서 내용에 관한 더 자세한 정보가 필요하다면, 외교부가 온라인상에 제공하는 『대한민국 외교사료요약집』 1991년과 1992년 자료를 참조할 수 있다.

| 차례

정/리/보/존/문/서/목/록					
기록물종류	문서-일반공문서철	등록번호	17776	등록일자	2001-06-12
분류번호	729.415	국가코드		주제	
문서철명	SOFA 한·미국 합동위원회 재무분과위원회, 1982				
생산과	안보과	생산년도	1982 - 1982	보존기간	영구
담당과(그룹)	미주	안보	서가번호	--	
참조분류					
권차명					
내용목차					

마/이/크/로/필/름/사/항				
촬영연도	*롤 번호	화일 번호	후레임 번호	보관함 번호

재　　　　무　　　　부

관협 1272 -89　　　　(720-3227)　　　　1982. 2. 19

수신 외무부장관

참조 미주국장

제목 SOFA 재무분과위원회 위원 변경 통보

SOFA 재무분과위원회 한국측 위원 간사인 당부 관세국 관세협력과장이 인사발령으로 '82. 2. 9 일자로 다음과 같이 변경 되었음을 통보합니다.

다　　　음

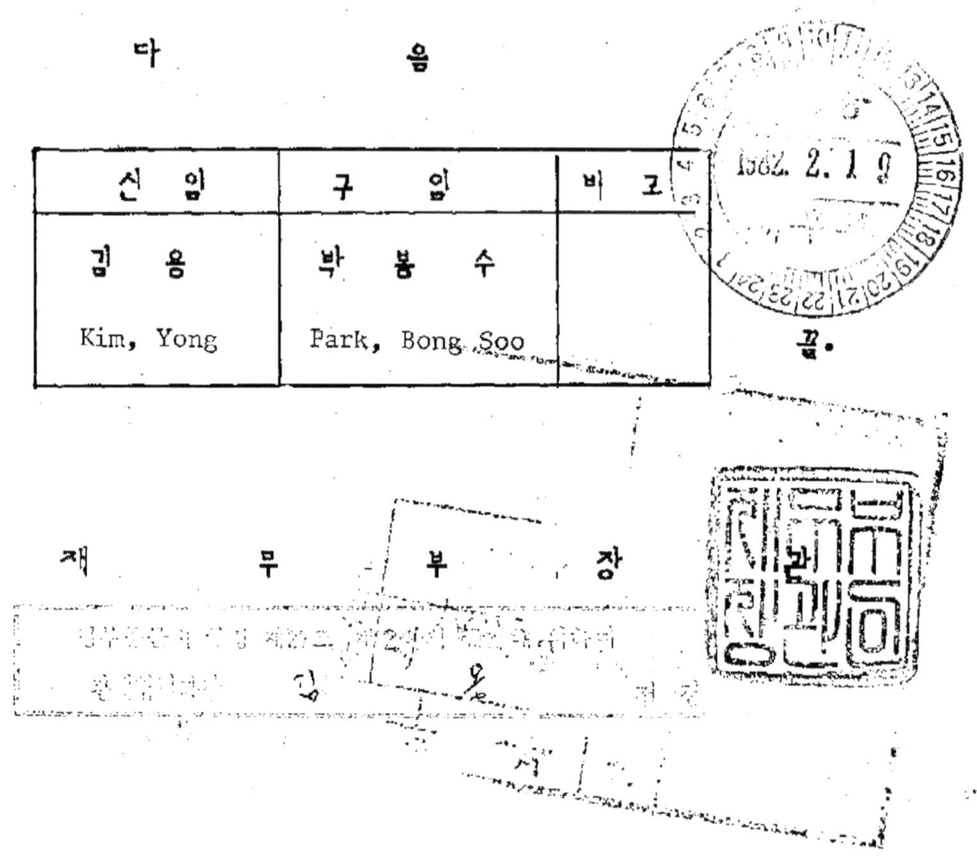

신　임	구　임	비　고
김　용 Kim, Yong	박　봉　수 Park, Bong Soo	

끝.

재　　　무　　　부　　　장

2

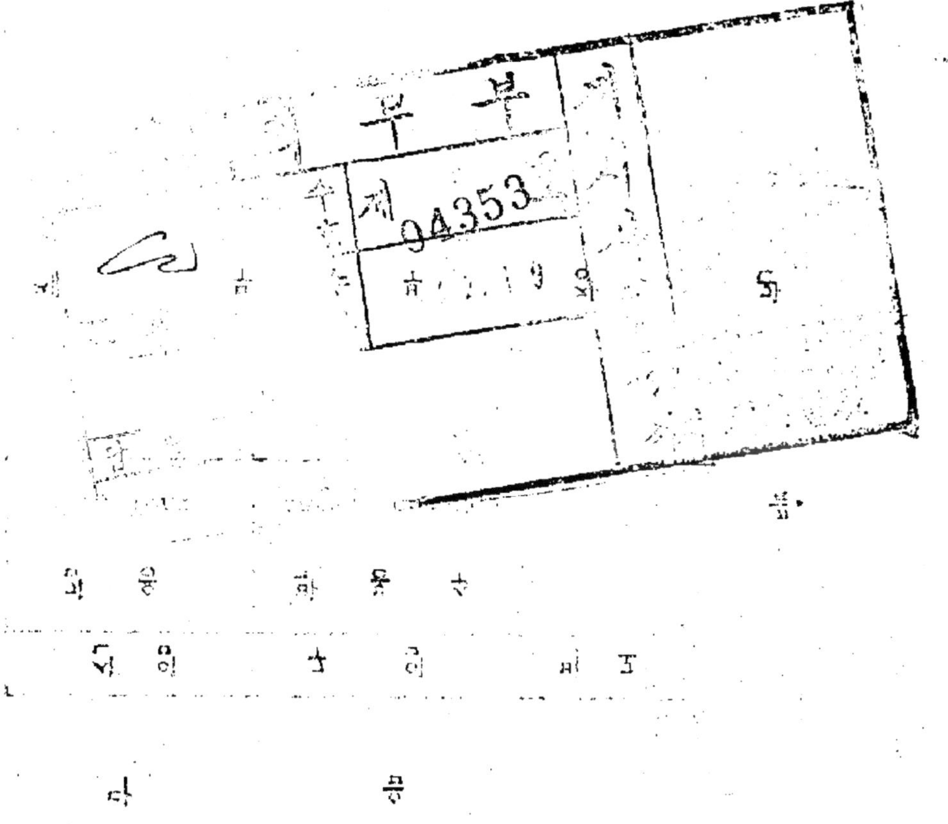

재 무 부

외무부 접수 제 04353호 일시 82.2.19

[illegible]

문번 1072 - (720-3387) 1982. 2. 19

수신 외무부장관

참조 미주국장

제목 재무분과위원회 위원 변경 통보

재무분과위원회 한국측 위원 [illegible]
과장이 인사발령으로 '82. 2. 9 일자로 아래와 같이 변경 되었음을 통보합니다.

다 음

[illegible]	[illegible]	[illegible]	비 고
[illegible]	[illegible]	[illegible]	

재 무 부

3

메 모

19 . . .

전 화

SOFA 재무분과위원회소집
(참조 : 67년도 SOFA JC 8次회의)

1. 일일 : 2. 26
(※ 2.18 아측 재무위 간사는
Fedale 미측 합동위 고체간사와
면담 후, 합동회의소집에 합의)

2. 참석범위 : 양측 실무자

3. 토의 안건 :

1. 미군 이사화물의통관절차개선 :
(GBL中 個人用品에 대해서는 개장
검사 : 아측주장, SOFA 9조 3항근거)

2. APO 화물검사 : 현재는 10% 표본검사만 함.
(대형 X-Ray 를통한 검사로 이를
미측에통보함으로써 미측이 부정유출을
방지하도록 합참의 의견을 ...)

0202—1—35(2—1) A
1972. 3. 20. 승인

134 mm×190 mm(신문용지)
(조 달 청)(600,000매 인쇄)

4

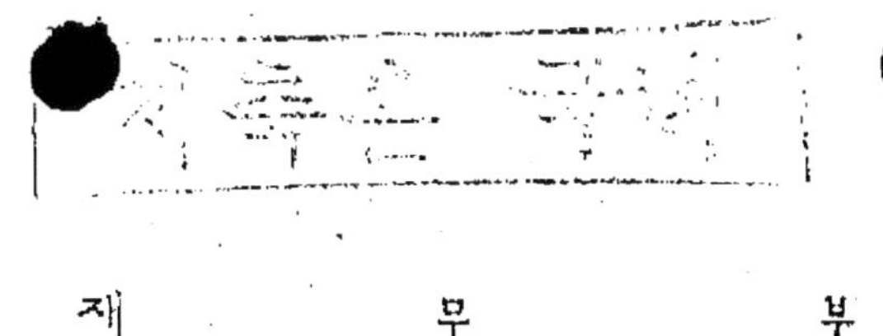

재 무 부

관협 1272 -513 (720-3227) 1982. 6. 30

수신 수신처 참조

제목 SOFA 재무분과위원회 회의 개최

1. SOFA 협정 제9조에 대한 합의양해 사항 제1-4호에서 규정한 미군사 우체국을 통한 우편 소포에 대한 한국세관검사 절차를 개정하기 위하여 다음과 같이 재무분과 위원회를 개최코자 하오니 참석 바랍니다.

다 음

가. 일 시 : 1982. 7. 9 (금) 14:30

나. 장 소 : 관세청 회의실 (7층)

다. 참석범위 : 한.미 재무분과위 관계관

라. 토의 의제 : 미군사 우체국 경로를 통하여 한국에 우송되는 비공용 소화물의 검사비율 확대 "끝".

- 위원변경(미측)
- 학동(강남구청주변)

재 무 부 장 관

수신처 : 외무부장관 (미주국장), 상공부장관 (통상진흥국장), 관세청장(직세국장, 관세국장)

5

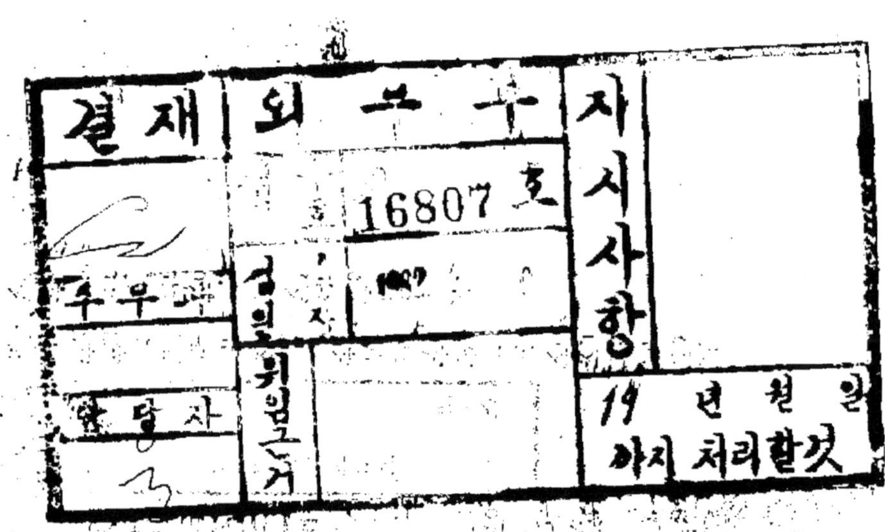

6

재 무 부

관협 1272 - 415 (720-3227) 1982. 7. 6

수신 수신처 참조

제목 SOFA 재무분과위원회 회의개최 연기

1. 관협 1272 - 394 ('82. 6. 30)와 관련입니다.

2. 미군측의 재무분과위 위원장 교체등의 사정으로 인하여 표제 회의를 '82. 7. 30 (금) 14:30 으로 연기 개최할 예정이니 착오 없길 바랍니다. "끝"

재 무 부 장 관

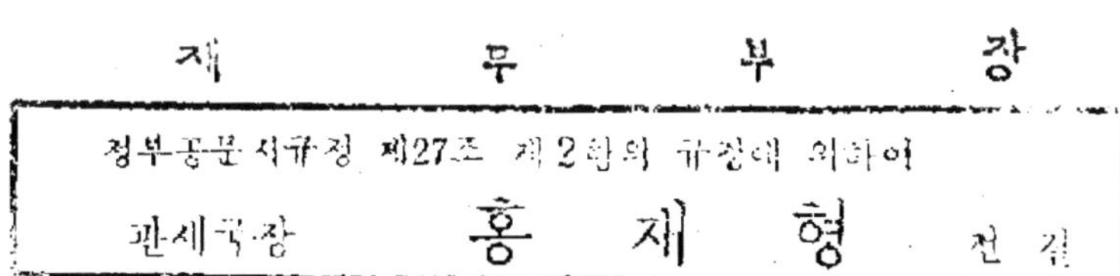

정부공문서규정 제27조 제2항의 규정에 의하여

관세국장 홍 재 형 전결

수신처 : 외무부장관 (미주국장), 상공부장관 (통상진흥국장), 관세청 (지도국장), 국세청 (직세국장, 관세국장)

7

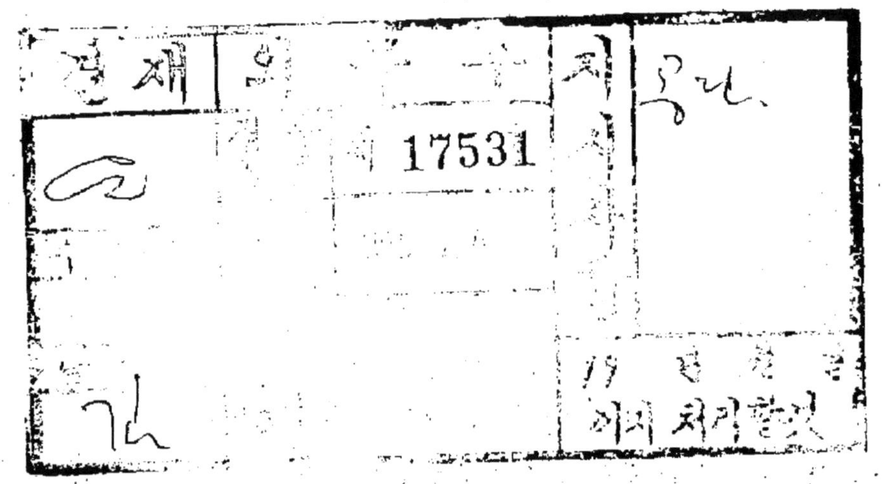

8

JOINT COMMITTEE
UNDER
THE REPUBLIC OF KOREA AND THE UNITED STATES
STATUS OF FORCES AGREEMENT

2 August 1982

Dear Director KWON:

In June of this year, the National Tax Administration informed the AFRC Duty Free Shop concessionaire at the Naija Hotel, Dae Lim Industrial Co., that their application for Value Added Tax and Special Excise Tax exemption had been denied, and that Dae Lim owes the ROKG approximately 60 million won for past taxes. This denial may have been based on a misunderstanding by the tax authorities that the concessionaire was acting as an independent businessman dealing directly with USFK personnel.

The Naija Hotel Armed Forces Recreation Center, a Non-appropriated Fund Instrumentality, established a duty-free shop in order to provide a service to SOFA personnel and US Forces personnel visiting Korea. The duty-free shop provides a convenient outlet where those US Forces personnel who are authorized NAFI privileges under Article XIII of the SOFA can purchase electronic items of Korean manufacture at a substantial savings. Such an outlet is beneficial to both the US Forces and the ROK economy, and is similar to other duty-free stores in Korea.

I respectfully request your assistance in this matter. We would greatly appreciate it if Dae Lim were relieved of liability for the Value Added and Special Excise Taxes on the sales made to US Forces personnel authorized duty-free privileges.

Sincerely,

CARROLL B. HODGES
United States SOFA Secretary

Mr KWON Soon Tae
Republic of Korea SOFA Secretary
Security Division, American Affairs Bureau
Ministry of Foreign Affairs, Seoul, Korea

9

통화 : 82. 8. 7. 재무부 국제조사과 임
사무관(720-3233) 및 간접세과
(720-3222)

* 세금의 종류

직접세 ...소득세, 상속세, 자산재평가세 ...

간접세 ...부가가치세, 특별소비세, 인지세, 주세 ...
(77.7.1부터시행)

목적세 ...~~(77.7.1. 부터 시행)~~ 방위세, 주민세 ...

* o SOFA 제 16조 제 3항의 조세는 대부분 부가가치세로 통합되었으며 일부는 특별소비세로도 적용됨. (부가세 및 특별세 부칙에)

* o 외국인 전용판매장에서 물품을 판매하며, 16개 면세 물품~~품목~~에 해당하는 경우, 면세가능 (특소세법 시행령 제 27조)

* o 부가세법상 영세율 적용 (부가세법 시행령 제 26조 제 1항 제1호~제 6호 해당자)

– 제 6호에 의하면 주한 국제연합군 또는 미군지역내의 사업자로서 소관세무서장이 지정하는 자가 국내에서 공급하는 재화 또는 용역으로서 그 대가를 외화로 받고 그 외화를 외국환은행 또는 금융기관인 환전상에서 환전하는 경우, 영세율 적용됨.

10

追錄回數	內容現在			加除整理			整理者印	追錄回數	內容現在			加除整理			整理者印
第 91 回	年	月	日	年	月	日		第 107 回	年	月	日	年	月	日	
第 92 回	年	月	日	年	月	日		第 108 回	年	月	日	年	月	日	
第 93 回	年	月	日	年	月	日		第 109 回	年	月	日	年	月	日	
第 94 回	年	月	日	年	月	日		第 110 回	年	月	日	年	月	日	
第 95 回	年	月	日	年	月	日		第 111 回	年	月	日	年	月	日	
第 96 回	年	月	日	年	月	日		第 112 回	年	月	日	年	月	日	
第 97 回	年	月	日	年	月	日		第 113 回	年	月	日	年	月	日	
第 98 回	年	月	日	年	月	日		第 114 回	年	月	日	年	月	日	
第 99 回	年	月	日	年	月	日		第 115 回	年	月	日	年	月	日	
第 100 回	年	月	日	年	月	日		第 116 回	年	月	日	年	月	日	
第 101 回	年	月	日	年	月	日		第 117 回	年	月	日	年	月	日	
第 102 回	年	月	日	年	月	日		第 118 回	年	月	日	年	月	日	
第 103 回	年	月	日	年	月	日		第 119 回	年	月	日	年	月	日	
第 104 回	年	月	日	年	月	日		第 120 回	年	月	日	年	月	日	
第 105 回	年	月	日	年	月	日		第 121 回	年	月	日	年	月	日	
第 106 回	年	月	日	年	月	日		第 122 回	年	月	日	年	月	日	

第9巻 目 次

第11編 內國稅

第1章 行政組織・通則

第2章 租稅通則

11

第3章 直接稅

第4章 間接稅

第5章 租稅犯團束

(추 68)

第5章 租稅犯團束

〔별지 제2호서식〕

재 산 재 평 가 대 장

주 소						
법인 또는 상호						
대 표 자 성 명						
재산의 종 류	신 고 액			부인결정증감액		비 고
	재평가액	장부가액	재 평 가 차 액	재 평 가 액	재평가 차 액	

명 세								
재산의소재지	재 산 종 류	수량	신 고 액			부인결정증 감 액		비고
			재평 가액	장부 가액	재평가 차 액	재평 가액	재평가 차 액	

〔별지 제3호서식〕

재 평 가 세 연 부 연 납 대 장

주 소				
법인 또는 상호				
대 표 자 성 명				
납 부 한 재 평		신 고 년월일	년 월 일	
가 세 의 총 액	원	결 정 년월일	년 월 일	
구 분		세 액	납 부 기 한	납부 년 월 일
재평가세의 납부명세	제 1 회(액년)			
	제 2 회(2년)			
	조 상 징 수			
	합 계			

(주 34)

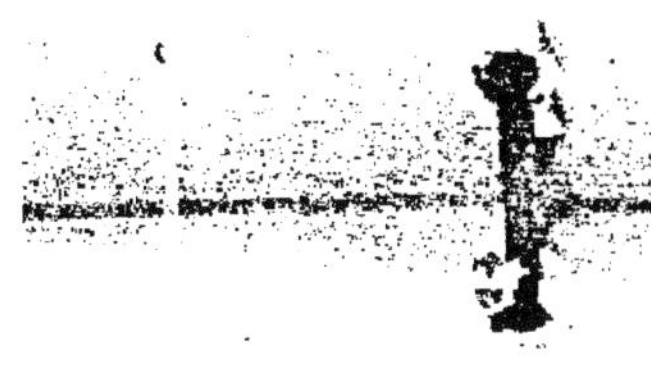

(주 57)

第4章 間接稅

●附加價値稅法 〔1976・12・22 法律第2934號〕

改正 1977・12・19 法律第3016號
1978・12・ 5 法律第3100號
1980・12・13 法律第3273號

第1章 總 則

第1條 (課稅對象) ①附加價値稅는 다음 各號의 去來에 對하여 賦課한다.

1. 財貨 또는 用役의 供給
2. 財貨의 輸入

②第1項에서 財貨라 함은 財産的 價値가 있는 모든 有體物과 無體物을 말한다.

③第1項에서 用役이라 함은 財貨이외의 財産的 價値가 있는 모든 役務 및 기타 行爲를 말한다.

④主된 去來인 財貨의 供給에 必須的으로 附隨되는 財貨 또는 用役의 供給은 主된 去來인 財貨의 供給에 포함되고 主된 去來인 用役의 供給에 必須的으로 附隨되는 財貨 또는 用役의 供給은 主된 去來인 用役의 供給에 포함되는 것으로 본다.

⑤第1項의 財貨와 用役의 범위에 관하여 필요한 事項은 大統領令으로 정한다.

第2條 (納稅義務者) ①營利目的의 有無에 불구하고 事業上 獨立的으로 財貨(第1條에 規定하는 財貨를 말한다. 이하 같다.) 또는 用役(第1條에 規定하는 用役을 말한다. 이하 같다)을 供給하는 者(이하 "事業者"라 한다)는 이 法에 의하여 附加價値稅를 納付할 義務가 있다.

②第1項의 規定에 의한 納稅義務者에는 個人・法人(國家・地方自治團體와 地方自治團體組合을 포함한다)과 法人格없는 社團・財團 기타 團體를 포함한다.

第3條 (課稅期間) ①事業者에 대한 附加價値稅의 課稅期間은 다음과 같다.

第1期 : 1月 1日부터 6月 30日까지

第2期 : 7月 1日부터 12月 31日까지

②新規로 事業을 開始하는 者에 대한 最初의 課稅期間은 事業開始日부터 그 날이 속하는 課稅期間의 終了日까지로 한다. 다만, 第5條第1項 但書의 規定에 의하여 登錄한 경우에는 그 登錄日로부터 그 날이 속하는 課稅期間의 終了日까지로 한다.

③事業者가 廢業하는 경우의 課稅期間은 廢業日이 속하는 課稅期間의 開始日로부터 廢業日까지로 한다. 다만, 第5條第1項但

書의 規定에 의하여 登錄한 후 事業을 開始하지 아니하게 되는 때에는 事實上 그 事業을 開始하지 아니하게 되는 날까지로 한다.

第4條 (納稅地) ①附加價値稅는 事業場마다 納付하여야 한다.

②事業者에게 2이상의 事業場이 있는 경우에는 大統領令이 定하는 바에 의하여 主된 事業場에서 總括하여 納付할 수 있다.

③第2項의 規定에 의하여 主된 事業場에서 總括하여 納付하고자하는 者는 大統領令이 定하는 바에 의하여 政府에 申請하여 그 承認을 얻어야 한다.

④第1項의 事業場의 범위는 大統領令으로 정한다.

第5條 (登錄) ①新規로 事業을 開始하는 者는 事業場마다 大統領令이 정하는 바에 의하여 事業開始日부터 20日내에 政府에 登錄하여야 한다. 다만, 新規로 事業을 開始하고자 하는 者는 事業開始日전이라도 登錄할 수 있다.

②政府는 第1項의 規定에 의하여 登錄한 事業者에게 大統領令이 정하는 바에 의하여 登錄番號가 賦與된 登錄證(이하 "事業者登錄證"이라 한다)을 交付하여야 한다.

③事業者登錄證은 大統領令이 정하는 바에 의하여 每年 1月1日부터 1月31日까지와 7月1日부터 7月31日까지 政府에 申請하여 그 檢閱을 받아야 한다.

④第1項의 規定에 의하여 登錄한 事業者가 休業 또는 廢業하거나 기타 登錄事項에 變動이 발생한 때에는 大統領令이 정하는 바에 의하여 지체없이 政府에 申告하여야 한다. 第1項但書의 規定에 의하여 登錄한 者가 事實上 事業을 開始하지 아니하게 되는 때에도 또한 같다.

⑤事業者가 廢業하거나 第1項 但書의 規定에 의하여 登錄한 후 事實上 事業을 開始하지 아니하게 되는 때에는 政府는 지체없이 그 登錄을 抹消하여야 한다.

⑥政府는 필요하다고 인정하는 때에는 大統領令이 정하는 바에 의하여 事業者登錄證을 更新交付할 수 있다.

第2章 課稅去來

第6條 (財貨의 供給) ①財貨의 供給은 契約上 또는 法律上의 모든 原因에 의하여 財貨를 引渡 또는 讓渡하는 것으로 한다.

②事業者가 자기의 事業과 관련하여 生産하거나 取得한 財貨를 자기의 事業을 위하여 직접사용·消費하는 경우에 大統領令이 정하는 것은 財貨의 供給으로 본다.〈改正 77·12·19 法3016〉

③事業者가 자기의 事業과 관련하여 生産하거나 取扱한 財貨를

第12條 (免稅) ①다음 各號의 財貨 또는 用役의 供給에 대하여는 附加價値稅를 免除한다.〈改正 80·12·13 法3273〉

1. 加工되지 아니한 食料品(食用에 供하는 農産物·畜産物·水産物과 林産物을 포함한다) 및 우리나라에서 生産된 食用에 供하지 아니하는 農産物·畜産物·水産物과 林産物로서 大統領令이 정하는 것.
2. 수도물
3. 煉炭과 無煙炭
4. 醫療保健用役(獸醫師의 用役을 포함한다)으로서 大統領令이 정하는 것과 血液
5. 敎育用役으로서 大統領令이 정하는 것.
6. 旅客運送用役. 다만, 航空機·高速버스·傳貰버스·택시·特殊自動車 또는 特種船舶에 의한 旅客運送用役으로서 大統領令이 정하는 것은 제외한다.
7. 圖書·新聞·雜誌·官報·通信 및 放送으로서 大統領令이 정하는 것. 다만, 廣告는 제외한다.
8. 郵票(蒐集用 郵票를 제외한다)·印紙·證紙·福券과 公衆電話
9. 專賣品
10. 金融·保險用役으로서 大統領令이 정하는 것.
11. 住宅과 이에 附隨되는 土地의 賃貸用役으로서 大統領令이 정하는 것.
12. 土地
13. 辯護士·公認會計士·稅務士·關稅士 기타 大統領令이 정하는 者가 職業上 제공하는 人的用役
14. 藝術創作品·純粹藝術行事·文化行事와 非職業運動競技로서 大統領令이 정하는 것.
15. 圖書館·科學館·博物館·美術館·動物園 또는 植物園에의 入場
16. 宗敎·慈善·學術·救護 기타 公益을 目的으로 하는 團體가 供給하는 財貨 또는 用役으로서 大統領令이 정하는 것
17. 國家·地方自治團體·地方自治團體組合 또는 大統領令이 정하는 政府業務를 代行하는 團體가 供給하는 財貨 또는 用役
18. 國家·地方自治團體·地方自治團體組合 또는 大統領令이 정하는 公益團體에 無償으로 供給하는 財貨 또는 用役

②다음 各號의 財貨의 輸入에 대하여는 附加價値稅를 免除한다.〈改正 80·12·13 法3273〉

1. 加工되지 아니한 食料品(食用에 供하는 農産物·畜産物·水産物과 林産物을 포함한다)으로서 大統領令이 정하는 것
2. 圖書·新聞 및 雜誌로서 大統領令이 정하는 것.
3. 學術研究團體·敎育機關 또는 文化團體가 科學·敎育·文化用으로 輸入하는 財貨로서 大統領令이 정하는 것.
4. 宗敎儀式·慈善·救護 기타 公益을 目的으로 外國으로부터 宗敎團體·慈善團體 또는 救護團體에 寄贈되는 財貨로서 大統領令이 정하는 것.

5. 外國으로부터 國家·地方自治團[illegible]는 地方自治團體組合에 寄贈되는 財貨

6. 居住者에게 寄贈되는 少額物品으로서 寄贈받는 者가 직접 사용할 것으로 인정되어 關稅가 免除되는 財貨

7. 移住·移民 또는 相續으로 인하여 輸入하는 財貨

8. 旅行者携帶品·別送品과 郵送品으로서 關稅가 免除되거나 그 簡易稅率이 適用되는 財貨

9. 輸入하는 商品見本과 廣告用物品으로서 關稅가 免除되는 財貨

10. 우리나라에서 開催되는 博覽會·展示會·品評會·映畵祭 또는 이와 類似한 行事에 出品하기 위하여 無償으로 輸入하는 物品으로서 關稅가 免除되는 財貨

11. 條約·國際法規 또는 國際慣習에 의하여 關稅가 免除되는 財貨로서 大統領令이 정하는 것

12. 輸出된 후 다시 輸入하는 財貨로서 關稅가 減免되는 것중 大統領令이 정하는 것. 다만, 輕減의 경우에는 輕減되는 分에 限한다.

13. 다시 輸出하는 條件으로 一時 輸入하는 財貨로서 關稅가 減免되는 것중 大統領令이 정하는 것. 다만, 輕減의 경우에는 輕減되는 分에 限한다.

14. 第6號 및 第8號 내지 第13號이외에 關稅가 無稅이거나 減免되는 財貨로서 大[illegible]令이 정하는 것. 다만, 輕減의 경우에는 輕減되는 分에 限한다.

③第1項의 規定에 의하여 免稅되는 財貨 또는 用役의 供給에 必須的으로 附隨되는 財貨 또는 用役의 供給은 免稅되는 財貨 또는 用役의 供給에 포함되는 것으로 본다.

④事業者는 第1項의 規定에 의하여 附加價値稅가 免除되는 財貨 또는 用役의 供給으로서 第11條의 規定에 의하여 零稅率適用의 대상이 되는 것과 第1項第11號·第13號 및 第16號의 財貨 또는 用役의 供給에 대하여는 大統領令이 정하는 바에 의하여 附加價値稅의 免除를 받지 아니할 수 있다. <改正 77·12·16 法3016>

⑤第1項과 第2項에서 規定하는 財貨 또는 用役의 범위에 관하여 필요한 事項은 大統領令으로 정한다.

第4章 課稅標準과 稅額

第13條 (課稅標準) ①財貨 또는 用役의 供給에 대한 附加價値稅의 課稅標準은 다음 各號의 價額의 合計額(이하 "供給價額"이라 한다)으로 한다. 다만, 附加價値稅는 포함하지 아니한다.

1. 金錢으로 對價를 받는 경우에는 그 對價

2. 金錢이외의 對價를 받는 경우에는 자기가 供給한 財貨 또는 用役의 時價

(추 57)

(추 39)

3. 부당하게 낮은 對價를 받거나 對價를 받지 아니하는 경우에는 자기가 供給한 財貨 또는 用役의 時價

4. 廢業하는 경우의 在庫財貨에 대하여는 時價

②다음 各號의 金額은 課稅標準에 포함하지 아니한다.

1. 에누리액

2. 還入된 財貨의 價額

3. 供給받는 者에게 到達하기 전에 破損·毁損 또는 滅失된 財貨의 價額

4. 國庫補助金과 公共補助金

③財貨 또는 用役을 供給한 후의 그 供給價額에 대한 割引額·貸損金·奬勵金과 이와 類似한 金額은 課稅標準에서 控除하지 아니한다.

④財貨의 輸入에 대한 附加價値稅의 課稅標準은 關稅의 課稅價格과 關稅·特別消費稅 및 酒稅의 合計額으로 한다.

⑤第1項 내지 第4項이외에 課稅標準의 計算에 관하여 필요한 사항은 大統領令으로 정한다.

第14條 (稅率) ①附加價値稅의 稅率은 100분의 13으로 한다.

②第1項의 稅率은 그 稅率에 100分의 3을 加減한 범위안에서 大統領令으로 調整할 수 있다.

③削除 <78·12·5 法3100>

第15條 (去來徵收) 事業者가 財貨 또는 用役을 供給하는 때에는 第13條의 規定에 의한 課稅標準에 第14條의 規定에 의한 稅率을 適用하여 計算한 附加價値稅를 그 供給을 받는 者로부터 徵收하여야 한다.

第16條 (稅金計算書) ①納稅義務者로 登錄한 事業者가 財貨 또는 用役을 供給하는 때에는 第9條第1項 및 第2項에 規定하는 時期에 다음 各號의 事項을 記載한 計算書(이하 "稅金計算書"라 한다)를 大統領令이 정하는 바에 의하여 供給을 받은 者에게 交付하여야 한다.

1. 供給하는 事業者의 登錄番號와 姓名 또는 名稱

2. 供給받는 者의 登錄番號

3. 供給價額과 附加價値稅額

4. 作成年月日

5. 第1號 내지 第4號이외의 大統領令이 정하는 事項

②大統領令이 정하는 경우에는 供給받는 者와 附加價値稅額을 따로 記載하지 아니한 計算書(이하 "簡易稅金計算書"라 한다)를 交付하도록 한다.

야 한다.

②第1項의 경우에 用役의 供給을 받은 者가 同項의 規定에 의하여 附加價値稅를 政府에 納付하지 아니한 때에는 政府는 그 納付하지 아니한 稅額에 그 稅額의 100분의 10에 상당하는 金額을 加算하여 國稅徵收의 예에 의하여 徵收한다.

第35條 (質問·調査) ①附加價値稅에 관한 事務에 종사하는 公務員은 附加價値稅에 관한 事務를 위하여 필요한 때에는 納稅義務者, 納稅義務者와 去來가 있는 者, 納稅義務者가 加入한 同業組合 또는 이에 準하는 團體에 대하여 附加價値稅와 관계되는 事項을 質問하거나 그 帳簿·書類 기타의 物件을 調査할 수 있다.

②政府는 附加價値稅의 納稅保全 또는 調査를 위하여 納稅義務者에 대하여 帳簿·書類 기타의 物件의 제출 기타 필요한 事項을 命할 수 있다.

第36條 (施行令) 이 法 施行에 관하여 필요한 事項은 大統領令으로 정한다.

附 則

第1條 (施行日) 이 法은 1977年 7月1日부터 施行한다. 다만, 經濟與件의 推移에 비추어 필요하다고 인정되는 때에는 大統領令이 정하는 바에 의하여 그 施行을 延期할 수 있다.

第2條 (廢止法律) 다음 各號의 法律은 廢止한다.

1. 營業稅法
2. 物品稅法
3. 織物類稅法
4. 石油類稅法
5. 電氣까스稅法
6. 通行稅法
7. 入場稅法
8. 遊興飮食稅法

第3條 (一般的 經過措置) ①이 法 施行당시 종전의 稅法에 의하여 賦課하였거나 賦課하여야 할 營業稅·物品稅·織物類稅·石油類稅·電氣까스稅·通行稅·入場稅와 遊興飮食稅에 관하여는 종전의 예에 의한다. 다만, 이 法 施行日 이후에는 종전의 營業稅法 第40條의 規定에 의한 源泉徵收는 하지 아니한다.

②이 法 施行전의 營業에 대한 營業稅는 종전의 營業稅法 第4條의 規定에 의한 課稅期間 開始日부터 이 法 施行前日까지를 1課稅期間으로 하여 종전의 營業稅法에 의하여 賦課한다.

③第2項에 規定하는 課稅期間에 대한 종전의 營業稅法 第31條

(추 21)

6

(추 30)

의 規定에 의한 告知稅額의 納期는 大統領令으로 정한다.

第4條 (在庫品의 間接稅에 관한 措置) ①이 法 施行日 現在 在庫狀態에 있는 販賣用 商品과 事業用原資材의 價額에 포함된 종전의 稅法에 의한 間接稅額중 附加價値稅와 代替되는 稅額에 대하여는 당해 事業者의 申告에 의하여 附加價値稅의 納付稅額에서 控除한다.

②第1項의 規定은 課稅特例者 또는 國外나 保稅區域내의 財貨에 대하여는 適用하지 아니한다.

③第1項의 경우에 販賣用商品 또는 事業用原資材의 價額을 虛僞로 申告한 때에는 그 虛僞로 申告한 價額의 100분의 10에 상당하는 金額을 加算稅로 徵收한다.

④第1項의 規定에 의한 申告·控除되는 金額과 그 控除에 관하여는 大統領令으로 정한다.

第5條 (不動産에 관한 措置) 이 法 施行전에 取得한 不動産에 대하여는 第6條第2項 내지 第4項의 規定을 適用하지 아니한다. 다만, 이 法 施行후에 增築 또는 改築함으로써 不動産의 價額이 顯著하게 增加된 경우에 그 增加된 部分은 그러하지 아니하다.

第6條 (去來徵收에 관한 措置) ①이 法 施行전에 契約을 締結하고 이 法 施行후에 第9條第1項 및 第2項에 規定하는 供給時期가 到來하는 경우에 그 財貨 또는 用役을 供給하는 者는 당초의 契約에 관계없이 그 契約金額을 課稅標準으로 하여 第14條에 規定하는 稅率을 適用하여 計算한 附加價値稅를 徵收하여야 한다.

②第1項의 規定에 의하여 附加價値稅를 徵收하는 경우에 그 契約金額에 종전의 稅法에 의한 物品稅·織物類稅 또는 石油類稅가 포함되어 있고 特別消費稅가 賦課되지 아니하는 때에는 그 稅額을 控除한 金額을 課稅標準으로 하여 計算한 附加價値稅額에서 종전의 당해 間接稅를 控除한 差額을 徵收하여야 한다.

③課稅特例者에 대하여는 第1項과 第2項의 規定을 適用하지 아니한다.

第7條 (登錄에 관한 措置) ①이 法 施行전에 事業을 開始한 者는 이 法 施行 20日전까지 第5條의 規定에 의한 登錄을 하여야 한다.

②이 法 施行전 20日이후에 事業을 開始한 者는 그 事業開始日부터 20日내에 第5條의 規定에 의한 登錄을 하여야 한다.

第8條 (課稅特例에 관한 經過措置) ①이 法 施行후 最初의 年度에 있어서는 종전의 營業稅法에 의한 收入金額을 供給對價로 보아 第7章의 規定을 適用한다.

②이 法 施行전에 事業을 開始한 者로서 第1項의 規定에 의하여 課稅特例者에 해당하는 者는 이 法 施行후 10日내에 第30條 第2項의 規定에 의한 申告를 할 수 있다.

附 則 〈77·12·19 法3016〉

①(施行日) 이 法은 1978年 1月 1日부터 施行한다.

②(適用例) 이 法은 이 法 施行후의 去來分부터 適用한다. 다만, 第19條와 第27條의 規定은 이 法 施行후 최초의 申告分부터 適用한다.

附 則 〈78·12·5 法3100〉

①(施行日) 이 法은 公布한 날로부터 施行한다.

②(適用例) 이 法은 1979年 1月 1日이후 最初로 開始하는 課稅期間分부터 適用한다. 다만, 第22條第4項의 規定은 이 法 適用후 最初로 確定申告하는 分부터 適用한다.

附 則 〈80·12·13 法3273〉

第1條 (施行日) 이 法은 1981年 1月 1日부터 施行한다.

第2條 (一般的適用例) 이 法은 이 法 施行후 最初로 供給하거나 供給받는 分부터 適用한다.

第3條 (不動產賃貸用役에 관한 經過措置) 이 法 施行전에 賃貸契約이 締結된 不動產賃貸用役에 있어서는 이 法 施行후에 해당하는 賃貸分에 대하여 附加價値稅를 賦課한다.

第4條 (事業用財貨의 供給契約에 따른 經過措置) 이 法 施行전에 附加價値稅가 免除되던 不動產賃貸用役 또는 旅客運送用役의 供給이 이 法 施行으로 인하여 附加價値稅가 賦課되는 경우에 당해 事業을 經營하는 者(이하 "課稅轉換事業者"라 한다)가 이 法 施行전에 그 事業用財貨에 대하여 延拂販賣 또는 中間支給條件附로 供給契約을 締結하고, 이에 따라 당해 財貨를 引渡(利用可能하게 하는 것을 포함한다. 이하 이 條에서 같다)한 경우에는 종전의 例에 의하고, 그 對價의 一部는 領收하였으나 당해 財貨를 이 法 施行전에 引渡하지 아니한 경우에는 이 法 施行후에 供給時期가 到來하는 分에 限하여 이 法의 規定을 適用한다.

第5條 (課稅標準 및 供給時期에 관한 經過措置) ①課稅轉換事業者가 이 法 施行전에 供給契約을 締結하고 이 法 施行으로 인하여 附加價値稅가 賦課되는 경우에 當事者의 合意에 의하여 契約金額을 供給價額 또는 供給對價로 修正하지 아니하는 경우에는 契約金額을 供給價額 또는 供給對價로 본다.

②課稅轉換事業者가 이 法 施行전에 供給契約을 締結하고 이 法 施行으로 인하여 附加價値稅가 賦課되는 경우에 이 法 施行후

(추 57)

(추 57)

供給되는 財貨 또는 用役에 대한 對價를 이 法 施行전에 받거나 받기로 한 때에는 이 法 施行후 最初의 豫定申告期間終了日을 그 供給時期로 본다.

第6條 (事業者登錄에 관한 經過措置) ①課稅轉換事業者는 事業場別로 이 法 施行日로 부터 20日내에 第5條의 規定에 의하여 登錄을 하여야 한다.

②課稅轉換事業者가 이미 登錄되어 있는 경우에는 事業場所管稅務署長은 이 法 施行후부터 10日내에 大統領令이 정하는 바에 의하여 登錄된 事項을 基準으로 하여 第5條第2項에 規定하는 事業者登錄證을 交付하여야 한다.

第7條 (課稅特例者에 관한 經過措置) ①이 法 施行후 最初의 年度에 있어서 課稅轉換事業者가 課稅特例者에 해당되는 與否에 관하여는 所得稅法의 規定에 의한 收入金額을 供給對價로 보아 第25條의 規定을 適用한다.

②第1項의 規定에 의한 課稅特例者에게 이 法 施行후 最初의 豫定申告期間에 대하여 第27條第1項의 規定을 適用함에 있어서 直前課稅期間에 대한 納付稅額은 第1項에 規定하는 收入金額을 6個月에 상당하는 金額으로 換算하고 第26條第1項에 規定하는 稅率을 適用하여 計算한 金額으로 한다.

③第1項의 規定에 의한 課稅特例者는 이 法 施行후 10日內에 第30條第2項의 規定에 의한 申告를 할 수 있다.

④第28條第2項 但書의 規定은 이 法 施行후 最初로 開始되는 課稅期間에 대한 更正分부터 適用한다.

⑤第28條第3項 但書의 規定은 이 法 施行후 最初로 申告하는 分부터 適用한다.

第8條 (買入稅額 控除에 관한 經過措置) 第17條第2項第1號 및 第3號의2의 規定은 이 法 施行후 開始되는 課稅期間에 대한 納付稅額計算分부터 適用한다.

第9條 (不動產등에 관한 經過措置) 課稅轉換事業者가 이 法 施行전에 取得한 不動產과 特種船舶에 대하여는 第6條第2項 내지 第4項의 規定을 適用하지 아니한다. 다만, 이 法 施行후에 당해 財貨에 대한 資本的支出로 인하여 그 財貨의 價値가 현저히 增加된 경우에는 그 增加된 部分에 관하여는 그러하지 아니하다.

17

한 때.
3. 반환조건부판매·동의조건부판매 기타 조건부 및 기한부 판매의 경우에는 그 조건이 성취되거나 기한이 경과되어 판매가 확정되는 때.
4. 완성도기준지급 또는 중간지급조건부로 재화를 공급하거나 전력 기타 공급단위를 구획할 수 없는 재화를 계속적으로 공급하는 경우는 대가의 각 부분을 받기로 한 때.
5. 재화의 공급으로 보는 가공의 경우에는 가공된 재화를 인도하는 때.
6. 법 제6조제2항 및 제3항의 규정에 의하여 재화의 공급으로 보는 경우에는 재화가 사용 또는 소비되는 때.
7. 법 제6조제4항의 경우에는 폐업하는 때.
8. 무인판매기를 이용하여 재화를 공급하는 경우에는 당해 사업자가 무인판매기에서 현금을 인취하는 때.
9. 기타의 경우에는 재화가 인도되거나 인도가능한 때.
10. 수출면허를 받은 수출재화의 경우에는 수출면허일.
11. 보세구역내의 사업자가 보세구역 이외의 국내에 재화를 공급하는 경우에 당해 재화가 수입재화에 해당하는 때에는 수입면허일.

②위탁판매 또는 대리인에 의한 매매의 경우에는 수탁자 또는 대리인의 공급을 기준으로 하여 제1항의 규정을 적용한다. 다만, 법 제6조제5항 단서의 경우에는 위탁자와 수탁자 또는 본인과 대리인 사이에도 공급이 이루어진 것으로 보아 제1항의 규정을 적용한다.

③납세의무있는 사업자가 시설대여산업육성법에 의하여 인가를 받은 시설대여회사로부터 시설등을 임차하고, 당해 시설등을 공급자 또는 세관장으로부터 직접 인도받은 경우에는 당해 사업자가 공급자로부터 재화를 직접 공급받거나 외국으로부터 재화를 직접 수입한 것으로 보아 제1항의 규정을 적용한다. 〈신설 77·6·29 대령8607〉

④제1항제2호의 할부판매는 일정한 판매조건을 정한 전형적인 약관에 의하여 재화를 공급하고, 그 대가를 월부·연부 기타 부불방법에 따라 받는 것중 다음 각호에 해당하는 것으로 한다. 〈신설 77·9·12 대령8689〉
1. 3회이상으로 분할하여 대가를 받는 것.
2. 당해 재화의 인도기일이 속하는 달의 다음 달부터 최종의 부불금의 지급기일이 속하는 달까지의 기간이 3월이상 2년미만인 것.

⑤제1항제2호의 연불판매는 할부판매에 해당하지 아니하는 것으로서 개별약관에 의하여 재화를 공급하고 그 대가를 월부·연부 기타 부불방법에 따라 받는 것중 다음 각호에 해당하는 것으로 한다. 〈신설 77·9·12 대령8689〉
1. 3회이상으로 분할하여 대가를 받는 것.
2. 당해 재화의 인도기일이 속하는 달의 다음 달부터 최종의 부불금의 지급기일이 속하는 달까지의 기간이 2년이상인 것.

제22조 (용역의 공급시기) 법 제9조제2항에 규정하는 용역의 공급시기는 다음 각호의 규정에 의한다. 다만, 폐업전에 공급한 용역의 공급시기가 폐업일 이후에 도래하는 경우에는 그 폐업일을 공급시기로 본다. 〈개정 77·12·30 대령8787, 78·12·30 대령9233, 80·12·31 대령10121〉
1. 통상적인 공급의 경우에는 역무의 제공이 완료되는 때.
2. 완성도기준지급·중간지급·연불 또는 기타 조건부로 용역

(수 58)

(수 58)

을 공급하거나 그 공급단위를 구획할 수 없는 용역을 계속적으로 공급하는 경우에는 그 대가의 각 부분을 받기로 한 때.
3. 제1호 및 제2호의 규정을 적용할 수 없는 경우에는 역무의 제공이 완료되고 그 공급가액이 확정되는 때.
4. 제49조의2제1항의 규정에 의하여 계산하는 공급가액의 경우에는 예정신고기간 또는 과세기간의 종료일

제23조 (비거주자 및 외국법인의 정의) 법 제10조제2항제2호·법 제11조제2항 및 법 제31조제1항과 제4조제4항에 규정하는 비거주자 또는 외국법인은 소득세법 제1조와 법인세법 제1조에 규정하는 바에 의한다. 〈개정 77·6·29 대령8607〉

제3장 영세율적용과 면세

제24조 (수출의 범위) ①법 제11조제1항제1호에 규정하는 수출은 내국물품(우리나라 선박에 의하여 채포된 수산물을 포함한다)을 외국으로 반출하는 것으로 한다.

②법 제11조제1항제1호에 규정하는 수출하는 재화에는 사업자가 내국신용장(제2차 내국신용장을 포함한다. 이하 같다)과 수출용원자재구매승인서(수출용원자재부구매승인서를 포함한다. 이하 같다)에 의하여 공급하는 재화를 포함한다. 〈개정 77·12·30 대령8787, 78·12·30 대령9233〉

제25조 (외국항행용역의 범위) 법 제11조제1항제3호에 규정하는 외국항행용역은 선박 또는 항공기에 의하여 여객이나 화물을 국내에서 국외로, 국외에서 국내로 또는 국외에서 국외로 수송하는 것을 말하며 외국항행사업자가 자기의 사업에 부수하여 행하는 재화 또는 용역의 공급으로서 다음 각호에 게기하는 것을 포함한다. 〈개정 77·6·29 대령8607〉
1. 다른 외국항행사업자가 운용하는 선박 또는 항공기의 탑승권을 판매하거나 화물운송계약을 체결하는 것.
2. 외국을 항행하는 선박내 또는 항공기내에서 승객에게 공급하는 것.
3. 자기의 승객만이 전용하는 버스를 탑승하게 하는 것.
4. 자기의 승객만이 전용하는 호텔에 투숙하게 하는 것.

제26조 (기타 외화획득재화 및 용역의 범위) ①법 제11조제1항제4호에 규정하는 외화를 획득하는 재화 또는 용역은 다음 각호에 게기하는 것으로 한다. 〈개정 77·6·29 대령8607, 77·9·12 대령8689, 77·12·30 대령8787, 78·12·30 대령9233, 79·12·31 대령9604, 80·9·27 대령10034〉
1. 국내에서 국내사업장이 없는 비거주자 또는 외국법인에게 공급되는 재화 또는 용역으로서 그 대금을 외국환은행에서 외환증서 또는 원화로 받는 것.
2. 수출업자와 직접 도급계약에 의하여 수출재화를 임가공하는 수출재화임가공용역(수출재화염색임가공을 포함한다)
3. 외국을 항행하는 선박 및 항공기 또는 원양어선에 공급하는 재화 또는 용역.
4. 국내에 주재하는 외국정부기관·국제기구·국제연합군 또는 미국군에게 공급하는 재화 또는 용역으로서 그 대금을 외국환은행에서 외환증서 또는 원화로 받은 것. 이 경우에 대한민국과 아메리카합중국간의 상호방위조약제4조에 의한시설과구역 및 대한민국에서의 합중국군대의지위에관한협정 제16조제3항의 규정에 의하여 우리나라에 주재하는 미국군(공인된 조달기

18

관을 포함한다)에 물품을 납품하거나 용역을 제공하고 그 대금을 우리나라 은행의 비거주자원화계정을 통하여 원화로 받는 경우를 포함한다.

5. 관광사업법에 의한 국제여행알선업자·관광숙박업자 또는 관광기념품판매업자가 외국인 관광객(음식·숙박용역의 경우에는 비거주자로 한다)에게 공급하는 관광알선용역·숙박용역·음식용역(숙박용역과 함께 공급하는경우에 한한다)및 관광기념품으로서 숙박인의 성명·국적·여권번호등이 기재된 외국인 음식·숙박기록표·구매자의 성명·국적·여권번호·품명·수량·공급·가액등이 기재된 물품판매기록표 또는 기타의 방법에 의하여 외국인과의 거래임이 표시되는 것. 다만, 국제여행알선업의 경우에는 그 대가를 외국환은행에서 외환증서 또는 원화로 받는 것으로 한다.

6. 주한국제연합군 또는 미국군이 주둔하는 지역내의 사업자로서 소관세무서장이 지정하는 자가 국내에서 공급하는 재화 또는 용역으로서 그 대가를 외화로 받고 그 외화를 외국환은행 또는 금융기관인 환전상에서 원화로 환전하는 것.

7. 우리나라에 주재하거나 파견된 외교관 또는 외교사절이 국세청장이 정하는 바에 따라 소관세무서장의 지정을 받은 사업장(특별소비세법시행령 제28조의 규정에 의하여 지정을 받은 판매장을 포함한다)에서 외무부장관이 발행하는 외교관면세카드를 제시하여 공급받는 다음 각호에 게기하는 재화 또는 용역으로서 당해 외교관 또는 외교사절의 성명·국적·외교관면세카드번호·품명·수량·공급가액등이 기재된 외교관면세판매기록표에 의하여 외교관 또는 외교사절과의 거래임이 표시되는 것.

가. 음식·숙박용역

나. 특별소비세법시행령 제24조제1항 및 제27조에 규정하는 물품 또는 주세법에 의한 주류

다. 가 및 나 이외에 재무부장관이 외무부장관과 협의하여 재무부령으로 정하는 재화 또는 용역

8. 외국공공기관또는국제금융기구에의가입조치에관한법률 제2조에 게기하는 국제금융기구로부터 국내사업을 위하여 받은 차관자금으로 국제경쟁입찰에 의하여 직접 공급하는 재화 또는 용역

9. 문화공보부장관의 허가를 받아 설립한 외신기자클럽이 공급하는 재화 또는 용역으로서 그 재화 또는 용역을 공급받는 자의 성명·국적·여권번호·주민등록번호 등이 기재된 재화 또는 용역공급기록표 기타의 방법에 의하여 외신기자와의 거래임이 표시되는 것.

②제1항의 외화획득의 증명에 관하여 필요한 사항은 재무부령으로 정한다.

제27조 (상호면세의 범위) 법 제11조제2항에 규정하는 동일한 면세를 하는 때는 당해 외국의 조세로서 우리나라의 부가가치세 또는 이와 유사한 성질의 조세를 면세하는 때와 그 외국에 우리나라의 부가가치세 또는 이와 유사한 성질의 조세가 없는 때로 한다.

제28조 (미가공식료품의 범위) ①법 제12조제1항제1호에 규정

(추 56)

(추 63)

하는 가공되지 아니한 식료품은 다음 각호에 게거하는 것으로서 가공되지 아니하거나 탈곡·정미·정맥·제분·정육·건조·냉동·염장·포장 기타 원생산물의 본래의 성질이 변하지 아니하는 정도의 1차가공을 거쳐 식용에 공하는 것으로 한다. 〈개정 77·6·29 대령8607〉

1. 곡 류
2. 서 류
3. 특용작물류
4. 과실류
5. 채소류
6. 수축류
7. 수육류
8. 유란유(우유 및 분유를 포함한다.)
9. 생선류(고래를 포함한다.)
10. 패 류
11. 해조류
12. 제1호 내지 제11호 이외에 식용에 공하는 농산물·축산물·수산물·임산물과 기타 재무부령이 정하는 단순가공식료품
13. 소 금

②법 제12조제1항제1호에 규정하는 농산물·축산물·수산물·임산물은 원생산물 또는 원생산물의 본래의 성상이 변하지 아니하는 정도의 원시가공을 거친 것으로 한다. 〈신설 77·12·30 대령8787〉

③제1항 각호의 미가공식료품의 범위에 관하여 필요한 사항은 재무부령으로 정한다.

제29조 (의료보건용역의 범위) 법 제12조제1항제4호에 규정하는 의료보건용역은 다음 각호에 게기하는 것(의료법 또는 수의사법의 규정에 의하여 의료기관 또는 동물병원을 개설한 자가 제공하는 것을 포함한다)으로 한다. 〈개정 81·6·9 대령10338〉

1. 의료법에 규정하는 의사·치과의사·한의사·조산원 또는 간호원이 제공하는 용역.
2. 의료법에 규정하는 접골사·침사·구사 또는 안마사가 제공하는 용역.
3. 의료기사법에 규정하는 임상병리사·방사선사·물리치료사·작업치료사·치과기공사 또는 치과위생사가 제공하는 용역.
4. 약사법에 규정하는 약사가 제공하는 의약품의 제조용역.
5. 수의사법에 규정하는 수의사가 제공하는 용역.
6. 장의업자가 제공하는 장의용역.
7. 기타 재무부령이 정하는 의료보건위생용역.

〔전문개정 80·12·31 대령10121〕

제30조 (교육용역의 범위) 법 제12조제1항제5항에 규정하는 교육용역은 정부의 허가 또는 인가를 받은 학교·학원·강습소·훈련원·교습소 기타 비영리단체에서 학생·수강생·훈련생·교습생 또는 청강생에게 지식·기술 등을 가르치는 것으로 한다.

제31조 (항공기·고속버스 등에 의한 여객운송 용역의 범위) 법 제12조제1항제6호 단서에 규정하는 항공기·고속버스·전세버스·택시·특수자동차 또는 특종선박에 의한 여객운송용역은 다음 각호에 게기하는 것으로 한다.

1. 항공법에 규정하는 항공기에 의한 여객운송용역

●특별소비세법시행령 〔1976·12·31 대통령령제8408호〕

개정 1977·6·29 대통령령제 8608호
1977·11·30 대통령령제 8760호
1978·10·5 대통령령제 9182호
1978·12·30 대통령령제 9235호
1979·3·7 대통령령제 9360호
1979·5·18 대통령령제 9466호
1979·12·31 대통령령제 9695호
1980·4·1 대통령령제 9830호
1980·9·12 대통령령제10023호
1980·11·13 대통령령제10066호
1980·11·24 대통령령제10080호
1981·5·26 대통령령제10320호
1981·6·15 대통령령제10349호
1981·12·31 대통령령제10700호

제 1 조 (과세물품·과세장소 및 과세유흥장소의 세목등) 특별소비세법(이하 "법"이라 한다) 제 1 조제 5 항의 규정에 의한 과세물품의 세목은 별표 1과 같이 하고, 과세장소의 종류는 별표 2와 같이 하며, 과세유흥장소의 종류는 카바레·나이트크럽·요정·외국인전용 유흥음식점 및 기타 이와 유사한 장소로 한다.
〔전문개정 81·12·31 대령10700〕

제 2 조 (용어의 정의) ①법 또는 이 영에서 사용하는 용어의 정의는 다음 각호와 같다. 〈개정 78·12·30 대령9235, 81·6·15 대령10349, 81·12·31 대령10700〉

1. "수출"이라 함은 다음에 게기하는 것을 말한다.

가. 내국물품을 국외로 반출하고 그 대금을 외화 또는 물품으로 결제하는 것

나. 외국공공기관 또는 국제금융기관으로부터 받은 차관자금으로 물품을 구매하기 위하여 실시되는 국제경쟁입찰의 낙찰자가 당해 계약내용에 따라 국내에서 생산된 물품을 납품하고 그 대금을 외화로 결제하는 것

다. 상용견본·기능시험용품 또는 광고용 물품을 무상으로 국외로 반출하는 것

라. 건설공사용 자재를 국외로 반출하는 것

마. 해외취업근로자가 해외에서 외화로 구입한 국산품을 그 물품이 외화면세판매물품임을 증명하는 서류(이하 "면세쿠폰"이라 한다)에 의하여 국내의 일정한 장소에서 인도하는 것. 다만, 해외취업근로자가 해외에서 반입하는 동일한 품목의 휴대품·별송품·탁송품등에 대하여 면세하지 아니하는 경우에 한한다.

2. "주한외국군에 납품하는 것"이라 함은 주한외국군기관에 매각하거나 그 기관의 공사 및 용역의 시공을 위하여 사용하는 물품을 말한다.

3. 삭제 〈81·12·31 대령10700〉

(주 66)

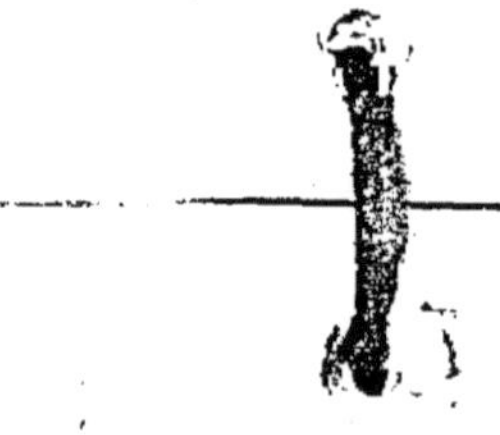

(주 66)

4. "조"라 함은 2개이상이 함께 사용되는 물품으로서 보통 짝을 이루어 거래되는 것을 말한다.

5. "이미 특별소비세가 납부되었거나 납부될 물품의 원재료"라 함은 다음에 게기하는 것을 말한다.

가. 과세물품 또는 수출물품을 형성하는 원재료

나. 과세물품 또는 수출물품을 상품화하는데 소요되는 포장 또는 용기

다. 과세물품 또는 수출물품을 형성하지는 아니하나 당해 물품의 제조·가공에 직접적으로 사용되는 것으로서 화학반응을 하는 물품과 당해 과세물품과 당해 과세물품 또는 수출물품의 제조·가공 과정에서 당해 물품이 직접적으로 사용되는 단용원자재

6. "사"라 함은 섬유를 꼬아 만든 것으로서 방적공정을 거쳐 꼬아진 것을 말한다.

7. "비거주자"라 함은 외국환관리법의 규정에 의하여 비거주자로 인정되는 자를 말한다.

8. "입장료"라 함은 그 명목 여하를 불문하고 입장자 또는 설비이용자(용품이용자를 포함한다)로부터 입장 또는 설비이용의 대가로 영수하는 금액을 말한다.

9. "제조장과 특수한 관계가 있는 곳"이라 함은 다음에 게기하는 장소를 말한다.

가. 제조자가 자기의 제품을 직접 판매하기 위하여 특설한 판매장(하치장을 포함한다)

나. 제조자와 친족관계에 있거나 생계를 같이 하는 자가 경영하는 판매장

다. 제조자와 사실상 혼인관계에 있는 자 또는 그의 친족으로서 생계를 같이 하는 자가 경영하는 판매장

라. 제조자와 고용관계에 있는 자가 따로 경영하는 판매장

마. 제조자에게 속하는 자본 또는 출자총액이 판매장의 자본 또는 출자총액의 100분의 51이상이 되거나 판매자에게 속하는 자본 또는 출자총액이 제조장의 자본 또는 출자총액의 100분의 51이상이 되는 판매장

바. 제조자가 법인인 경우에 그 법인 또는 그 법인의 주주·사원·출자자(법인세법 제22조제 3 항제 2 호에 규정하는 소액주주를 제외하며, 이하 "출자자"라 한다) 및 이들과 특수한 관계가 있는 자에게 속하는 자본 또는 출자의 합계액이 판매장의 자본 또는 출자총액의 100분의 51이상이 되는 그 판매장. 이 경우에 법인 또는 출자자와 특수한 관계

20

④법 제15조제3항에서 "일정한 사유가 발생한 때"라 함은 제3항의 규정에 의하여 1인당 구입할 수 있는 물품의 수량을 초과하여 구입한 사실이 확인된 때를 말한다. 〈신설 81·12·31 대령10700〉

⑤면세물품의 구입절차와 확인방법에 관하여 필요한 사항은 재무부령으로 정한다.

〔본조신설 81·6·15 대령10349〕

제23조 (외교관 면세승인신청) ①법 제16조제1항 각호의 물품에 대하여 면세를 받고자 하는 자는 다음 각호의 사항을 기재한 신청서에 당해 주한외국공관장 또는 제25조에 규정하는 기관의 장이 당해 사실을 증명한 서류를 첨부하여 당해 물품을 판매 또는 반출할 때에(수입물품의 경우에는 그 수입신고시부터 수입면허전까지) 소관세무서장 또는 세관장에게 제출하여 그 승인을 얻어야 한다. 〈개정 78·12·30 대령9235〉

1. 신청자의 주소·성명·명칭·주민등록번호 또는 사업자등록번호
2. 판매 또는 반출장소
3. 종류호별·품명·수량·규격·단가·가격 및 세액
4. 반입장소
5. 반입자의 주소·성명·명칭
6. 반출예정연월일
7. 신청사유
8. 기타 참고사항

②제1항의 신청을 받은 소관세무서장 또는 세관장이 이를 승인한 때에는 그 신청서에 준하는 내용의 승인서를 교부하여야 한다.

제24조 (외국공관용 석유류에 대한 면세특례) ①법 제16조제1항제3호의 규정에 의하여 특별소비세가 면제되는 석유류를 제조장 또는 석유류판매장에서 구입하는 경우에는 제조자 또는 석유류의 판매자(이하 이 조에서 "판매자"라 한다)는 외무부장관이 발행한 외국공관별·유류별·사용량 기타 필요한 사항을 기재한 면세석유류구입추천서를 받고 특별소비세상당액을 그 가격에서 공제한 후 인도하여야 한다.

②제1항의 경우에 판매자는 당해 면세석유류구입추천서를 갖추어 매월분 판매량을 제조자에게 통보하여야 하며, 그 통보를 받은 제조자는 공제된 특별소비세상당액을 판매자에게 교부하여야 한다.

③제조자는 주한외국공관에 직접 판매한 석유류의 매월분판매량과 제2항의 규정에 의하여 통보받은 판매자의 매월분 판매량을 면세석유류구입추천서를 갖추어 소관세무서장에게 보고하여야 한다.

④제3항의 보고를 받은 소관세무서장은 판매자가 판매한 석유류에 대하여 이미 납부한 특별소비세액을 제조자에게 환급하여야 한다. 다만, 환급을 받을 자의 신청에 의하여 이후에 납부할 세

(추 66)

(추 66)

액에서 공제할 수 있다.

제25조 (주한외국공관 및 외교관의 범위) ①법 제16조제1항제1호 및 제3호의 규정에 의하여 특별소비세를 면제할 기관은 협정에 의한 주한외국공관 및 주한외국공관에 준하는 대우를 받는 외국기관과 문화공보부장관의 인가를 받아 설립한 외신기자크럽으로 한다. 다만, 외신기자크럽에 대하여 면세할 물품은 청량음료와 기호음료에 한한다. 〈개정 78·12·30 대령9235〉

②법 제16조제1항제2호 및 법 제19조의2제3호의 규정에 의하여 특별소비세를 면제한 자는 주한외국공관(명예영사의 경우를 제외한다)에 근무하는 외국인으로서 당해 국의 공무원의 신분을 가진 자, 정부의 초청으로 우리나라에 파견된 고문관 및 기술단원과 제1항의 기관의 외국인직원으로 한다. 〈개정 81·12·31 대령 10700〉

제26조 (외국인전용판매장에서 판매한 물품의 면세승인신청) ①법 제17조제1항의 규정에 의하여 면세를 받고자 하는 자는 다음 각호의 사항을 기재한 신청서에 외국인전용판매장의 소관세무서장이 발행한 사업자등록증 사본과 외국인전용판매장지정증 사본을 첨부하여 당해 물품을 판매 또는 반출하는 때에 소관세무서장에게 제출하여 그 승인을 얻어야 한다. 〈개정 78·12·30 대령9235〉

1. 신청자의 주소·성명·명칭·주민등록번호 또는 사업자등록번호
2. 판매 또는 반출장소
3. 종류호별·품명·수량·규격·단가·가격 및 세액
4. 반입장소
5. 반입자의 주소·성명·명칭
6. 판매 또는 반출예정연월일
7. 반입증명서 제출기한
8. 신청사유
9. 기타 참고사항

②제1항의 신청을 받은 소관세무서장이 이를 승인한 때에는 그 신청서에 준하는 내용의 승인서를 교부하고 반입지 소관세무서장에게 그 뜻을 통지하여야 한다. 〈개정 78·12·30 대령9235〉

제27조 (외국인전용판매장에서 판매하는 면세물품의 범위) 법 제17조제1항의 규정에 의하여 특별소비세의 면제를 받을 수 있는 물품은 다음 각호와 같다.

1. 보석과 이를 사용한 제품
2. 귀금속제품
3. 골페와 화무류
4. 가구
5. 특수화장품
6. 공기조절기
7. 냉장고
8. 텔레비전수상기

9. 녹음기.

10. 삭제<79·12·31 대령9695>

11. 사탕.

12. 청량음료.

13. 기호음료.

14. 자양강장품(인삼을 원료로 하여 제조한 제품으로서 전매청장이 허가하여 국세청장에게 통지한 것에 한한다)

15. 모사와 능 직물.

16. 융단.

제28조 (외국인전용판매장의 지정 및 그 취소) ①법 제17조제1항의 규정에 의하여 외국인 전용판매장의 지정을 받고자 하는 자는 다음 각호의 사항을 기재한 신청서에 판매장 소관세무서장이 발행한 사업자 등록증사본을 첨부하여 판매장 소관세무서장에게 제출하여야 한다. 이 경우에 외국인이 전용하는 매점으로서 법령에 의하여 정부의 허가 또는 등록을 받아야 하는 것에 있어서는 당해 허가증 또는 등록증사본을 첨부하여 제출하여야 한다. <개정 79·12·31 대령9695>

1. 신청자의 주소·성명·명칭·생년월일 및 주민등록번호

2. 판매장의 소재지 및 상호와 대표자의 성명 및 주민등록번호

3. 판매하고자 하는 물품의 품명.

②제1항의 지정을 한 소관세무서장은 다음 각호의 사항을 기재한 지정증을 교부하여야 한다.

1. 지정번호.

2. 판매장의 소재지 및 상호.

3. 대표자의 주소·성명·생년월일 및 주민등록번호.

4. 면세판매물품의 품명.

③소관세무서장은 제1항의 지정을 받은 자가 다음 각호의 1에 해당하는 경우에는 그 지정을 취소할 수 있다. <개정 79·12·31 대령9695>

1. 면세물품을 부정하게 판매한 사실이 있은 때.

2. 법 제25조의 규정에 의한 국세청장·소관지방국세청장 또는 소관세무서장의 명령에 위반하여 처벌 또는 처분을 받은 때.

3. 관계법령에 의한 허가 또는 등록이 취소되거나 기타 처분을 받은 때.

4. 사업자 또는 법인의 임원이 국세 또는 지방세를 50만원 이상 포탈하여 처벌 또는 처분을 받은 때.

(추 49)

(추 49)

5. 당해 판매장을 양도 또는 대여한 때.

6. 제1항의 서류에 불실한 기재를 한 사실이 발견된 때.

7. 국내에 거주하지 아니하거나 실종된 사실이 발견된 때. 다만, 관리인이 따로 있는 경우는 제외한다.

④제1항의 신청을 받은 소관세무서장은 신청인이 다음 각호의 1에 해당하는 경우에는 그 지정을 하지 아니할 수 있다. <신설 79·12·31 대령9695>

1. 외국인의 이용도가 낮다고 인정되는 장소에서 판매장을 경영하고자 하는 자

2. 판매에 필요한 인원 및 물적시설이 구비되지 아니한 자

3. 신청일로부터 기산하여 과거 1년내에 국세에 관한 법칙행위를 한 자

4. 판매장 경영에 필요한 자력 및 신용을 갖추지 못하였다고 인정되는 자

제29조 (외국인전용판매장에서 판매하는 면세물품의 구입방법 및 판매보고) ①제28조제1항의 규정에 의하여 외국인전용판매장의 지정을 받은 자가 면세물품을 판매하는 때에는 당해물품의 구입자의 신분을 확인한 후 다음 각호의 사항을 기재한 면세물품구입기록표를 작성하여 구입자의 여권에 첨부하고 간인하여야 한다

1. 판매장소관세무서명, 판매장의 소재지와 판매자의 성명·명칭

2. 구입자의 성명·국적·입국항·근무처명·직위·입국연월일·입국목적·출국예정항·출국예정연월일 및 출국방법.

3. 신분증 또는 여권의 종류, 신분증번호, 여권번호, 통과상륙허가서번호 또는 기항상륙허가서번호.

4. 면세물품의 품명·수량·규격·단가·판매가격·과세표준·세율 및 세액

②제1항의 물품을 판매한 자는 동항 각호의 사항 이외에 면세구매물품의 휴대여부 또는 세액의 징수내용을 기재한 면세물품판매확인서 2통을 작성하여 그 중 1통은 구입자(주한 외교관 및 주한외국군 장병의 경우를 제외한다)의 출국예정항 소관세관장에게 판매한 때마다 제출하고, 다른 1통은 판매장소관세무서장에게 법 제17조제3항의 규정에 의한 신고를 하는 때에 면세물품판매명세서에 첨부하여 각각 제출하여야 한다. 다만, 보세구역내에 있는 판매장에서 판매한 경우에는 당해 소관세관장에게는 제출하지 아니하여도 된다.

③제2항의 확인서를 받은 세관장은 구입자가 출국할 때에 제1

기 안 용 지

분류기호 문서번호	미안 723-	(전화번호)	전결규정 조 항 전결사항
처리기간		차 관	장 관
시행일자	1982. 8. 12.		
보존년한			
보조기관 국 장	전결		협조
과 장			
기안책임자	김영준	안보과	
경유		발신	통제
수신	재무부장관		
참조	세제국장		
제목	주한미군 현지조달 물품에 대한 면세		

주한미군 당국은 별첨서한을 통해 대림기업(주)이 미군전용 내자호텔 내 면세물품 상점에 납품한 국산품에 대해 면세받을 수 없다는 국세청의 통보로 6천만원의 세금을 부담하게 되었다고 하면서 이의 시정을 요청하여 왔는 바, 이에대한 귀부의 견해를 알려주시기 바랍니다.

첨부 : 주둔군 지위 협정 (SOFA) 합동위 미측 간사 서한 사본 1부. 끝.

정서 / 관인 / 발송

0281-1-8A(갑) 1969. 11. 10. 승인

정직 질서 창조

190mm×268mm (2급인쇄용지 60g/m²) 조달청

23

August 18, 1982

Dear Dr. Hodges :

With reference to your letter dated August 2, 1982 concerning the request to exempt Dae Lim Industrial Co. from Value Added Tax and Special Excise Tax, it is with regret to inform you that we reached a negative decision on the following grounds :

Since it is impossible for Korean business firms to become Non-appropriated Fund organizations, Dae Lim Industrial Co. can not but be considered as a supplier to the Naija Hotel AFRC, if not an independent businessman dealing directly with USFK personnel.

According to paragraph 3 of SOFA Article XVI, the exemption from Korean taxes on materials, supplies, equipment and services is limited to the procurement for official purposes by the USFK including their authorized procurement agencies. More specifically, paragraph 2 of Article XIII stipulates that purchases within the Republic of Korea of merchandise and supplies by Non-appropriated Fund organizations shall be subject to the Korean taxes to which other purchasers of such merchandise and supplies are subject.

Sincerely,

Soon Tae Kwon
ROK Secretary
SOFA Joint Committee

Dr. C.B. Hodges
US Secretary
SOFA Joint Committee

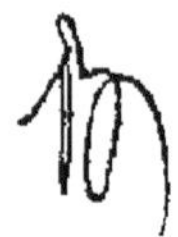

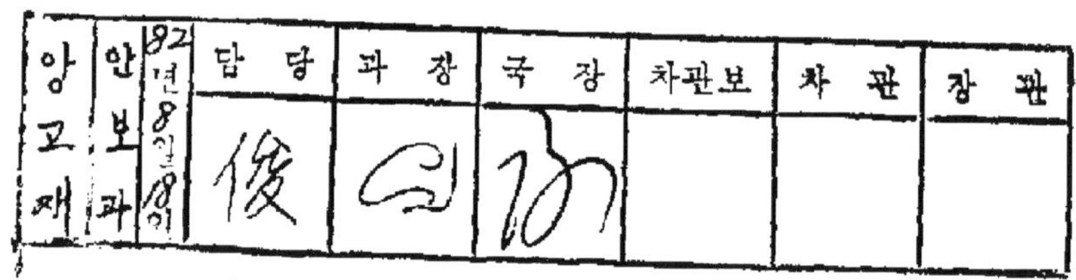

양고재	안보과	82년 8월 18일	담 당	과 장	국 장	차관보	차 관	장 관

24

JOINT COMMITTEE
UNDER
THE REPUBLIC OF KOREA AND THE UNITED STATES
STATUS OF FORCES AGREEMENT

August 18, 1982

Dear Dr. Hodges :

With reference to your letter dated August 2, 1982 concerning the request to exempt Dae Lim Industrial Co. from Value Added Tax and Special Excise Tax, it is with regret to inform you that we reached a negative decision on the following grounds :

According to paragraph 3 of SOFA Article XVI, the exemption from Korean taxes on materials, supplies, equipment and services is limited to the procurement for official purposes by the USFK including their authorized procurement agencies. More specifically, paragraph 2 of Article XIII stipulates that purchases within the Republic of Korea of merchandise and supplies by Non-appropriated Fund organizations shall be subject to the Korean taxes to which other purchasers of such merchandise and supplies are subject.

Sincerely,

Soon Tae Kwon
ROK Secretary
SOFA Joint Committee

Dr. C.B. Hodges
US Secretary
SOFA Joint Committee

25

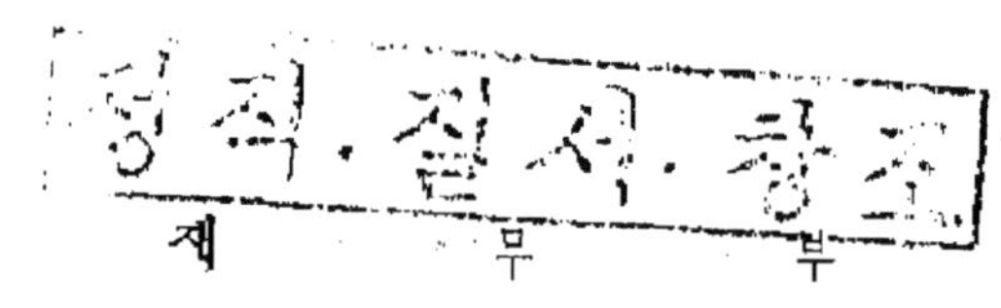

국조 1261·51-104p. 720-3223 1982. 9. 4.

수신 외무부장관

참조 미주국장

제목 SOFA 협정 제13조 제2항에 관한 합의사항 확인

1. 미안 723-27562 (82. 8. 12)에 관련됩니다

2. SOFA 협정 제13조 제2항에 의하면, 비세출 자금 기관에 의한 상품 및 수용품의 대한민국 안에서의 구입에 대하여는 양 정부간에 달리 합의하지 아니하는 한 과세되는 것으로 규정하고 있는바, 동 조항의 적용과 관련하여 양 정부간에 별도의 합의 기록이 있는지 여부를 확인하여, 조속히 통보해 주시기 바랍니다. 끝.

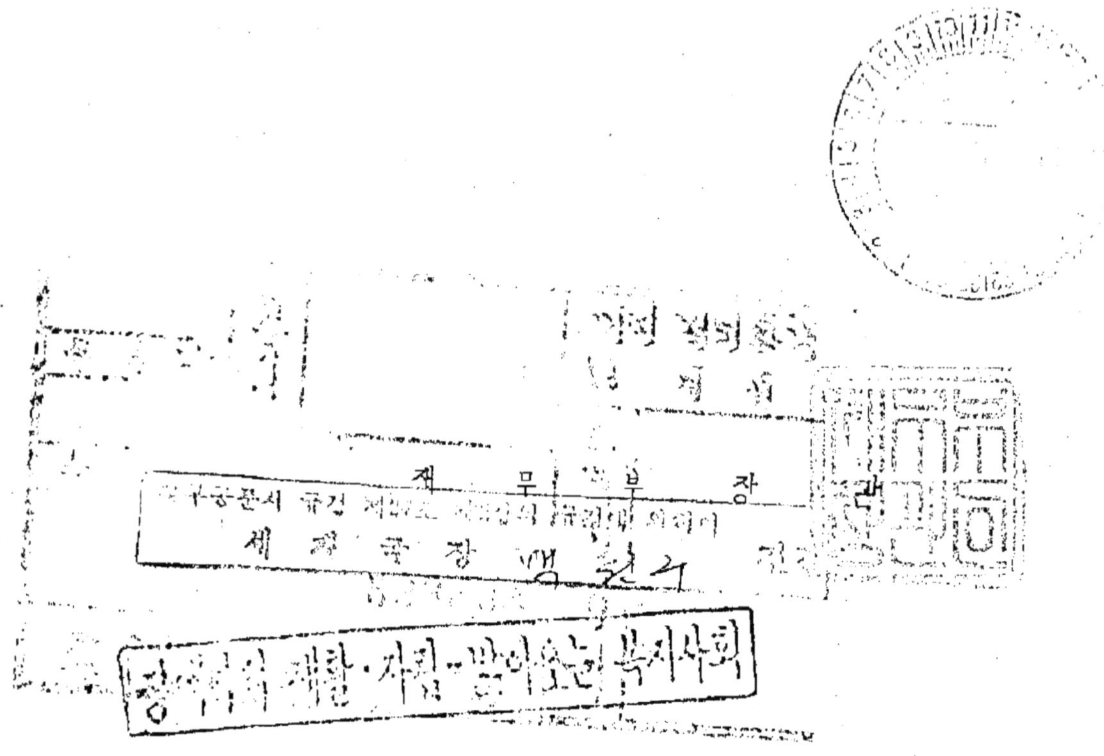

26

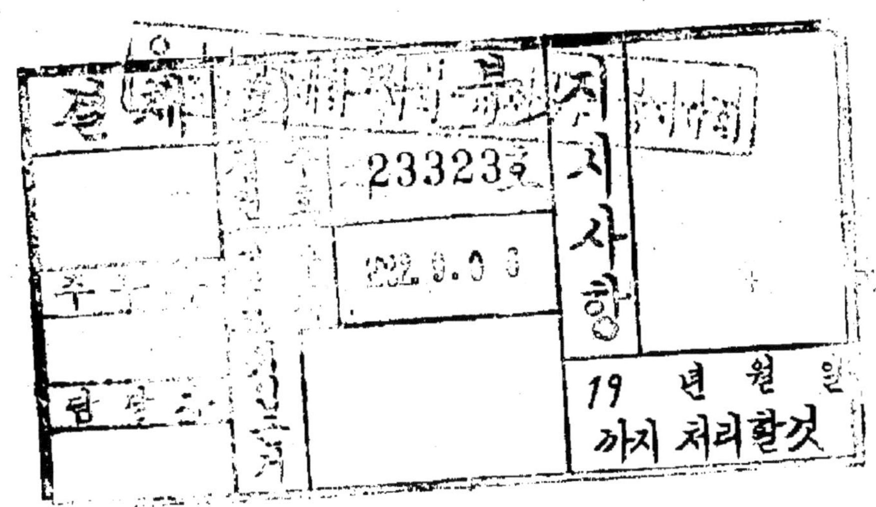
23323호
1982. 9. 0 3
지시사항
19 년 월 일
까지 처리할것

27

기안용지

분류기호 문서번호	미안 723-	(전화번호)	전결규정 조 항 전결사항
처리기간		장 관	
시행일자	1982. 9. 7.		
보존년한			
보조기관 국 장	전결		협조
과 장			
기안책임자	김영준	안보과	

경 유		통제
수 신	재무부 장관	
참 조	세제국장	
제 목	주둔군 지위협정 문의에 대한 회신	

1982.9.10 / 19224 / 외무부

대 : 국조 1261.51-1049 (82. 9. 4.)

연 : 미안 723-27562 (82. 8. 12.)

대호로 문의한 주둔군 지위협정 (SOFA) 제 13조 제 2항의 양정부간 별도합의 사항은 없음을 알려드립니다. 끝.

정서

관인

발송

0201 - 1 - 8 A(갑) 1969. 11. 10. 승인

정직 질서 창조

190mm×268mm (2급인쇄용지 60g/m²) 조 달 청(3,000,000매 인 쇄)

28

기안용지

분류기호 문서번호	미안 723-	(전화번호)	전결규정 조 항 전결사항
처리기간		장 관	
시행일자	1982. 9. 8.		
보존년한			
보조기관	국 장 전결		협조
	과 장		
기안책임자	김영준	안보과	
경 유		발신 1982. 9. 9	통제
수 신	재무부 장관		
참 조	관세국장		
제 목	군대지위협정 (SOFA) 대상자의 여권상 기재		

1982. 9. 7. 한미주둔군 지위협정 (SOFA) 합동위원회 미측 간사는 별첨서한을 통해 합동위 제 120차 회의에서의 합의에도 불구하고 세관당국이 휴가차 출국하는 SOFA 대상자에게 부당히 불편을 주고있다 하고 이에대한 시정 (여권상의 휴대품 기재중지, 이미 한 기재의 말소)을 요청하여 왔는 바, 관련 사항 파악, 시정하여 주시고 결과를 알려 주시기 바랍니다.

첨부 : 미측 SOFA 합동위 간사 서한 사본 1부.

동 제 120차 합동위 합의사항 사본 1부. 끝.

정서 관인 발송

대 한 민 국
외 무 부

미안 723- 720-2239 1982. 9. 9.

수신 재무부 장관

참조 관세국장

제목 군대지위협정 (SOFA) 대상자의 여권상 기재

1982. 9. 7. 한미주둔군 지위협정 (SOFA) 합동위원회 미측 간사는 별첨서한을 통해 합동위 제 120차회의에서의 합의에도 불구하고 세관당국이 휴가차 출국하는 SOFA 대상자에게 휴대품과 관련, 여권상의 기재된 물품의 반출이나 유치등을 강요하는등 부당한 불편을 주고 있다하고 이에대한 시정(여권상의 휴대품 기재행위 중지, 이미한 기재의 말소)을 요청하여 왔는바, 관련사항의 파악, 시정하여 주시고 결과를 알려 주시기 바랍니다.

첨부 : 미측 SOFA합동위간사 서한 사본 1부.
동 제 120차 합동위 합의사항 사본 1부. 끝.

외 무 부 장 관

정부 공문서 규정 제27조 제2항의 규정에 의하여
미 주 국 장 김 석 규 전결

30

저축은 국력

재 무 부

관협 1272 - 767 (720-3227) 1982. 11. 29

수신 외무부장관

참조 미주국장

제목 SOFA 대상자의 여권상 기재

1. 관련 : 관협 1272 - 710 ('82. 10. 25)

2. 관련 공문중 SOFA 대상자의 휴대반출 확인서 양식을 별첨과 같이 수정하여 영문 번역한바, 조치하여 주시기 바랍니다.

첨부 : Declaration Card For Accompanying Goods

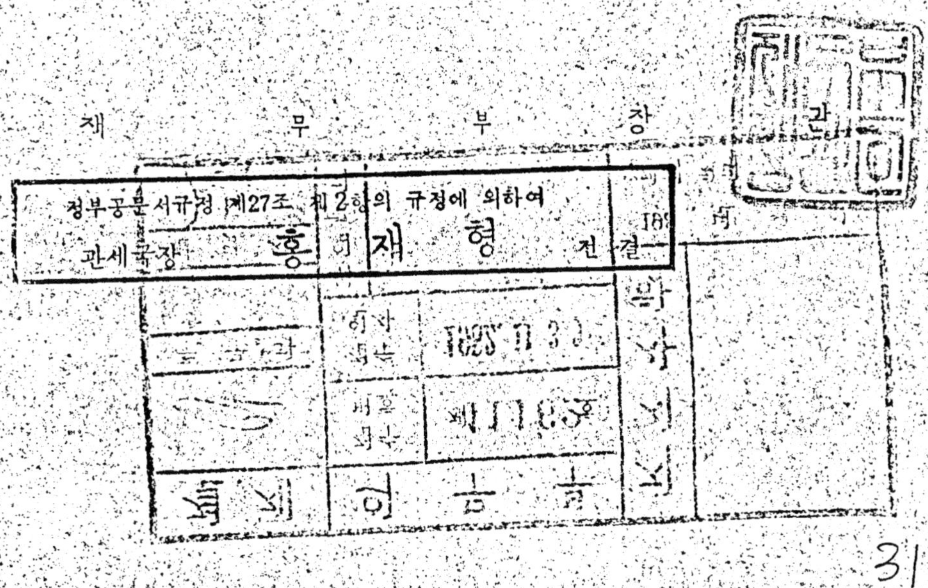

31

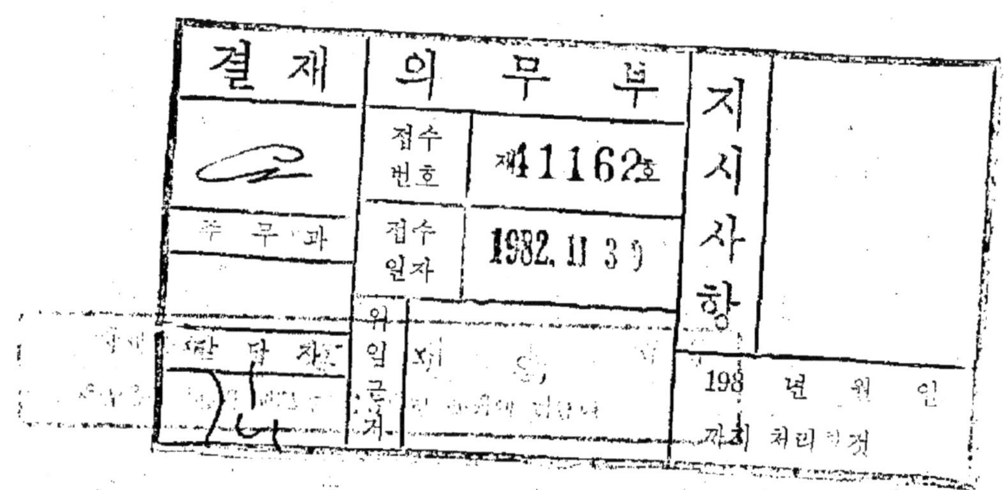

결 재	외 무 부		지시사항
	접수번호	제41162호	
주무과	접수일자	1982. 11 3 0	
담당자	위임근거		198 년 월 일 까지 처리할 것

32

Declaration Card For Accompanying Goods

1. Declarant

   Name :

   Rank (Position) :

2. Date of Departure :

3. Accompanying Goods

Description	Specification	Quantity	Other Information

4. Signature

   A. Declarant

   B. Verifying Customs Officer

Name and Position

* The declarant must show this card to customs officers concerned, to benefit from SOFA on the above mentioned items when returning to Korea.

33

To SOFA US Secretary

SOFA 대상자의 여권상 기재

(making entries regarding personal effects in the passports of SOFA personnel)

1. 현 황

- 최초 입국시, 반입물품등에 대한 여권상 기재는 하지 않고 있음.

- 휴가차 출국시, 본인이 휴대 반출 사실 확인을 요구하는 경우에 한하여 반출 사실을 여권에 기재하고 있음.

- 휴가후 입국시, 국내 관세법령에 따라 일반 외국인과 동일하게 취급하고 있음.

2. 의견 문의

상기 여권상 기재에 따른 불편 완화를 위해 반출 사실 확인 제도 (휴대 반출 확인서 발급)를 실시하고자 하는바, 귀하의 의견은 ?

3. 요청 사항

다만 미측은 휴가자에게 1) 휴대 반출시 세관에 신고, 확인을 받고 2) 입국시 신분을 명백히 밝힐 것을 사전에 주지시켜 줄 것.

※ 재무부에 통보 조치됨 (82. 12. 10 관세협력과 [illegible])
미측입장 : - 현재 문제의 되고 있는 것은 최초 입국시 여권상 기재로 인한 불편 야기등인바 이를 시정하여 주기 바람.
- 휴가후의 휴대반출 신고 확인제도 실시는 [illegible] 불편 [illegible] 않고 있음.

34

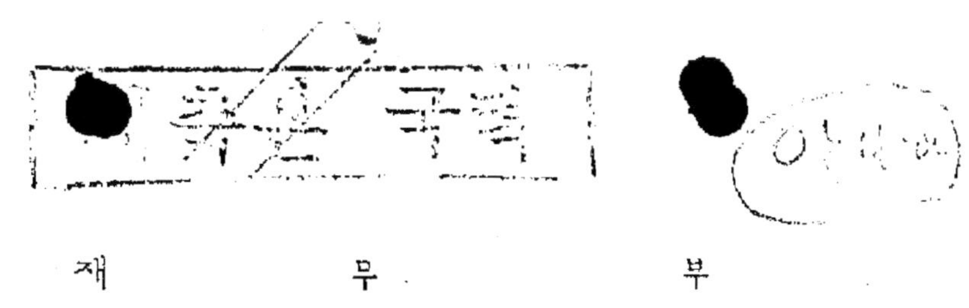

재 무 부

관협 1272 - 710 (720-3227) 1982. 10. 25

수신 외무부장관

참조 미주국장

제목 SOFA 대상자의 여권상 기재

1. 관련 : 미안 723 - 31458 ('82. 9. 9)

2. 소파 대상자의 최초 입국시 반입물품등에 대하여 여권상 각종 사항을 기재하는 사실은 없으며,

3. 휴가차 출입국하는 소파 대상자의 경우,

가. 휴가차 출국시 본인이 휴대반출 사실 확인을 요구하는 경우에 한하여 반출사실을 여권에 기재하고 있으며,

나. 휴가후 입국시 과세대상물품을 휴대반입하는 경우에는 휴대반입을 불허하고 소파 제9조 제1항, 제3항 및 제5항에 의하여 처리하고 있으나, 소파 대상자가 자신의 신분을 밝히지 않고 여권만을 제시할때는 신분 확인 방법이 없어 일반 비거주 여행자에 준하여 휴대반입을 허용하고 있으며,

/계속/

35

결 재	외 무 부		지 시 사 항	
	접수 번호	2재7867 호		
주 무 과	접수 일자	1982. 10. 26		
담 당 자	위임근거		198 년 월 일	

36

관협 1272 - 1982. 10. 25

4. 이권상의 기재에 따르는 불편등을 완화하기 위하여 출국시 휴대반출하는 물품에 대하여 별지 (휴대 반출확인서)에 따른 반출 사실 확인제도를 실시하고자 하는바, 이에 대한 미측의 의견을 통보하여 주시기 바랍니다.

5. 다만, 휴대반출 여부등으로 검사시 분쟁의 소지가 있으므로 휴대반출시 세관에 신고, 확인을 받도록 하는 사항과 입국시 신분을 명백히 밝히도록 휴가자에게 미측에서 사전에 주지교육을 시켜 주도록 요청하여 주시기 바랍니다.

첨부 : 소파대상자의 휴대품 반출 확인서 (안) 1 매 "끝".

재 무 부 장

관세국장 홍 기 선

37

첨부

SOFA 대상자의 휴대반출 확인서

반출자 직 성명	직급 성명
품 명	
규 격	
수 량	
반출 년 월 일	
반출 확인자	0 0 세관 직급 성명 (인)

38

Dae Kim Industrial Co., Ltd.
C. P. O. Box 929) Seoul, Korea
Cable address : DL Chong 대 김 기 업 주 식 회 사 Telephone: 778-8054

No. 대김 제 12003 호 Date: 1981. 12. 3.

[82. 12. 21]

수 신: 국세청장

참 조: 관세국장

제 목: 당사가 미8군 구매처 (K.C.A.)와 체결한 군납계약서가 계약내용과 같이 행정 협정 제16조의 면세 사항을 적용하여도 되는지 여부에 대한 질의 건.

당사는 첨부한 계약서 사본과 같이 미8군 구매처 (K.C.A.)및 KOAX 와 국산 전자 제품을 미8군 영내인 PX CONCESSION ARCADE 및 내자 USFK RECREATION CENTER에서 한미간에 체결된 행정 협정 제16조의 규정에 의거 주한미군 기관및 SOFA 대상자들에게 면세로 국산 전자 제품을 공급및 판매 할수 있는 조항이 들어 있는 장기 계약을 체결하였읍니다.

그럼으로 당사는 국내전자제품 생산업자로부터 미국의 전자제품 안전 수칙 규정 (UL)을 취득한 국산제품을 공급받아 체결된 군납계약을 수행하여 옴에 있어서 미8군 측이 계약서에 제시한 면세적용 사항에 의거하여 제조업체로부터 상품을 공급받을때 제세에 대하여 한미행정 협정 제16조와 같이 면세율을 적용 하여도 무방한지의 유권 해석을 의뢰하오니 적절한 유권해석을 조속히 내려 주시길 바랍니다.

당사의 입장이나 국가적인 차원에서 생각하여도 유효 적절한 세제상의 혜택이 있다고 하면 현시점에서 미8군 PX 내에서 국산전자 제품도 30여년만에 외국산

39

[82.12.21] 재무부 세제국 국제조세과로부터 접수

(일본, 미국, 독일등)과 경쟁하여 외화 획득을 할수있는 절호의 기회라고 확신하며 나아가 수출입국에 다소라도 이바지 할수 있는 기회라고 확신합니다.

반면 대부분의 군납업자는 미8군 군납용으로 외국에서 상품및 자재를 수입할 경우 한미 행정 협정에 준하여 JK FORM 78-1,1 JUNE79 에 의거하여 필요한 상품및 자재를 수입 시점부터 제세금을 면세받을수 있으나 국내에서 조달 받을때에는 적절한 면세적용을 받을수 있는 명문이 없음으로 국내에서 조달할수 있는 국산물품도 외국에서 수입하는 여가 비일 비재한 실정이며 국가적인 차원에서 보아도 외화 가득면에서 위배된다고 사료됩니다.

만일 당사가 미8군과 체결한 제반사항이 세법에 위배된다면 위배되는 사항을 유권해석상에 명확히 명시하여 주시기 바랍니다.

왜냐하면 당사의 입장에서 미지급 상태에 있는 미8군 영업장 사용료및 수수료를 지불하지 않을수 있는 법적인 근거를 제시할수 있을뿐만 아니라 본 계약을 미8군 구매처 (K.C.A.)에 반납할수 있는 합법적인 근거를 제시할수 있기 때문입니다.

첨부서류: 1. 한미협정 제16조 사본 및 해석
2. 군납계약서 사본 3 종
3. 상공부 군납업자 등록 필증 사본
4. 주한 미군 계약용 수입물자 증명서 사본 (JK FORM 78-1)

大林企業株式會社
代表理事 張 敎 哲

40

EXHIBIT A

SOLICITATION NO. KO-81-18-81-43

ARMY AND AIR FORCE EXCHANGE SERVICE

GENERAL PROVISIONS
(CONTRACT FOR SERVICES)

1. DEFINITIONS: As used throughout this contract, the following terms shall have the meaning set out below:

a. "AAFES" refers to the Army and Air Force Exchange Service.

b. "Contract" identifies this contract or any amendment thereto.

c. "Contracting Officer" means a person authorized in writing to execute and administer the contract on behalf of AAFES or said contracting officer's successor or successors.

d. "Contractor" means the individual, partnership, corporation, or other entity which is a party to this contract and who is responsible for all actions, performance and work thereunder, to include that of any subcontractor.

2. LEGAL STATUS: AAFES–including its activities, offices, individual exchanges and oversea exchange systems–is an integral part of the Departments of the Army and the Air Force and is an instrumentality of the U.S. Government. AAFES contracts are United States contracts; however, they do not obligate appropriated funds of the United States, except for a judgment or compromise settlement in suits brought in the Federal District courts (28 USC 1346) and in the U.S. Court of Claims (28 USC 1491)–in which event, AAFES will reimburse the U.S. Government [31 USC 724(a)]. [NOTE: The Armed Services Procurement Act applies only to procurements for which payment is to be made from appropriated funds [10 USC 2303(a)] and does not govern AAFES procurements. The Defense Acquisition Regulation (DAR), published pursuant to the Armed Services Procurement Act, is likewise inapplicable except for those DAR provisions that have been administratively adopted by AAFES and that are either incorporated into or specifically referenced in this contract.]

3. GRATUITIES AND CONTINGENT FEES: Contractor warrants that no person or selling agency has been employed or retained to secure this contract upon an agreement or understanding for a commission, percentage, brokerage, or contingent fee excepting bona fide employees or bona fide established commercial selling agencies retained by Contractor for the purpose of securing business. Contractor warrants that no gratuities (entertainment, gifts, etc.) were or will be offered or given by the Contractor or any person representing the Contractor to any AAFES officer or employee or any other officer or employee of the U.S. Government or member of their family or household. For breach of either of the warranties, AAFES may terminate this and all other AAFES contracts for default and deduct from amounts due under this or other contracts, or bill Contractor for, the total value of any contingent fee or gratuity.

4. ORAL REPRESENTATIONS: This written contract includes the entire agreement between the parties. AAFES will not be bound by any oral or written representation not included in the written contract or a change or amendments thereto. AAFES will not be bound by any terms on contractor forms or letters unless such terms are specifically agreed to and incorporated in the contract and signed by the Contracting Officer.

5. MODIFICATIONS AND ADDITIONS: Except as otherwise specifically provided in this contract, all changes, modifications, additions, or deletions to this contract must be prepared in writing as formal amendments signed by both parties and approved in accordance with provisions of applicable regulations.

6. SUBCONTRACTORS: Contractor shall not subcontract any part of the work to be performed without the prior written consent of the Contracting Officer. Any subcontractor so approved and used in connection with this contract is the agent of the Contractor and not the agent of AAFES.

AAFES FORM 4450-15 (REV MAY 81) (JUL 78 - MAR 80 EDITIONS USABLE)

41

82. 12. 21 재무부 국제조세과로부터 접수

7. <u>ASSIGNMENT</u>: Contractor may not assign his rights or delegate his obligations under this contract without the prior written consent of the Contracting Officer.

8. <u>CONTRACT EXTENSION</u>: It is expressly understood this contract will be in effect only for the stated period. The Contracting Officer may, within the guidelines established in AAFES Procurement Instructions, negotiate an extension for a like or lesser period. No representation that this contract will be extended beyond its original period is binding on AAFES unless in writing signed by the Contractor and Contracting Officer and approved by any required approval authority. In no event will the total contract period exceed an accumulated period of five(5) years from the date established in the original contract for commencement of service.

9. <u>TERMINATION</u>: Relative to termination of this contract, it is mutually agreed:

a. This contract may be terminated in whole or in part by either party immediately upon written notice to the other party in the event of breach of this contract by the other party.

b. This contract may be terminated in whole or in part by either party upon thirty (30) days notice [ninety (90) days for vending contracts]in writing to the other party.

c. This contract is automatically terminated upon the dispatch of written notice to Contractor in the event the exchange is inactivated or the installation at which the exchange is located is inactivated. If this contract covers services to be performed at various exchanges or installations and only one or more of the exchanges or installations is inactivated, then only that portion of the contract being performed at the inactivated exchange or installation is terminated.

10. <u>PERMITS AND LICENSES</u>: Contractor will, at his own expense, obtain all necessary permits, give all notices, pay all license fees and comply with all laws, rules, ordinances, and regulations relating to the preservation of the public health or applicable to the service or business carried on under this contract. The burden of determining applicability of licensing requirements, laws, ordinances, and regulations for Contractor and his employees rests with the Contractor.

11. <u>INDEMNIFY AND HOLD HARMLESS</u>: Contractor will indemnify, hold harmless and defend AAFES and all other agencies and instrumentalities of the United States, their agents, representatives, employees and customers from any and all suits, judgments and claims, including those established by or pursuant to court decisions, to international agreements, or duly promulgated regulations of the U.S. Government, and all charges and expenses incident thereto which arise out of:

a. The alleged or established violation or infringement of any patent, copyright or trademark rights asserted by any third party with regard to items or services provided by Contractor;

b. Loss, damage or injury alleged or established to have arisen out of or in connection with items or services provided by Contractor, unless such loss, damage, or injury was caused by or resulted solely from the acts or omissions of AAFES, its agents, representatives, or employees;

c. Any loss, damage, or injury alleged or established to have arisen out of or in connection with any other acts or omissions of Contractor;

AAFES will give Contractor notice and an opportunity to defend.

12. <u>CLAIMS</u>: No claim by Contractor may be considered unless submitted in writing to the Contracting Officer no later than 90 days after termination of performance under the contract; provided, however, this clause will not extend the period for filing claims which is further limited by another clause of the contract.

42

13. DISPUTES:

a. (1) Contractor must submit any request for monetary or other relief relating to this contract in writing to the Contracting Officer. The request must specify the amount of money or the other relief requested and include all supporting data. In addition, with the request or any amendment thereto, Contractor must submit a signed certificate reading as follows:

> "I certify that this request and any ensuing claim are made in good faith, that the supporting data are accurate and complete to the best of my knowledge and belief, and that any amount requested accurately reflects the amount for which Contractor believes AAFES is liable."

____
(Signature of individual authorized to bind Contractor)

(NOTE: SUBMISSION OF FALSE CLAIMS IS A VIOLATION OF FEDERAL LAW AND MAY RESULT IN CIVIL AND/OR CRIMINAL PENALTIES.)

(2) Contractor's request for payment of money or other relief is not a "claim" until:

(a) A written request has been received by the Contracting Officer complying fully with subparagraph (1) above,

(b) A dispute arises between the parties after a reasonable time for review and disposition, and

(c) Contractor requests the Contracting Officer to issue a final decision.

(3) Contractor's request for a contract amendment or for relief which is discretionary with the Contracting Officer will not be considered a "claim."

b. All disputed claims relating to this contract will be decided by the Contracting Officer, who will issue a written Final Decision and mail or otherwise furnish a copy thereof to Contractor. The Contracting Officer's decision will be final and conclusive unless:

(1) Within 90 days from the date of Contractor's receipt of the Contracting Officer's Final Decision, Contractor mails or otherwise furnishes the Contracting Officer a written appeal (two copies) addressed to the Armed Services Board of Contract Appeals (ASBCA); or

(2) Within 12 months from the date of Contractor's receipt of the Contracting Officer's Final Decision, Contractor brings an action in the United States Court of Claims.

c. The decision of the ASBCA is final and conclusive except:

(1) Contractor may appeal such a decision to the United States Court of Claims within 120 days from the date of Contractor's receipt of a copy of the decision of the ASBCA.

(2) AAFES may transmit the decision of the ASBCA to the United States Court of Claims for judicial review within 120 days from the date of AAFES' receipt of a copy of the decision of the ASBCA.

(3) ASBCA decisions made under the Board's small claims (expedited) procedures ($10,000 or less) may be set aside only in case of fraud. In all other cases, the ASBCA decisions on questions of fact may be set aside only where the decisions are fraudulent, arbitrary, capricious, or so grossly erroneous as to necessarily imply bad faith, or if such decisions are not supported by substantial evidence. The decisions of the ASBCA on any questions of law will not be final or conclusive as to the United States Court of Claims.

d. Pending final resolution on any request for relief, disputed claim, appeal, or action, related to this contract, Contractor will proceed diligently with the performance of this contract and will comply with the Contracting Officer's decisions.

e. If Contractor cannot support any part of its claim as a result of fraud or misrepresentation of fact, then, in addition to other remedies or penalties provided for by law, Contractor will pay AAFES an amount equal to the unsupported part of the claim plus all AAFES costs attributable to reviewing that part of the claim.

f. The Contract Disputes Act of 1978 and the provisions of this contract contain the sole procedures for resolving disputed claims relating to this contract. A copy of the Act may be obtained from the Contracting Officer.

14. NON-WAIVER OF DEFAULTS: Any failure by AAFES at any time or from time to time to enforce or require strict performance of any terms or conditions of this contract will not constitute waiver thereof and will not affect or impair such terms and conditions in any way or AAFES' right at any time to avail itself of such remedies as it may have for breach or breaches of such terms and conditions.

15. REPRESENTATIONS: The Contractor will not represent himself to be an agent or representative of AAFES, or any other agency or instrumentality of the United States.

16. ADVERTISEMENTS: The Contractor will not represent in any manner, expressly or by implication, that items or services purchased or sold under this contract are approved or endorsed by any element of the U.S. Government. Any advertisement, including cents-off coupons, by the Contractor which refers to a military resale activity will contain a statement that the advertisement was neither paid for nor sponsored, in whole or in part, by the particular activity.

17. EXAMINATION OF RECORDS:

a. This clause is applicable if the amount of this contract exceeds $2,500 and was entered into by means of negotiation. The Contractor agrees that the Contracting Officer or his duly authorized representatives will have the right to examine and audit the books and records of the Contractor directly pertaining to the contract during the period of the contract and until the expiration of three (3) years after final payment under the contract.

b. The Contractor agrees to include clause "a" in all his subcontracts hereunder, except purchase orders not exceeding $2,500.

18. REPRESENTATIVES: Contractor is fully responsible for the actions of all employees and contracted representatives. Books and records of contracted representatives are subject to examination and audit under the Examination of Records clause of the contract.

19. ENVIRONMENTAL PROTECTION:

a. This clause will apply to any contract in excess of $100,000, indefinite quantity contracts estimated to exceed $100,000 in one year; provided, however, it shall not apply to use of facilities located outside the United States or to contracts otherwise excepted in accordance with 40 CFR part 15.

b. Unless this contract is exempt, by acceptance of this contract, Contractor (and where appropriate subcontractor) stipulates:

(1) that any facility to be utilized in the performance of any nonexempt contract or subcontract is not listed on the EPA List of Violating Facilities as of the date of contract award.

(2) his (their) agreement to comply with all requirements of Section 114 of the Air Act and Section 308 of the Water Act relating to inspection, monitoring, entry, reports, and information, as well as all other requirements specified in Sections 114 and 308 of the Air Act and the Water Act, respectively, and all regulations and guidelines issued thereunder.

44

4

(3) that as a condition of award of contract, he shall promptly notify the Contracting Officer of the receipt of any communication from the Director, Office of Federal Activities, U.S. Environmental Protection Agency, or his delegee, indicating that a facility to be utilized for the contract is under consideration to be listed on the EPA List of Violating Facilities.

(4) his (their) agreement to include the criteria and requirements in subparagraphs (1) through (4) in every nonexempt subcontract, and to take such action as the Government may direct as a means of enforcing such provisions.

EXHIBIT C

SOLICITATION NO.
KO-81-18-81-43

ARMY AND AIR FORCE EXCHANGE SERVICE

INDEX

SPECIAL PROVISIONS (CONCESSION CONTRACTS)

ACTIVITY (DEC 1979)

FACILITIES/MAINTENANCE (DEC 1979)

EQUIPMENT, FURNITURE, AND MOVABLE TRADE FIXTURES (DEC 1979)

TOOLS AND SUPPLIES (JUN 1980)

PROHIBITED ACTIVITIES (DEC 1979)

SCOPE OF SERVICE (NOV 1980)

MINIMUM QUALITY (JUL 1976)

PRICES (AUG 1978)

AUTHORIZED CUSTOMERS (JUL 1976)

CUSTOMER COMPLAINTS AND CLAIMS (NOV 1980)

SIGNS (JUN 1980)

UTILITIES (MAY 1978)

INTERNAL CONTROLS (NOV 1980)

CONCESSIONAIRE SETTLEMENT REPORT (MAY 1978)

FEE PAYMENT (DEC 1979)

16. TAXES (AUG 1978)

17. CONCESSIONAIRE AND CONCESSIONAIRE EMPLOYEES (CONCESSION PERSONNEL) (NOV 1980)

18. ACTIONS TO BE TAKEN UPON TERMINATION (INCLUDING EXPIRATION) (AUG 1978)

19. UNCALLED-FOR CUSTOMER PROPERTY (DEC 1979)

20. LOST, ABANDONED, AND UNCLAIMED PROPERTY (JUL 1976)

21. INVENTORY TRANSFER (NOV 1980)

22. INDEBTEDNESS (DEC 1979)

23. PRICE/FEE REVISIONS (OCT 1977)

24. INSURANCE (MAR 1979)

25. PROMOTIONAL EVENTS (NOV 1980)

26. AAFES SPECIAL SALES COUPONS (SEP 1980)

27. REFUNDS (DEC 1979)

28. DISHONORED CHECKS (JUL 1976)

29. SAFEGUARDING OF CONCESSIONAIRE FUNDS ON ARMY AND AIR FORCE INSTALLATIONS (AUG 1978)

46

SED NOV 1980

ARMY AND AIR FORCE EXCHANGE SERVICE

SPECIAL PROVISIONS

(CONCESSION CONTRACTS)

ACTIVITY (DEC 1979).

a. AAFES grants to concessionaire a concession to operate the activity described in the Schedule. ssignment of space for concession use is a revocable license and is not a tenancy. In the event ises furnished by or through AAFES are destroyed either in whole or in substantial part (so as to icantly hinder or prevent normal operations by concessionaire) by act of God, such as, but not d to, fire, flood, hurricane, unusually severe weather conditions, or as a result of any other unusual rence not caused by AAFES negligence, AAFES will not be responsible for repair/restoration of the ises or for lost profits, damage to concessionaire property, or any consequential costs incurred.

b. During the period of this contract, the contracting officer may require relocation of the ession activity. Concessionaire will be given at least 30 days advance notice of such relocation. s associated with moving and installing of AAFES-owned equipment, furniture, trade fixtures and s of the trade, and provision of utility lines for concessionaire hookup will be borne by AAFES. All costs related to relocation of the concession activity, such as movement and installation of cessionaire furnished equipment, will be borne by concessionaire.

FACILITIES/MAINTENANCE (DEC 1979).

a. Investment for buildings and installed property or fixtures will not be required of concessionaire. FES will repair and maintain AAFES furnished premises and assume all costs of ordinary running airs and interior decorating. Concessionaire will be liable for any damage to the premises resulting n acts or omissions of concessionaire, his employees, or agents. AAFES may inspect the premises at time.

b. Concessionaire will keep the premises clean, orderly, secure, and sanitary. Concessionaire will ply with the installation/exchange fire and safety regulations, the provisions of Exchange Service al 17-1, entitled "Occupational Safety and Health Program," and applicable health and sanitation ulations.

c. Concessionaire will perform custodial maintenance on the exterior of the facility and grounds if a lding is assigned to the concessionaire for his use. If the facility is shared with other concessionaires, erior custodial maintenance will be assigned by exchange management. If the concession is located in exchange complex and predominant tenancy is by AAFES direct-operated activities, AAFES will form exterior custodial maintenance, except those tasks described in "d" below. The equipment and to perform exterior custodial maintenance, assigned to the concessionaire, will be furnished by the cessionaire at no cost to AAFES.

d. Concessionaire will, as needed, but at least daily, clean the entrance door, exterior of storefront dows, entranceway and customer walkways, empty and thoroughly clean all waste and smoking eptacles, and check exterior lighting. Exterior lighting failures will be promptly reported to AAFES.

EQUIPMENT, FURNITURE, AND MOVABLE TRADE FIXTURES (DEC 1979).

a. AAFES Furnished — The item list, agreed value, and condition of equipment, furniture and trade tures furnished by AAFES are stated in an exhibit to this contract. Concessionaire will sign a custody eipt for the items furnished. Repairs of and replacement parts for AAFES furnished equipment, niture, and fixtures will be provided by AAFES or at AAFES' option by concessionaire at AAFES' cost. cessionaire will perform routine preventive maintenance and keep the equipment, furniture and

47

fixtures clean, sanitary, and secure. AAFES property will not be removed from the premises without the prior written approval of the contracting officer. AAFES property will only be used for performance of this contract. AAFES may inspect AAFES furnished equipment, furniture, and fixtures at any time.

b. Concessionaire Furnished -- Concessionaire will provide and install all the equipment, furniture and movable trade fixtures listed in an exhibit to this contract. All concessionaire furnished property is subject to the approval of the contracting officer. All electrical equipment will carry the Underwriters' Laboratories (UL) Seal of Approval. Not less than 10 working days prior to the commencement date of services under this contract, concessionaire will submit to the contracting officer a typed list of all equipment, furniture and movable trade fixtures to be used in performing this contract. Each item on the list will be identified by manufacturer, model name/number, serial number or concessionaire's fixed asset number, as appropriate. Concessionaire will not sell or remove any equipment, furniture or fixtures from the concession premises without the prior written approval of the contracting officer. Concessionaire will maintain and repair or replace, as necessary, all concessionaire furnished equipment, furniture, and fixtures. Title to concessionaire furnished equipment, furniture and fixtures remains with the concessionaire. Concessionaire investment, in equipment, furniture and fixtures required by this contract, is a business risk which concessionaire assumes. It is expressly understood and agreed that neither AAFES nor any other agency or instrumentality of the United States is or shall be liable to concessionaire for costs of concessionaire's investment in equipment, furniture or movable trade fixtures in the event of termination of this contract without renewal.

4. TOOLS AND SUPPLIES (JUN 1980). Tools of the trade and supplies required for performing this contract will not be furnished by AAFES.

5. PROHIBITED ACTIVITIES (DEC 1979). Concessionaire will not, in or about the premises of the military installation, engage in or permit gambling or the use of any device which savors gambling (such as punch cards or slot machines) or loan money to customers or to others. Facilities will not be used for performance or support of other contracts with AAFES or otherwise, or for performance or support of other commercial business activities.

6. SCOPE OF SERVICE (NOV 1980). Concessionaire will sell only that merchandise and render only those services which are specifically enumerated in the Price Schedule exhibit of this contract. Items sold under this contract will be in good taste.

7. MINIMUM QUALITY (JUL 1976). Items of merchandise or service provided under this contract will, as a minimum, be equal to those provided by first quality commercial establishments.

8. PRICES (AUG 1978).

a. Concessionaire will post a standard AAFES price list sign in a place conspicuous to customers, and maintain a standard AAFES price list binder (except automotive). Articles stocked for sale will be individually price marked.

b. Concessionaire will charge for merchandise or services only those prices established in the Price Schedule exhibit of this contract.

c. Where a state law imposes a sales tax on the sale of the item and/or service by concessionaire to the authorized customer, the sales tax will be separately stated from the sales price, added to the price set out in the Price Schedule exhibit, and collected from the customer.

9. AUTHORIZED CUSTOMERS (JUL 1976). Concessionaire will render service or sell merchandise only to personnel authorized to patronize AAFES facilities. Concessionaire will comply with patron identification procedures required by AAFES.

10. CUSTOMER COMPLAINTS AND CLAIMS (NOV 1980). Concessionaire will adhere to AAFES' policy of customer satisfaction guaranteed. All customer complaints and claims, including but not limited to claims for loss or damage to customer property, will be resolved at concessionaire's expense. Any disagreement that cannot be resolved between concessionaire and the customer will be referred to the

ntracting officer, whose decision will be final and not subject to the Disputes clause. If concessionaire fails to process complaints and claims timely, AAFES may, in addition to other rights and remedies available under this contract, settle customer complaints and claims and charge them to concessionaire's account. If concessionaire receives a customer complaint or claim based on merchandise sold or services performed by a predecessor concessionaire, the matter will be referred to the contracting officer.

11. SIGNS (JUN 1980). AAFES will furnish (as applicable) and the concessionaire will keep posted the following signs:

a. Standard AAFES Price List Sign.

b. Exterior Facility Sign.

c. Hours of Operation.

d. Emergency Contact Sign/Decal.

e. Cash Register Discrepancy Sign.

12. UTILITIES (MAY 1978).

a. AAFES is responsible for provision of heat, power, water, sewage service, and trash removal from designated areas.

b. Concessionaire is responsible for costs of connecting or disconnecting utilities to concessionaire furnished equipment.

c. Concessionaire is responsible for costs of telephone service used in performance of this contract.

d. Concessionaire furnished equipment requiring utilities hookup will comply with AAFES energy conservation policy. Concessionaire furnished equipment which is determined by the contracting officer be inefficient in use of energy will be removed and replaced with acceptable equipment at oncessionaire's expense.

e. Concessionaire and concessionaire employees will comply with AAFES energy conservation programs.

13. INTERNAL CONTROLS (NOV 1980).

a. Concessionaire will establish procedures for a complete and accurate accounting of all transactions.

b. Cash Register Procedure.

(1) Each sales transaction (cash, charge card or deposit) will be recorded on the cash register at time the transaction is made.

(2) An underring will be corrected by ringing up the additional amount.

(3) An overring will be corrected by ringing up the correct amount and completing a Concessionaire Cash Register Adjustment Voucher, AAFES Form 6550-24, for the amount of the erroneous ring. Under no circumstances will overrings be adjusted by not registering subsequent sales.

(4) If ring-ups are made for other than recording sales (e.g., repair), readings will be taken before and after test rings and reported on a Concessionaire Cash Register Adjustment Voucher, AAFES Form 6550-24.

(5) The Concessionaire Cash Register Adjustment Voucher, AAFES Form 6550-24, will be used to record necessary refunds and will be signed by the customer and concessionaire.

(6) One copy of completed vouchers will be attached to the cash register tape to substantiate refunds and adjustments of overrings and will be submitted with the Concessionaire Settlement Report, AAFES Form 6550-10.

-19

(7) Cash registers will be read at close of business daily, and the date for the day's sales will be indicated on the register tape. The register tape will be removed from the register at the monthly cut-off (10th calendar day of the month), folded to show the opening and closing readings for the reporting period and annotated to indicate date removed, cash register number and facility number. If the tape is changed during the month, the tapes will be fastened together to form a continuous tape for the reporting period.

(8) Cash register tapes for each settlement period will be attached to the Concessionaire Settlement Report, AAFES Form 6550-10, for submission to the supporting exchange accounting office.

(9) New or transferred cash registers will be read by exchange supervisor before put into use. Readings will be verified and recorded on the first Concessionaire Settlement Report, AAFES Form 6550-10.

(10) If a cash register is taken out of use, the closing register reading(s) and date will be recorded on the settlement report. The reason for removal of the cash register will be noted on the reverse side of the form. If the register is again placed in operation, these readings will appear as the opening readings on the next settlement report.

c. Customer Daily Sales Register -- If specified in the Schedule, concessionaire may use Customer Daily Sales Register, AAFES Form 6550-9, in lieu of a cash register. One copy of the completed Customer Daily Sales Register will be attached to the Concessionaire Settlement Report instead of the cash register tape.

d. Multiple Keys -- If service concessionaires sell retail merchandise or if more than one fee is applicable, concessionaire will:

(1) Record each sale of service and sale of retail merchandise on a separate key of the cash register if the cash register has multiple keys; or,

(2) (Excluding automotive activities) record the sale of services on the cash register and record the sale of retail merchandise on a Customer Daily Sales Register (attach to settlement report) if the cash register is a one key model.

(3) (Automotive activities only) ring all sales on the available key. Labor sales will be determined by totaling the labor charges listed on each work order used during the settlement period.

e. Sales Form Procedure (applicable if customer property is accepted for servicing, or a deposit is collected, or items rented).

(1) Concessionaire will provide prenumbered claim tickets, sales slips, work orders, or order blanks as appropriate, in addition to the cash register procedure set out above, acceptable to the contracting officer. Sales forms will list personal or firm names, followed by the phrase "Exchange Service Concessionaire." A separate prenumbered series of forms will be used for each outlet. Distribution of copies will be as prescribed by the contracting officer.

(2) Concession activities which accept customer property for servicing or processing will use claim tickets providing spaces for the following information: (a) date property received, (b) customer's name, rank, organization or address, and telephone number, (c) description of property, customer estimate of dollar value, and condition, (d) services performed, individually listed, (e) charges for each service, and sales tax if applicable, and (f) the following: "If the property identified on this order is not picked up within 90 days after the item is ready, the customer donates and transfers all right, title, and interest in the property to the Army and Air Force Exchange Service." (In case of privately owned vehicles left for servicing, the customer will be required to sign adjacent to the clause on the concessionaire copy of the order.)

(3) Concessionaire will submit a list of the prenumbered sales forms, by outlet or route, for the initial and each subsequent printing of forms, to the supporting exchange accounting office.

(4) A service sales form will be filled out for each transaction. Forms will be used in serial number order. Voided service sales forms will be annotated with the number of the ticket used to replace it and be processed as a complete transaction. A full description of each product sold, or service performed, will be listed on the form and the charge for each individual item listed. Under no circumstances will parts and/or products be commingled with service as a single charge.

(5) The customer will be furnished with a copy of the completed claim ticket, work order, or order blank. If a customer calls for his property without a claim ticket, the salesclerk will require proper identification, obtain the customer's signature for the property on the control copy, countersign, and indicate the date of pickup.

(6) If pickup and delivery to quarters are a part of the sales transaction, one copy of the claim ticket or sales form will be left at a mutually determined location for the customer. Route sales will be shown separately on the settlement report for purposes of audit and verification of sequence of serially numbered forms used, and included in total gross sales of the activity for purpose of fee application.

(7) If a customer picks up a portion of the items listed on a sales ticket, the unclaimed items will be listed on a new sales ticket, and the customer furnished a copy as a claim ticket.

(8) If a deposit is required from the customer, concessionaire will complete an order form detailing the customer order, charges, amount of deposit, and balance due. (The deposit will also be rung on the cash register.) When the completed order is picked up by the customer, the balance due will be rung on the cash register and supported by one copy of the order form.

(9) Completed sales forms will be retained in the originating activity for 90 days (1 year for automotive activities) after the applicable settlement report date.

f. Charge Card Sales -- Concessionaire may accept those national charge cards customarily recognized in their commercial trade. Concessionaire will be responsible for the payment of any fees, charge backs, and other arranged costs levied by the charge card issuing companies. All charge card transactions will be rung on the cash register at the time of the sale.

g. Inspections. The AAFES contracting officer, or any person designated by the contracting officer, may conduct inspections as may be considered necessary to insure strict compliance by the concessionaire with all provisions of this contract.

14. <u>CONCESSIONAIRE SETTLEMENT REPORT (MAY 1978).</u>

a. Concessionaire will prepare a Concessionaire Settlement Report, AAFES Form 6550-10, for each reporting period, listing each facility separately on the report. Copies of all cash register tapes, Concessionaire Cash Register Adjustment Vouchers, AAFES Form 6550-24, and Customer Daily Sales Register, AAFES Form 6550-9 (if authorized for use), for the reporting period will be attached.

b. The reporting period will be from the 11th calendar day of the month through the 10th calendar day of the next month.

c. A copy of the Concessionaire Settlement Report must be forwarded to arrive in the supporting exchange accounting office no later than the 20th calendar day of each month for the reporting period.

15. <u>FEE PAYMENT (DEC 1979).</u>

a. The amount and frequency of fee payments will be based on the "Estimated Fee" which is determined by applying the contract fee to the estimated monthly sales in the contract. The estimated sales may be revised by amendment if there is significant variance from the actual. Payments must be made to arrive in the supporting exchange accounting office as follows:

(1) If the "Estimated Fee" is less than $1,000, the actual fee payment for the monthly reporting period is due no later than the 20th calendar day of each month;

(2) If the "Estimated Fee" is $1,000 or more, concessionaire will make three partial payments, each equal to one-fourth of the "Estimated Fee," no later than the 27th, the 6th, and the 13th day of the calendar month. The balance (the fee based on actual sales for the monthly reporting period, less the three partial payments) will be paid no later than the 20th calendar day of the month.

b. Fee (and settlement report) for less than a full reporting period upon termination or expiration of the contract will be forwarded to arrive no later than 10 calendar days after termination or expiration of the contract.

c. Payments due on Saturday, Sunday, or national holidays will be due on the next working day.

TAXES (AUG 1978).

a. Concessionaire is responsible for determining the applicability of and for payment of all federal, state, host country, and local taxes applicable to the property, income, and transactions of concessionaire, and if required by applicable laws and regulations, will collect and remit sales taxes to the state. Sales taxes which have been collected in the manner required by Clause 8, Prices, will be excluded from the computation of gross receipts, and the amount excluded will be listed on the Concessionaire Settlement Report. The amount of taxes so excluded will not exceed the actual sum payable to the state. If required by state law or regulation, concessionaire will obtain and conspicuously display the state sales tax permit.

b. Concessionaire warrants that the contract prices or other consideration do not include any tax or duty from which concessionaire is exempt under the laws or agreements of the United States Government, state or host country where this contract is performed. If any such tax or duty has been included in the pricing or consideration through error or otherwise, the contract pricing or consideration will be correspondingly reduced or adjusted. If for any reason after the contract date, concessionaire is relieved, in whole or in part, from the payment or the burden of any tax or duty included in the contract pricing or other consideration, the contract pricing and/or other consideration will be correspondingly reduced or adjusted.

c. If this contract covers an activity involving a Federal Occupational Tax, concessionaire agrees as a condition precedent to engaging in or operating such activity, to tender to AAFES the amount of any Federal Occupational Tax applicable thereto if payment has not been accomplished by concessionaire, or to reimburse AAFES the amount of any such tax AAFES has paid as a result of the operation of such activity by concessionaire. As between the parties of this contract, notice or demand for payment from an office of the U.S. Internal Revenue Service will be conclusive that the Federal Occupational Tax is payable and in the amount so specified to be due.

'. **CONCESSIONAIRE AND CONCESSIONAIRE EMPLOYEES (CONCESSION PERSONNEL) (NOV 1980).**

a. Responsible management will be available during all hours of operation at the concession activity. The manager or designated representative will be completely knowledgeable of the terms and conditions of this contract and will be delegated authority to conduct business as required by this contract. Authority will include, but will not be limited to, purchase of operating supplies, maintenance and repair of equipment, training of employees, maintaining prescribed hours of operation, supervision of concessionaire employees, and settlement of customer complaints or claims. The concessionaire will provide the contracting officer with written notification naming the person appointed manager or representative.

b. Concessionaire will furnish a sufficient number of trained, qualified employees to ensure the efficient performance of this contract. New concessionaires will give first consideration to employment of employees of the previous concessionaire.

c. If requested by exchange management, the concessionaire will, at his expense, make his employees available for any applicable training in accordance with training dates determined by exchange management.

d. Concession personnel must meet the health and security standards prescribed by the contract and applicable regulations, and must obtain installation passes, permits, and security clearances as applicable.

e. Concession personnel will be neatly dressed and meticulous in their personal grooming at all times. Customer contact personnel will be required to wear attire typical of styles commonly used by the better local commercial facilities of the same trade and as approved by the contracting officer. The standard AAFES nameplate will be worn in the manner prescribed by current directives. Nameplates will be furnished by AAFES, and the concessionaire will reimburse AAFES the cost thereof (approximately $1.00 per nameplate).

f. Concession personnel will give prompt and courteous treatment to authorized customers.

g. Concession personnel will abide by applicable regulations and directives and conduct themselves so as not to reflect discredit on AAFES.

h. Concessionaire will discontinue the use of any employee for performance of this contract upon written notice from the contracting officer that the individual is not (or no longer) acceptable for performance under this contract. Concessionaire will not use any such employee in performance of other AAFES contracts without the prior written consent of the applicable contracting officer.

18. ACTIONS TO BE TAKEN UPON TERMINATION (INCLUDING EXPIRATION) (AUG 1978).

a. AAFES will have the option and first right to purchase any or all of the concessionaire furnished property including equipment, furniture and movable trade fixtures, etc., used in the facility by concessionaire to perform this contract. In the event of exercise of this option by AAFES, the value of such property will be determined by an independent appraiser obtained by the contracting officer.

b. Concessionaire will promptly settle his account with AAFES including payment in full of all amounts due AAFES; yield up the premises, installed property and fixtures, and all AAFES furnished property, clean and in as good order and condition as when received (damage due to acts of God or the U.S. Government, and ordinary wear and tear excepted); surrender all installation passes, decals, etc., for himself and his employees; and complete satisfactory settlement of all customer complaints and claims. Termination of the contract does not release concessionaire from the obligation to satisfactorily settle customer complaints and claims.

c. Concessionaire will promptly remove all concessionaire furnished property including equipment, furniture and movable trade fixtures, etc., not purchased by AAFES, identified in an exhibit in this contract, and all concessionaire owned tools of the trade and supplies. Upon failure to yield up the premises or remove concessionaire's property, the contracting officer may enter the premises, cause concessionaire's property to be removed and stored in a warehouse at concessionaire's expense, and cause the premises to be cleaned and restored at concessionaire's expense. If concessionaire is indebted to AAFES, concessionaire authorizes and empowers the contracting officer to take possession of concessionaire's property and dispose of same by public or private sale without notice, and out of the proceeds of sale, satisfy all costs to AAFES including the costs of sale, handling, storage, etc., and any other indebtedness to AAFES.

19. UNCALLED-FOR CUSTOMER PROPERTY (DEC 1979). Customer property not picked up within 90 days from the ready date is uncalled-for customer property and will be handled as follows:

a. The sales ticket/claim check (both customer and concessionaire copies acknowledging receipt of customer property) must contain the statement set out in Clause 13e(2) of this exhibit. Concessionaire will contact the customer if the property is not picked up within a reasonable time after it's ready and will maintain a record of contacts. If required by the contracting officer, concessionaire will provide a list of uncalled-for customer property indicating the order/ticket number, customer name, description of item(s), and amount due.

b. The contracting officer will determine disposition of uncalled-for customer property. Uncalled-for customer property valued at more than $100.00 released to concessionaire must be accounted for. Items sold will be handled as a sale. Fees will be paid on these transactions.

c. Customer vehicles will be turned over to the exchange with a copy of the customer order, a copy of the work order, a copy of the notification to the customer, and all other available documentation.

LOST, ABANDONED, AND UNCLAIMED PROPERTY (JUL 1976). Personal property left in the concession area will be returned promptly to the owner if the owner can be identified. If return to the owner cannot be promptly accomplished, the items will be turned over to the appropriate military office for lost, abandoned or unclaimed items. (Example, a customer leaves his umbrella in the concession.)

INVENTORY TRANSFER (NOV 1980).

a. If this contract is not awarded to the incumbent concessionaire or is for converting an AAFES direct operated service activity to concession operation, the new concessionaire will purchase all unclaimed customer orders — which involve processing or repair of customer-owned property -- from the previous concessionaire or AAFES. This does not include uncalled-for customer property, as defined in clause 19 of this exhibit. The unclaimed customer orders are to be purchased by the commencement date of service under this contract, and the purchase price will be the full charge(s) in effect at time customer(s) turned the item(s) in for processing or repair, less any cash deposit(s) and less AAFES' fee under any previous contract. The new concessionaire assumes full responsibility for servicing unfinished orders purchased and delivering the finished orders to customers at the original price. Payment of fee to AAFES will be at the rate set out in either the previous contract or, if previously an AAFES direct operation, this contract. Prior to the service commencement date under this contract, a listing of such transferred inventory — by finished and unfinished work -- signed by both the outgoing and incoming concessionaires will be furnished the contracting officer.

b. Upon expiration or termination of this contract, concessionaire will transfer all undelivered customer orders to any new concessionaire or to AAFES, as determined by the contracting officer. Payment to concessionaire will be on the basis of the full charge(s) in effect under this contract, less any cash deposit(s) and less AAFES' fee. Contracting officer will determine appropriate disposal for uncalled-for customer orders. Any monies derived from the sale of such uncalled-for customer property will be remitted by AAFES to concessionaire, to the extent of concessionaire's share of the customer charges for services rendered.

22. **INDEBTEDNESS (DEC 1979).**

a. Concessionaire will pay promptly and in accordance with the terms of this contract, all indebtedness incurred in connection with performing the contract. If a due date is not specifically set out elsewhere, such payments due AAFES must be received by AAFES no later than 15 days after receipt of notice of amounts due. If all amounts due under this contract or due under other contracts are not received, at any time thereafter, the contracting officer may at his option direct by written order that daily receipts be turned over to AAFES for the period or periods of time until all amounts owing AAFES are paid.

b. AAFES may charge concessionaire for a dishonored check received from concessionaire, except when (1) the bank acknowledges the return to be the result of bank error or (2) the return is the result of an AAFES error. The amount charged by AAFES will not exceed the administrative amount normally charged AAFES customers by AAFES for dishonored checks. The contracting officer may, at his option, require payment to be made in cash, certified check, or cashier's check.

23. **PRICE/FEE REVISIONS (OCT 1977).** The prices and fees established in this contract will remain firm throughout the term of the contract unless revised in accordance with the following:

a. Price Revisions.

(1) The contracting officer may, on his own initiative or on request of concessionaire, increase or decrease prices at his sole discretion. In the event of a price decrease, the fee to AAFES will be decreased by a percentage which will result in the reduction in income generated by the price decrease being absorbed by AAFES. Any increase/decrease in concessionaire expenses directly attributable to price revisions will be taken into consideration by the contracting officer in computing the appropriate percentage of fee change.

8

54

(2) The contracting officer will effect such price/fee revisions by issuing an unilateral contract mendment to become effective on the date indicated in the amendment. The concessionaire will mplement the prices on the date established in the amendment. The fee revision will be considered final nless concessionaire submits a request for reconsideration to the contracting officer within 30 days after eceipt of the amendment by the concessionaire. Such request for reconsideration may only be based on e fact that the contracting officer's fee revision will result in loss of income to the concessionaire hich can be directly attributed to the price revision. After receipt of a request for reconsideration, the ontracting officer will reconsider his action and issue a final decision under the Disputes clause of this contract. However, nothing in this clause will excuse the concessionaire from proceeding with mplementation of the revised prices on the date established in the amendment.

b. Fee Revisions.

(1) Fee revisions may be effected as indicated in subparagraph "a" above in conjunction with price revisions.

(2) A decrease in AAFES' fee may be requested by the concessionaire in the event of increase in his operating costs which were unforeseen at the time of execution of contract, execution of a novation of the contract, amendment of the contract to revise prices and/or fees, or extension of the contract. Such request must be in writing, directed to the contracting officer, and must include factual information and data to substantiate the requested revisions. The information and data must include detailed identification of higher or newly applicable costs of operation. This subparagraph will not be construed to grant concessionaire any right to a fee revision due to unforeseen increased costs; rather, favorable consideration of concessionaire requests for fee revisions hereunder is solely at the discretion of the contracting officer. In the event the contracting officer agrees to grant concessionaire's requested revision, in whole or in part, a fee revision will become effective on the date established in the amendment or on the date of execution by both parties, whichever is later. In no event will the fee revision be made effective retroactively. Failure to grant requested relief under this subparagraph will not be subject to the Disputes clause.

24. INSURANCE (MAR 1979).

a. Concessionaire will maintain in full force and effect, during the period of the contract, at least e insurance coverage set out in the Insurance Requirements exhibit of this contract.

b. Concessionaire will be liable for damage, loss or injury to property or persons resulting from acts or omissions of concessionaire, his employees or agents, whether or not covered by required insurance.

25. PROMOTIONAL EVENTS (NOV 1980).

a. Concessionaire agrees to participate in the annual AAFES anniversary sale. The contracting officer will select services and/or items listed in the Price Schedule to be sold at reduced prices, and establish duration and percent of price reduction. The period of the anniversary sale will not exceed 3 days, and prices will be reduced by not more than 15 percent. However, price reductions may be greater than 15 percent and offered for more than 3 days, subject to written agreement between concessionaire and contracting officer. The agreement need not be in the form of a contract amendment.

b. Concessionaire may at any time offer voluntary price reductions for limited time periods upon written agreement between concessionaire and the contracting officer. The agreement need not be in the form of a contract amendment.

c. Other promotional price reductions for limited time periods may be provided upon written agreement between concessionaire and the contracting officer. Such written agreement may provide for temporarily reducing fee in conjunction with the promotional price reduction. The agreement need not be in the form of a contract amendment.

AAFES SPECIAL SALES COUPONS (SEP 1980).

(This clause applies to all activities except automotive.)

a. Periodically, AAFES may provide its customers with special sales coupons for use in purchasing merchandise or services provided under this contract at reduced prices. The coupons will show the specific amount of discount customers will be entitled to receive.

b. Concessionaire will honor and redeem coupons presented by exchange customers. The coupons are redeemable at face value towards purchase of specific items indicated, subject to compliance with any time limit and other restrictions that may be specified. Coupons will not be redeemed for cash.

c. The regular sell price (price before discount) will be rung on the cash register. The amount of monies collected from the customer will equal the regular sell price discounted by the coupon's face value. Concessionaire will calculate fee to AAFES based on regular sell price, before considering any discount customers are entitled to resulting from redeeming the special sales coupons.

d. Concessionaire will have customers print their name, address and telephone number on reverse side of the coupon. Concessionaire will annotate the coupons with the cash register transaction number and/or sales receipt number, along with the date accepted.

e. AAFES will reimburse concessionaire for amount of valid coupons redeemed by exchange customers, as follows:

(1) Concessionaire will enter the total face value amount of coupons redeemed, during a reporting period, on the Concessionaire Settlement Report, AAFES Form 6550-10, and deduct the coupon amount from fee payment due AAFES.

(2) The coupons received and redeemed will be submitted to the supporting exchange accounting office with the settlement report. The supporting exchange accounting office will verify the coupon amount.

REFUNDS (DEC 1979).

a. Concessionaire will be responsible for refunds to customers due to customer dissatisfaction with any item or service or due to any overcharges made on items or services furnished under this contract. Should concessionaire refuse or fail to promptly make any refund of overcharges to a customer, AAFES may make such refund and charge such amount to concessionaire's account. If a customer cannot be located or if refund to a customer is otherwise not practicable as determined by the contracting officer, concessionaire will pay the amount of the overcharge to AAFES within 15 calendar days from date of demand by AAFES.

b. Requests for refunds not promptly honored will be considered complaints or claims and will be subject to the provisions of the Customer Complaints and Claims clause.

8. DISHONORED CHECKS (JUL 1976). Concessionaire may charge the customer for a dishonored check received from the customer, except that the charge will not be applicable when (1) the bank acknowledges its return to be the result of bank error or (2) the return is the result of a concessionaire error. The amount charged by concessionaire will not exceed the administrative amount charged by AAFES for dishonored checks. Losses due to dishonored checks are concessionaire's responsibility.

9. SAFEGUARDING OF CONCESSIONAIRE FUNDS ON ARMY AND AIR FORCE INSTALLATIONS (AUG 1978).

a. When funds in excess of $100 are kept in the concessionaire facility during nonoperational hours, they will be secured in a steel safe equipped with a three-position combination tumbler locking device.

b. When funds in excess of $500 are held in the concessionaire facility during nonoperational hours, the safe must --

(1) be secured to the premises by being encased in a concrete bed; or

(2) be bolted or steel-strapped to a floor beam or an internal wall support beam with the bolts or straps concealed to prevent cutting or prying; or

(3) weigh in excess of 1,000 pounds.

57

PRICE SCHEDULE

PART I - MERCHANDISING POLICY

. The concessionaire is required to stock for sale the categories of merchandise indicated Part IV below which comply with the provisions of Exhibit I, Additional Special Provisions r Commodity Concession Contracts, and Exhibit J, Performance Specifications. The concessionaire will keep a sufficient quantity and selection of items available at all times to tisfactorily meet customer demand and the requirements of the Contracting Officer.

. The concessionaire will frequently add or delete individual items in authorized categories of his stock assortment to vary the selection, test new merchandise, respond to customer requests and purge the inventory of slow moving items. Items may be added to or leted from the stock assortment only upon approval of the Contracting Officer or his signated representative. Approval will be indicated by verification of the price and dition to the concession price list as per Part III, paragraph 7.

. Entire categories of merchandise may be added to or deleted from the stock assortment nly after approval by the Contracting Officer and appropriate amendment of the contract.

. Merchandise in authorized categories, but not regularly stocked due to price, infrequent mand, space limitations, etc., may be special ordered for customers. Current AAFES licies regarding deposits and refunds relative to Exchange special orders are applicable special orders by concessionaire.

. At the request of the Contracting Officer, or his designated representative, the concessionaire will eliminate any item from the concession stock assortment which duplicates AAFES rect retail merchandise, another concessionaire's merchandise, or is otherwise found objectionable for sale to AAFES customers. The removal request will specify whether the tem is to be removed from sale immediately or discontinued when existing supplies are xhausted.

. All merchandise on display at the point of sale will be price marked using price marking r or similar mechanical price marking device.

T II - DEFINITION OF TERMS

. Supplier: A firm or individual from whom the concessionaire purchases merchandise.

. Supplier's Invoice: The original statement showing supplier's name and business address; description and cost price of the merchandise delivered or shipped, and when and to whom old.

. Cost Price: The concessionaire's "Landed Cost," determined by one of the following thod:

a. For F.O.B. destination purchases, the price that is shown on the supplier's invoice.

58

EXHIBIT D (Cont'd)

b. For F.O.B. origin purchases, the price that is shown on the supplier's invoice plus, where applicable, actual packing, transportation, customs and other charges incurred by the concessionaire in getting the merchandise to the concession sales outlet(s). The actual transportation charges should be reasonable and in conformance with commonly accepted tariffs.

c. When the concessionaire is also the manufacturer/supplier of an item, the cost price will be the average unit production cost from typical production run plus, where applicable, other costs normally associated with F.O.B. origin purchases for resale. The concessionaire will submit his cost analysis showing amounts for materials, labor, overhead, transportation, taxes, etc., to the Contracting Officer for approval.

4. Sell Price: The price that the AAFES customer must pay for the item.

PART III - PRICING POLICY

1. The pricing method and percentage factor listed in Part IV, for the respective category of merchandise, will be applied according to the appropriate formula below to determine the maximum sell price of all concession items.

Markup on Cost Method: Multiply the cost price by the markup percentage for the merchandise category as listed in Part IV, and add the product to the cost price. Resulting sell prices less than $50.00 will be rounded to the nearest nickel (5¢); sell prices $50.00 and above will be rounded to the nearest dollar ($1.00).

2. The sell price computed as above, is the maximum authorized for any item in the stock assortment. This does not restrict the concessionaire from selling an item at a lesser price to clear slow moving, aged or excess merchandise; meet the competition of the local economy or participate in special promotional events. Any reduction in price is a part of the normal routine of doing business and will not be considered for a fee reduction except as otherwise provided for in the contract.

3. Price Changes:

a. Prices will be changed on merchandise in stock that was originally priced by the Markup on Cost Method whenever there is a change in the concessionaire's cost price. Such changes will be effected upon receipt of the first delivery of replenishment merchandise at the concessionaire's new cost price. Approval of the Contracting Officer or his designated representative must be obtained prior to increasing sell prices.

b. Prices will be changed on merchandise in stock when the exchange established currency conversion rate, where applicable, is revised. Concessionaires will be notified of the effective date of price changes due to currency fluctuation by the Contracting Officer or his designated representative.

c. Price increases/decreases will be made effective in all sales outlets simultaneously.

4. Special Order Merchandise:

a. The sell price for special order merchandise will be determined by the same method as if the item was being purchased for stock.

59

AAFES FORM 4450-3 (REV JAN 79) (PREV EDITION USABLE)

ARMY AND AIR FORCE EXCHANGE SERVICE	SOLICITATION OR CONTRACT NO.	PAGE OF PAGES
EXHIBIT D (Cont'd)	KO-81-18-81-43	3 4

b. Where expeditious delivery, over and above normal transportation or handling charges is requested by the customer, the customer will be advised that such additional cost will be added to the sell price, and that additional cost can be avoided by agreeing to normal transportation or handling charges. If such handling is still requested by the customer after the required explanation, the sell price will be determined by adding the actual additional freight or handling charges incurred to the sell price computed by application of a pricing method in Paragraph 1 above. For example: An item with a cost price of $10.00, a markup of 40%, for which actual additional freight and handling charges of $.75 were incurred because the customer requested expeditious delivery involving above normal transportation or handling charges, would sell for $14.75 ($10.00 x 140% + $.75 = $14.75). All special orders that have a special handling charge will be recorded on a sales slip showing the total price plus a notation of the special handling charge. Special handling charges may be excluded from calculation of gross sales for fee computation purposes.

c. All price lists and merchandise on display at the point of sale will be price marked in dollars. Invoices priced in other currencies and locality survey results in local currency will be converted to dollar currency using the current conversion rate established by the exchange for commodity concessions.

6. Verification of Prices:

a. The concessionaire will furnish copies of most recent supplier's invoices, manufacturing cost analysis, and local prevailing prices being used as a basis for pricing every item in the proposed concessionaire stock assortment to the contracting officer or his designated representative for approval of items and verification of pricing. Copies of these price verification documents will be kept on file in the area services operations office.

b. When the Markup on Cost method is used to determine the maximum authorized sell price, the supplier's invoice cost and the pro rata costs associated with getting the merchandise to the concession sales outlet(s) will be clearly identified and stated in a "per unit" cost price. The percentage markup on cost will be applied to determine the exchange concession sell price. Each merchandise item will be cross-referenced to its price list item number.

7. Concessionaire Price List:

AUTHORIZED STOCK ASSORTMENT & PRICE LIST

The concessionaire will establish a price list for use in the sales outlet by concessionaire employees as a reference document in the format shown below, or as modified by the contracting officer. Merchandise will be listed by category, subcategory, or individual items as stated in Part IV below. The initial stock assortment and price list will be signed and dated by the contracting officer or his designated representative in the "approved by" and "date" blocks. The addition/deletion of items from this stock assortment and subsequent price changes will be accomplished by issuance of revised price list pages. Revised pages will be verified, signed and dated with the effective date in the same manner as the initial stock assortment and price list.

60

ARMY AND AIR FORCE EXCHANGE SERVICE | SOLICITATION/CONTRACT NO. | PAGE OF PAGES

EXHIBIT D (Cont'd) | KO-81-18-81-43 | 4 4

Contract No. ______________ Page ____ of ____

AUTHORIZED STOCK ASSORTMENT AND PRICE LIST

MERCHANDISE CATEGORY/SUB CATEGORY/ITEM DESCRIPTION	PRICING METHOD MARKUP ON COST Cost Price	Exchange Price
1.	1.	1.
-	-	-
-	-	-
-	-	-

Approved By______________ Date ______________ Currency Conversion Rate: = $1 Price List Effective Date ______

PART IV - AUTHORIZED MERCHANDISE AND PRICING METHOD

The maximum sell price for items in the following categories of merchandise will be determined by application of the pricing method and percentage factor according to the procedures in Part III above.

Merchandise Category/Sub Category/Item Description	PRICING METHOD Markup on Cost (%)
1. TV Sets, Color/Black and White	40%
2. Radio/Cassette Recorders, Portable/Stereo	40%
3. Stereo Components	40%
4. Air Conditioners	40%
5. Refrigerators	40%
6. Fans	40%

61

AFE FORM 4450-2 (REV JAN 78)

ARMY AND AIR FORCE EXCHANGE SERVICE	SOLICITATION OR CONTRACT NO.	PAGE OF PAGES
EXHIBIT E	KO-81-18-81-43	1 1

FEE SCHEDULE

Offerors shall enter below the single percentage fee offered to AAFES. Fee shall be paid based on total combined volume of all locations included in this contract. Settlement of fee shall be in accordance with the Clause 15, Exhibit C, Special Provisions, as altered by Exhibit H.

FEE

________________%

OFFEROR

AAFES FORM 4480-8 (REV JAN 70) (PREV EDITION USABLE)

62

ARMY AND AIR FORCE EXCHANGE SERVICE EXHIBIT F	Solicitation No. KO-81-18-81-43	PAGE 1 OF 2 PAGES

INSURANCE REQUIREMENTS

1. The concessionaire will maintain, during any contract period, insurance coverage listed herein, in insurance company(ies) acceptable to AAFES. All liability insurance coverage will name the United States and AAFES as additional insured and include a severability of interest clause with respect to claims, demands, suits, judgments, cost, charges, and expenses arising out of or in connection with any loss, damage, or injury resulting from the negligence or other fault of concessionaire, or concessionaire's agents, representatives, or employees. The insurance coverages to be maintained are:

a. The following with coverage limits complying with state or military installation requirements, whichever is greater, where this contract is performed:

(1) Worker's Compensation and Employer's Liability Insurance.

(2) Automobile Bodily Injury and Property Damage Liability for vehicles operated in performance of this contract by the concessionaire or concessionaire's agents or employees on the military installation, whether or not owned by concessionaire.

b. The following coverage will be maintained and as required by the contracting officer, the concessionaire will furnish Certificate of Insurance, AAFES Form 7500-3, evidencing that insurance is in effect:

(1) Comprehensive General Liability in minimum limits of $100,000 for personal injury for each occurrence or $200,000 aggregate and $25,000 for each occurrence for property damage or $50,000 aggregate.

(2) Products Liability Insurance in minimum limits of $50,000 for injury to or death of any one person, $100,000 for each accident or occurrence, $100,000 for aggregate products bodily injury liability, $25,000 for property damage liability, and $25,000 for aggregate products property damage liability.

AAFES FORM 4450-8 (REV JAN 79) (PREV EDITION USABLE)

63

ARMY AND AIR FORCE EXCHANGE SERVICE	SOLICITATION/CONTRACT NO.	PAGE	OF PAGES
EXHIBIT F (Continued)	KO-81-18-81-43	2	2

AAFES-PAC BLANKET INSURANCE PROCEDURES
(Concession Contracts)

2. AAFES-PAC COMPREHENSIVE GENERAL LIABILITY INSURANCE

a. To satisfy the insurance requirements in paragraph 1 of this Exhibit to the extent covered by the AAFES-PAC General Liability Insurance for Concessionaires (Blanket Policy), the contractor may subscribe by signing the declaration below.

b. In the event the contractor chooses to obtain his own insurance but fails to submit a certificate of insurance or other acceptable evidence of insurance to the Contracting Officer within fourteen (14) days after award of contract, the contractor will automatically be included in the Blanket Policy and the amounts stated in the paragraphs below will be charged. If the contractor's insurance is due to expire during the term of the contract, the contractor will be included in the Blanket Policy immediately upon expiration of his insurance policy unless the Contracting Officer receives evidence of renewal at least ten (10) days prior to the expiration of insurance.

c. The contractor, when enrolled in the Blanket Policy, agrees to pay the premium rate as established annually by the insurance company. Currently the premium rates are as follows:

(1) For Workmen's Compensation Insurance at the rate of ___.05___ percent of gross monthly receipts regardless of the number of employees.

(2) For all other types of insurance required above except Workmen's Compensation and Automobile Liability, at the rate of ___.028___ percent of the gross monthly receipts.

(3) Other liability (list):

d. The AAFES-PAC Blanket Insurance Policy excludes (among other things itemized in the policy) automobile liability, losses from acts of terrorism and loss of any of the contractor-owned equipment and supplies.

3. ACCEPTANCE DECLARATION

I (We) do elect to be enrolled in the AAFES-PAC Blanket Insurance Policy at the rate specified above, subject to annual adjustment by the insurance company. I (We) further agree that in the event I (we) wish to terminate this insurance I (we) will provide at the time of termination a certificate of insurance for the required coverage. The date of any termination will be effective on the last day of the Exchange fiscal period in which the notice of termination is received by the Contracting Officer.

____________________ ____________________
(Date) (Signature)

AAFES FORM 4450-9 (REV JAN 79) (PREV EDITION USABLE)

64

AND AIR FORCE EXCHANGE SERVICE	SOLICITATION NO.	PAGE OF PAGES
EXHIBIT G	KO-81-16-81-43	1 1

AAFES FURNISHED EQUIPMENT

1. The following Exchange owned equipment is available for use by the concessionaire rental free in the performance of the contract.

Acq. Date	Description	Q'ty	Acq. Cost
Unknown	Swag/Table Lamp Gondola Fix No. 503	3 ea	$630.00 (for 3 ea)
Jun 74	Full Vision Showcase Fix No. 312	1 ea	275.00
Jun 74	Cash Register Stand - 36" Fix No. 323	1 ea	90.00
Unknown	Cash Register 500 Series	1 ea	Unknown

2. The concessionaire shall perform maintenance and repairs necessary to keep the items in good condition, reasonable wear and tear expected, shall use the items solely for the operation of its exchange concession, shall not remove the items from the United States military installation wherein the concession is located without the written consent of the Contracting Officer, and shall return the items to the Exchange upon expiration or termination of the contract.

3. Certification of Equipment: Concessionaire may be required to furnish periodic certification as to the location of all AAFES-furnished equipment for which the concessionaire has not taken legal title. The frequency and format of such certification shall be as determined by the Contracting Officer.

AAFES FORM 4450-9 (REV JAN 79) (PREV EDITION USABLE)

65

[ARMY] AND AIR FORCE EXCHANGE SERVICE	SOLICITATION OR CONTRACT NO.	PAGE OF PAGES
EXHIBIT H	KO-81-18-81-43	1 4

AAFES-PAC ALTERATIONS

(FEB 1980)

The following alterations have been made in the provisions of this solicitation/contract:

1. Subparagraph a of the "DEFINITIONS" clause, Exhibit A, General Provisions, is deleted in its entirety, and the following is substituted in lieu thereof:

"a. "AAFES" identifies the Army and Air Force Exchange Service, and its subordinate elements including, but not limited to, the Army and Air Force Exchange Service-Pacific (AAFES-PAC), and the Korea Area Exchange (KOAX). The term "Exchange" is synonymous with the term "AAFES".

2. The following clauses are added to Exhibit A, General Provisions:

"CONFLICT IN TRANSLATION (1976). In the event of a disagreement between the English text of this contract and any translation thereof or any ambiguity in any translation, the English text shall govern."

"APPLICABLE LAW (JUN 1979). The rights and remedies of the parties are governed by the terms and provisions of this contract. The validity and interpretation of this contract and all rights and obligations thereunder shall be governed by the laws of the United States of America."

3. Subparagraph b of the "ACTIVITY" clause, Exhibit C, Special Provisions, is revised by deleting the second sentence in its entirety, and substituting the following in lieu thereof:

". . . If such relocation to building(s) or location(s) other than as indicated in the Schedule is required, AAFES will attempt to provide thirty days advance notice; however, if due to military exigency, a thirty day notice is not possible, the AAFES will not be responsible for any excess costs resulting from the short notification. . ."

4. The "FACILITIES/MAINTENANCE" clause, Exhibit C, Special Provisions, is amended by adding the following as subparagraph e:

"e. Concessionaire's use of facilities will be limited to performance of this contract. Concessionaire shall not, in or about the premises of the military installation, engage in or permit gambling or the use of any device which savors gambling such as punch cards, or slot machines; sell or deal in or permit to be sold any form of intoxicating beverages, drugs, depressants, stimulants or hallucinogens; loan money to customers or to others; or sell merchandise or services on credit, unless specifically provided for elsewhere in this contract. However, nothing in this clause shall limit or restrict the sale of authorized merchandise or services in or about the premises by AAFES through vending machines or other means."

AAFES FORM 4450-9 (REV JAN 78) (PREV EDITION USABLE)

66

AAFES-PAC ALTERATIONS (FEB 1980)

5. Subparagraph c of the "PRICES" clause, Exhibit C, Special Provisions, is hereby deleted.

6. The "CONCESSION SETTLEMENT REPORT" clause, Exhibit C, Special Provisions, is deleted in its entirety.

7. The "FEE PAYMENT" clause, Exhibit C, Special Provisions, is hereby deleted in its entirety, and the following is substituted in lieu thereof:

"FEE PAYMENT (1976). The concessionaire shall pay to the AAFES the fee percentage of the total combined sales of all locations included in this contract in accordance with the fee schedule in Exhibit E. The procedure for payment of fee shall be as prescribed below.

a. At the close of each business day, the concessionaire will turn in the total receipts for the day and the following documentation to the designated AAFES cashier:

(1) The Salesclerk's Daily Report/Register Summary Report, AAFES Form 7200-12 (in triplicate), Concessionaire Cash Register Adjustment Vouchers, and

(2) Cash register audit tapes, or the original(s) of the Customer Daily Sales Register, AAFES Form 6550-9; and

(3) Duplicate copies of prenumbered sales forms, claim tickets, work order, as may be required by this contract.

b. The AAFES cahsier will, in the presence of the concessionaire verify the amount received, sign and return one copy of the Salesclerk's Daily Report/Register Summary Report, AAFES Form 7200-12 as a receipt for monies turned in.

c. Computation of fee will be based on the net register sales plus any noted cash overages. In instances of cash shortages, the computation of fee will be based on the net register sales.

d. Should a check be received by the concessionaire payable to AAFES, payment of which is refused by the payee bank, such check will not constitute a valid receipt and the records of receipts and computation of fee will be adjusted accordingly.

e. Reimbursement will be made within 20 days following the close of the Exchange fiscal accounting month by an Exchange check drawn in Republic of Korea Won at the official Eighth Army accommodation dollar-won rate of exchange in effect on the date of payment."

8. Subparagraph a of the "TAXES" clause, Exhibit C, Special Provisions, is hereby deleted in its entirety, and the following is substituted in lieu thereof:

"a. Concessionaire assumes complete and sole liability for all host country and local taxes applicable to the property, income, and transactions of the concessionaire."

ARMY AND AIR FORCE EXCHANGE SERVICE EXHIBIT H (Cont'd)	SOLICITATION OR CONTRACT NO. KO-81-18-81-43	PAGE 3 OF PAGES 4

AAFES-PAC ALTERATIONS (FEB 1980)

9. The "DISHONORED CHECKS" clause, Exhibit C, Special Provisions, is hereby deleted in its entirety, and the following is substituted in lieu thereof:

"RISK OF LOSS (1976).

a. Concessionaire assumes the risk of loss of all receipts until delivered to the authorized AAFES cashier. In the event of loss of receipts prior to delivery to the cashier, concessionaire shall pay AAFES, or AAFES shall deduct from payments due concessionaire such amounts as shall be established by AAFES audit.

b. Concessionaire may accept customer's check for the amount of the purchase made or services rendered. Third party checks will not be accepted. While AAFES will assist wherever possible, the concessionaire assumes the risk of loss from dishonored checks. Concessionaire may charge the customer for a dishonored check received from the customer, except that the charge will not be applicable when (a) the bank acknowledges the return to the result of bank error or (b) the return is the result of a concessionaire error. The amount charged by the concessionaire will not exceed the administrative amount charge by AAFES for dishonored checks.

c. Concessionaire assumes the risk of loss from acceptance of counterfeit money.

d. Concessionaire assumes the risk of loss or damage from any cause whatsoever to his stock, equipment, fixtures and property, and to customer's property left with him for service.

e. If the sale of merchandise or services on credit is authorized by this contract, concessionaire assumes responsibility for all deferred charges."

10. The following clauses are added to the AAFES Furnished Equipment Exhibit:

"a. PURCHASES FROM AAFES (FEB 1980). Concessionaire may purchase from AAFES, on a reimburseable basis, equipment, merchandise and supplies required in the performance of the contract. All such purchases shall be in accordance with applicable AAFES, U.S. Military, and Host Country regulations."

b. The concessionaire is cautioned that any equipment, merchandise and supplies obtained by means of the AAFES conditional sales agreement, other than expendable supplies, remains the property of AAFES and title to the items may not be obtained by the concessionaire unless AAFES first determines that it (AAFES) does not need the equipment, merchandise and supplies for future use. After this determination, the concessionaire may obtain title to the items by satisfying all the terms of the conditional sales agreement. Before entering into any conditional sales agreement with AAFES, the concessionaire should determine if any prohibitions against obtaining title to the items exist under Host Country laws or regulation."

11. The following clause is hereby added to Exhibit A, General Provisions:

AAFES FORM 4450-2 (REV JAN 78) (PREV EDITION USABLE)

68

AAFES-PAC ALTERATIONS (FEB 1980)

"CERTAIN COMMUNIST AREAS:

a. Contractor shall not acquire for use in the performance of this contract:

(1) any supplies or services originating from sources within the communist areas of North Korea, Vietnam, Cambodia, or Cuba; or

(2) any supplies, however processed, which are or were located in or transported from or through North Korea, Vietnam, Cambodia, or Cuba:

b. Contractor agrees to insert the provisions of this clause, including this paragraph (b.), in all subcontracts hereunder."

12. Paragraph 6 entitled "Late Proposals and Modifications", shown on page 3, AAFES Form 4450-5, (Instructions to Offerors) is hereby deleted and the following is substituted therefor:

"6. LATE PROPOSALS AND MODIFICATIONS.

a. Any proposal received at the office designated in the solicitation after the exact time specified for receipt will not be considered unless it is received before award is made; and

(1) it was sent by mail (or telegram if authorized) and the late receipt was due to mishandling by AAFES after receipt; (A telegram proposal is the hard copy of the telegram, not oral notification.) or

(2) it is the only proposal received; or

(3) all proposals are received late.

b. Any modifications of a proposal, except a modification resulting from further negotiations, is subject to the same conditions as in a (1).

c. A modification resulting from further negotiations received after the time and date specified by the Contracting Officer will not be considered unless received before award and the late receipt is due to mishandling by AAFES after receipt.

d. The only acceptable evidence to establish the time of receipt by AAFES is the time/date stamp on the proposal wrapper or other documentary evidence of receipt.

e. A late modification of an otherwise successful proposal which makes its terms more favorable to AAFES will be considered and may be accepted.

f. Proposals may be withdrawn by written notice or telegram received at any time prior to award."

ARMY AND AIR FORCE EXCHANGE SERVICE

SCHEDULE

SOLICITATION OR CONTRACT NO.	PAGE	OF PAGES
KO-81-18-81-43	1	3

EXHIBIT I

ADDITIONAL SPECIAL PROVISIONS
FOR COMMODITY CONCESSION CONTRACTS

1. INSPECTION/QUALITY CONTROL:

a. All items listed in this contract are subject to inspection and test at all reasonable times and at all reasonable places including, but not limited to, the manufacturing plant, shipping point, depot, and the sales outlet(s). Additionally, AAFES may remove merchandise items from the sales outlet(s) for inspection/testing at AAFES or other testing facilities, in which case AAFES assumes responsibility for the cost of shipment to and from the testing facility and for the safe return of the merchandise to the sales outlet(s). Items for resale may be inspected after sale to an AAFES customer. AAFES may at its option inspect items in accordance with Military Standard 105, Sampling Procedures and Tables of Inspection by Attributes (copy available upon request), or in accordance with any other normal inspection procedure.

b. Merchandise found by AAFES to be defective/nonconforming will be immediately removed from sale. However, the Contracting Officer, at his option, may allow these items to be offered for sale after the Contractor, at Contractor's expense, exercises one of the following options:

(1) Screen (100% inspect) and repair or replace defective/nonconforming items, and resubmit the merchandise for inspection, or

(2) Make an equitable adjustment in sell price, as determined by the Contracting Officer.

c. Contractor is responsible for all losses and costs incurred in connection with the removal from sale, screening, repair, or replacement of defective/nonconforming merchandise.

2. LATENT DEFECTS: Any item or items found to have latent defect(s) will be immediately removed from sale. Contractor will be fully responsible for all losses and costs incurred in connection with the removal from sale of defective items.

3. WARRANTY: Contractor warrants that:

a. All merchandise furnished under this contract will be merchantable, and fit and sufficient for the use intended and will not be "seconds" as the term is normally understood in the trade. This warranty will survive acceptance or approval of merchandise by the Contracting Officer, and sale to AAFES customers, and is in addition to other warranties of additional scope given by the Contractor to AAFES.

b. The merchandise or services furnished under this contract are covered by the most favorable warranties the Contractor gives to any customer for such merchandise or services and that the rights and remedies provided in the Contractor's warranties are in addition to and do not limit any rights afforded to AAFES by any other clause of this contract.

CONTINUED ON NEXT PAGE

OFFEROR

70

AAFES FORM 4450.9 (REV NOV 72) (PREV EDITION USABLE) UNIT OF ISSUE: 25 CUT SHEETS

ARMY AND AIR FORCE EXCHANGE SERVICE	SOLICITATION OR CONTRACT NO.	PAGE OF PAGES
EXHIBIT J	KO-81-18-81-43	1 1

PERFORMANCE SPECIFICATIONS

1. Concessionaire will sell Korean manufactured items of such brand name products as Gold Star, T.E.C., Samsung, Korea National and Chunilsa only. Any other brand name product must be specifically approved by the contracting officer prior to offering for sale.

2. All items offered for sale shall be new and free of defects in workmanship and parts used to manufacture the item. Concessionaire will offer for sale only those latest models which best meet customer demands.

3. Concessionaire must provide a sales clerk who can readily explain and demonstrate operation of products on display. A sample of each item offered for sale must be on display for customer review.

4. All items offered for sale must be manufactured for export to the United States and are provided with fiberboard boxes suitable for overseas shipping and a product information booklet which describes specifications and operation procedures.

5. Warranty/Guarantee: In addition to manufacturers warranty/guarantee, concessionaire will provide a 90-day warranty or guarantee with each item provided under this contract. The warranty/guarantee shall provide that the item furnished will perform the service stipulated by the manufacturer for a fixed period after delivery to the exchange customer and that defects discovered in materials or workmanship within a fixed period will be corrected at no expense to the exchange or exchange customer. If the item does not meet the conditions of the warranty/guarantee, the concessionaire agrees to revise, replace or recondition the item in a manner calculated by the concessionaire to correct the unsatisfactory conditions at the concessionaire's own expense.

AAFES FORM 4450-? (REV JAN 78) (PREV EDITION USABLE)

171

ARMY AND AIR FORCE EXCHANGE SERVICE	SOLICITATION NO.	PAGE 1 OF 2 PAGES
EXHIBIT K	KO-81-18-81-43	

ROK TAXES

TAXES:

1. The Status of Forces Agreement between the Republic of Korea and United States exempts the US Forces, including Korea Area Exchange, from paying any and all ROK taxes; including commodity, traffic, petroleum, electricity, gas, and business taxes plus all other taxes found to constitute a significant and readily identifiable part of the gross purchase price of materials, supplies, equipment, and services. Also, the SOFA excludes USFK including Korea Area Exchange from payment of customs tax on items imported specifically for the USFK contract.

2. The following listed taxes are exempted from Korean taxes for items or services used on this contract:

a. Value Added Taxed Items: This clause is in implementation of Article XVI of the Status of Forces Agreement between the Republic of Korea and the United States granting contractors exemption from Republic of Korea Value Added Taxes. At the time this contract is awarded, the contractor will certify to the contracting officer that all supplies, services, and construction he will purchase for the contract have been proposed to the government value added tax exclusive and further that the contract price includes no value added tax whatsoever. He will indicate to the contracting officer the total amount of value added tax excluded from the contract price. The contractor will purchase supplies, services, and construction for use on the contract value added tax inclusive. Sample certificate format to be submitted by the concessionaire is provided in Exhibit L to this contract. He will be required to obtain refunds for these value added tax amounts from his ROK District Tax Office. These refunds will be accomplished by a contractor submission to his governing ROK District Tax Office of the tax invoices obtained from purchases of supplies, services, and construction for the USFK contract. The first purchase tax invoice submission will be accompanied by a copy of the USFK contract. Subsequent purchase tax invoice submissions will be accompanied by a letter reference to the USFK contract previously submitted. The contractor's ROK District Tax Office will refund to the contractor the full amount of value added tax paid by the contractor in the purchase price of the supplies, services, and construction.

b. POL Products. This clause is in implementation of Article XVI of the Status of Forces Agreement between the Republic of Korea and the United States granting contractors exemption from Republic of Korea taxes for petroleum products (POL) utilized on USFK procurements in the Republic of Korea. At the time this contract is awarded the contractor will make a final nomination in writing of the oil company from which he will purchase POL products required for performance of this contract, the estimated quantities of each POL product for performance, the estimated value of the POL products, and the value of the tax exemption for this quantity and value of POL products. Sample certificate format to be submitted by the concessionaire is provided in Exhibit L to this contract. The contracting officer will verify the reasonableness of the quantities claimed and will issue POL Tax Exemption Coupons to the contractor. The POL Tax Exemption Coupons for construction and single delivery supply/service contracts will be issued at award. The

OFFEROR

72

AAFES FORM 4150-9 (REV NOV 72) (PREV EDITION USABLE) UNIT OF ISSUE: 25 CUT SHEE

ARMY AND AIR FORCE EXCHANGE SERVICE	SOLICITATION OR CONTRACT NO.	PAGE 2 OF 2 PAGES
EXHIBIT K (Cont'd)	KO-81-18-81-43	

POL Tax Exemption Coupons for requirements contracts will be issued with individual delivery orders. The contractor will present the POL Tax Exemption Coupons to gasoline stations affiliated with the POL manufacturer of his choice. These coupons will permit tax free purchase of the amounts of POL covered by the coupon(s).

c. Special Excise Taxed Items: This clause is in implementation of Article XVI of the Status of Forces Agreement between the Republic of Korea and the United States granting contractors exemption from Republic of Korea Special Excise Taxes. At the time this contract is awarded the contractor will indicate to the contracting officer which items he will purchase for the contract are subject to special excise tax. He will indicate the name of the item, the number of units to be purchased, the cost per unit w/o tax, the percentage of tax, the tax amount per unit, the total tax, and the manufacturer of the item. The contracting officer will verify the reasonableness of the quantities claimed. Sample certificate format to be submitted by the concessionaire is provided in Exhibit L to this contract. The contractor will purchase the special excise taxed items from the item manufacturer tax inclusive. For construction and single delivery type supply and service contracts he will employ the following procedure: At the time he purchases the items he will present the manufacturer with a notification letter requesting refund of the special excise tax. (Copies of this letter can be obtained from the KOAX contracting officer). The manufacturer will indorse the letter to the Manufacturer's District Tax Office which will make refund to the manufacturer. The Manufacturer will make subsequent refund to the contractor. Requests for refund under requirements type contracts will be submitted monthly and will be accompanied by copies of the USFK delivery orders issued during the monthly period.

OFFEROR

73

AAFES FORM 4450-9 (REV NOV 7...)

SOLICITATION NO. KO-81-18-81-43

EXHIBIT L

CERTIFICATE FOR TAX EXEMPTION

TO: KOAX Contracting Office
APO 96301

TAX INFORMATION (JULY 1977)

A. References:

(1) Special Provisions Clause entitled "Taxes (Aug 1978)".

(2) US/ROK Status of Forces Agreement (SOFA) Articles IX and XVI.

(3) ROK Custom Tax Law #32, dated 30 December 1972, or any superseding law.

(4) ROK Value Added Tax Law, dated 8 December 1976 (effective date 1 July 1977).

(5) ROK Special Excise Tax Law, dated 8 December 1976 (effective date 1 July 1977).

B. US Government Procurement Regulations require the Contracting Officer to obtain and make a part of the contract file specific taxes and the amounts thereof, normally applicable to the contract, from which the US Government is exempt under the provisions of applicable tax agreements.

C. In addition to the ROK Tax Laws cited above, the SOFA and its interpretations exempts US Government contractors from the following Korean taxes upon appropriate certification in advance by the US Armed Forces:

(1) Custom Tax.

(2) Value Added Tax (VAT).

(3) Special Excise Tax (SET).

D. Request an estimate be furnished for type and amount of taxes that would normally apply to the transaction but are exempt from this proposal.

Type of Tax	Number of Units	Cost/Unit W/O Tax	% of Tax	Tax/Unit	Tax Total
(1) Custom Tax:					
________	________	________	________	________	________

Name of Item
This item will be imported specifically for this contract? Yes________
No________

74

Type of Tax	Number of Units	Cost/Unit W/O Tax	% of Tax	Tax/Unit	Tax Total
______	______	______	______	______	______

Name of Item
This item will be imported specifically for this contract? Yes______
No______

______	______	______	______	______	______

Name of Item
This item will be imported specifically for this contract? Yes______
No______

(2) Value Added Tax:

Input VAT on materials purchased for this contract.	10%	______
Input VAT on transportation leased/rented for this contract.	10%	______
Input VAT on equipment leased/rented for this contract.	10%	______
Input VAT on services purchased for this contract.	10%	______
Output VAT on total contract amount.	10%	______

(3) Special Excise Tax:

______	______	______	______	______	______

Name of Item

______
Name of item manufacturer

______	______	______	______	______	______

Name of Item

______
Name of item manufacturer

______	______	______	______	______	______

Name of Item

______
Name of item manufacturer

(4) Special Excise (Petroleum) Tax:

Regular Gasoline __________(L)__________ ₩__________ __________

Premium Gasoline __________(L)__________ ₩__________ __________

Diesel __________(L)__________ ₩__________ __________

Other __________(L)__________ ₩__________ __________

Other __________(L)__________ ₩__________ __________

E. Supplementing the information on Petroleum Tax under subparagraph (D) (4) above is the following information which shall serve as the advance information for purposes of the clause of this contract entitled "Exemption from Korean Taxes for POL Products used on this contract".

Name of the oil company from which POL products will be purchased:

Oil Company:____ (name only).

F. Request an estimate be furnished for type and amount of any taxes that are not exempt from this transactions and are included in the proposed price:

Type of Tax	Number of Units	Cost/Unit W/O Tax	% of Tax	Tax/Unit	Tax Total

G. I certify by this submission that all supplies and services to be purchased for this contract have been proposed Value Added Tax and Special Excise Tax Exclusive. I also certify that the prices on all items to be imported for this contract do not contain any customs tax.

____
Signed (Chop)

76

UNIT OF ISSUE: 25 CUT SHEET

3. (continued)

c. Any product that can reasonably be used to carry subsistence and made of a substance prone to heavy metal leaching, such as and to include pewterware, earthenware, ceramicware, chinaware, ironware, lacquerware, bronzeware, brassware, and coated/plated items with a heavy metal base furnished under this contract contains no leachable levels of heavy metal dangerous to users. (This excludes glassware and flatware products.) Maximum leachable levels are 0.5 parts per million (ppm) for cadmium and 7.0 ppm for lead, when tested in accordance with the current United States (U.S.) Government Food and Drug Administration test methods. Additionally, suppliers of such merchandise of foreign origin must be certified by the Japan Pottery Inspection Association (JPIA) or Japan Metal Tableware Inspection Association (JMTIA) (or an equivalent agency). AAFES additionally reserves the right to test Contractor's product on an unannounced basis. If a heavy metal leaching failure is found, Contractor agrees to reimburse AAFES for all follow-up costs to sample test the remainder of his items for the duration of the contract. This provision does not supersede, replace or cancel other remedial provisions allowed by contract. The Contracting Officer may at his sole discretion, and in lieu of the foregoing, allow such products that reasonabl can be used for subsistence carrying purposes, but are intended for display purposes only, to be rendered unsuitable for food use. The article may be considered unsuitable for food use if:

(1) It is made or rendered unsuitable for such purpose by some artifice such as holes bored through the potential food contact surface or

(2) A label, incapable of obliteration, is permanently affixed to the article's potential food contact surface; and if such label states that the article is "not for food use" along with a statement of the hazard associated with the article when used for food purposes.

d. Any electrical/electronic merchandise furnished under this contract has been manufactured in accordance with the United States Underwriters Laboratories, Inc. (UL) standards, or equivalent regulatory agency standards for foreign origin items, e.g., Japan, Ministry of International Trade and Industry (MITI); Canada, Canadian Standard Association Testing Laboratories (CSA); Germany, Verein Deutscher Electro-Techniker (VDE); United Kingdom, British Standards System (BSS), or Internation Safety Standards (ISS/ISO), and, except as indicated below, that the applicable merchandise carries the seal of approval authorized by the applicable regulatory agency. In addition to the foregoing, Contractor warrants that the items furnished under this contract will operate as intended without defect or presentation of hazard by the electrical characteristics of the geographical area of intended sale.

EXCEPTION: The following electrical/electronic merchandise, not UL or equivalent agency certified, may be furnished under this contract in accordance with the following

(1) Electric lamps that are not of American manufacture; provided, however, that all electrical components (socket, cord, plug, etc.) are certified by and carry the seal of approval authorized by UL or equivalent agency, and further provided that sample lots successfully pass the AAFES lamp housing safety inspection.

CONTINUED ON NEXT PAGE

OFFEROR

AAFES FORM 4450-9 (REV NOV 72) (PREV EDITION USABLE) UNIT OF ISSUE: 25 CUT S

UNIT OF ISSUE: 25 CUT SHI

AAFES FORM 4450-1 (REV JAN 79) (PREV EDITION USABLE)

ARMY AND AIR FORCE EXCHANGE SERVICE	SOLICITATION OR CONTRACT NO.	PAGE	OF	P
SCHEDULE		3	3	

3. (continued)

(2) Electrical/electronic merchandise from Japan in which switchable voltage in the 100/200 volt range is required, provided such requirement prevents application of the appropriate safety seal.

(3) Prior to offering merchandise described in (1) and (2) above for sale, Contractor is required to furnish a Certificate of Compliance stating that the item(s) meet or exceed UL or equivalent standards. This Certificate is required in addition to the component certification required for items in (1) above, and is subject to the approval of the Contracting Officer.

OFFEROR

AAFES FORM 4450-9 (REV NOV 72) (PREV EDITION USABLE) 78 UNIT OF ISSUE: 23 CUT SHE

FOR USFK CONTRACT
(SOFA AGREEMENT, 4 MAY 78)
주한미군 계약용 수입물품 증명서

27 July 1981

CONTRACT No.: 계약 번호
DAJB03-81-C-4046

NAME AND ADDRESS OF CONTRACTOR 계약업자의 주소 및 성명

NAME: 이름
Dae Lim Industrial Co., Ltd.

ADDRESS: 주소
#453-30, pachu kun, chunae-myon, pachu-ri, kyonggi-pro

BRIEF DESCRIPTION OF CONTRACT: 계약 내용 개요
Replacing Deteriorated seculity lamp.

SCH'D COMPL/DLVR DATE: 완공 또는 납품 예정일
14 November 1981

DESCRIPTION OF IMPORTED MATERIALS 수입물자소요 명세서

ITEM 품목	SPECIFICATION 규격	QUANTITY 수량	IMPORT PRICE W/O TAX 수입 단가	EXPLANATION OF QTY CALCULATION 수량산출 근거: ANALYSIS OF PERCENTAGE OR COMPOSITION 배합 또는조성비율	EXPLANATION OF QTY CALCULATION 수량산출 근거: EXPLANATION OF CALCULATION 산출 근거
Low pressure Sodium Vapor Lamp	W90/120V	135	DFL 6,750	N/A	By Commercial Offer.

THE ABOVE GOODS ARE TO BE IMPORTED FOR THE ABOVE USFK CONTRACT.
상기물품은 주한미군과의 상기계약을 위하여 수입할 것임.

DATE: 날자
29 July 1981

SIGNATURE OF CONTRACTOR: 계약업자의 서명
Chang Kyo Chol - President
Dae Lim Industrial Co., Ltd.

I CERTIFY THAT THE ABOVE GOODS ARE TO BE DELIVERED TO USFK IN ACCORDANCE WITH PARA 2. ARTICLE IX OF ROK/USA SOFA.
상기물품은 한미 지위협정 제9조 2항에 의거, 주한미군 당국에 납품될 것임을 증명함.

DATE: 날자
29July 1981

SIGNATURE OF USFK CONTRACTING OFFICER: 주한미군 계약관의 서명
LOUISE H. PLANK

I CERTIFY THAT THE ABOVE CONTRACTING OFFICER'S SIGNATURE IS TRUE AND CORRECT TO THE BEST OF MY KNOWLEDGE. 본인은 상기 계약관의 서명이 확실이고 유효함을 증명함.

FOR THE COMMANDER:
USFK PROCUREMENT AGENCY
주한미군구매처 사령관을 대리하여

NAME, TITLE, GRADE, ORG & SIGNATURE: 성명, 직위, 계급, 소속 기관 및 서명
29 July 81
JOHN L. WILLIAMS
CPT, AGC, Adjutant, usakca

USFK FORM 78
JUN 78
1 JUN 78 10-1

79

PPC-Korea

CERTIFICATE OF DELIVERY OF IMPORTED MATERIALS FOR USFK CONTRACT
(SOFA AGREEMENT, 4 MAY 78)
주한미군용 수입물자 납품완료 증명서

DATE OF CONTRACT: 계약 일자
27 July 1981

CONTRACT No.: 계약 번호
DAJB03-81-C-4046

NAME AND ADDRESS OF CONTRACTOR 계약업자의 성명 및 주소

NAME: 이름
Dae Lim Industrial Co., Ltd.

ADDRESS: 주 소
#453-30, pachu-kun, chuwae-myon, pachu-ri, kyonggi-pro

BRIEF DESCRIPTION OF CONTRACT: 계약 내용 개요
Replacing Deteriorated security lamp.

ACTUAL COMPL/DLVR DATE: 완공 또는 납품 일자
14 November 1981

DESCRIPTION OF IMPORTED MATERIALS 수입물자초요 명세서

ITEM 품 목	SPECIFICATION 규 격	QUANTITY 수 량	EXPLANATION OF QTY CALCULATION 수량 산출 근거: ANALYSIS OF PERCENTAGE OR COMPOSITION 백분 또는조성비율	EXPLANATION OF CALCULATION 산출 근거	IMPORT PERMIT No. 수입허가번호
Low pressure Sodium Vapor Lamp	W90/120V	135	DFL 6,750.-	N/A	By Commercial Offer.
	* Unit Price:	CIF Kimpo	DFL 50.-		I-1902-107-AS-00018
					DATED: July 31, 1981

THE ABOVE GOODS WERE DELIVERED FOR THE ABOVE USFK CONTRACT.
상기 품목은 주한미군과의 상기 계약을 위하여 납품되었음.

DATE: 날자
9 November 1981

SIGNATURE OF CONTRACTOR: 계약업자의 서명
Chang Kyo Chol - President
Dae Lim Industrial Co., Ltd.

I CERTIFY THAT THE ABOVE GOODS WERE DELIVERED TO USFK/INSTALLED TO USFK PROPERTY IN ACCORDANCE WITH PARA 2, ARTICLE IX OF ROK/USA SOFA.
상기 품목은 한미 지위협정 제9조 2항에 의거 주한미군의 재산에 설치 또는 주한미군 당국에 납품되었음을 증명함.

DATE: 날자
9 November 1981

SIGNATURE OF USFK CONTRACTING OFFICER: 주한미군 계약관의 서명
LOUISE H. PLANK

I CERTIFY THAT THE ABOVE CONTRACTING OFFICER'S SIGNATURE IS TRUE AND CORRECT TO THE BEST OF MY KNOWLEDGE. 본인은 상기 계약관의 서명이 확실하고 유효함을 증명함.

FOR THE COMMANDER:
USFK PROCUREMENT AGENCY
주한미군구매처 사령관을 대리하여

NAME, TITLE, GRADE, ORG & SIGNATURE: 성명, 직위, 계급, 소속 기관 및 서명
9 Nov, 1981
JOHN L. WILLIAMS
CPT, AGC, Adjutant, usakca

USFK FORM 78-1
1 JUN 78

FPC Korea

80

I N D E X

81

A

AMENDMENT OF SOLICITATION/MODIFICATION OF CONTRACT *(Nonappropriated Fund)*

For use of this form, see DA Pam 27-154; the proponent agency is the ODCSPER.

PAGE 1 OF 1

1. AMENDMENT/MODIFICATION NO.	2. EFFECTIVE DATE	3. REQUISITION/PURCHASE REQUEST NO.	4. PROJECT NO. *(If applicable)*
P00007	1 Jul 82	DF, EAGY-DPCA-NH, dtd 22 Dec 82	

5. ISSUED BY

Commander, USAKCA
ATTN: EAKC-CSS
APO SF 96301 Buyer: Yim S.O.

6. ADMINISTERED BY *(If other than block 5)*

7. CONTRACTOR NAME AND ADDRESS *(Street, city, county, state, and ZIP Code)*

Dae Lin Industrial Co., Ltd.
Rm #508, YWCA Bldg
1-3, 1-ka, Myong-dong, Chung-ku
Tel: 778-8054

8. ☐ AMENDMENT OF SOLICITATION NO. ____ DATED ____ *(See block 9)*

☒ MODIFICATION OF CONTRACT/ORDER NO. KCANAF-80-C-V065

DATED ~~22 Feb 80~~ *(See block 11)*

9. THIS BLOCK APPLIES ONLY TO AMENDMENTS OF SOLICITATIONS

☐ The above numbered solicitation is amended as set forth in block 12. The hour and date specified for receipt of Offers ☐ is extended, ☐ is not extended.

Offerors must acknowledge receipt of this amendment prior to the hour and date specified in the solicitation, or as amended, by one of the following methods:

(a) By signing and returning ____ copies of this amendment; (b) by acknowledging receipt of this amendment on each copy of the offer submitted; or (c) by separate letter or telegram which includes a reference to the solicitation and amendment numbers. FAILURE OF YOUR ACKNOWLEDGMENT TO BE RECEIVED AT THE ISSUING OFFICE PRIOR TO THE HOUR AND DATE SPECIFIED MAY RESULT IN REJECTION OF YOUR OFFER. If, by virtue of this amendment you desire to change an offer already submitted, such change may be made by telegram or letter, provided such telegram or letter makes reference to the solicitation and this amendment, and is received prior to the opening hour and date specified.

10.

No appropriated funds of the United States shall become due, or be paid, the Contractor by reason of this contract.

11. THIS BLOCK APPLIES ONLY TO MODIFICATIONS OF CONTRACTS/ORDERS

(a) ☐ This Change Order is issued pursuant to ____

The Changes set forth in block 12 are made to the above numbered contract/order.

(b) ☐ The above numbered contract/order is modified to reflect the administrative changes (such as changes in paying office, etc.) set forth in block 12.

(c) ☒ This Supplemental Agreement modifies the above numbered contract as set forth in block 12.

12. DESCRIPTION OF AMENDMENT/MODIFICATION

1. Pursuant to Section J, Paragraph 19, OPTION TO EXTEND THE TERM OF THE CONTRACT, of the contract terms and conditions, the contract period of one (1) month from 1 Jul 82, as specified in the Modification No. P00006, dated 20 May 82 is hereby extended through 31 Jul 82.

2. The contractor waives the requirement for a 60-day preliminary notice of this exercise of the said option.

Except as provided herein, all terms and conditions of the document referenced in block 8, as heretofore changed, remain unchanged and in full force and effect.

13. ☐ CONTRACTOR/OFFEROR IS NOT REQUIRED TO SIGN THIS DOCUMENT ☒ CONTRACTOR/OFFEROR IS REQUIRED TO SIGN THIS DOCUMENT AND RETURN 1 COPIES TO ISSUING OFFICE

14. NAME OF CONTRACTOR/OFFEROR	17. NAME AND SIGNATURE OF CONTRACTING OFFICER	18. DATE SIGNED
BY [signature] (Signature of person authorized to sign)	RAYMOND L. URCH	JUN 21 82

15. NAME AND TITLE OF SIGNER *(Type or print)*	16. DATE SIGNED	19. NAME AND SIGNATURE OF INSTALLATION COMMANDER *(If required)*
CHANG KYO CHO., President	21 June 82	Raymond L. Urch

DA FORM 4073-R

AMENDMENT OF SOLICITATION/MODIFICATION OF CONTRACT *(Nonappropriated Fund)*
For use of this form, see DA Pam 27-154; the proponent agency is the ODCSPER.

PAGE 1 OF

1. AMENDMENT/MODIFICATION NO.	2. EFFECTIVE DATE	3. REQUISITION/PURCHASE REQUEST NO.	4. PROJECT NO. *(If applicable)*
P00006	1 Jun 82	95, EAGY-DPCA-UH dtd 22 Dec 81 (NAF 8177-82)	

5. ISSUED BY
Commander
US Army Korea Contracting Agency
ATTN: EAKC-CSS
APO San Francisco, CA 96301 Buyer: YIM S.O

6. ADMINISTERED BY *(If other than block 5)*

7. CONTRACTOR NAME AND ADDRESS *(Street, city, county, state, and ZIP Code)*
Dae Lim Industrial Co., Ltd.
Rm #508, YWCA Bldg
1-3, 1-Ka, Myong-dong, Chung-Ku,
Tel: 778-8054

8.
☐ AMENDMENT OF SOLICITATION NO. ____
DATED ____ *(See block 9)*
☒ MODIFICATION OF CONTRACT/ORDER NO. KCANAF-80-C-V06
DATED 22 Feb 80 *(See block 11)*

9. THIS BLOCK APPLIES ONLY TO AMENDMENTS OF SOLICITATIONS

☐ The above numbered solicitation is amended as set forth in block 12. The hour and date specified for receipt of Offers ☐ is extended, ☐ is not extended.

Offerors must acknowledge receipt of this amendment prior to the hour and date specified in the solicitation, or as amended, by one of the following methods:

(a) By signing and returning ____ copies of this amendment; (b) By acknowledging receipt of this amendment on each copy of the offer submitted; or (c) By separate letter or telegram which includes a reference to the solicitation and amendment numbers. FAILURE OF YOUR ACKNOWLEDGMENT TO BE RECEIVED AT THE ISSUING OFFICE PRIOR TO THE HOUR AND DATE SPECIFIED MAY RESULT IN REJECTION OF YOUR OFFER. If, by virtue of this amendment you desire to change an offer already submitted, such change may be made by telegram or letter, provided such telegram or letter makes reference to the solicitation and this amendment, and is received prior to the opening hour and date specified.

10. *No appropriated funds of the United States shall become due, or be paid, the Contractor by reason of this contract.*

11. THIS BLOCK APPLIES ONLY TO MODIFICATIONS OF CONTRACTS/ORDERS

(a) ☐ This Change Order is issued pursuant to ____
The Changes set forth in block 12 are made to the above numbered contract/order.

(b) ☐ The above numbered contract/order is modified to reflect the administrative changes (such as changes in paying office, etc.) set forth in block 12.

(c) ☒ This Supplemental Agreement modifies the above numbered contract as set forth in block 12.

12. DESCRIPTION OF AMENDMENT/MODIFICATION

1. Pursuant to Section J, Paragraph 19, OPTION TO EXTEND THE TERM OF THE CONTRACT of the contract terms and conditions, the contract period of one (1) month from 31 May 1982, as specified in the Modification No. P00005, dated 29 Apr 1982 is hereby extended through 30 Jun 82.

2. The contractor waives the requirement for a 60-day preliminary notice of this exercise of the said option.

Except as provided herein, all terms and conditions of the document referenced in block 8, as heretofore changed, remain unchanged and in full force and effect.

13. ☐ CONTRACTOR/OFFEROR IS NOT REQUIRED TO SIGN THIS DOCUMENT ☒ CONTRACTOR/OFFEROR IS REQUIRED TO SIGN THIS DOCUMENT AND RETURN 1 COPIES TO ISSUING OFFICE

14. NAME OF CONTRACTOR/OFFEROR	17. NAME AND SIGNATURE OF CONTRACTING OFFICER	18. DATE SIGNED
BY (Signature of person authorized to sign)	LEONARD LAZOFF	MAY 20 19[illegible]

15. NAME AND TITLE OF SIGNER *(Type or print)*	16. DATE SIGNED	19. NAME AND SIGNATURE OF INSTALLATION COMMANDER *(If required)*
CHANG KYO CHOL, President		

DA FORM 1 MAY 73 4073-R

PPC-Kore

83

AMENDMENT OF SOLICITATION/MODIFICATION OF CONTRACT *(Nonappropriated Fund)*

For use of this form, see DA Pam 27-154; the proponent agency is the ODCSPER.

PAGE 1 OF 1

1. AMENDMENT/MODIFICATION NO.	2. EFFECTIVE DATE	3. REQUISITION/PURCHASE REQUEST NO.	4. PROJECT NO. *(If applicable)*
P00005	1 May 82	DF, EAGY-DFCA-HG, dtd 22 Dec 81 (MAF 8177-80)	

5. ISSUED BY

Commander
US Army Korea Contracting Agency
ATTN:EAKC-CSS
APO San Francisco, CA 96301 : Buyer: YIM, S.O.

6. ADMINISTERED BY *(If other than block 5)*

7. CONTRACTOR NAME AND ADDRESS *(Street, city, county, state, and ZIP Code)*

Dae Lim Industrial Co., Ltd.
Rm #508, YWCA Bldg
1-3, 1-Ka, Myong-dong, Chung-Ku,
Seoul, Korea
Tel: 778-8054

8. ☐ AMENDMENT OF SOLICITATION NO. ______

DATED ______ *(See block 9)*

☒ MODIFICATION OF CONTRACT/ORDER NO. KCANAF-80-C-V065

DATED 22 Feb 80 *(See block 11)*

9. THIS BLOCK APPLIES ONLY TO AMENDMENTS OF SOLICITATIONS

☐ The above numbered solicitation is amended as set forth in block 12. The hour and date specified for receipt of Offers ☐ is extended, ☐ is not extended.

Offerors must acknowledge receipt of this amendment prior to the hour and date specified in the solicitation, or as amended, by one of the following methods:

(a) By signing and returning ______ copies of this amendment; (b) By acknowledging receipt of this amendment on each copy of the offer submitted; or (c) By separate letter or telegram which includes a reference to the solicitation and amendment numbers. FAILURE OF YOUR ACKNOWLEDGMENT TO BE RECEIVED AT THE ISSUING OFFICE PRIOR TO THE HOUR AND DATE SPECIFIED MAY RESULT IN REJECTION OF YOUR OFFER. If, by virtue of this amendment you desire to change an offer already submitted, such change may be made by telegram or letter, provided such telegram or letter makes reference to the solicitation and this amendment, and is received prior to the opening hour and date specified.

10. *No appropriated funds of the United States shall become due, or be paid, the Contractor by reason of this contract.*

11. THIS BLOCK APPLIES ONLY TO MODIFICATIONS OF CONTRACTS/ORDERS

(a) ☐ This Change Order is issued pursuant to ______

The Changes set forth in block 12 are made to the above numbered contract/order.

(b) ☐ The above numbered contract/order is modified to reflect the administrative changes (such as changes in paying office, etc.) set forth in block 12.

(c) ☒ This Supplemental Agreement modifies the above numbered contract as set forth in block 12.

12. DESCRIPTION OF AMENDMENT/MODIFICATION

1. Pursuant to Section J, paragraph 19, OPTION TO EXTEND THE TERM OF THE CONTRACT, of the contract terms and conditions, the contract period of one (1) month from 30 April 1982, as specified in the Modification No. P00004, dated 9 March 1982 is hereby extended through 31 May 1982.

2. The contractor waives the requirement for a 60-day preliminary notice of this exercise of the said option.

Except as provided herein, all terms and conditions of the document referenced in block 8, as heretofore changed, remain unchanged and in full force and effect.

13. ☐ CONTRACTOR/OFFEROR IS NOT REQUIRED TO SIGN THIS DOCUMENT ☒ CONTRACTOR/OFFEROR IS REQUIRED TO SIGN THIS DOCUMENT AND RETURN 1 COPIES TO ISSUING OFFICE

14. NAME OF CONTRACTOR/OFFEROR	17. NAME AND SIGNATURE OF CONTRACTING OFFICER	18. DATE SIGNED
BY [signature] (Signature of person authorized to sign)	LEONARD LAZOFF	29 Apr 82
15. NAME AND TITLE OF SIGNER *(Type or print)* / **16. DATE SIGNED**	**19. NAME AND SIGNATURE OF INSTALLATION COMMANDER** *(If required.)*	
CHANG KYO CHOL, President / 29 Apr 82		

DA FORM 4073-R PPC-Korea

84.

AMENDMENT OF SOLICITATION/MODIFICATION OF CONTRACT *(Nonappropriated Fund)* PAGE 1 OF 1

For use of this form, see DA Pam 27-154; the proponent agency is the ODCSPER.

1. AMENDMENT/MODIFICATION NO.	2. EFFECTIVE DATE	3. REQUISITION/PURCHASE REQUEST NO.	4. PROJECT NO. *(If applicable)*
P00003	9 Apr 81		

5. ISSUED BY

Cdr, US Army Korea Contracting Agency
Sup., Sub. & NAF Br., COD
APO S.F. 96301
~~Buyer: Kang H. S.~~

6. ADMINISTERED BY *(If other than block 5)*

7. CONTRACTOR NAME AND ADDRESS *(Street, city, county, state, and ZIP Code)*

Dae Lim Industrial Co, Ltd.
Rm 508 YWCA Bldg. #1-3, 1-ka
Myongtong, Chung-ku
Seoul, Korea (776-8054)

8. ☐ AMENDMENT OF SOLICITATION NO. ______ DATED ______ *(See block 9)*

☒ MODIFICATION OF CONTRACT/ORDER NO. KCANAF-80-C-V065 DATED 26 Mar 80 *(See block 11)*

9. THIS BLOCK APPLIES ONLY TO AMENDMENTS OF SOLICITATIONS

☐ The above numbered solicitation is amended as set forth in block 12. The hour and date specified for receipt of Offers ☐ is extended, ☐ is not extended.

Offerors must acknowledge receipt of this amendment prior to the hour and date specified in the solicitation, or as amended, by one of the following methods:

(a) By signing and returning ______ copies of this amendment; (b) By acknowledging receipt of this amendment on each copy of the offer submitted; or (c) By separate letter or telegram which includes a reference to the solicitation and amendment numbers. FAILURE OF YOUR ACKNOWLEDGMENT TO BE RECEIVED AT THE ISSUING OFFICE PRIOR TO THE HOUR AND DATE SPECIFIED MAY RESULT IN REJECTION OF YOUR OFFER. If, by virtue of this amendment you desire to change an offer already submitted, such change may be made by telegram or letter, provided such telegram or letter makes reference to the solicitation and this amendment, and is received prior to the opening hour and date specified.

10. *No appropriated funds of the United States shall become due, or be paid, the Contractor by reason of this contract.*

11. THIS BLOCK APPLIES ONLY TO MODIFICATIONS OF CONTRACTS/ORDERS

(a) ☐ This Change Order is issued pursuant to ______
The Changes set forth in block 12 are made to the above numbered contract/order.

(b) ☐ The above numbered contract/order is modified to reflect the administrative changes (such as changes in paying office, etc.) set forth in block 12.

(c) ☒ This Supplemental Agreement modifies the above numbered contract as set forth in block 12.

12. DESCRIPTION OF AMENDMENT/MODIFICATION

1. Delete "Viedo" on the face of Standard Form 26, and insert "Video" in lieu thereof.

2. Delete "as the appointed Contracting Officer's Representative" in paragraph 2, Section I.

3. Delete "NAF Branch, CED" in paragraph 4, Section J and insert "SSN Branch, COD" in lieu thereof.

4. Add "See paragraph 21, Section J" to Clause 28, General Provisions.

5. Delete Page G-8 and insert the attached in lieu thereof.

Except as provided herein, all terms and conditions of the document referenced in block 8, as heretofore changed, remain unchanged and in full force and effect.

13. ☐ CONTRACTOR/OFFEROR IS NOT REQUIRED TO SIGN THIS DOCUMENT ☒ CONTRACTOR/OFFEROR IS REQUIRED TO SIGN THIS DOCUMENT AND RETURN 1 COPIES TO ISSUING OFFICE

14. NAME OF CONTRACTOR/OFFEROR	17. NAME AND SIGNATURE OF CONTRACTING OFFICER	18. DATE SIGNED
BY (Signature of person authorized to sign)	LEONARD MAZOFF	9 Apr 81
15. NAME AND TITLE OF SIGNER *(Type or print)* / 16. DATE SIGNED: 17 Apr	19. NAME AND SIGNATURE OF INSTALLATION COMMANDER *(If required)*	

85

AMENDMENT OF SOLICITATION/MODIFICATION OF CONTRACT (Nonappropriated Fund)
For use of this form, see DA Pam 27-154; the proponent agency is the ODCSPER.

PAGE 1 OF 1

1. AMENDMENT/MODIFICATION NO.	2. EFFECTIVE DATE	3. REQUISITION/PURCHASE REQUEST NO.	4. PROJECT NO. (If applicable)
P00002	23 Feb 81		

5. ISSUED BY
Cdr, US Army Korea Contracting Agency
Sup., Sub. & NAF Br., COD
APO S.F. 96301 Buyer: Kang H. S.

6. ADMINISTERED BY (If other than block 5)

7. CONTRACTOR
NAME AND ADDRESS (Street, city, county, state, and ZIP Code)
Dae Lim Industrial Co, Ltd.
Rm 508 YWCA Bldg. #1-3, 1-ka
Myongtong, Chung-ku
Seoul, Korea (778-8054)

8.
☐ AMENDMENT OF SOLICITATION NO. ____
DATED ____ (See block 9)
☒ MODIFICATION OF CONTRACT/ORDER NO. KCANAF-80-C-V065
DATED 26 Mar 80 (See block 11)

9. THIS BLOCK APPLIES ONLY TO AMENDMENTS OF SOLICITATIONS
☐ The above numbered solicitation is amended as set forth in block 12. The hour and date specified for receipt of Offers ☐ is extended, ☐ is not extended.
Offerors must acknowledge receipt of this amendment prior to the hour and date specified in the solicitation, or as amended, by one of the following methods:
(a) By signing and returning ____ copies of this amendment; (b) By acknowledging receipt of this amendment on each copy of the offer submitted; or (c) By separate letter or telegram which includes a reference to the solicitation and amendment numbers. FAILURE OF YOUR ACKNOWLEDGMENT TO BE RECEIVED AT THE ISSUING OFFICE PRIOR TO THE HOUR AND DATE SPECIFIED MAY RESULT IN REJECTION OF YOUR OFFER. If, by virtue of this amendment you desire to change an offer already submitted, such change may be made by telegram or letter, provided such telegram or letter makes reference to the solicitation and this amendment, and is received prior to the opening hour and date specified.

10. *No appropriated funds of the United States shall become due, or be paid, the Contractor by reason of this contract.*

11. THIS BLOCK APPLIES ONLY TO MODIFICATIONS OF CONTRACTS/ORDERS
(a) ☐ This Change Order is issued pursuant to ____
The Changes set forth in block 12 are made to the above numbered contract/order.
(b) ☐ The above numbered contract/order is modified to reflect the administrative changes (such as changes in paying office, etc.) set forth in block 12.
(c) ☒ This Supplemental Agreement modifies the above numbered contract as set forth in block 12.

12. DESCRIPTION OF AMENDMENT/MODIFICATION
Pursuant to Section J, paragraph 19, OPTION TO EXTEND THE TERM OF THE CONTRACT, of the contract terms and conditions, the contract period of 1 Apr 80 thru 31 Mar 81, as specified in modification No. P00001, dated 26 Mar 80 is hereby extended through 31 Mar 82.

Except as provided herein, all terms and conditions of the document referenced in block 8, as heretofore changed, remain unchanged and in full force and effect.

13. ☐ CONTRACTOR/OFFEROR IS NOT REQUIRED TO SIGN THIS DOCUMENT ☒ CONTRACTOR/OFFEROR IS REQUIRED TO SIGN THIS DOCUMENT AND RETURN 1 COPIES TO ISSUING OFFICE

14. NAME OF CONTRACTOR/OFFEROR	17. NAME AND SIGNATURE OF CONTRACTING OFFICER	18. DATE SIGNED
BY (Signature of person authorized to sign)	LEONARD LAZOFF	23 Feb 81
15. NAME AND TITLE OF SIGNER (Type or print) / 16. DATE SIGNED 25 Feb 81	19. NAME AND SIGNATURE OF INSTALLATION COMMANDER (If required.)	

86

AMENDMENT OF SOLICITATION/MODIFICATION OF CONTRACT *(Nonappropriated Fund)* PAGE 1 OF

For use of this form, see DA Pam 27-154; the proponent agency is the ODCSPER.

1. AMENDMENT/MODIFICATION NO.	2. EFFECTIVE DATE	3. REQUISITION/PURCHASE REQUEST NO.	4. PROJECT NO. *(If applicable)*
P00001	26 Mar 80	Ltr, 3 Jan 80(8409-80)	

5. ISSUED BY

Cdr, US Army Korea Contracting Agency
Sup., Sub. & NAF Br., COD
APO S.F. 96301
~~Buyer: Kang H. S.~~

6. ADMINISTERED BY *(If other than block 5)*

7. CONTRACTOR NAME AND ADDRESS *(Street, city, county, state, and ZIP Code)*

Dae Lim Industrial Co, Ltd.
Rm 508 YWCA Bldg, #1-3, 1-ka
Myongtong, Chung-ku
Seoul, Korea (778-8054)

8. ☐ AMENDMENT OF SOLICITATION NO. ________
DATED ________ *(See block 9)*

☒ MODIFICATION OF CONTRACT/ORDER NO. ~~KCANAF-80-C-~~ V065
DATED ~~26 Mar 80~~ *(See block 11)*

9. THIS BLOCK APPLIES ONLY TO AMENDMENTS OF SOLICITATIONS

☐ The above numbered solicitation is amended as set forth in block 12. The hour and date specified for receipt of Offers ☐ is extended, ☐ is not extended.

Offerors must acknowledge receipt of this amendment prior to the hour and date specified in the solicitation, or as amended, by one of the following methods:

(a) By signing and returning ____ copies of this amendment; (b) By acknowledging receipt of this amendment on each copy of the offer submitted; or (c) By separate letter or telegram which includes a reference to the solicitation and amendment numbers. FAILURE OF YOUR ACKNOWLEDGMENT TO BE RECEIVED AT THE ISSUING OFFICE PRIOR TO THE HOUR AND DATE SPECIFIED MAY RESULT IN REJECTION OF YOUR OFFER. If, by virtue of this amendment you desire to change an offer already submitted, such change may be made by telegram or letter, provided such telegram or letter makes reference to the solicitation and this amendment, and is received prior to the opening hour and date specified.

10. *No appropriated funds of the United States shall become due, or be paid, the Contractor by reason of this contract.*

11. THIS BLOCK APPLIES ONLY TO MODIFICATIONS OF CONTRACTS/ORDERS

(a) ☐ This Change Order is issued pursuant to ________
The Changes set forth in block 12 are made to the above numbered contract/order.

(b) ☐ The above numbered contract/order is modified to reflect the administrative changes (such as changes in paying office, etc.) set forth in block 12.

(c) ☒ This Supplemental Agreement modifies the above numbered contract as set forth in block 12.

12. DESCRIPTION OF AMENDMENT/MODIFICATION

1. Effective date, as specified in block #2 is amended from 15 Mar 80 to read 1 Apr 80.

2. Contract Period, as specified in para 1. of Section H is deleted and the following is substituted in lieu thereof:

"The contract period is for one year to begin on the effective date of 1 Apr 80 to 31 Mar 81."

Except as provided herein, all terms and conditions of the document referenced in block 8, as heretofore changed, remain unchanged and in full force and effect.

13. ☐ CONTRACTOR/OFFEROR IS NOT REQUIRED TO SIGN THIS DOCUMENT ☒ CONTRACTOR/OFFEROR IS REQUIRED TO SIGN THIS DOCUMENT AND RETURN 1 COPIES TO ISSUING OFFICE

14. NAME OF CONTRACTOR/OFFEROR	17. NAME AND SIGNATURE OF CONTRACTING OFFICER	18. DATE SIGNED
BY ________ (Signature of person authorized to sign)	LEONARD LAZOFF	26 Mar 80

15. NAME AND TITLE OF SIGNER *(Type or print)*	16. DATE SIGNED	19. NAME AND SIGNATURE OF INSTALLATION COMMANDER *(If required.)*

87

STANDARD FORM 26, JULY 1966
GENERAL SERVICES ADMINISTRATION
FED. PROC. REG. (41CFR) 1-16.101

AWARD/CONTRACT

PAGE 1 OF

1. CONTRACT (Proc. Inst. Ident.) NO.: KCANAF-80-C.-V065
2. EFFECTIVE DATE: 15 Mar 80
3. REQUISITION/PURCHASE REQUEST/PROJECT NO.: Ltr, 3 Jan 80 (NAF 8409-80)
4. CERTIFIED FOR NATIONAL DEFENSE UNDER BDSA REG. 2 AND/OR DMS REG. 1. RATING:

5. ISSUED BY CODE
Cdr, US Army Korea Contracting Agency
Sup., Sub., & NAF Br., CQD
APO S. F. 96301
Buyer: Kang H. S.

6. ADMINISTERED BY (If other than block 5) CODE

7. DELIVERY
[X] FOR DESTINATION
[ ] OTHER (See below)

8. CONTRACTOR CODE FACILITY CODE
NAME AND ADDRESS (Street, city, county, State, and ZIP code)
Dae Lim Industrial Co, Ltd.
Rm 508 YWCA Bldg, #1-3, 1ka, Myong-Tong,
Chung-ku, Seoul, Korea (778-8054)

9. DISCOUNT FOR PROMPT PAYMENT
N/A

10. SUBMIT INVOICES (4 copies unless otherwise specified) TO ADDRESS SHOWN IN BLOCK 12

11. SHIP TO/MARK FOR CODE
See Schedule

12. PAYMENT WILL BE MADE BY CODE
Commander
FAO-K (CAO)
APO SF 96301

13. THIS PROCUREMENT WAS [ ] ADVERTISED, [ ] NEGOTIATED, PURSUANT TO: [X] XXXXXXXXXXXXX AR 230-1, para 1-19 and [X] XXXXXXXXXXXX DA Pamphlet 27-154

14. ACCOUNTING AND APPROPRIATION DATA
No appropriated funds of the United States shall become due or be paid the contractor by reason of this contract.

THE FOLLOWING CHECKED SECTIONS ARE CONTAINED IN THE CONTRACT

X	SEC	TABLE OF CONTENTS	PAGE	X	SEC		PAGE
		PART I - GENERAL INSTRUCTIONS			G	Preservation/Packaging/Packing	
	A	Cover Sheet (DD Form 1707)			H	Deliveries or Performance	3
	B	Contract Form and Representations, Certifications, (SF 26)	1		I	Inspection & Acceptance	3
					J	Special Provisions	3 - 9
					K	Contract Administration Data	9 - 10
	C	Instructions, Conditions, and Notices to Offerors				PART III - GENERAL PROVISIONS	
					L	General Provisions	G1-G6
	D	Evaluation & Award Factors				PART IV - LIST OF DOCUMENTS AND ATTACHMENTS	
		PART II - THE SCHEDULE					
	E	Supplies/Services & Prices	2		M	List of Documents, Exhibits, and Other Attachments	G7-G8
	F	Description/Specifications	2				

Operation of Hi-Fi, Stereo Equipment, Viedo (Video) and Audio Ship for the Naija Hotel, Armed Forces Recreation Center, US Army Garrison, Yongsan, APO96301.

21. TOTAL AMOUNT OF CONTRACT ₩ $30,012.00

CONTRACTING OFFICER WILL COMPLETE BLOCK 22 OR 26 AS APPLICABLE

22. [X] CONTRACTOR'S NEGOTIATED AGREEMENT (Contractor is required to sign this document and return 3 copies to issuing office.) Contractor agrees to furnish and deliver all items or perform all the services set forth or otherwise identified above and on any continuation sheets for the consideration stated herein. The rights and obligations of the parties to this contract shall be subject to and governed by the following documents: (a) this award/contract, (b) the solicitation, if any, and (c) such provisions, representations, certifications, and specifications, as are attached or incorporated by reference herein. (Attachments are listed herein.)

26. [ ] AWARD (Contractor is not required to sign this document.) Your offer on Solicitation Number ________, including the additions or changes made by you which additions or changes are set forth in full above, is hereby accepted as to the items listed above and on any continuation sheets. This award consummates the contract which consists of the following documents: (a) the Government's solicitation and your offer, and (b) this award/contract. No further contractual document is necessary.

23. NAME OF CONTRACTOR
BY Dae Lim Ind Co, Ltd
(Signature of person authorized to sign)

27. 8th US Army C?/NAF Activities
BY
(Signature of Contracting Officer)

24. NAME AND TITLE OF SIGNER (Type or print)
CHANG. KYO-CHOL, Chair Man

25. DATE SIGNED
22 Feb 80

28. NAME OF CONTRACTING OFFICER (Type or print)
LEONARD LAZOFF

29. DATE SIGNED
15 Mar 80

88

PART II--THE SCHEDULE

SECTION E - Services

Item No.	Service	Fixed Fee
0001	Operate an electronic equipment and stereo shop in the Naija Hotel. Merchandise to be sold shall consist of Hi-Fi, Stereo Equipment, Video Equipment, and Various Electronic Equipment that are manufactured locally for export to the United States. Merchandise shall carry a customer warranty and meet USA standards.	$ 2,501.00 Monthly Rent

SECTION F - Description

1. Scope of Services:

a. Contractor shall furnish services, merchandise, and supplies required to operate the shop listed in the Schedule, Section E.

b. The location of the facility is the Naija Hotel R&R Center, Bldg. No. P-2 downtown Seoul, in the #7 Naija-dong, Chongro-ku, Seoul Korea.

c. Contractor personnel shall communicate with customers in the English language.

d. Contractor shall ensure that merchandise presented for sale shall be neatly displayed and that the premises are clean and orderly.

89

SECTION H - Performance

1. Contract Period: The contract period is for one year to begin on the effective date of **1 February 1980, or settlement date, whichever is later.**

2. Hours of Operation: The hours of operation shall be from 1000 hours to 2200 hours, Monday through Sunday (seven days a week). No holiday shall be observed by contractor personnel unless mutually agreed upon between the contractor and the General Manager of the Naija Hotel R&R Center, 72 hours prior to the expected holiday.

SECTION I - Inspection and Acceptance

1. The General Manager of the Naija Hotel, R&R Center, U.S. Army Garrison, Yongsan, APO 96301, shall retain physical control over the facilities and fund furnished equipment. He shall coordinate with contractor on prices to be charged.

2. The General Manager of the Naija Hotel~~, as the appointed Contracting Officer's Representative~~, reserves the right to inspect contractor's operation and sales accounts at any time deemed necessary.

3. Contractor's operation may be audited by the Fund or any audit agency employed by the Fund, not less frequently than semiannually (AR-230-60, para 9-6(d)(5), and para 9-6(d)(6)).

SECTION J - Special Provisions

1. Authorized Customers: Contractor shall render services only to authorized personnel. Authorized personnel shall be defined by the General Manager of the Naija Hotel.

2. Authorized Services: Contractor shall render only those services specified in Part II, Section E hereof.

3. Authorized Prices:

a. Within ten (10) days after award of this contract and prior to selling any merchandise or services under this contract, contractor shall submit to the General Manager of the Naija Hotel, a price list for merchandise proposed to be sold at the Naija Hotel. Contractor and the General Manager of the Naija Hotel shall negotiate and reach agreement on a price for each item of merchandise or service, prior to that item or service being sold. The General Manager of the Naija Hotel shall then sign the price list noting his agreement. After the prices are initially approved, contractor shall submit a price list of items at least quarterly and before introducing new items of merchandise or services, he shall receive written agreement on prices from the General Manager of the Naija Hotel prior to selling the item or service. During the period of the contract, the prices of items or services shall conform to the approved price list and shall be no greater than the market prices of the items or services performed. Merchandise shall have a selling price sticker attached to it. 90

4

b. Contractor shall maintain the approved price list of articles or services to be furnished. This list shall state that it has been approved by the General Manager of the Naija Hotel and this price list shall be conspicuously posted at the place of business.

4. Changes in Prices and Fee: Contractor fixed fee shall remain firm for the period of the contract, or any renewal, unless changes are authorized by the Contracting Officer, NAF Branch, CFD, USAKCA. Merchandise or services prices, if changed, shall conform to the price list as approved by the General Manager of the Naija Hotel.

5. Quality of Merchandise and Customer Complaints: Merchandise sold or services performed shall be a consistently high quality. Contractor shall adhere to the fund policy of customer satisfaction guaranteed. Disagreements that cannot be resolved between contractor and customer shall be referred by contractor to the General Manager of the Naija Hotel. Customers shall be treated in a courteous manner and without discrimination to rank, race, sex, creed, color or national origin. When items are returned due to inferior quality or workmanship, contractor shall either refund the money, redo services, or replace the merchandise, as the customer requests.

6. Restrictions: Contractor shall not, in or about premises or the military installation, engage in or permit gambling or the use of any device which savors of gambling, such as punch cards, or slot machines; sell or deal in or permit to be sold any form of intoxicating beverages, drugs, depressants, stimulants or hallucinogens; loan money to customers or to others; or sell merchandise or services on credit.

7. Abandoned Customer Property:

a. Customer property abandoned with contractor shall be turned over to the fund within the same day on which the property was left with contractor. Before turning over the property contractor shall make a diligent effort to locate the owner.

b. Customer property turned over to the fund shall be disposed of by the fund in accordance with pertinent Army and Air Force regulations and fund's directives relating to abandoned property.

8. Risk of Loss:

a. Contractor assumes the risk of loss of receipts until delivered to the custodian of fund. Custodian of fund shall accept only receipts in U.S. currency and/or personal U.S. check.

b. Contractor assumes the risk of loss or damage to his stock, equipment, fixtures and property.

91

9. Signs:

Contractor shall provide sign boards which include the following information;

a. Identification Sign

b. Emergency Contact Sign

c. Hours of Operation

Signs shall be approved by the fund custodian prior to posting and shall be posted in conspicuous places.

10. Indebtedness: Contractor shall pay promptly and in accordance with the terms thereof, indebtedness incurred in connection with the performance of this contract.

11. Personnel:

a. Qualification of Employees: Contractor shall provide a sufficient number of qualified employees possessing the necessary health certificates in compliance with the rules and regulations as required by the fund and the US Government. For the efficient performance of this contract employees shall be subject to a physical examination and immunization prior to and during the performance of the contract.

b. Contractor shall procure and maintain, at his own cost and expense, a distinctive uniform and shall require his employees to wear the uniform throughout the hours of operation. Contractor shall provide sufficient number of uniforms to employees to insure that they are kept clean, neat, in good repair, and properly fitted. Uniforms that are unpresentable or worn beyond repair shall be expeditiously replaced.

c. Contractor and his employees are subject to security clearance procedures and shall obtain such installation passes and permits as are provided for in installation regulations.

d. Contractor and his employees shall obey the national and local laws and regulations of the country in which the contract is being performed, and the regulations, orders and directives applicable to the military installation upon which the contract is being performed.

e. If, in the opinion of the fund custodian, the conduct or efficiency of contractor or any of his employees interferes with proper service or proper discipline, or if contractor or any employee fails to meet prescribed health standards, or if contractor or any employee fails to obtain or loses a required security clearance or installation pass or permit, or if contractor or any employee fails to comply with laws

92

5

or regulations referred to above, the fund custodian may at his discretion, direct contractor to remove the employees subject to the approval of the contracting officer (in which event contractor shall effect such removal), or terminate this contract for default pursuant to paragraph 7, General Provisions.

f. Contractor is responsible for supervision over his employees to insure that their actions are in accordance with the terms of this contract and for handling all problems which may arise in this operation.

g. Contractor's employees shall have a working knowledge of the English language, sufficient to perform their duties, be well groomed, wear conservative makeup, maintain haircuts and in general, conform to the standards prescribed by the military services in regard to appearance. In addition, they shall be courteous, prompt and provide efficient service.

h. Contractor employees shall wear a plastic name plate, clutch back, 3/4" x 3" with 1/4" white letters indicating the employee's family name in the English alphabet. The name plate shall be worn over the left breast.

12. Internal Control:

a. Accounting procedures involving concessionaire activities shall be in compliance with standards prescribed in AR 230-65.

b. Contractor shall keep a complete and accurate account of concession transactions and maintain methods of internal control to allow fund custodian to accurately certify sales revenues for ROK Tax purposes only.

13. Utilities: Contractor shall be furnished required utilities without charge. Contractor shall be provided with a class "B" army telephone by the fund on a reimbursable basis.

14. Maintenance: Contractor shall keep the premises clean, orderly, and perform regular housekeeping, to the satisfaction of the fund custodian. Contractor shall comply with installation fire, sanitation, and safety regulations and shall take prompt corrective action on reports of violations thereof.

15. Buildings, Fixtures and Improvements:

a. Wherever the word "fixtures" appears in this contract it shall be interpreted to mean the fittings attached to the premises and considered legally as part of the premises, such as light fixtures.

b. Fund shall repair and maintain fund furnished fixtures and fund furnished premises, which includes interior decorating.

c. Contractor shall furnish, install, move, maintain, repair and replace contractor furnished fixtures at his own expense.

93

d. Building improvements to fund furnished premises shall have prior approval from General Manager, Naija Hotel, and from AFE, Yongsan. Contractor shall be required to submit blueprints of proposed improvements along with their request. Building improvements shall be made at the expense of contractor.

e. Contractor investment in fixtures and/or building improvements to be used in the performance of this contract is a business risk which contractor shall assume. Title to contractor furnished fixtures shall remain with contractor. It is expressly understood and agreed that the United States, the Departments and Fund are not and shall not be liable for costs of contractor investments in fixtures and building improvements in the event of termination of this contract or expiration of this contract without renewal.

16. Equipment and Furniture:

a. Fund shall not furnish fund owned equipment or furniture to contractor for the performance of services herein specified.

b. Contractor shall furnish, install, move, maintain, repair and replace contractor furnished equipment and furniture at his own expense.

c. Contractor furnished equipment and furniture shall be approved by General Manager, Naija Hotel, prior to being used in the performance of this contract.

d. Contractor investment in equipment and furniture to be used in the performance of this contract is a business risk which the contractor shall assume. Title to contractor furnished equipment and furniture shall remain with contractor. It is expressly understood and agreed that the United States, the Departments and Fund are not and shall not be liable for costs of contractor investments in equipment and furniture in the event of termination of this contract or expiration of this contract without renewal.

17. Supplies and Inventory: Contractor shall furnish at his expense merchandise inventory, tools of the trade, supplies and materials required for the efficient operations of the activity.

18. Settlement of Accounts upon Termination or Expiration:

Upon termination of this contract under other contract provisions contained herein, or expiration of contract period, the following requirements shall be fulfilled;

a. Contractor shall promptly settle his account with fund; yield up fund furnished premises and fixtures in as good order and condition as when the contract commenced, ordinary wear and tear excepted; surrender installation passes for himself and his employees; and complete settlement of customer claims satisfactorily.

94

b. Contractor shall promptly remove contractor owned property and supplies from the installation. Upon failure to do so the fund custodian may cause the contractor's property to be removed and stored in a public warehouse at contractor's expense. If contractor is indebted to the fund, the contractor authorizes the fund custodian to take possession of contractor's property and dispose of same by public or private sale without notice, and satisfy out of the proceeds of sale, the cost of sale and contractor's indebtedness to the fund.

19. Option to Extend the Term of the Contract: This contract is renewable, at the option of the fund, by the contracting officer giving written notice of renewal to contractor within the period specified in the schedule; provided, that the contracting officer shall have given preliminary notice of the funds intention to renew at least sixty (60) days before this contract is to expire. (Such a preliminary notice shall not be deemed to commit the fund to renewals.) If the fund exercises this option for renewal, the contract as renewed shall be deemed to include this option provision. However, the total duration of this contract, including the exercise of options under this clause, shall not exceed five (5) years.

The contracting officer shall give written notice of renewal fifteen (15) days or more before the contract would otherwise expire.

20. Government: As used herein or in references, the term "Government means nonappropriated fund activities of the Department of the Army.

21. Insurance:

Contractor shall procure and maintain at its own cost and expense, from an insurance company or companies acceptable to the Fund Custodian, insurance coverage as set forth below and shall furnish the Fund Custodian and the contracting officer with certificates of insurance evidencing that such insurance is in effect. Not less than ten (10) days prior notice shall be given to the Fund Custodian and the contracting officer by the contractor in the event of modification, cancellation or nonrenewal of such insurance coverage. Public Liability Insurance contracts shall name the nonappropriated fund activity and the United States of America as co-insured parties, in addition to concessionaire, with a severability of interest clause, with respect to claims, demands, suits, judgments, costs, charges and expenses arising out of or in connection with losses, damages, or injuries resulting from the negligence or other fault of contractor, his agents, representatives and employees.

a. Workmen's Compensation Insurance and Employer's Liability Insurance: Aside from Host Country Requirements as to the minimum number of employees, contractor's insurance coverage hereunder shall comply with the requirements and benefits established by the Ministry of Finance of the Republic of Korea.

b. Comprehensive General Liability Insurance: Minimum limits of fifty thousand dollars ($50,000.00) for injury to or death of each person, one hundred thousand

95

dollars ($100,000.00) for each accident or occurrence for property damage liability.

c. Contractors operating vehicles on the military installation for any purpose, whether or not owned by them (owned by them and operated by another) shall provide automobile Bodily Injury and Property Damage Liability Insurance with minimum limits as required by EA Reg. 190-1. Contractor shall provide non-ownership Automobile Liability Insurance with limits as aforementioned if their employee(s) operate vehicles not owned by contractor but which are used in the conduct of contractor's business.

The insurance requirements prescribed above are stated in equivalent won denomination at the exchange rate which is in effect as of contract date. In the event that the won/dollar rate in effect at the time of the contract changes, contractor shall nevertheless maintain insurance in an amount equal to the dollar value stated above.

22. Liabilities Taxes and Limitation: Contractor assumes complete liability for taxes applicable to the property, income, and transactions of contractor. The limitations imposed upon the sales and services, which may be provided by open messes, apply equally to open mess contractors.

SECTION K - Contract Administration Data

1. Sales Accounting Procedure: Sales transactions shall be conducted either in US currency, personal US check or in Korean won. Personal checks received from the customer shall be made payable to the Naija Hotel AFRC. However, should a check be received by the custodian payable to the Fund, payment of which is refused by the payor's bank, such check shall not constitute a valid receipt and the record or receipts shall be adjusted accordingly.

2. Fee Payment Procedure:

a. At the close of each business day contractor shall turn in the following:

(1) All sales receipts made in US currency and/or personal US check.

(2) Sales Clerk's Daily Report:
This report shall be made in triplicate. Fund custodian or his duly authorized/designated cashier shall, in the presence of contractor, verify the amount of receipts, sign and return one copy of the Sales Clerk's Daily Report, as a receipt for monies turned in.

b. Fund shall reimburse contractor an amount equal to the total daily receipts turned in during Fund fiscal period less amounts due and payable to Fund by contractor. Payment to contractor shall be made twice monthly by Fund directly to contractor in won at the official US Government exchange rate on the date of payment.

96

c. Contractor shall pay Fund the full amount of said fee no later than the last day of the month for which payment is due. For periods less than one (1) month this amount shall be prorated at the rate of 1/30 per day.

3. Accounting (AR 230-65, para 7-2d): Separate physical inventories will be made of fund and Government owned equipment at the time the concessionaire accepts the premises. Subsequently, physical inventories will be made every 6 months and at the date the agreement is terminated.

97

PART III - GENERAL PROVISIONS

SECTION I - General Provisions

1. General Provisions, Nonappropriated Fund Supply and Services Contracts, DA Form 4074-R, dated 1 May 73 is attached hereto and made a part thereof.

2. Alterations in Contract:

The following alterations have been made in the provisions of this contract, which are set forth in DA 4074-R (1 May 73).

The following clauses are deleted in their entirety:

(1) Clause No. 1, "Definitions".

(2) Clause No. 2, "Nonappropriated Fund Activity".

(3) Paragraph b, Clause No. 11, "Disputes".

(4) Clause No. 12, "Convict Labor".

(5) Clause No. 17, "Communist Areas".

(6) Clause No. 18, "Buy American".

(7) Clause No. 22, "Labor Provisions".

3. Additional Provisions:

The following additional provisions are incorporated herein and are set forth in full.

(1) Clause No. 1, "Definition".

(2) Clause No. 17, "Rhodesia and Certain Communist Areas".

(3) Clause No. 35, "Endorsement and/or Advertisement".

(4) Liability and Security.

(5) Exemption from Korean Taxes for POL Products Used on this contract.

(6) Exemption from Korean Customs Taxes for Items Used on this contract.

(7) Exemption from Korean Taxes for Value Added Taxed Items Used on this contract.

(8) Exemption from Korean Taxes for Special Excise Taxed Items Used on this contract.

(9) Tax Information Clause, 1 July 77.

GENERAL PROVISIONS
NONAPPROPRIATED FUND SUPPLY AND SERVICE CONTRACTS
For use of this form, see DA Pam 27-154, the proponent agency is the OCCSPER.

FUND NAME AND ADDRESS	CONTRACTOR NAME AND ADDRESS
Same as block #14	Same as block #8

1. DELETED
2. DELETED [illegible]IATED FUND ACTIVITY
3. INSPECTION AND ACCEPTANCE
4. VARIATION IN QUANTITY
5. PAYMENTS
6. DISCOUNTS
7. TERMINATION FOR DEFAULT
8. TERMINATION FOR CONVENIENCE
9. CHANGES
10. EXTRAS
11. DISPUTES
12. DELETED [illegible]OR
13. OFFICIALS NOT TO BENEFIT
14. CONVENANT AGAINST CONTINGENT FEES
15. CONVENANT AGAINST GRATUITIES
16. FUND PROPERTY
17. DELETED [illegible]READ
18. DELETED [illegible]AN
19. PERMITS AND LICENSES
20. ASSIGNMENT OF RIGHTS
21. TAXES
22. LABOR PROVISION
23. EMPLOYEES
24. DISCRIMINATION
25. NEW MATERIAL
26. PRICE CONTROL
27. ACCIDENT PREVENTION, FIRE PREVENTION, AND SANITATION
28. INSURANCE
29. SAVE HARMLESS
30. COMMERCIAL WARRANTY
31. NON-WAIVER OF DEFAULTS
32. SUBJECT TO REGULATIONS
33. MODIFICATION AND ADDITIONS
34. EXAMINATION OF RECORDS

~~1. DEFINITION~~
~~"Contracting Officer" means the person executing or administering this contract on behalf of the nonappropriated fund which is [illegible], or his successor or successors.~~

~~2. NONAPPROPRIATED FUND ACTIVITY~~
~~The Fund herein is a nonappropriated fund activity of the Department of the Army. No appropriated funds of the United States shall become due, or be paid, the Contractor by reason of this contract.~~

3. INSPECTION AND ACCEPTANCE
Inspection and acceptance will be at destination, unless otherwise provided. Until delivery and acceptance, and after any rejections, risk of loss will be on the Contractor unless loss results from negligence of the Fund.

4. VARIATION IN QUANTITY
No variation in the quantity of any item called for by this contract will be accepted unless such variation has been caused by conditions of loading, shipping, or packing, or allowances in manufacturing processes, and then only to the extent, if any, specified elsewhere in this contract.

5. PAYMENTS
Invoices shall be submitted in triplicate (one copy shall be marked "Original") unless otherwise specified, and shall contain the following information: Contract or Order number, Item number, contract description of supplies or services, sizes, quantities, unit prices and extended totals. Bills of lading number and weight of shipment will be shown for shipments on Government Bills of Lading. Unless otherwise specified, payment will be made on partial deliveries accepted by the Fund when the amount due on such deliveries so warrants.

6. DISCOUNTS
Discount time will be computed from date of delivery at the place of acceptance or from receipt of correct invoice at the office specified by the Fund, whichever is later. Payment is made, for discount purposes, when check is mailed.

7. TERMINATION FOR DEFAULT
The Contracting Officer, by written notice, may terminate this contract, in whole or in part, for failure of the Contractor to perform any of the provisions hereof. In such event, the Contractor shall be liable for damages, including the excess cost of reprocuring similar supplies or services; provided that, if
(i) it is determined for any reason that the Contractor was not in default or
(ii) the Contractor's failure to perform is without his and his subcontractor's control, fault or negligence, the termination shall be deemed to be a termination for convenience under Paragraph 8.

DA FORM 1 MAY 73 4074-R

99

8. TERMINATION FOR CONVENIENCE

The Contracting Officer, by written notice, may terminate this contract, in whole or in part, when it is in the best interest of the Fund. If this contract is for supplies and is so terminated, the Contractor shall be compensated in accordance with Section VIII of the Armed Services Procurement Regulation, in effect on this contract's date. To the extent that this contract is for services, and is so terminated, the Fund shall be liable only for payment in accordance with the payment provisions of this contract for services rendered prior to the effective date of termination.

9. CHANGES

The Contracting Officer may at any time, by written order, and without notice to the sureties, make changes, within the general scope of this contract, in

(i) drawings, designs, or specifications, where the supplies to be furnished are to be specially manufactured for the Fund in accordance therewith;

(ii) method of shipment or packing; and

(iii) place of delivery. If any such change causes an increase or decrease in the cost of, or the time required for performance of this contract, whether changed or not changed by any such order, an equitable adjustment shall be made by written modification of this contract. Any claim by the Contractor for adjustment under this clause must be asserted within 30 days from the date of receipt by the Contractor of the notification of change provided that the Contracting Officer, if he decides that the facts justify such action, may receive and act upon any such claim if asserted prior to final payment, under this contract. Failure to agree to any adjustment shall be a dispute concerning a question of fact within the meaning of the clause of this contract entitled "Disputes." However, nothing in this clause shall release the Contractor from proceeding with the contract as changed.

10. EXTRAS

Except as otherwise provided in this contract, no payment for extras shall be made unless such extras and the price therefor have been authorized in writing by the Contracting Officer.

11. DISPUTES

a. The following applies to contracts, purchase orders, or agreements entered into by any fund except contracts, purchase orders, or agreements entered into by a fund located in United States Army, Europe, and which to be performed outside the United States. Except as otherwise provided in this contract, any dispute or claim concerning this contract which is not disposed of by agreement shall be decided by the Contracting Officer, who shall reduce his decision to writing and mail or otherwise furnish a copy thereof to the Contractor. Within 30 days from the date of receipt of such copy, the Contractor may appeal by mailing or otherwise furnishing to the Contracting Officer a written appeal addressed to the Armed Services Board of Contract Appeals, and the decision of the Board shall be final and conclusive. In connection with any appeal proceeding under this clause, the Contractor shall be afforded an opportunity to be heard and to offer evidence in support of his appeal. Pending final decision of a dispute hereunder, the Contractor shall proceed diligently with the performance of the contract and in accordance with the Contracting Officer's decision.

~~b. The following applies to contracts, purchase orders, or agreements entered into by the fund in United States Army, Europe to be performed outside the United States: Except as otherwise provided in this contract, any dispute or claim concerning this contract which is not disposed of by agreement shall be decided by the Contracting Officer, who shall reduce his decision to writing and mail or otherwise furnish a copy thereof to the Contractor. The decision of the Contracting Officer shall be final and conclusive unless, within 30 days of the receipt of such copy, the Contractor mails or otherwise furnishes to the Contracting Officer a written appeal addressed to the Commander in Chief, United States Army, Europe. The decision of the Commander in Chief, United States Army, Europe, or his duly authorized representative (other than the Contracting Officer under this contract) for the determination of such appeals shall be final and conclusive if the amount involved in the appeal is $50,000 or less. If the amount involved exceeds $50,000 such decision shall be final and conclusive unless, within 30 days after receipt by the Contractor thereof, the Contractor furnishes to the Contracting Officer a written appeal addressed to the Armed Services Board of Contract Appeals. The decision of the Board shall be final and conclusive. In connection with any appeal proceeding under this clause, the Contractor shall be afforded an opportunity to be heard and to offer evidence in support of his appeal. Pending final decision of a dispute hereunder, the Contractor shall proceed diligently with the performance of the contract and in accordance with the Contracting Officer's decision.~~

~~12. CONVICT LABOR~~

~~The Contractor agrees not to employ for work under this contract any person undergoing sentence of imprisonment at hard labor.~~

13. OFFICIALS NOT TO BENEFIT

No official or employee of the United States Government or its nonappropriated fund instrumentalities shall be admitted to any share or part of this contract or any benefit that may arise therefrom.

14. COVENANT AGAINST CONTINGENT FEES

The Contractor warrants that no person or selling agency has been employed or retained to solicit or secure this contract upon an agreement or understanding for a commission, percentage, brokerage, or contingent fee, excepting bona fide employees or bona fide established commercial or selling agencies maintained by the Contractor for the purpose of securing business. For breach or violation of this warranty the Fund shall have the right to annul this contract without liability or in its discretion, to deduct from the contract price or consideration, or otherwise recover, the full amount of such commission, percentage, brokerage, or contingent fee.

15. COVENANT AGAINST GRATUITIES

The Contractor warrants that no gratuities (in the form of entertainment, gifts, or otherwise) were offered or given by the Contractor, or any agent or representative of the Contractor, to any officer, agent, or employee of the Fund with a view toward securing a contract or securing favorable treatment with respect to the awarding or amending, or making of any determinations with respect to the performance of such contract. For breach or violation of this warranty, the Fund shall have the right to terminate this contract without liability and, in its discretion, to deduct from the contract, price, consideration, or any other sums due or to become due the Contractor under this or any other contract the full amount of any such gratuities or the value thereof.

2

100

15. FUND PROPERTY

The Contractor shall sign a receipt for any property furnished by the Fund and upon expiration of this contract shall return such property to the Fund in the same condition as when received, fair wear and tear excepted. If any such property is lost, damaged or destroyed and not returned or returned in a damaged condition in excess of fair wear and tear, the Contractor shall pay the Fund for the cost of repairs of damages or the fair market value of the property as determined by the Contracting Officer.

[illegible]

[illegible] the written approval of the Contracting Officer, the Contractor shall not acquire for use in performance of this co[illegible]

[illegible] services originating from sources within the following communist areas:

[illegible] China, excluding Taiwan (Formosa), but including Manchuria, Inner Mongolia, the province of Tsinghai and Sinkiang, Sinkiang, Tibet, the former Kwantung Leased Territory, the present Port Arthur Naval Base area and Liaotung [illegible]; Communist controlled area of Vietnam and communist controlled area of Laos; Cuba; Czechoslovakia; East Germany (Soviet Zone of Germany and Soviet Sector of Berlin); Estonia; Hungary; Latvia-Lithuania; North Korea; Outer Mongolia; Poland and Danzig; Rumania; and Union of Soviet Socialist Republics.

(ii) any supplies, however processed which are or were located in or transported from or through China (as described in (i) above), North Korea, North Vietnam, or Cuba.

b. The Contractor agrees to insert the provisions of this clause, including this paragraph b., in all subcontracts hereunder.

18. BUY AMERICAN ACT

[illegible] products, the Buy American Act (41 U.S. Code 10 a-d) as implemented by Executive Order 10582, 17 Dec 1954, pr[illegible] give preference to domestic source end products. For the purpose of this clause:

(i) "Components" means those articles, materials, and supplies, which are directly incorporated in the end product;

(ii) "End products" means those articles, materials and supplies, which are to be acquired under this contract for public use; and

(iii) A "domestic source end product" means (A) an unmanufactured end product which has been mined or produced in the United States and (B) an end product manufactured in the United States if the cost of the components thereof which are mined, produced, or manufactured in the United States exceeds 50 percent of the cost of all its components. For the purpose of the a(iii)(B) components of foreign origin of the same type or kind as the products referred to in b(ii) or (iii) of this clause shall be treated as components mined, produced or manufactured in the United States.

b. The Contractor agrees that there will be delivered under this contract only domestic source end products, except end products:

(i) Which are for use outside the United States;

(ii) Which the Government determines are not mined, produced, or manufactured in the United States in sufficient and reasonably available commercial quantities and of a satisfactory quality;

(iii) As to which the Secretary of the Army determines the domestic preference to be inconsistent with the public interest; or

~~(iv) As to which the Secretary determines the cost to the Government to be unreasonable.~~

19. PERMITS AND LICENSES

The Contractor will procure all necessary permits and licenses at no cost to the Fund.

20. ASSIGNMENT OF RIGHTS

The Contractor cannot assign his rights or delegate his obligations under this contract without the prior written permission of the Fund.

21. TAXES

(a) Except as may be otherwise provided in this contract, the contract price includes all taxes, duties or other public charges in effect and applicable to this contract on the contract date, except any tax, duty, or other public charge which by law, regulation or governmental agreement is not applicable to expenditures made by the Fund or on its behalf; or any tax, duty, or other public charge from which the Contractor, or any subcontractor hereunder, is exempt by law, regulation of otherwise. If any such tax, duty or other public charge has been included in the contract price, through error or otherwise, the contract price shall be correspondingly reduced.

(b) If for any reason, after the contract date of execution, the Contractor or subcontractor is relieved in whole or in part from the payment or the burden of any tax, duty or other public charge included in the contract price, the contract price shall be correspondingly reduced; or if the Contractor or a subcontractor is required to pay in whole or in part any tax, duty or other public charge which was not included in the contract price and which was not applicable at the contract date of execution the contract price shall be correspondingly increased.

(c) No adjustment of less than $100 shall be made in the contract price pursuant to this paragraph.

22. LABOR PROVISION

(This clause applies if this contract is for services and is not exempted by applicable regulations of the Department of Labor.) *Service Contract Act of 1965.* Except to the extent that an exemption, variation, or tolerance would apply pursuant to 29 CFR 4.6 if this were a contract in excess of $2,500, the Contractor and any subcontractor hereunder shall pay all of his employees engaged in performing work on the contract not less than the minimum wage specified under section 6(a)(1) of the Fair Labor Standards Act of 1938, as amended ($1.60 per hour). However, in cases where section 6(e)(2) of the Fair Labor Standards Act of 1938 is applicable, the rates specified therein will apply. All regulations and interpretations of the Service Contract Act of 1965 expressed in 29 CFR Part 4 are hereby incorporated by reference in this contract.

23. EMPLOYEES

In the performance of services, the Contractor agrees to use only employees who meet the standards prescribed by the Fund. The Contractor will cease the use of any agent or employee who, in the opinion of the Fund, is considered undesirable.

24. DISCRIMINATION

Contractor agrees that in the performance of work under this contract there will be no discrimination against any employee or applicant for employment because of race, creed, color, or national origin.

3

9-4

101

25. NEW MATERIAL

Except as to any supplies and components which the Specification or Schedule specifically provides need not be new, the Contractor represents that the supplies and components to be provided under this contract are new. If at any time during the performance of this contract, the Contractor believes that the furnishing of supplies or components which are not new is necessary or desirable, he shall notify the Contracting Officer immediately, in writing, including the reasons therefore and proposing any consideration which will flow to the Fund if authorization to use such supplies is granted.

26. PRICE CONTROL

The Contractor warrants that the contract prices, including the prices in subcontracts hereunder, are not in excess of the prices allowed under price control laws and regulations of the Contractor's Government. If the contract prices are in excess of such allowable prices, through error or otherwise, the contract prices shall be correspondingly reduced.

27. ACCIDENT PREVENTION, FIRE PREVENTION, AND SANITATION

If this contract is performed in whole or in part on premises owned or under the control of the United States Government and/or the Fund, the Contractor shall conform to all safety regulations and requirements covering such premises in effect any any time during the performance of the contract and take all necessary steps and precautions to prevent accidents. Any violation of safety regulations, unless immediately corrected as directed by the Contracting Officer, shall be grounds of termination of the Contract under the "Termination For Default" clause.

28. INSURANCE

(a) The Contractor will, at his own expense, procure and maintain during the entire performance period of this contract insurance of at least the kinds and minimum amounts set forth below:

(b) At all times during performance, the Contractor shall maintain with the Contracting Officer a current Certificate of Insurance showing at least the insurance required by the Schedule, and providing for thirty (30) days' written notice to the Contracting Officer by the insurance company prior to cancellation or material change in policy coverage.

29. SAVE HARMLESS

The Contractor shall save harmless the Fund and the United States Government from any claims of third parties arising out of or from accidents or incidents involving acts or omissions of the Contractor, its officers, agents, or employees, occuring as a result of performance of the terms and conditions of this contract or as a result of operation of Fund furnished equipment or materials, if any, or of the performance of the services under this contract.

30. COMMERCIAL WARRANTY

The Contractor agrees that the supplies or services furnished under this contract shall be covered by the most favorable commercial warranties the Contractor gives to any customer for such supplies or services and that the rights and remedies provided herein are in addition to and do not limit any rights afforded to the Fund by any other clause of this contract.

31. NON-WAIVER OF DEFAULTS

Any failure by the Fund at any time, or from time to time, to enforce or require strict performance of any terms or conditions of this contract will not constitute waiver thereof and shall not effect or impair such terms or conditions in any way or the Fund's right at any time to avail itself of such remedies as it may have for any breach or breaches of such terms and conditions.

32. SUBJECT TO REGULATIONS

This contract is subject to all applicable statutes, treaties, conventions, executive agreements, and regulations.

33. MODIFICATIONS AND ADDITIONS

All modifications, additions, or deletions to this contract are considered to be amendments hereto and must be prepared in writing as formal amendments to this contract and must be signed by both parties in the same manner as this contract in order to be effective.

34.(This clause shall be incorporated in all nonappropriated fund contracts except those contracts with a foreign contractor in a country where such clause is precluded by law or when the Secretary of the Army determines that the inclusion of the clause would not be in the public interest.)

EXAMINATION OF RECORDS

a. This clause is applicable if the amount of this contract exceeds $2,500 and was entered into by means of negotiation. The contractor agrees that the contracting officer or his duly authorized representatives shall have the right to examine and audit the books and records of the contractor directly pertaining to the contract during the period of the contract and until the expiration of three years after final payment under the contract.

b. The contractor agrees to include the clause in paragraph a. in all his subcontracts hereunder, except purchase orders not exceeding $2,500.

4

102

G-5

Clause 1. DEFINITION

Contracting Officer: as used in this contract, the term means the person executing or administering this contract on behalf of the NAFI which is a party hereto, or his successor or successors.

Nonappropriated Fund Activity: The "Activity" as specified in Block #13 is a Nonappropriated Fund Activity of the Department of the Army. No appropriated funds of the United States shall become due, or be paid to the Contractor by reason of this contract.

Fund Custodian, General Manager, The Manager: Wherever these words appear in this contract they shall be interpreted to mean the contracting officer's representative appointed by the contracting officer for administration of the contract on behalf of the contracting officer.

Clause 17: RHODESIA AND CERTAIN COMMUNIST AREAS

a. Unless he first obtains the written approval of the contracting officer, the contractor shall not acquire for use in the performance of this contract:

(i) Any supplies or services originating from sources within Rhodesia and the communist areas of North Korea, Vietnam, or Cuba; or

(ii) Any supplies, however processed, which are or were located in or transported from or through North Korea, Vietnam, or Cuba; or

(iii) Ferrochromium or steel mill products in their basic shapes and forms which contain more than three percent (3%) chromium if they are produced outside of the United States and contain Rhodesian chromium.

b. The contractor shall insert the provisions of this clause, including this paragraph (b), in all subcontracts hereunder.

Clause 35: ENDORSEMENT AND/OR ADVERTISEMENT

Contractor shall not represent in any manner, expressly or by implication, that products purchased under the contract are approved or endorsed by any element of the United States Government. Advertisements, including cents-off coupons by contractor, which refers to a military resale activity shall contain a statement that the advertisement was neither paid for nor sponsored, in whole or in part, by the particular activity.

103

LIABILITY AND SECURITY

1. LIABILITY:

a. Contractor shall be:

(i) liable to the Government for loss of or damage to property, real and personal, owned by the Government or for which the Government is liable;

(ii) responsible for, and hold the Government harmless from loss of or damage to property not included in (i) above, and

(iii) responsible for, and hold the Government harmless from, bodily injury and death of persons,

occasioned either in whole or in part by the negligence or fault of the Contractor, his officers, agents, or employees in the performance of work under this contract.

b. Decisions of the contracting officer with respect to liability shall be subject to the "Disputes" article of the contract.

2. PREVENTION OF PILFERAGE:

a. Contractor shall throughout the term of this contract institute and maintain adequate controls and security measures to prevent pilferage during the time that property, as described in 1(a)(i) and 1(a)(ii) above, is under the contractor's control.

b. In the event that contractor's employees by direct act, or otherwise, commit, condone, fail to report, or otherwise are illegally involved in the theft of any Government property, contractor shall remove such individual from work under this contract, if so directed by the contracting officer.

3. GOVERNMENT'S RIGHTS:

The rights of the government arising from this article are in addition to any other rights set forth in the contract or any other rights to which the government is otherwise entitled. Nothing in this article shall be construed to limit these rights nor shall any other provision of this contract be construed to limit the rights of the government under this provision.

104

EXEMPTION FROM KOREAN TAXES FOR VALUE ADDED TAXED ITEMS USED ON THIS CONTRACT

This clause is in implementation of Article XVI of the Status of Forces Agreement between the Republic of Korea and the United States granting contractors exemption from Republic of Korea Value Added Taxes (VAT). At the time this contract is awarded, the contractor shall certify to the contracting officer that all supplies, services, and construction he shall purchase for the contract have been proposed to the government VAT exclusive and further that the contract price includes no VAT whatsoever. He shall indicate to the contracting officer the total amount of VAT excluded from the contract price. The contractor shall purchase supplies, services, and construction for use on the contract VAT inclusive. He shall be required to obtain a refund for these VAT amounts from his ROK District Tax Office. These refunds shall be accomplished by a contractor submission to his governing ROK District Tax Office of the tax invoices obtained from purchase of supplies, services, and construction for the USFK contract. The first purchase tax invoice submission shall be accompanied by a copy of the USFK contract. Subsequent purchase tax invoice submissions shall be accompanied by a letter reference to the USFK contract previously submitted. The contractor's ROK District Tax Office will refund to the contractor the full amount of the VAT paid by the contractor in the purchase price of the supplies, services, and construction.

This page Insert To Amendment #1 paragraph K. Section I

105

EXEMPTION FROM KOREAN TAXES FOR SPECIAL EXCISE TAXED ITEMS USED ON THIS CONTRACT

This clause is in implementation of Article XVI of the Status of Forces Agreement between the Republic of Korea and the United States granting contractors exemption from Republic of Korea Special Excise Taxes (SET). At the time this contract is awarded the contractor shall indicate to the contracting officer which items he shall purchase for the contract are subject to SET. He shall indicate the name of the item, the number of units to be purchased, the cost per unit w/o tax, the percentage of tax, the tax amount per unit, the total tax, and the manufacturer of the item. The contracting officer shall verify the reasonableness of the quantities claimed. The contractor shall purchase the SET items from the item manufacturer tax inclusive. For construction and single delivery type supply and service contracts he shall employ the following procedure: At the time he purchases the items he shall present the manufacturer with a notification letter requesting a refund of the SET. (Copies of this letter can be obtained from the USAKPA contracting officer.) The manufacturer will indorse the letter to the manufacturer's District Tax Office which will make the refund to the manufacturer. The manufacturer will make subsequent refunds to the contractor. Requests for refund under requirements type contracts shall be submitted monthly and shall be accompanied by copies of the USFK delivery orders issued during the monthly period.

G-9

106

-G-3. EXEMPTION FROM KOREAN TAXES FOR VALUE-ADDED TAXED ITEMS USED ON THIS CONTRACT

This clause implements Article XVI of the Status of Forces Agreement between the Republic of Korea and the United States of America, which exempts contractors from paying the Republic of Korea Value Added Taxes. When the contractor submits an offer, he shall certify to the Contracting Officer that all the costs in the offer will be exclusive of any Value-Added Tax and, further, that the proposed contract price includes no Value-Added Tax. Contractor shall also indicate the amount and type of Value-Added Taxes exluded from the contract price. If supplies and/or services which the contractor purchases for this contract inlcudes Value-Added Taxes, he can obtain a full refund for the amount of the Value-Added Taxes from his ROK District Tax Office. Contractor can receive Value-Added Tax refunds by submitting to ROK District Tax Office tax invoices which he receives when he purchases materials and/or services for this contract. The contractor must submit a copy of the USFK contract with his first tax invoice submission. Subsequent tax invoice submissions must be accompanied by a letter which references the USFK contract submitted with the first tax invoice submission.

KCA LOI 29
1 Jul 80

MINISTRY OF FINANCE
REPUBLIC OF KOREA

July 2, 1980

Issue No. 1265.1-2064
Indirect Tax Section

To : Mr. Chung, Se Young
President,
Hyundai Automobile Co., Ltd.

Subject : Inquiry concerning the application of tariff for small industries.

Dear Sir:

1. This is a reply to your inquiry No. 5-15 dated May 14, 1980.

2. The provision of Paragraph ~~1,~~ Section 1, Article 11 of Value Added Tax Law does not include commodity supplied to the U.S. Armed Forces stationed in Korea by Korean supplier based on agreement conclued between the supplier and the U.S. Armed Forces and internal letter of credit.

/Official Seal Affixed/
Minister of Finance,
Republic of Korea

108

재 무 부

관세 1265.1- 70-3222 1980. 7. 8.

수신 서울 종로구 계동 140-2

현대자동차주식회사 대표이사 정 세 영

제목 영세율 적용에 관한 질의

1. 현자관 제5-15호 (80. 5. 14)에 대한 회신입니다.

2. 부가가치세법 제11조 제1항 제1호에 규정하는 수출하는 재화에는 사업자가 미국군납계약서에 의하여 개설된 내국신용장에 의하여 공급하는 재화는 포함되지 아니하는 것입니다. 끝.

재 무 부 장 관

109

REQUEST FOR NOTARIZATION

This is to request a notarization of the true and faithful translation of the Inquiry to Chung, Se Young.

Requested by: Hyun Sook Tak

CERTIFICATE

This is to certify that the translation of the Inquiry to Chung, Se Young is true and correct from the Korean original.

Date: 1982. 12. 22

등·부 제 [illegible] 호
별지 번역된 영문은 별지 국문으로된
원문과 부합 일치하다
이에 이를 인증하다
서기 壹九八 [illegible] 년 [illegible] 월 [illegible] 일
서울특별시중구을지로2가21번지
서울지방검찰청소속
공증인 홍 순 엽

Sun-yup HONG
Notary Public
Seoul District prosecutor's Office
Seoul, Korea

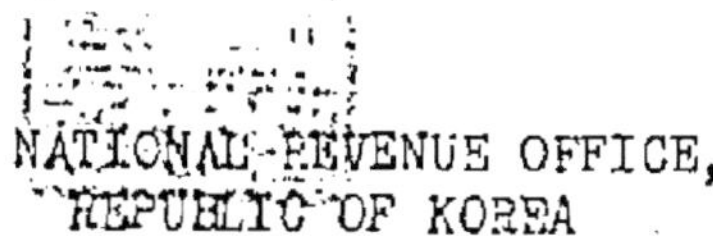

NATIONAL REVENUE OFFICE,
REPUBLIC OF KOREA

December 8, 1980

Issue No. 1265.1-2618,
Value Additional Tax Section.

To : Yu, Tong Sik,
President,
Dae Lim Industrial Co., Ltd.
Rm. 508, Y.W.C.A. Bldg.,
203, 1-ka, Myung-dong, Chung-ku,
Seoul, Korea

Subject : Reply to inquiry concerning the authoritative interpretation of Value Added Tax.

Dear Sir:

1. This refers to your inquiry forwarded on November 21, 1980.

2. In the event when any business oprator receives Certificate of Payment for Foreign Currency issue by Korea Foreign Exchange Bank or foreign currency from the same bank or Korean currency through the account of non-indigenous person from the same bank as a compensation for supply of commodity or service to the U.S. Army stationed in Korea, tariff for small industries will be applied, pursuant to the provisions of Paragraph 4, Section 1, Article 11 of Value Added Tax Law and Paragraph 4, Section 1, Article 26 of the Enforcement Regulation of the above law.

3. In the event when tariff for small business is applied for supply of commodity or service based on internal Letter of Credit, the provision of Paragraph 1, Section 1, Article 11 of Value Added Tax Law will be applied for only supply of commodity to foreign buyer for the purpose of export of the said commodity.

/s/
Han, Yong Suk
Suprintendent,
National Revenue Office,
Seoul, Korea

///

국 세 청

부가 1265.1 - 2618 ˋ 633 - 1363 1980. 12. 8.

수신 서울 중구 명동 1가 203 Y.W.C.A 508호

대림기업(주) 대표 유 동 식

제목 부가가치세법에 대한 유권해석 질의 회신

1. 1980. 11. 21일자 귀 질의에 대한 회신입니다.

2. 사업자가 미국군에게 직접 재화나 용역을 공급하고 그 대가를 외국환 은행에서 외환증서 또는 원화로 받거나 비거주자 원화계정을 통하여 원화로 받는 경우 부가가치세법 제11조 1항 4호 및 동 법시행령 제26조 1항 4호 규정에 의거 영세율이 적용되는 것임.

3. 내국신용장에 의하여 공급되는 재화가 영세율이 적용되는 경우는 부가가치세법 제11조 제1항 1호 규정에 의한 수출재화를 외국으로 반출하는 사업자에게 공급하는 때에 한하는 것입니다. 끝.

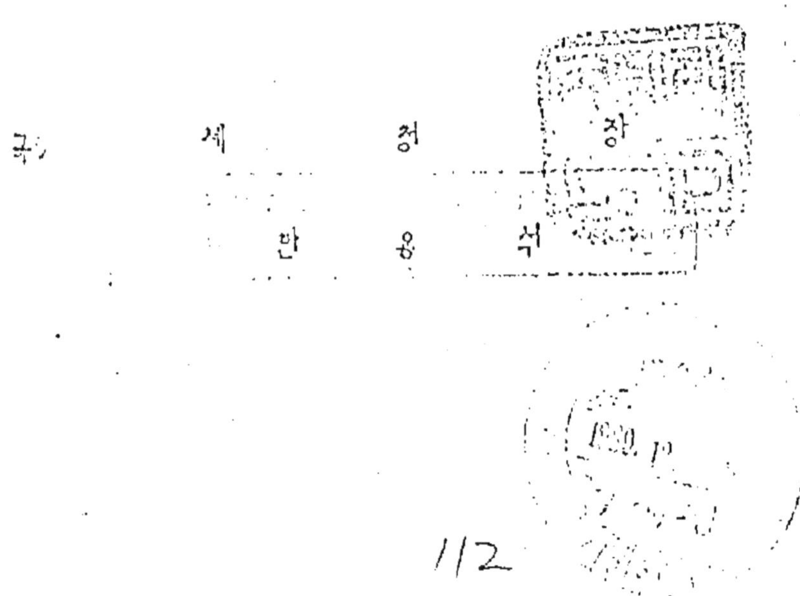

국 세 청 장

안 용 석

112

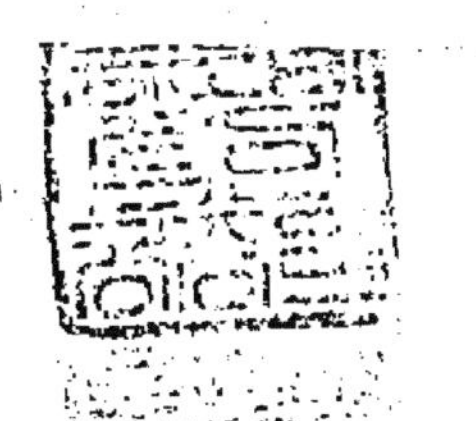

REQUEST FOR NOTARIZATION

This is to request a notarization of the true and faithful translation of the Reply to Yu, Tong Sik.

Requested by: [illegible]

CERTIFICATE

This is to certify that the translation of the Reply to Yu, Tong Sik.

is true and correct from the Korean original.

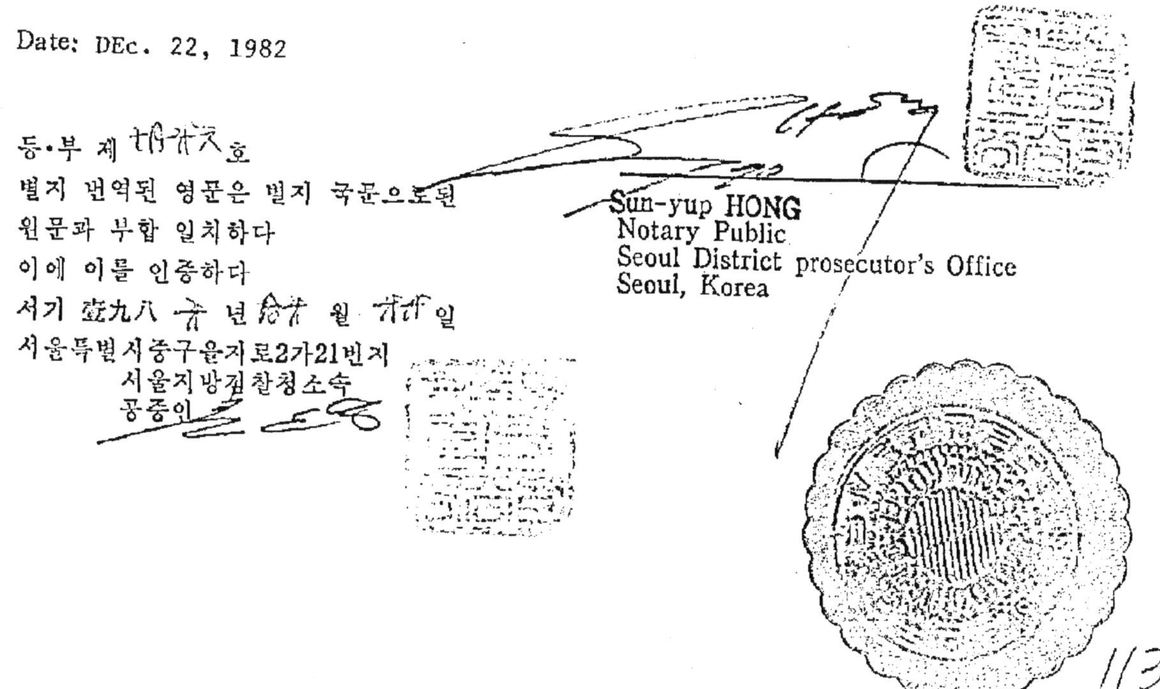

Date: DEc. 22, 1982

등·부 제 [illegible] 호
별지 번역된 영문은 별지 국문으로된
원문과 부합 일치하다
이에 이를 인증하다
서기 一九八[illegible] 년 [illegible] 월 二十二 일
서울특별시중구을지로2가21번지
서울지방검찰청소속
공증인

Sun-yup HONG
Notary Public
Seoul District prosecutor's Office
Seoul, Korea

113

C.

The United States of America

and the Republic of Korea

STATUS OF FORCES AGREEMENT

with

Related Documents

HEADQUARTERS

UNITED STATES FORCES, KOREA

Fourth Edition January 1978

114

punishable by the law of the Republic of Korea. In recognition of the role of such persons in the defense of the Republic of Korea, they shall be subject to the provisions of paragraphs 5, 7(b), and 9 and the related Agreed Minutes, of Article XXII. In those cases in which the authorities of the Republic of Korea decide not to exercise jurisdiction they shall notify the military authorities of the United States as soon as possible. Upon such notification the military authorities of the United States shall have the right to exercise such jurisdiction over the persons referred to as is conferred on them by the law of the United States.

ARTICLE XVI

Local Procurement

1. The United States may contract for any materials, supplies, equipment and services (including construction work) to be furnished or undertaken in the Republic of Korea for purposes of, or authorized by, this Agreement, without restriction as to choice of contractor, supplier or person who provides such services. Such materials, supplies, equipment and services may, upon agreement between the appropriate authorities of the two Governments, also be procured through the Government of the Republic of Korea.

2. Materials, supplies, equipment and services which are required from local sources for the maintenance of the United States armed forces and the procurement of which may have an adverse effect on the economy of the Republic of Korea shall be procured in coordination with, and, when desirable, through or with the assistance of, the competent authorities of the Republic of Korea.

3. Materials, supplies, equipment and services procured for official purposes in the Republic of Korea by the United States armed forces, including their authorized procurement agencies, or procured for ultimate use by the United States armed forces shall be exempt from the following Korean taxes upon appropriate certification in advance by the United States armed forces:

(a) commodity tax;
(b) traffic tax;
(c) petroleum tax;
(d) electricity and gas tax;
(e) business tax.

With respect to any present or future Korean taxes not specifically referred to in this Article which might be found to constitute a significant and readily identifiable part of the gross purchase price of materials, supplies, equipment and services procured by the United States armed forces, or for ultimate use by such forces, the two Governments will agree upon a procedure for granting such exemption or relief therefrom as is consistent with the purpose of this Article.

4. Neither members of the United States armed forces, civilian component, nor their dependents, shall by reason of this Article enjoy any exemption from taxes or similar charges relating to personal purchases of goods and services in the Republic of Korea chargeable under legislation of the Republic of Korea.

5. Except as such disposal may be authorized by the authorities of the United States and the Republic of Korea in accordance with mutually agreed conditions, goods purchased in the Republic of Korea exempt from taxes referred to in paragraph 3, shall not be disposed of in the Republic of Korea to persons not entitled to purchase such goods exempt from such taxes.

ARTICLE XVII

Labor

1. In this Article the expression;

(a) "employer" refers to the United States armed forces (including nonappropriated fund organizations) and the persons referred to in the first paragraph of Article XV;

(b) "employee" refers to any civilian (other than a member of the civilian com-

IX, take up the matter with the appropriate authorities of the United States armed forces.

6. The words "The United States armed forces shall render all assistance within their power," etc., in paragraph 9(b) and (c) refer to reasonable and practicable measures by the United States armed forces.

7. It is understood that the duty-free treatment provided in paragraph 2 shall apply to materials, supplies, and equipment imported for sale through commissaries and non-appropriated fund organizations, under such regulations as the United States armed forces may promulgate, to those individuals and organizations referred to in Article XIII and its Agreed Minute.

ARTICLE X

1. "United States and foreign vessels . . . operated by, for, or under the control of the United States for official purposes" means public vessels and chartered vessels (bare boat charter, voyage charter and time charter). Space charter is not included. Commercial cargo and private passengers are carried by them only in exceptional cases.

2. The ports of the Republic of Korea mentioned herein will ordinarily mean "open ports".

3. The exemption from making the "appropriate notification" referred to in paragraph 3 will apply only in unusual cases where such is required for security of the United States armed forces or similar reasons.

4. The laws and regulations of the Republic of Korea will be applicable except as specifically provided otherwise in this Article.

ARTICLE XII

Installation by the United States armed forces of permanent navigational aids for vessels and aircraft outside of facilities and areas in use by the United States armed forces will be effected in accordance with the procedures established under paragraph 1 of Article III.

ARTICLE XIII

The United States armed forces may grant the use of the organizations referred to in paragraph 1 of Article XIII to: (a) other officers or personnel of the Government of the United States ordinarily accorded such privileges; (b) those other non-Korean armed forces in the Republic of Korea under the Unified Command which receive logistical support from the United States armed forces, and their members; (c) those non-Korean persons whose presence in the Republic of Korea is solely for the purpose of providing contract services financed by the Government of the United States; (d) those organizations which are present in the Republic of Korea primarily for the benefit and service of the United States armed forces, such as the American Red Cross and the United Service Organizations, and their non-Korean personnel; (e) dependents of the foregoing; and (f) other persons and organizations with the express consent of the Government of the Republic of Korea.

ARTICLE XV

1. The execution of contracts with the United States in addition to those specified in paragraph 1 of Article XV shall not exclude the persons provided for in Article XV from the application of that Article.

2. Contractor employees who are present in the Republic of Korea on the effective date of this Agreement and who would qualify for the privileges contained in Article XV but for the fact that they are not ordinarily resident in the United States shall be entitled to enjoy such privileges so long as their presence is for the purpose stated in paragraph 1 of Article XV.

ARTICLE XVI

1. The United States armed forces will furnish the authorities of the Republic of

Korea with appropriate information as far in advance as practicable on anticipated major changes in their procurement program in the Republic of Korea.

2. The problem of a satisfactory settlement of difficulties with respect to procurement contracts arising out of differences between economic laws and business practices of the Republic of Korea and the United States will be studied by the Joint Committee or other appropriate representatives.

3. The procedures for securing exemptions from taxation on purchases of goods for ultimate use by the United States armed forces will be as follows:

(a) Upon appropriate certification by the United States armed forces that materials, supplies and equipment consigned to or destined for such forces, are to be used, or wholly or partially used up, under the supervision of such forces, exclusively in the execution of contracts for the construction, maintenance or operation of the facilities and areas referred to in Article V or for the support of the forces therein, or are ultimately to be incorporated into articles or facilities used by such forces, an authorized representative of such forces shall take delivery of such materials, supplies and equipment directly from manufacturers thereof. In such circumstances the collection of taxes referred to in Article XVI, paragraph 3, shall be held in abeyance.

(b) The receipt of such materials, supplies and equipment in the facilities and areas shall be confirmed by an authorized representative of the United States armed forces to the authorities of the Republic of Korea.

(c) Collection of the taxes on such materials, supplies and equipment shall be held in abeyance until

(i) the United States armed forces confirm and certify the quantity or degree of consumption of the above referred to materials, supplies and equipment, or

(ii) the United States armed forces confirm and certify the amount of the above referred to materials, supplies, and equipment which have been incorporated into articles or facilities used by the United States armed forces.

(d) Materials, supplies and equipment certified under (c)(i) or (ii) shall be exempt from taxes referred to in Article XVI, paragraph 3, insofar as the price thereof is paid out of appropriations of the Government of the United States or out of funds contributed by the Government of the Republic of Korea for disbursement by the Government of the United States.

4. Regarding paragraph 3 it is understood that "materials, supplies, equipment and services procured for official purposes" refers to direct procurement by the United States armed forces or their authorized procurement agencies from Korean suppliers. "Materials, supplies, equipment and services procured for ultimate use" refers to procurement by contractors of the United States armed forces from Korean suppliers of items to be incorporated into or necessary for the production of the end product of their contracts with the United States armed forces.

ARTICLE XVII

1. It is understood that the Government of the Republic of Korea shall be reimbursed for direct costs incurred in providing assistance requested pursuant to paragraph 2.

2. The undertaking of the Government of the United States to conform to the provisions of labor legislation of the Republic of Korea does not imply any waiver by the Government of the United States of its immunities under international law. The Government of the United States may terminate employment at any time the continuation of such employment is inconsistent with the military requirements of the United States armed forces.

117

제 16 조

국내 조달

제 1 절 미합중국은, 본 협정의 목적에 따르거나 허용되는바 대한민국내에서 공급 또는 청부될 물자 보급 장비와 용역 (건설공사 포함)에 관한 계약을 이를 제공하는 청부업자 조달자 혹은 자연인의 선택에 제한없이 체결할수 있다. 이러한 물자보급 장비 용역은, 양국 정부간의 적절한 기관간의 합의에 의하여 대한민국 정부를 통하여 조달될수도 있다.

제 2 절 미합중국군 유지를 위한 국내에서 조달 되어야할 물자 보급 장비 용역과 이러한 조달이 대한민국 경제에 유해한 효과를 가져올경우 필요하다면 대한민국 정부의 적절한 당국을 통하거나 이의 협조를 받어 조달 되어야 한다.

제 3 절 미합중국군과 이로부터 허가된대리인에 의하여 대한민국내에서 공적 목적을 위하고 미합중국군에 의해 최종적으로 사용되기 위한 물자 보급 장비 용역은, 미합중국군으로부터의 사전에 적절한 보증 에 의거 면세된다.

(a) 물품세

(b) 교통세

(c) 석유세

(d) 전기및깨스 세

(e) 사업세

이 조항에서 특별히 명시되지 않은 대한민국의 현재 또는 장래의 세제에 관련해서 미합중국군에 의해 또는 미합중국군의 최종사용을 위한 물자 보급 장비 용역의 구매 총액중에 점하는 쉽게 식별이 되는 상당부분에 대한 과세에 대해 양국 정부는 본절의 목적에 일치하듯이 면세와 구제책을 허용하는 절차를 설정함에 합의한다.

제 4 절 미합중국군 장병 구성민간인 또는 계열가족중에 여하한 자도 본조의 이유에 의해 대한민국 정부의 법율제정에 의거 대한민국내에서 구매한 개인적인 물자와 용역에 대하여 부가되는 세금과 유사한 과세로 부터의 면세 혜택을 받을수 없다.

118

제 5 절 미합중국과 대한민국 당국의 상호의 합의조건에 따라 허가된 처분을 제외하고 제3절에서 면세된 대한민국내에서 구매된 물자는 대한민국에서 면세 특혜자가 아닌 타인에게로의 처분을 하지 못한다.

제 16 조

제 1 절 미합중국군은 대한민국 당국에게 대한민국내에 있어서의 조달계획상의 예측된 중요변동사항에 관해 가능한 속한 시일내에 적절한 정보를 사전 제공한다.

제 2 절 대한민국과 미합중국의 경제법령과 사업관습의 차이에서 야기되는 조달계획에 관한 이외의 만족한 해결의 문제는 양국대표의 합동위원회에 위해 검토된다.

제 3 절 미합중국군에 위해 최종적으로 사용되는 물품에 대해 면세를 취득하는 절차는 다음과 같다.

(a) 미합중국군에 위한 물자 보급 장비가 미합중국군의 위해 출하되거나 또한 미합중국군이 최종 수송지가 되며 그의 전부 또는 일부가 해당 미합중국군의 감독하에, 제5조에 명시된 시설의 건설, 유지혹은 운영과 그 시설내에 주둔하고 있는 부대의 지원을 위한 계약의 유일 독점이행을 위하여 사용될 것인지 또는 사용되었는지, 또한 본조에 최종적으로 명문화 될 것인지, 또는 미합중국군에 위해 그 시설이 사용되었었는지 를 근거로 하는 보증에 의해 해당부대의 법정대표는 생산자로부터 직접 물자 보급 그리고 자비를 수송하여야 한다. 이러한 경우 제16조 제3절에 명시된 세금징수는 중지 되어야한다.

(b) 그러한 물자보급 장비가 수령되는 시설과 지역은 미합중국군의 법정대표에 위해 대한민국 당국에 확인 되어야 한다.

(c) 이러한 물자보급 및 장비에 대한 세금징수는 다음의 시기까지 보류된다.

(i) 미합중국군이 물자 보급 장비의 소비량과 상태를 확인 증명할때까지

(ii) 미합중국군이 상술한 물자 보급 장비의 소비량이 본조에 명문화 이나, 혹은 미합중국군에 위해 시설의 사용여부를 확인증명이 될때까지

(D) (c) 항의 (i) 이나 (ii) 에 위하여 증명된 물자 보급 장비는 제16조 제3절에 명시된 과세로 부터 미합중국정부로 하여금 지출이 가능 한 대한민국 정부로 부터 기증된 기금, 혹은 미국정부의 충당금 에서 지출하는한 면제된다

119

제 4 절 제3절에 관하여 공식 목적을 위한 물자 보급 용역의 조달이란 미합중국군 혹은 그의 허가된 조달기관이 한국의 조달자로부터의 직접 허가품목의 또는 미합중국군과의 계약의 위한 최종 제품의 생산을 의한 필요한 물품의 직접 구매를 말한다.

120

서 약 서

본인은 별첨 영문 으로 된 한미행정협정일부조문 을 한글로 번역함에 있어서 차후 오역으로 인한 사고가 발생할 때에는 모든 책임을 본인이 지겠기에 이에 서약하나이다

서기 1978/년 12월 4일

주 소 : 서울시종로구운니동178-114

성 명 : 황기영 ㉞

주민등록번호 : 321208-1002215

등•부제 7065 호
우자등는 본직면전에서 서명날인 하다
본직은 이를 인증함
서기 1978년 12월 12일
서울특별시 중구 을지로2가21번지
서울지방검찰청소속
공증인

121

NATIONAL REVENUE OFFICE,
REPUBLIC OF KOREA

December 22, 1981

Issue No. 1265.1-3334,
Value Added Tax Section

To : Mr. Chang Kyo Chol
Dae Lim Industrial Co., Ltd.
Rm. 508, Y.W.C.A. Bldg.,
1-3, 1-ka, Myung-dong, Chung-ku,
Seoul, Korea

Subject : Inquiry concerning the exemption from Special Consumption Tax and application of tariff for small industries.

Dear Sir:

1. This refers to your inquiry forwarded on December 7, 1981.

2. When any supplier purchases commodity from manufacturer for supply to armed forces, the provisions of Article 11 of Value Added Tax Law and Article 24 to Article 26 of the Enforcement Regulation of the above law are not applied. Accordingly, tariff for small industries is not applied either.

3. With regard to the exemption from Special Consumption Tax, we have forwarded an inquiry to Minister of Finance and we will notify you later.

/Official Seal Affixed/
Oh, Hyok Ju
Suprintendent,
National Revenue Office,
Seoul, Korea

122

③

국 세 청

부가 1265.1-3334 634-0101(513) 1981. 12. 22.

수신 서울 중구 명동 1가 1-3 Y.W.C.A 508호

대림기업주식회사 장 교 섭

제목 영세율 적용 및 특별소비세 면세여부 질의

1. 81. 12. 7 귀 질의에 대한 회신입니다.

2. 군납업자가 군납에 필요한 물품을 생산업자로 부터 구입하는 것은 부가가치세법 제11조 및 동법시행령 제24조 내지 제26조의 규정에 해당되지 아니하는 것으로 영세율이 적용되지 아니하는 것이며,

3. 특별소비세의 면세여부는 재무부장관에게 질의중이므로 추후 회신하겠습니다. 끝.

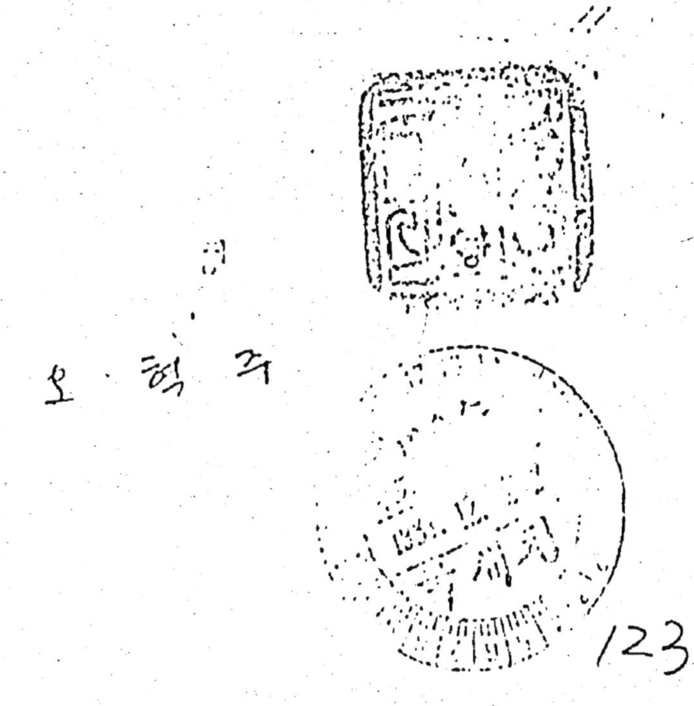

국 세 청 장

오 혁 주

123

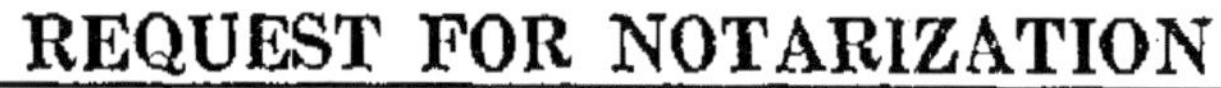

REQUEST FOR NOTARIZATION

This is to request a notarization of the true and faithful translation of the Inquiry concerning the exemption to Chang, Kyo Chol.

Requested by: [signature]

CERTIFICATE

This is to certify that the translation of the Inquiry concerning the exemption to Chang, Kyo Chol is true and correct from the Korean original.

Date: 1982. 12. 2 2

등·부 제 [illegible] 호
별지 번역된 영문은 별지 국문으로된
원문과 부합 일치하다
이에 이를 인증하다
서기 壹九八二 년 拾貳 월 貳拾貳 일
서울특별시중구을지로2가21번지
서울지방검찰청소속
공증인

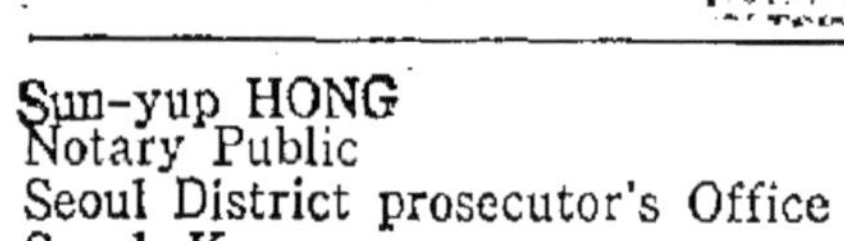

Sun-yup HONG
Notary Public
Seoul District prosecutor's Office
Seoul, Korea

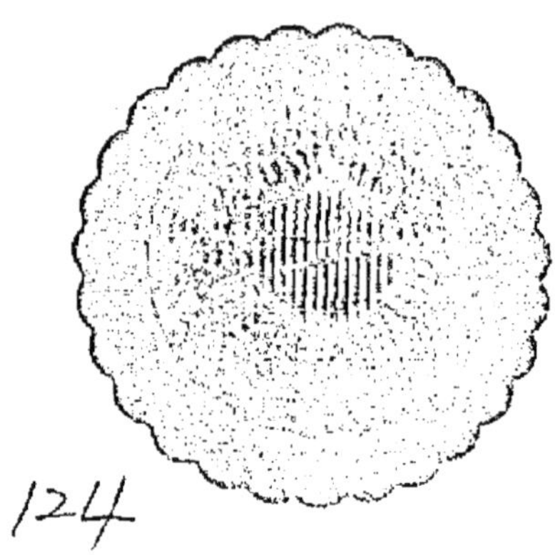

124

GENERAL CIVIL ADMINISTRATION OFFICE
REPUBLIC OF KOREA

January 13, 1982

Issue No. 125.4-523

To : Mr. Chang, Kyo Chol
Dae Lim Industrial Co., Ltd.
Rm. 508, Y.W.C.A. Bldg.,
1-3, 1-ka Myung-dong, Chung-ku
Seoul, Korea

Subject: Transfer of Civil Inquiry Case

Dear Sir:

1. Our examination of your inquiry filed by this office on January 9, 1982 indicates that your purport was to verify whether tariff for small business is applied to you or whether you are entitled for exemption from Special Consumption Tax.

   However, we judged that this matter is concerned with Ministry of Finance. In view of this, we have transferred your inquiry to the same ministry for further examination, investigation and disposition of your inquiry and we are pleased to notify you that the results of such examination, investigation will be notified to you until January 23, 1982.

2. In case the reply from Ministry of Finance is delayed or you will have further questions concerning the same matters, please feel free to contact with us. (Telephone number of Civil Administrative Disposition Office is 725-0114).

/Official Seal Affixed/

Director
General Civil Administrative Office

125

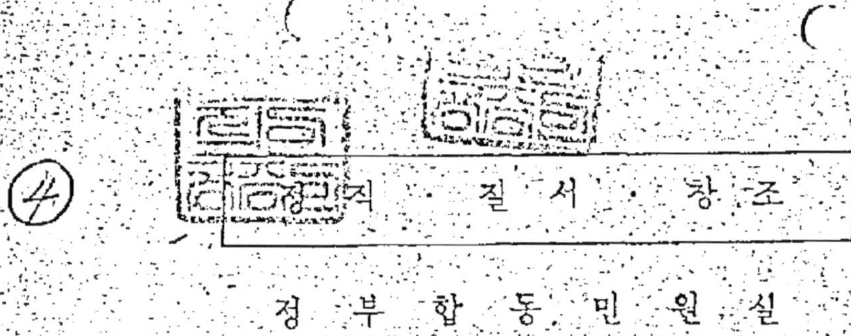

④

정 부 합 동 민 원 실

민처 125.4- 523 (725-0114) 1982. 1. 13.

수신 중구 명동 1가 1-3 YMCA508호 대림기업주식회사 장고걸귀하

제목 민원사안 이첩통보

1. 1982. 1. 9. 당실에 접수된 귀하의 민원사안을 검토한 바, 동 사안은 "영세율 적용 및 특별소비세면세여부 질의" 내용으로 이는 재무부 의 소관사항으로 판단되어 동 기관에 이첩하여 조사.처리케하고 그 결과를 1982. 1. 23. 까지 귀하에게 회신토록 조치하였음을 알려드립니다.

2. 동 기관으로부터 회신이 지체되거나 또는 회신내용에 대하여 상당한 이의가 있을 경우에는 당실(민원처리과 725-0114)에 재차 연락하시기 바랍니다. 끝.

정 부 합 동 민 원 실 장

126

REQUEST FOR NOTARIZATION

This is to request a notarization of the true and faithful translation of the attached transfer of civil inquiry case.

Requested by: Hyun Sook Tak
Tak, Hyun Sook

CERTIFICATE

This is to certify that the translation of the attached Transfer of Civil Inquiry Case is true and correct from the Korean original.

Date: 1982. 12. 2 2

등·부 제 [illegible] 호
별지 번역된 영문은 별지 국문으로된
원문과 부합 일치하다
이에 이를 인증하다
서기 壹九八 [illegible] 년 [illegible] 월 [illegible] 일
서울특별시중구을지로2가21번지
서울지방검찰청소속
공증인

Sun-yup HONG
Notary Public
Seoul District prosecutor's Office
Seoul, Korea

127

MINISTRY OF FINANCE,
REPUBLIC OF KOREA

January 14, 1982

Issue No. 1264-48

To : Suprintendent,
National Revenue Office

Reference: Director,
Indirect Tax Bureau

Subject : Reply to inquiry concerning the exemption from Special Consumption Tax based on the provision of Korea-America Administrative Agreement.

Dear Sir:

1. This is relevant with Consumption Tax No. 1265.3-3346 (December 23, 1981).

2. In regard to this matter, we forward the following replies:

The provision of Section 3, Article 16 of Korea-America Administrative Agreement means the exemption of tax for supply by Korean business organization to the U.S. Armed Forces or any agency approved by the U.S. Armed Forces for the use of the U.S. Government.

However, despite the virtue of the said provision, the member of the U.S. Armed Forces or any civilian employee of the U.S. Armed Forces or the family of such employee are not entitled for the exemption of tax for the purchase of commodity in Korean market for personal use.

/Official Seal Affixed/
Minister of Finance,
Republic of Korea

128

재 무 부

국조 1264-45 720-3223 1982. 1. 14.

수신 국세청장

참조 간세국장

제목 한·미 행정 협정에 의한 특별소비세 면제 질의(회신)

1. 소비 1265.3-3346 (81. 12. [illegible]) 관련입니다.

2. 본건에 대하여 다음과 같이 회신합니다.

한·미 행정 협정 제16조 제3항의 규정은, 합중국군대 또는 그 공인조달기관이 공용을 위하여 대한민국의 공급자로부터 물품을 조달할 경우의 조세면제를 뜻하는 것이므로, 합중국 군대의 구성원, 군속 및 그들의 가족은 본조를 이유로 하여 대한민국 안에서 조세를 부과할 수 있는 물품의 개인적 구입에 대한 조세의 면제를 받을 수 없습니다. 끝.

재 무 부 장 관

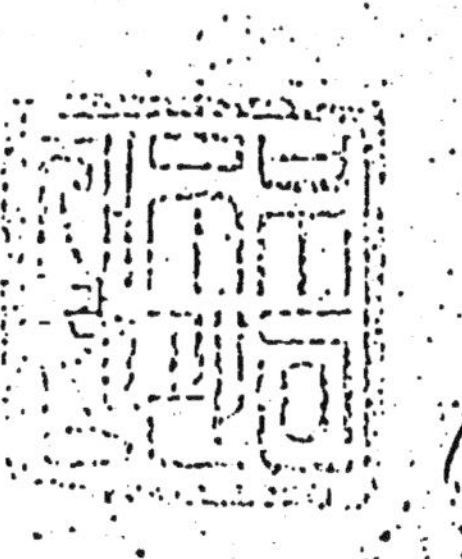

129

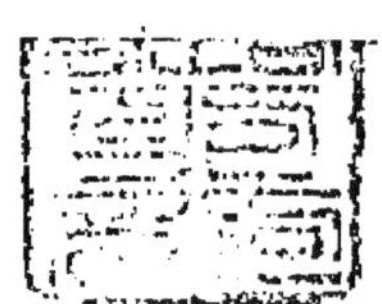

REQUEST FOR NOTARIZATION

This is to request a notarization of the true and faithful translation of the Reply to Superintendent of National Revenue Office.

Requested by: Hyun Sook Tak

CERTIFICATE

This is to certify that the translation of the Reply to Superintendent to National Revenue Office is true and correct from the Korean original.

Date: 1982. 12. 2 2

등·부 제 七百六十八 호
별지 번역된 영문은 별지 국문으로된
원문과 부합 일치하다
이에 이를 인증하다
서기 壹九八二 년 拾貳 월 貳拾貳 일
서울특별시중구을지로2가21번지
서울지방검찰청소속
공증인

Sun-yup HONG
Notary Public
Seoul District prosecutor's Office
Seoul, Korea

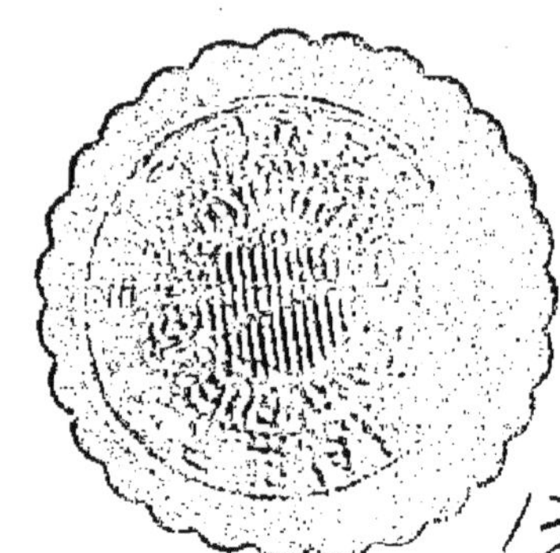

130

JIN OUK KIM
WOONG SHIK SHIN
ROK SANG YU
YONG YIL PARK
BYONG JOON KIM

KYU HWAN HAN
(PATENT ATTORNEY)

LAW OFFICES OF
KIM, SHIN & YU

C. P. O. BOX 3238
24TH FL. SAMILRO BLDG.
10, KWANCHUL-DONG, CHONGRO-KU,
SEOUL, KOREA

CABLE ADDRESS
"ATTKSY SEOUL"
TELEPHONE
725-5822 725-5824
725-3782 725-2662
TELEX: ATTKSY K23168

9.

July 20, 1982

Mr. K.C. Chang
Chairman
Dae Lim Industrial Co., Ltd.
C.P.O. Box 9291
Seoul, Korea

Dear Mr. Chang:

Please find enclosed our draft of the claim letter addressed to the Contracting Officer, US Army Korea Contracting Agency for your review.

Sincerely yours,

fr Woong Shik Shin

SWS/kic
Encl.

131

(Letterhead of Dae Lim)

(Date) May

Contracting Officer
Department of the Army
U.S. Army Korea Contracting Agency
APO San Francisco 96301
U. S. A.

Re: Claim with respect to Contract No. KCANAF-80-C-V065

Dear Sir:

In March of 1980, the U.S. Army Korea Contracting Agency ("KCA") and Dae Lim Industrial Co., Ltd. ("Dae Lim") entered into a contract No. KCANAF-80-C-V065 (the "Contract"). Under this Contract, Dae Lim was suppose to run a "tax-free" electronic equipment and stereo shop (the "Shop") in the Naija Hotel R & R Center, Building No. P-2 downtown Seoul, in the #7 Naija-dong, Chongro-ku, Seoul, Korea.

The Contract explicitly provided that the sales at the Shop was exempt from any taxes from Korean authorities. Dae Lim was contractually prohibited in charging any taxes on the sales at the Shop and accordingly the price were exclusive of any local taxes.

However, it came to the attention of Dae Lim around October of 1980, that Dae Lim was in violation of the tax laws of the Republic of Korea in carrying on business under the Contract. Dae Lim tried to obtain a clarification from

132

the Korean tax authorities on this matter and the reply from the National Tax Office and the Minister of Finance was that the activities of Dae Lim under the Contract was in violation of the tax laws. (The rulings of the National Tax Office and the Minister of Finance are attached hereto.)

Due to the abovementioned violation of the tax laws, the local suppliers of the electronic and stereo equipment discontinued the sales to Dae Lim starting from around the end of 1980. Since the equipments are manufactured for export, the manufacturers are prohibited from selling locally. Without new supplies of the equipment, Dae Lim could not carry on effective business.

Dae Lim relied on the assurances and representations of KCA that the Shop enjoyed tax-free status, in entering into this Contract. But, in fact, the Shop enjoyed no such tax-free status according to the relevant Korean tax authorities. Dae Lim has suffered and continues to suffer damages because it cannot carry on the business at the Shop and the pending tax assessment on Dae Lim. The damages are considerable and this should be absorbed by KCA because Dae Lim relied on KCA's representations and assurances in entering into the Contract and continuing to operate the Shop.

Therefore, Dae Lim now makes an official claim in the amount of US$183,678 as of June 30, 1982. The break down of the claims are as follows:

133

Claim Reason 1: So far we have made payment of ~~$50,878.00~~ monthly for rental fee under the Contract.

Claim Reason 2: Employee wage W380,000 per month x 32 = W12,160,000 ($16,888.00)

Claim Reason 3: Warehouse charge W240,000 x ~~26~~ 29 =6,240,000 ($8,666.00)

Claim Reason 4:

Nomenclature	Qty	Tax per unit	U/Total
CR 840 TV 19" Clr	210	W115,370	W24,227,700
CNR 842 TV 19" Clr	200	135,628	27,125,600
CR 402 TV 14" Clr	115	88,793	10,211,195
CNR 405 TV 14" Clr	145	107,950	15,652,750
			W77,217,245
			(US$107,246.00)

The foregoing does not include any penalties which may be imposed on Dae Lim nor any interest. These may be added at a later date.

We sincerely hope that KCA understands Dae Lim's predicament in this matter. And we are certain that after your due deliberation, this claim will be settled as soon as possible.

Very truly yours,

Chang Kyo Chol
President

134

Standard Form 1034-a (9-73)
Exception to SF 1034
approved by NARS, Feb 76
4 Treasury FRM 2000

PUBLIC VOUCHER FOR PURCHASES AND SERVICES OTHER THAN PERSONAL

653711

VOUCHER NO.

U.S. DEPARTMENT, BUREAU, OR ESTABLISHMENT AND LOCATION	DATE VOUCHER PREPARED	SCHEDULE NO.
USAFAAO-K APO SF 96301 (5)	22 Nov 82	
	CONTRACT NUMBER AND DATE DAJB03-82-C-2036	PAID BY USAFAAO-K DSSN 6411 APO SF 96301
	REQUISITION NUMBER AND DATE	

PAYEE'S NAME AND ADDRESS:
The Cho Heung Bank, Dongdaemun Branch
1-104 Chongro 4ga, Chongro-ku
Seoul Korea
FOR: Dae Lim Industrial Co.,Ltd.
Acct No. 303-1-1094916

4 DEC 1982

DATE INVOICE RECEIVED: 02 Nov 82

DISCOUNT TERMS

PAYEE'S ACCOUNT NUMBER

SHIPPED FROM / TO / WEIGHT / GOVERNMENT B/L NUMBER

NUMBER AND DATE OF ORDER	DATE OF DELIVERY OR SERVICE	ARTICLES OR SERVICES (Enter description, item number of contract or Federal supply schedule, and other information deemed necessary)	QUANTITY	UNIT PRICE COST	PER	AMOUNT
		Inv DDForm 250 dtd 15 Oct 82				$ 15,120.00
		Inv DDForm 250 15 Oct 82				151,620.00
		NOTICE TO CONTRACTOR: The sum of $19,446.95 is herewith deducted from this contract and placed in the USAFAAO-K SUSPENSE ACCOUNT. To offset debt to Contract No. KCAAAT 80-C-Y065. See attached DF from KCA Contracting Officer & Legal Officer.				($19,446.95)

(Use continuation sheet(s) if necessary) (Payee must NOT use the space below) TOTAL ₩ 109,980,615

PAYMENT:
- [ ] COMPLETE
- [ ] PARTIAL
- [x] FINAL
- [ ] PROGRESS
- [ ] ADVANCE

₩ 745

DIFFERENCES

Amount verified; correct for ₩ 109,980,615
(Signature or initials)

22 Nov 82

MEMORANDUM

R.J.DELANEY,LTC,FC,FAAO

ACCOUNTING CLASSIFICATION

2122020 78-1000 P200000 2612 592127 202494.X0075 IMAA KS $ 15,120.00
.X0000 IMCC 151,620.00
21X6875 78 592127 (19,446.95)
$ 147,293.05

PAID BY	CHECK NUMBER	ON TREASURER OF THE UNITED STATES	CHECK NUMBER	ON (Name of bank)
	₩ 109,980,615		162242	
	CASH $	DATE		

WC

1034-215-06

Dae Lim Industrial Co., Ltd.

C. P. O. Box 9291 Seoul, Korea

Coble address : DL Chang

Telephone : 778-8054

No.

Date: December 20, 1982

ABRIDGED STATEMENT FOR
THE AWARDED KCA CONTRACT PROCESS, KCA
CONTRACT NO. KCANAF-80-C-V065.

1) Mar. 15, 1982 : We, Dae Lim Industrial Co., Ltd. herein after call Dae Lim, awarded subjected contract from KCA, service for tax free local producted electric equipment in the Nae Ja Hotel R&R Center ref. : contract no. KCANAF-80-C-V065.

2) Oct. 1980 : However, it came to the attention of Dae Lim around October of 1980, that Dae Lim was in violation of the existing ROK tax laws in carrying on business under the contract. Because, Dae Lim provided merchandises under the tax free sell to each enlisted individure, not authorized US Army organizations.

3) Oct. 1980 : Dae Lim reported all this matter to general manager, Nae Ja to get an understandable legal support in compliance with Section 1, para 2 in contract.
But he could not believe about arised tax matter, and denied this matter by a word because he think that the contract was not violating to the ROK existing tax laws.

- 1 -

136

Dae Lim Industrial Co., Ltd.

C. P. O. Box 9291 Seoul, Korea

Cable address : DL Chang

Telephone : 778-8054

No.________________ Date: December 20, 1982

4) Oct. Nov. 1980 : Dae Lim not only studied ROK tax rules and also request to help officially authorized ROK tax accountant to justify the tax free clauses in contract.
But the result was very unclearness.

5) Nov. 21, 1980 : Dae Lim wrote an official letter to the department of ROK national tax administration to get an understandable letter of authoritative interpretation.

6) Dec. 8, 1980 ① : Dae Lim award negative authoritative interpretation for VAT tax as enclosed of this letter.

7) Dec. 1980 : Dae Lim,of course,reported this matter to general manager Nae Ja Hotel to get a fruitful solution, in result of many consult with general manager, there was not any believable consistency to clear this matter.

8) April 1981 ② : Dae Lim visit to ministry of treasure to clear the pending tax matter, but the result is very unsuccessful because we could award a copy of authoritative interpretation for the Hyun Dae Automobile Co., Ltd. dated July 8, 1980, Dae.Lim reported this matter to contracting officer representative, but his answere was very lukewarm only, for this reason I have been sick about four (4) months.

Dae Lim Industrial Co., Ltd.

C. P. O. Box 9291 Seoul, Korea

Cable address : DL Chang

Telephone : 778-8054

No.__________ Date: December 20, 1982

9) Oct. 1981 : We wrote a petition to ROK government civil service consultant center to justfy for Dae Lim effort during time of KCA contract.

10) Nov. 1981 : Dae Lim request to help to KCA contracting officer, also explained Dae Lim awarded KCA contract is violated to the ROK tax regulations.

④

11) Jan. 1982 : Dae Lim awarded a letter from government civil service consultant center, such as minister of finance will take care Dae Lim petition.

12) Jan. 14, 1982 : Dae Lim award very negative authoritative interpretation from the ministry of finance as attached.

13) Fev. 1982 : Dae Lim report all authoritative interpretation to KCA contracting officer and legal officer to provide understandable solusion.

14) July 1982 : Finally Dae Lim made a decision to report contract terminate because firstly related KCA people effort was lukewarm attitude and secondly total mounthly sales can not cover even the fixed rental fee since we award negative tax authority, dated Dec. 8, 1980 therefore, the debt arised to contractor, during the period, an amount of US$19,446.95 from uneffectable KCA contract under the existing ROK tax regulations.

Dae Lim Industrial Co., Ltd.

C. P. O. Box 9291 Seoul, Korea

Cable address : DL Chang Telephone : 778-8054

No.____________ Date: December 20, 1982

15) Nov. 3, 1982 ⑤ : The arised debt deducted from other of our KCA supplying contract with out have an agreement.

16) General abridgement : Beside of upon mention, so far we write many letters and request to legal support to KCA for the pending tax matter, however they are not absolutely any response to Dae Lim, and they just told us that US SOFA Committee will take care for Dae Lim tax matter and losses during the past years.

17) Nov. 1982 : Dae Lim questioned at KCA legal meeting, why only Dae Lim should pay such exolbitant prices for your contract? But they could not give us any understandable responses because the meeting just broken out in 5 or 10 minutes with by their provided drama. But legal officer recommend me to visit US SOFA Committee to get understandable solution prior to official claim.

18) View point of Dae Lim : Why Dae Lim have to involve in difficult tax penalty and heavy business bossed under the unproper KCA, contract. Dae Lim explicitly provided the sales at the shop was exempt from any taxes from Korea authorities. Dae Lim was contractually prohibited in charging any tax on the sales at the shop and accordingly the prices were exclusive of any local taxes. Ref. contract tax clauses.

- 4 - ... /5

139

Dae Lim Industrial Co., Ltd.

C. P. O. Box 9291 Seoul, Korea

Cable address : DL Chang | Telephone : 778-8054

No.________________ Date: December 20, 1982

Remark : Your cooperation and immediate attention for this matter shall be greatly appreciated and we shall be looking foreward to hear some from you.

Chang, K. C.

- 6 -

end.

140

기 안 용 지

분류기호 문서번호	미안 723-	(전화번호)	전결규정 조 항 전결사항
처리기간		장 관	
시행일자	1982. 12. 22.		
보존년한			

보조기관			협조	
국 장	전결			
과 장				
기안책임자	김영준	안보과		

경 유		발신	통제
수 신	재무부 장관	1982. 12. 22 외무부	1982.12.22 통제관
참 조	세제국장		
제 목	주한미군 현지조달 물품에 대한 면세		

연 : 미안 723-27562 (82. 8. 12.)

미안 723-31249 (82. 9. 7.)

대 : 국조 1261.51-1049 (82. 9. 4.)

국조 1261.51-1174 (82. 9. 29.)

1. 주한미군 당국은 연호에 이어 미군 전용 면세물품 납품과 관련 대림기업에 대한 면세혜택 조치를 재차 요청하여 왔는 바, 미군이 지적하는 하기 문제에 대한 귀부의 견해를 알려 주시기 바랍니다.

- 아 래 -

한.미 주둔군 지위협정 (SOFA) 제 13조 제 2항의 해석

정서 관인 발송

1205-25(2-1) A(갑) 1981. 12. 18 승인

정직 질서 창조

190mm×268mm (인쇄용지 2급 60g/m²) 조 달 청(000,000매 인 쇄)

/44

상 동항의 "다른 구입자 (other purchasers)"
에는 일차적으로 일반 외국인이 포함될 것이며 따라서
이들이 다른 면세점에서 동일품목을 면세로 구입할 수
있는한 문제의 내자호텔내 매점에서 구입한 것에 대해서
도 동일하게 적용되어야 한다고 봄.

2. 아울러 동건 관련 면세점 실태에 관한 다음 사항도
통보 바랍니다.

가. 허가된 면세점 (미군 지역내 명시)

나. 동 면세점 이용권자의 범위

다. 상기 면세점의 허가 기준 또는 자격

라. 동 면세점 판매물품의 종류

마. 문제의 대림기업 면세점의 지위

첨부 : SOFA 합동위 간사 서한 사본 1부. 끝.

142

JOINT COMMITTEE
UNDER
THE REPUBLIC OF KOREA AND THE UNITED STATES
STATUS OF FORCES AGREEMENT

15 December 1982

Dear Director KWON,

With reference to your letter dated August 18, 1982 concerning the request to exempt Dae Lim Industrial Co. from Value Added Tax and Special Excise Tax on items sold to U.S. Forces Korea personnel, I request your further consideration.

Your letter focuses upon the applicable exemptions provided by Article XIII. In this case, the critical point is interpretation of the Paragraph 2, Article XIII phrase "taxes to which other purchasers of such merchandise and supplies are subject..." Thus, Article XIII exempts Non-Appropriated Fund purchases of merchandise and supplies whenever other purchasers are exempted. It is U.S. Forces Korea's understanding that some "other purchasers," primarily foreigners, can buy the same items, exempt from Value Added Tax (VAT) and Special Excise Tax (SET), from various "tax-free shops" or "tax-free outlets." Since such tax-free stores exist and sell such items to "other purchasers" as Dae Lim sold, Article XIII clearly exempts the Naija Hotel purchasers in question. In both cases such items could equally be characterized as exported goods.

Even if the provisions of Article XIII were ambiguous, the interpretation favoring exemption in this case is more appropriate. The obvious intent of the SOFA provisions regarding customs, duties, and taxation generally is to permit members of the "United States armed forces, civilian components, and their dependents" to obtain and use, "reasonable quantities of personal effects and household goods." Restrictions upon these exemptions are imposed primarily to benefit ROK industry. Of course, VAT and SET do not serve exactly the same purpose as do the Customs tariffs, but the crucial point remains the same; tax-exempt sale of locally purchased, ROK-manufactured goods to U.S. Forces Korea personnel greatly benefits the ROK economy not only through direct increase of gross ROK sales to non-Koreans, but also through promotion of quality ROK products in the United States. The concerns to which the VAT and SET are directed can be satisfied by adequate enforcement of disposition restrictions imposed in accordance with Paragraph 3, Article XIII.

143

I again respectfully request your further consideration in this matter and that Dae Lim be relieved of Value Added Tax and Special Excise Tax on the sales to U.S. Forces Korea personnel.

CARROLL B. HODGES
United States Secretary
US-ROK SOFA

KWON Soon Tae
Republic of Korea Secretary
US-ROK SOFA
Ministry of Foreign Affairs
Republic of Korea

144

정 리 보 존 문 서 목 록					
기록물종류	일반공문서철	등록번호	29279	등록일자	2008-08-13
분류번호	729.416	국가코드		보존기간	영구
명 칭	SOFA 한.미국 합동위원회 - 상무분과위원회, 1984-85				
생 산 과	안보과	생산년도	1984~1985	담당그룹	북미국
내용목차	* SOFA 초청계약자의 국내 타사업 활동문제, 시설설계용역 초청계약자 지정 협의 간소화문제				

001

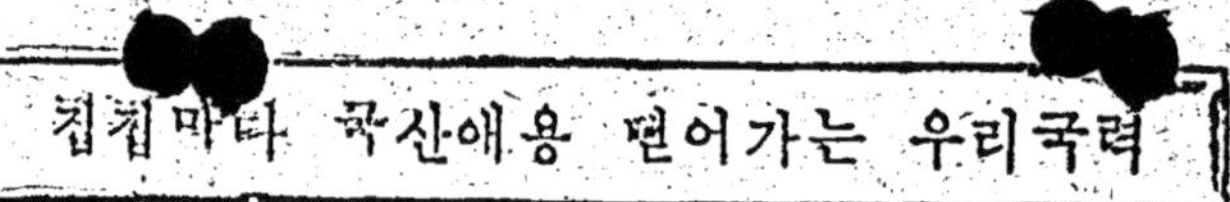
칩칩마다 국산애용 뻗어가는 우리국력

대 한 민 국
상 공 부

통충 1314- 652 (720- 3513) 1984. 3. 23.

수 신 외무부 장관

참 조 안보과장

제 목 SOFA 상무분과 위원회 관계관 명단 통보

SOFA 상무분과 위원회 관계관 명단을 아래와 같이 통보합니다.

아 래

구 분	성 명	당 부 소 속	비 고
위원장 Chairman	박 운 서 Un Suh ParK	상공부 통상진흥국 통상진흥국장 Director General, Bureau of Trade Promotion Ministry of Commerce & Industry	720-3512
교체위원장 Alternate Chairman	장 석 환 Sukan Chang	상공부 통상진흥국 통상진흥관 Deputy Director Geberal, Bureau of Trade Promotion Ministry of Commerce & Industry	
부간사 Alternate Secretary	이 태 숙 Tae Sook Lee	상공부 통상진흥국 통상총괄과 사무관 Deputy Director, Division of Trade Policy Bureau of Trade Promotion Ministry of Commerce and Industry	720-3513

끝.

상 공 부 장 관

정무공문서 규정 제27조 제2항의
통상총괄과장 이 상

002

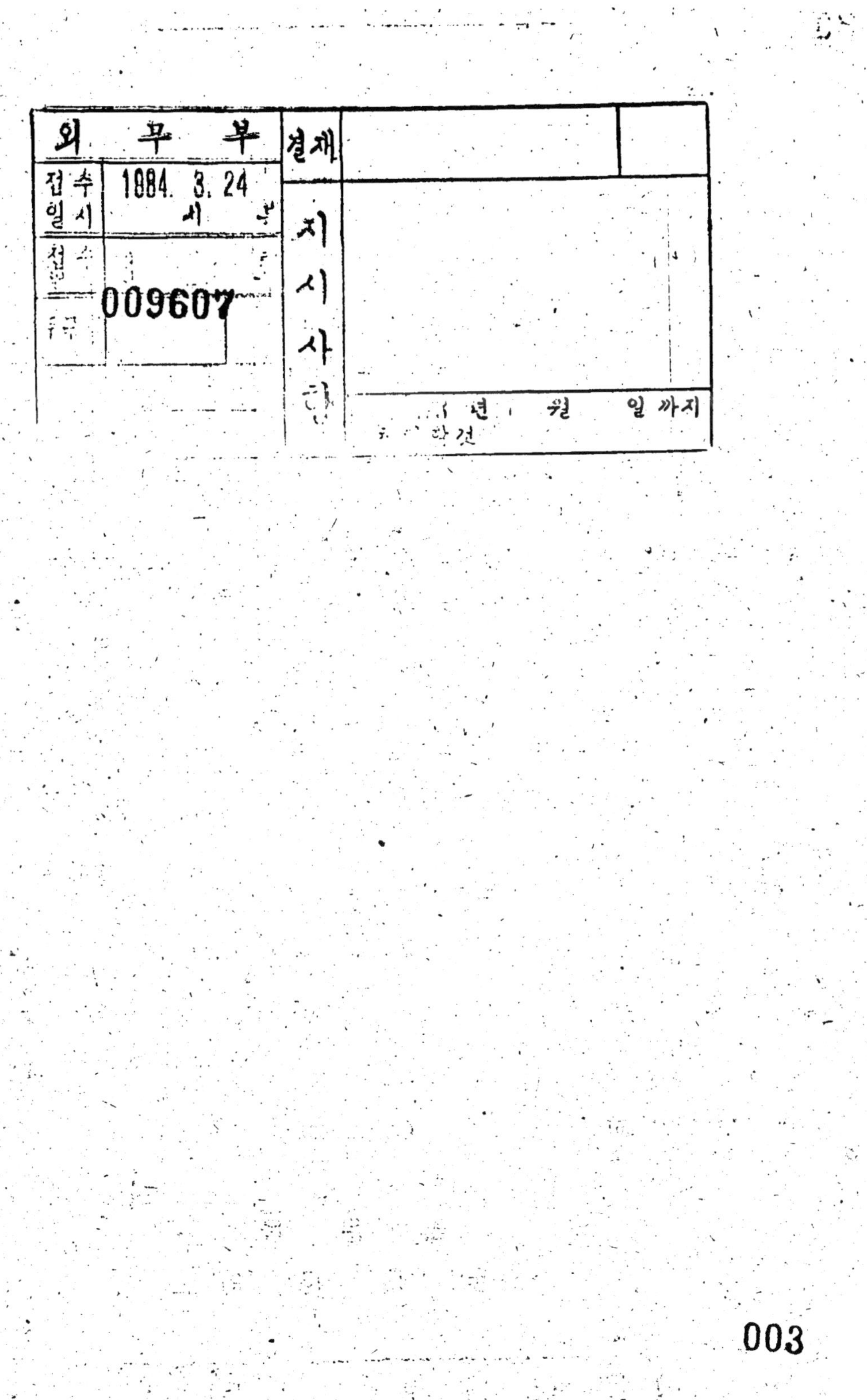

외 무 부		결재		
접수일시	1984. 3. 24 시 분			
처리	009607	지시사항	년 월 일까지	

003

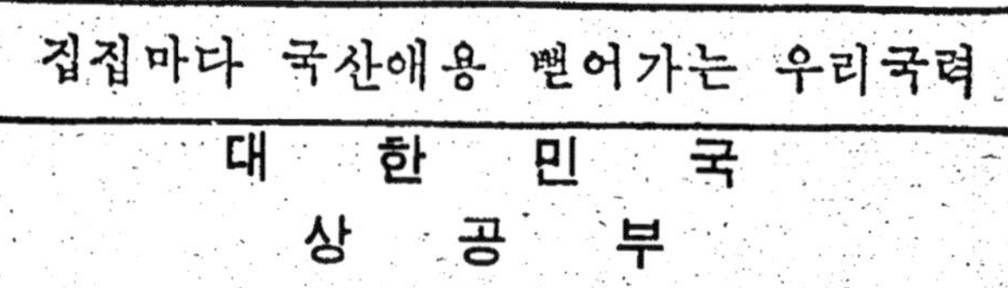

대 한 민 국
상 공 부

통총 1314-1550 (720-3513) 1984. 7. 19.
수신 외무부 장관
참조
제목 SOFA 초청계약자의 국내 타사업 활동 종사에 관한 질의

1. SOFA 제15조(초청계약자) 관련입니다.

2. 주한 미군 초청계약자인 trans-Asia Engineering Associates의 고문변호사(김진억)는 최근 해운항만청이 아시아 개발은행의 차관으로 건설하게 되는 항만공사의 계약과 관련하여 별첨과 같이 당부로 SOFA 초청계약자의 국내 타사업 활동에 종사함에 관한 질의가 있어, 당부는 본건의 처리를 신중히 하기 위하여 귀부의 이에 대한 의견을 문의하오니 검토하시어 회신하여 주시기 바랍니다.

첨부: 관련 질의서 사본 1부. 끝.

상 공 부 장 관

정부 공문서 규정 제27조 제2항의 규정에 의하여
통상진흥국장 박 운 서 전결

004

공람	통상기석과	84년 7월 21일	담당	과장	국장	차관	장관

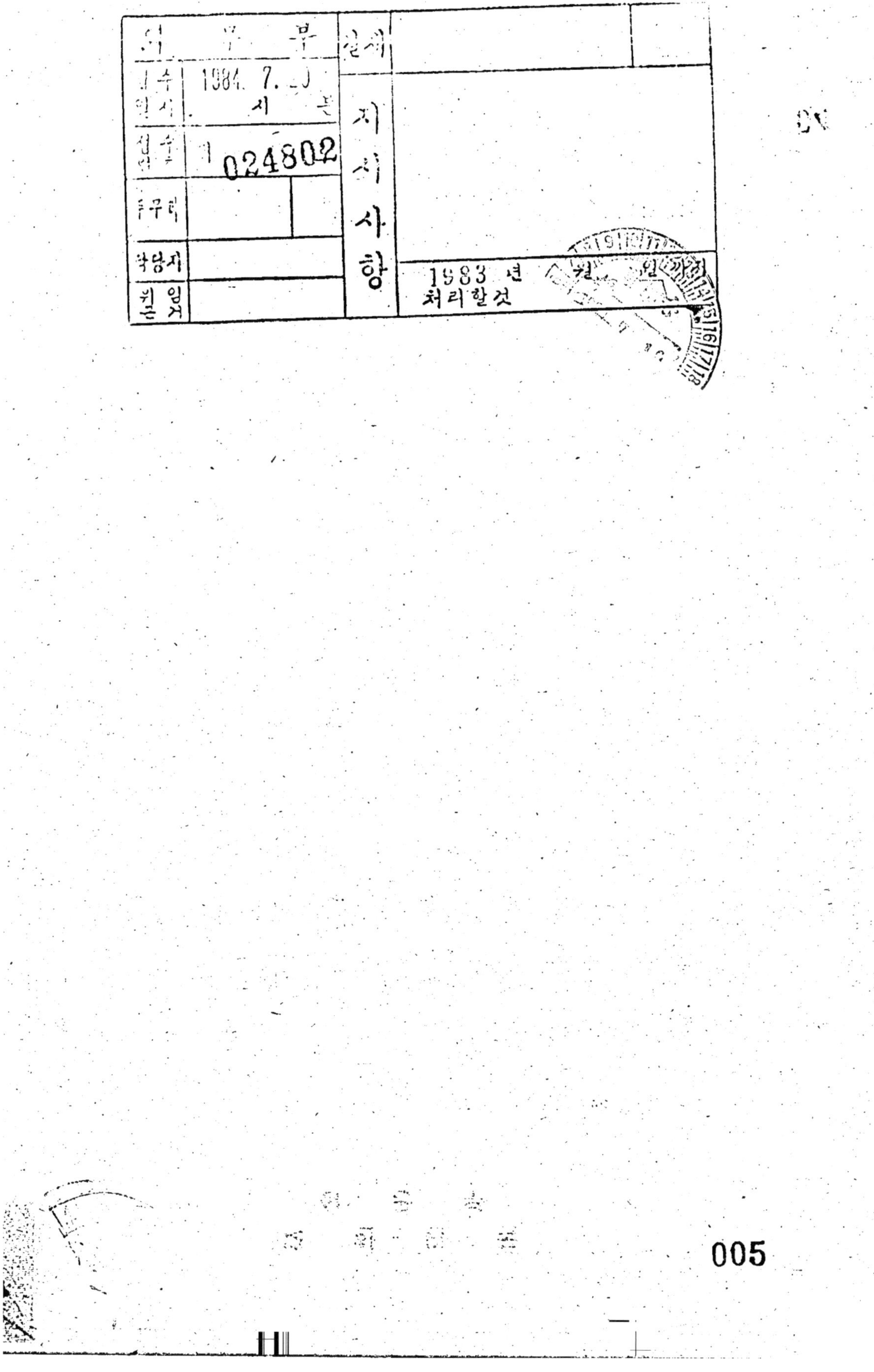

외 무 부		결재	
접수 일시	1984. 7. 20 시 분	지시사항	
접수 번호	024802		
주무과			
담당자			1983 년 월 일까지 처리할것
[illegible]			

005

JIN OUK KIM
WOONG SHIK SHIN
ROK SANG YU
YONG WHAN KIM
YONG YIL PARK
HAE DUK JUNG

KYU HWAN HAN
(PATENT ATTORNEY)

LAW OFFICES OF
KIM, SHIN & YU

C. P. O. BOX 3238
14TH FL. SAMILRO BLDG.
#10, KWANCHUL-DONG, CHONGRO-KU,
SEOUL, KOREA

CABLE ADDRESS
"ATTKSY SEOUL"
TELEPHONE
725-5822, 5823, 5824
3782, 2662
TELEX: ATTKSY K23168
FACSIMILE: (02) 744-6606 (GⅡ, GⅢ)

수 신 : Commerce Sub-committee (SOFA) 1984. 7. 12.

박운서 위원장 귀하

제 목 : SOFA 초청계약자의 국내 타사업활동에 종사함에 관한 질의

1. 본인은 Trans Asia Engineering (이하 "회사"라 함)의 고문변호사이며 위 회사는 건축사업, 건축설비 기계 전기 기타 시설물의 설계 및 기술상담, 건설설계 및 시공에 관한 기술용역, 토질기초 구조물에 관한 기술용역등을 사업목적으로 하는 종합 건축기술 회사로서 SOFA 초청계약자로 지정되어 있읍니다.

2. 위 회사는 최근에 해운항만청이 아시아 개발은행(Asian Development Bank)의 차관으로 건설하게 되는 항만공사에 초청계약자의 자격이 아닌 일반 사업자의 자격으로 응찰한바 있으며, 이와 관련하여 위 회사로 부터 본인에게 "만일 위 회사가 SOFA 프로젝트 이외의 사업에 SOFA 프로젝트를 위한 위 회사의 인원, 시설 및 자원과는 완전히 별개의 인원, 시설 및 자원등을 투입한다면, 그런 경우 위 회사가 위와 같은 공사에 종사하는 것이 SOFA 제15조에 위배되는지의 여부"를 검토해줄 것을 요청해 온바 있읍니다.

3. 이에 대하여 본인의 검토 의견으로는 SOFA 제15조는 초청 계약자가 초청계약자에게 부여되는 SOFA상의 제반 특권을

006

이용하여 SOFA 프로젝트 이외의 사업활동에 종사하는 것은 그와 같은 특전을 갖지 못한 일반 회사에 대하여는 불공평한 것이 되므로 이를 방지함에 그 목적이 있다 할 것이므로 SOFA의 초청계약자가 SOFA 프로젝트를 위하여 지정된 인원, 시설 및 자원을 다른 사업에 활용한다면 협정의 위반이 될 것이나 그 초청계약자가 수행하고자 하는 다른 사업활동에 전연 별개의 인원, 시설 및 자원등을 투입하는 경우라면 SOFA의 관계규정에 위반되지 않는다 할것이고 따라서 그러한 경우 초청계약자로서의 지정이 철회될 대상도 되지 않을 것으로 봄이 타당할 것으로 사료되오며 또한 1967년 8월 14일자 합동위원회 회의록에 의하면 당시 SOFA 초청계약자로 지정되어 있던 Collins Radio 사가 초청계약자로서의 자격을 취소하지 아니하고도 체신부와의 용역계약을 체결할수 있도록 한 Commercial Sub-committee의 추천을 승인한 선례도 있는바,

4. 사안의 처리를 보다 신중히 하기 위하여 Commercial Sub-committee의 위원장이신 귀하의 고견을 구하기에 이르렀아오니 국사 다망하신중 번거로우시겠아오나 모쪼록 검토하시와 회시하여 주시면 감사 하겠읍니다.

5. 본건에 관하여 Sub-committee의 미국측 대표로 부터는 별첨과 같이 본인의 의견과 같은 의견을 표시하는 서한을 받은바 있아오니 참고하여 주시기 바랍니다.

유 첨 : 주한 미합중국 군사령부 서한 및 번역문 각 1통

변호사 김 진 억

007

공 란

공 란

공 란

공 란

공 란

chei

JIN OUK KIM
WOONG SHIK SHIN
ROK SANG YU
YONG WHAN KIM
YONG YIL PARK
HAE DUK JUNG

KYU HWAN HAN
(PATENT ATTORNEY)

LAW OFFICES OF
KIM, SHIN & YU

C. P. O. BOX 3238
14TH FL. SAMILRO BLDG.
#10. KWANCHUL-DONG, CHONGRO-KU,
SEOUL, KOREA

CABLE ADDRESS
"ATTKSY SEOUL"
TELEPHONE
725-5822, 5823, 5824
3782, 2662
TELEX: ATTKSY K23168
FACSIMILE: (02 744-6606 GII, GIII)

수 신 : SOFA, Commercial Subcommittee 1984. 7. 20.
박운서 위원장 귀하
(상공부 통상진흥국장)

본인이 SOFA 초청계약자인 Trans Asia Engineering 사 (이하 T/A 라 약칭)가 SOFA 사업이외의 타사업을 수행할수 있는지의 여부에 관하여 1984년 7월 12일자로 위원장님께 제출한바 있는 질의 서신과 관련하여 다음 몇가지 점을 보완하여 말씀드리고자 하오니 참고하여 주시면 대단히 감사하겠읍니다.

(가) T/A 가 현재 참여하고자 하는 사업은 해운 항만청이 아시아 개발은행 차관 자금의 지원으로 시행하는 인천항 제3단계 개발 타당성 조사 용역사업으로서 아시아 개발은행은 차관 조건의 하나로서 외국 콘설턴트들을 참여시킬 것을 요구하고 있으므로 별첨 A 의 목록에서 보시다싶이 T/A 를 비롯한 많은 외국 콘설턴트들이 해운 항만청에 의하여 계약협의 대상자로 선정된 것입니다.

(나) 이 계약조건에 의하면 T/A 가 용역사업자로 선정되는 경우, T/A 는 회사 자체뿐만 아니라 그 용역사업에 종사하는 T/A 의 직원까지 대한민국내에서의 제반 세금이 완전히 면제되며 또한 T/A 가 이 계약을 이행하기 위하여 한국에 반입하고 계약종결후 반출하게 되는 모든 장비에 대해서도 어떠한 형태의 관세든지

013

면제받게 됩니다. (관계조항 발췌하여 별첨 B 로 첨부하였읍니다.)

(다) 다시 말씀드리자면 한국 회사들은 이미 계약 협의 대상자에서 제외되어 있으므로 T/A 가 위 용역사업의 계약자가 된다 하드라도 한국 회사에 대해서는 하등의 영향을 주지 않게 되며 또한 SOFA 초청계약자로서 받게되는 면세특전과 똑같은 내용의 면세특전을 용역사업 계약자로서 그 계약 조항에 따라 받게되어 있어 초청계약자로서의 지위를 손상시킬 하등의 사유도 없는 것입니다.

(라) 또한 T/A 가 위 용역사업의 이행을 위하여 사용하게될 직원들은 T/A 의 사무실과는 별도로, 해운 항만청이 제공할 해운 항만청 내의 사무실에서 일하게 되며 그 직원들은 지금까지 한번도 SOFA 사업에 종사한 일이 없는 사람들로서 항만기사, 장비관계 전문가, 경제학자 토질 및 구조기사, 평가사 및 설계사등 각 부분의 전문가들인바 미합중국에서 부터 직접 데려오게 됩니다.

(마) 별첨 C 에서 보시는 바와 같이 T/A 는 그동안 1969년 3월 20일자 제36차 및 1975년 3월 6일자 제102차 SOFA 합동위원회에서 T/A 가 SOFA 초청계약자로서의 지위와는 별도로 한국 정부와의 계약을 수행하는 것은 SOFA 초청계약자의 지위를 손상하지 않는다는 명백한 결정을 받은바 있으며 그중에서도 특히 제102차 합동위원회의 결정은 현재 계류되고 있는 것과 똑같은 내용인, 항만공사의 타당성 조사 사업에의 참여에 관한 것이었음을 첨언하고자 합니다.

— 2 —

014

위와 같은 선례가 위원장님의 본건 검토에 참고가 될수 있기를 바랍니다.

감사합니다.

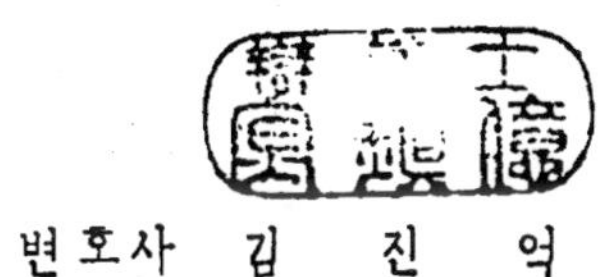

변호사 김 진 억

015

공 란

공　　　란

공 란

공 란

공 란

공 란

공　　　란

공 란

공 란

JIN OUK KIM
WOONG SHIK SHIN
ROK SANG YU
YONG WHAN KIM
YONG YIL PARK
HAE DUK JUNG

KYU HWAN HAN
(PATENT ATTORNEY)

LAW OFFICES OF
KIM, SHIN & YU

C. P. O. BOX 3238
14TH FL. SAMILRO BLDG.
#10, KWANCHUL-DONG, CHONGRO-KU,
SEOUL, KOREA

CABLE ADDRESS
"ATTKSY SEOUL"
TELEPHONE
725-5822, 5823, 5824
3782, 2662
TELEX: ATTKSY K23168
FACSIMILE: (02) 744-6606 (GII, GIII)

July 20, 1984

Translation

Mr. Park, Woon Suk
Chairman, Commerce Subcommittee (SOFA)
Director General
Bureau of International Trade Promotion
Ministry of Commerce and Industry
Republic of Korea

Dear Mr. Park:

1. By way of supplement to our letter to you of July 12, 1984 concerning the status of Trans-Asia Engineering Associates Incorporated ("Trans-Asia"), I wish to submit the following information to assist your full consideration of this matter.

2. The works for which Trans-Asia is bidding relates to an ADB (Asian Development Bank) project for the Port of Incheon. This is a feasibility study for the expansion of the port for the third phase. As this is an ADB contract, KMPA was required to have foreign consultants (enclosed as Exhibit A is a list of foreign consultants requested by KMPA to submit proposals) and under this contract, Trans-Asia is completely exempt from all taxes in Korea both as a firm and for personnel. Also, it is exempt from paying any type of duties

025

for any equipment brought into the country for use in the contract and to be taken out of the country after the contract completion. Enclosed as Exhibit B is the relevant provision. This means that (i) Trans-Asia's appointment as a contractor would not effect Korean companies as they are already excluded from participation and (ii) Trans-Asia's status for the project is tax free to the same extent as under SOFA which precludes any possible benefit for unlawful use of SOFA exempt resources.

3. The Trans-Asia personnel to be used in this contract will be in a completely separate office supplied by KMPA in their building. All such personnel have never worked previously in Korea on any SOFA projects. These people are specialists and will be brought in from the United States. They are Port Engineers, Equipment Specialists, Economist, Soils and Structural Engineers and Estimator and Specification Writer.

4. Lastly, I wish to call to your attention the fact that Trans-Asia has on at least two (2) previous occasions (Joint Committee meetings #36 dated 20 March 1969 and #102 dated 6 March 1975) received a clear interpretation that its

026

separate performance of Korean governmental contracts would not compromise its SOFA status. In fact, the second such determination was in regard to a seaport feasibility study just as that presently involved. Copies of these determinations are attached as Exhibit C.

5. I will be deeply appreciative of your further consideration of these compelling facts and precedents.

Sincerely yours,

Jin Ouk Kim

KJO/LLG/lan
cc: Mr. W.J. Curley
U.S. Component
SOFA Commerce Subcommittee

027

JIN OUK KIM
WOONG SHIK SHIN
ROK SANG YU
YONG YIL PARK

KYU HWAN HAN
(PATENT ATTORNEY)

LAW OFFICES OF
KIM, SHIN & YU

C. P. O. BOX 3238
14TH FL. SAMILRO BLDG.
#10, KWANCHUL-DONG, CHONGRO-KU,
SEOUL, KOREA

CABLE ADDRESS
"ATTKSY SEOUL"
TELEPHONE
725-5822~4
725-3782, 2662
TELEX: ATTKSY K23168

Translation

July 12, 1984

Mr. Park, Woon Suk
Chairman, Commerce Subcommittee (SOFA)
Director General
Bureau of International Trade Promotion
Ministry of Commerce and Industry
Republic of Korea

Dear Mr. Park:

1. I, the undersigned, act as legal counsel to Trans-Asia Engineering Associates Incorporated ("Trans-Asia") presently a U.S. Invested Contractor pursuant to Article XV of the Status of Forces Agreement ("SOFA").

Trans-Asia has submitted to the Korea Maritime Port Authority ("KMPA") its tender for the performance of certain works being undertaken by the KMPA which are being financed by an Asian Development Bank loan. We have been asked by Trans-Asia if its involvement in such a project would violate Article XV of SOFA if it utilized for such purpose personnel, premises and other resources which are entirely separate from Trans-Asia personnel, premises and resources "designated" for and engaged in SOFA projects.

028

3. As we read Article XV, the clear intent of this Article is to prevent an invited contractor from using its special SOFA privileges (unfairly by competing in other Korean business with companies which do not enjoy such previliges. Thus I am of the opinion that if an invited contractor were to use its existing personnel, premises and other resources "designated" for SOFA projects, this use would violate the treaty. Where however the other Korean business to be performed by the invited contractor does not involve the designated personnel, premises and resources Article XV would not be applicable. I accordingly would not consider that such an undertaking would require withdrawal of Trans-Asia's designation as an invited contractor under Article XV of SOFA. We believe that there is clear and accepted precedent for this position involving Collins-Raio Company, whereby such contractor has performed a Korean government project with the agreement of the SOFA Committee (the 12th meeting of the Joint Committee held on 14 August 1967).

4. Notwithstanding my legal view as described hereinbefore, I would like to have your kind opinion or comment thereon so that this matter may be treated more prudently. Please review this matter and advise me if you have the same opinion.

029

5. For your reference I am enclosing herewith an opinion letter (together with Korean translation thereof) obtained from the U.S. Component which concurs in my understanding.

Sincerely yours,

Jin Ouk Kim

KJO/LLG/lan

Enclosure

030

기안용지

분류기호 문서번호	미안 723-	(전화번호)	전결규정 조 항 전결사항
처리기간		장 관	
시행일자	1984. 8. 9.		
보존년한			

보조기관				협조
	국 장		심의관	
	과 장			
기안책임자		임성남	안보과	

경 유	
수 신	상공부 장관
참 조	통상진흥 국장
제 목	SOFA 초청 계약자의 국내 타사업 활동 종사

발송 030382 1984. 8. 10 외무부

접인 1984. 8. 10 통제관

통총 1314-1550(84.7.19)으로 질의하신 Trans-Asia Engineering Associates, Inc. 의 아국내 타사업 활동 종사 문제에 관한 당부 검토 의견작성에 참고코자 하오니, 다음사항에 관하여 해운 항만청등 관계부처와 협의, 당부에 회신하여 주시기 바랍니다.

- 다 음 -

1. 해운 항만청이 주관하는 표제건 관련 항만 공사에 참여 가능한 기술 수준등을 구비한 아국업체 또는 SOFA 상의 초청계약자가 아닌 외국 업체의 유무.

2. 동 항만 공사에 Trans-Asia Engineering Associates, Inc. 가 참여치 못하게 되는 경우, 아국이 입게 되는 실질적 불이익의 유무.

정서 / 관인 / 발송

0201-1-8A(갑)
1969. 11. 10. 승인

190mm×268mm(2급인쇄용지 60g/m²)
조 달 청(3,000,000매 인 쇄)

031

3. 만일 Trans-Asia Engineering Associates, Inc.

만이 동 항만 공사에 참여하여야 할 불가피한 이유가 있다면,

동 이유. 끝.

1205-25(2-2)(을)
1981. 12. 18 승인

190mm×268mm(인쇄용지 2급 60g/m²)
조 달 청(.,000,000매 인 쇄)

0133

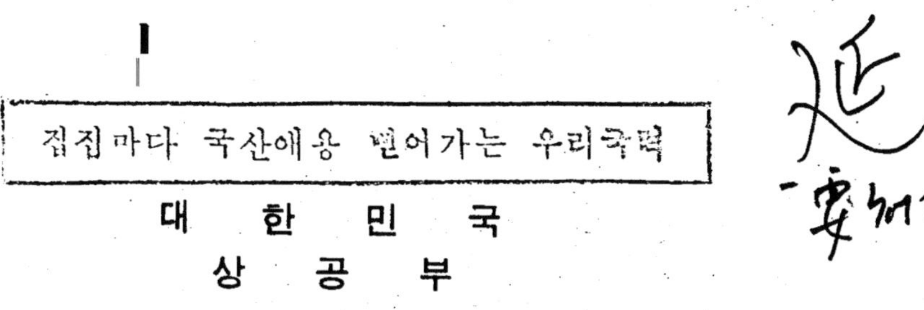

통 총 1314-1755 (720- 3513) 1984. 8. 20.

수 신 외무부 장관

참 조

제 목 SOFA 초청 계약자의 국내 타사업 활동 종사

1. 미안 723-030382 ('84. 8. 9)의 관련임

2. Frans-Asia Engineering Associates, Inc. 의 아국내 타사업 활동 종사 문제에 관하여 귀부에서 요청한 사항에 대한 해운항만청 의견을 별첨과 같이 송부하오니

3. 통총 1314-1550('84.7.19)으로 당부가 질의했던 초청계약자의 국내 타사업 활동 종사 여부를 조속 회신하여 주시기 바랍니다.

첨 부 : 해운항만청 공문 사본 1부. 끝.

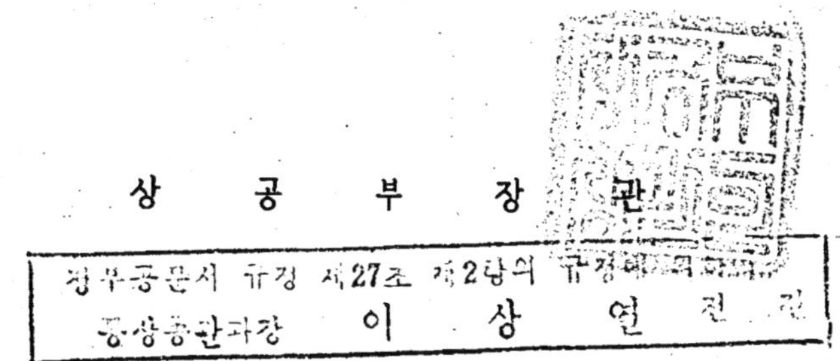

상 공 부 장 관

정부공문서 규정 제27조 제2항의 규정에 의하여
통상진흥관과장 이 상 연 전 결

033

외 무 부		관계		
접수일시	1984. 8. 시	지시사항		
접수번호	C28482			
주무과				
담당자				
원본 입거			1983 년 월 일까지 처리할것	

034

해 운 항 만 청

개발 351- 6085 (763-8149) '84. 8. 16

수신 상공부장관

참조 통상진흥국장

제목 SOFA 초청계약자의 국내 타사업 활동 종사 협의

1. 현재 당청에서 추진하고 있는 인천항 3단계 개발 타당성 조사는 인천항 항만시설 확장 및 항만운영의 효율화를 목적으로 아시아개발은행 (ADB)차관 지원자금으로서 사업 타당성 조사 및 일부 실시설계 용역을 발주코자 추진중에 있으며,

2. 본 용역에 참여할 용역사는 ADB 차관선과의 협의를 거쳐 Trans-Asia Engineering Associates, Inc. (T/A)와 Le Havre 항만청, 한국항만엔지니어링, 세광종합기술단등 4개 합작용역단이 최적업체로 선정되어 계약을 체결할 단계에 있읍니다.

3. 그러나 상기 4개 합작용역단중 T/A 는 주한미군 초청업체로서 한미행정협정 (SOFA) 제15조 2항에 관련되어 있다고 사료되오나, 별첨내용과 같이 동용역 수행상 가장 경험이 풍부한 최적업체이므로 계약이 이루어질수 있도록 협의하오니 회시하여 주시기 바랍니다.

첨부 : 인천항 3단계 개발 타당성 조사 개요 및 용역업체 선정 사유 1부. 끝

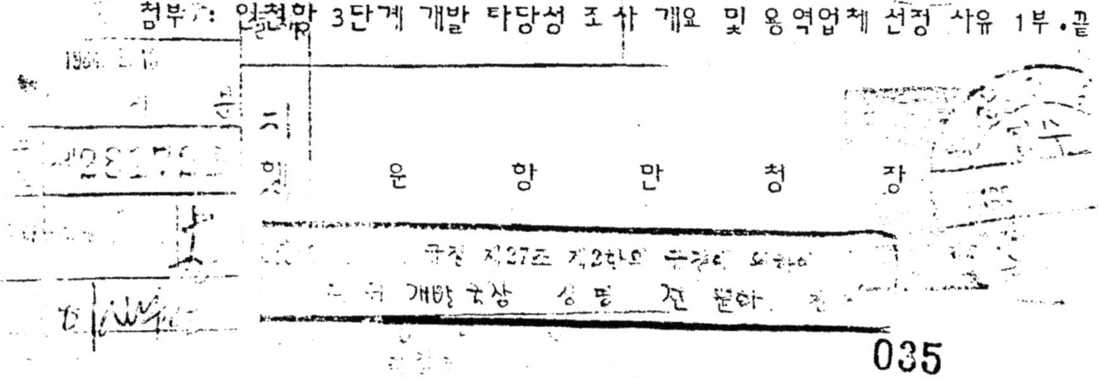

해 운 항 만 청 장

035

1. 용역 목적

o 인천항 화물량 증가에 대비한 항만시설 확장 및 정비계획 수립.

o 갑문 정기수리 기간중 (매 2-3년마다 약45일간 폐쇄) 항만운영 정상화를 위한 예비갑문설치 및 갑문운영효율화를 위한 갑문시설 개량 방안 강구

2. 과업내용

o 타당성 조사

- 화물량 증가에 대비한 항만시설의 기본계획수립

- 기존 갑문의 개량 방안 제시

- 50,000 DWT 갑문의 예비문비 설치 기본설계

o 실시설계

- 구 제1선거 구 갑벽제거 및 안벽 실시설계

036

3. 추진경위 및 계획

- '79. 3 - 9 ADB 기술지원 자금으로 인천항 2단계 타당성 조사 결과 3단계사업 타당성 인정
- '80. 7. 25 인천항 2단계 차관협정 (3단계 용역비 100만불 포함)
- '81. 12 인천항 3단계 개발사업 5차 5개년 계획 반영
- '82. 6 1차 투자심사 (경제기획원)
- '83. 3 2차 " (")
- '83. 6. 9 투자심사 완료 (")
- '84. 1. 21 용역 발주방법, 용역제의서 평가기준, 추진계획, 과업지시서 및 계약서 (안) 작성
- '84. 2. 24 " ADB 승인 요청
- '84. 3. 5 " ADB 승인
- '84. 3. 10 용역제의서 초청장 발송 (12개업체)
- '84. 4. 16 용역과업수행제의서 평가기준 작성
- '84. 5. 10 용역제의서 접수 마감
- '84. 5. 10 - '84. 6. 18 용역제의서 평가 및 ADB 협의 완료
- '84. 6. 18 - '84. 8. 30 용역협의 및 계약
- '84. 9 ADB, 관계부처 협의 및 용역착수 예정

037

4. 용역업체 선정 사유

가. 인천항 개발사업은 아시아개발은행 (ADB)차관 지원사업으로서 동항에 대한 조사 사업은 ADB 에 등록된 용역업체만이 사업에 참여 가능하며, 현재 ADB 에 등록된 국내 용역업체는 없읍니다.

나. 항만 차관사업에 대한 타당성 조사연구 및 갑문시설을 위한 조사 설계는 국내기술진 만으로 수행이 불가합니다.
(국내 용역업체는 외국기술 전수를 위해 합작 참여 배려)

다. T/A 는 인천항에 대해 유일하게 오랜 경험과 풍부한 기술진을 보유한 용역사로서 동용역 수행상 최적업체 입니다.

라. 특히 인천항은 조수간만의 차가 큰 불리한 여건을 갖고 있어 동항에 대한 경험이 풍부한 용역사라야만 가장 적합하고 확실한 조사성과를 얻을수 있읍니다.

마. 동 조사용역에 참여할 업체는 오랜시간동안 ADB 와의 협의를 거쳐 선정된 것이므로 번의하기 어려우며, 만약 재 선정하게 될시는 다시 차관선인 ADB 와 협의를 거치는등 상당한 시간이 소요되므로 현인천항 차관 협정상 '85년말까지 기한내 용역과업 수행이 불가하여, 본 차관사업의 수행에 차질이 우려됩니다.

038

기안용지

분류기호 문서번호	미안 723-	(전화번호)	전결규정 조 항 전결사항
처리기간		장 관	
시행일자	1984. 8.		
보존년한			

보조기관				협조
	국 장		심의관	
	과 장			
기안책임자		연상모	안보과	

		발신	통제
경 유		33614 발수송 1984. 8. 29 의무부	검열 1984. 8. 29 통제관
수 신	상공부 장관		
참 조	통상진흥국장		
제 목	SOFA 초청계약자의 국내 타사업 종사관련 의견회신		

대 : 통총 1314-1550(84.7.19), 통총 1755(84.8.20)

연 : 미안 723-030382(84.8.9)

SOFA상의 초청계약자인 Trans-Asia Engineering Associates,Inc.의 아국내 타사업 종사에 관한 당부의견을 다음과 같이 회신합니다.

– 다 음 –

1. SOFA 제 15조 제2항(나)에서 명시적으로 규정하고 있는바와 같이, SOFA상의 초청 계약자가 당초 주한미군과의 계약사업이 아닌 아국내 타사업 활동에 종사하게 되는 경우는, 원칙적으로 미측은 해당업체에 대한 초청계약자 지정을 철회하는 것이 타당하며, 이러한 원칙은 초청계약자의 종사가능 사업범위를 주한

/계속/

정서 | 관인 | 발송

0201-1-8A(갑) 1969. 11. 10. 승인

190mm×268mm(2급인쇄용지 60g/m²) 조달청(3,000,000매 인쇄)

039

미군과의 계약이행에만 한정시킨 SOFA 제 15조 제1항

("... solely for the purpose of executing contracts with the U.S. for the benefit of the U.S. armed forces ...") 에서도 분명하게 규정되어 있읍니다.

2. 그러나, SOFA 상의 초청계약자가 "아국정부에 즉각적이고 직접적으로 관련되는 아국내에서의 사업활동 (business activities in the Republic of Korea pertaining immediately and directly to the Government of the Republic of Korea)" 에 종사하는 것을,SOFA 합동위원회에서 일종의 특례조치로서 건의각서 처리 방식을 통해 승인해온 그간의 전례(67.7.13.제11차 합동위, 68.7.3.제28차 합동위, 69.3.20.제 36차 합동위, 72.5.3.제73차 합동위, 74.7.25.제 96차 합동위)를 고려하고, 금번 Trans-Asia Engineering Associates, Inc.의 해운 항만청 주관사업에의 종사가 필수적이라는 해운 항만청의 의견을 감안할때, SOFA 협정의 초청계약자 지위로서의 동 업체의 인원, 시설및 자원과 완전히 별개의 인원, 시설, 자원등을 동 사업에 투입하고 동 별개의 사업및 그 인원에 관하여는 SOFA제15조가 규정한 특권면제가 적용되지 않도록 보장되는 조치가 가능할 경우 동업체가 국내 사업에 종사하는 것이 가능하다고 사료됩니다. (예외적으로)

3. 이상과 같은 고려에 따라, Trans-Asia Engineering Associates,Inc.와 계약을 체결하는 경우에는, 이미 언급한

/계속/.

1205-25(2-2)(을)
1981. 12. 18 승인

190mm×268mm(인쇄용지 2급 60g/m²)
조 달 청(.,000,000매 인 쇄)

040

전례와 마찬가지로 SOFA 상무분과위의 건의 각서를 SOFA 합동 위원회에서 승인하는 절차를 취함으로써 형식적인 요건을 갖추는 것이 필요할 것으로 사료됩니다. 끝.

집집마다 국산애용 넘어가는 우리국력

대 한 민 국

상 공 부

통 총 1314- 2[illegible] (720 - 3513) 1984. 10. 23.

수 신 외무부 장관

참 조

제 목 시설설계용역 초청계약자 지정 협의 간소화

1. 미8군 시설설계용역계약은 아국업체와 초청계약자가 50:50으로 투자 설립한 7개 합작법인에 의하여 수행되어 온 전문성이 요구되고, 한국업체만의 단독 수행은 어려운 분야로서,

2. 시설설계용역 초청계약자 지정 협의가 미측으로부터 요구될때는 technical qualifications 상으로 협의, 거절의 전례가 없고, 우리업체의 수행 능력상으로도 불가하여 특기사항 없이 같은 내용의 승인만이 되풀이 협의됨으로써 한.미 양측에 시간과 인력의 문제를 초래하였음.

3. 미측 상무분과위원장은 시설설계용역 초청계약자를 사업단위별 지정에서 회계년도 내의 포괄지정제로 하자는 의견을 별첨과 같이 제출하여 왔기

4. 미측의 절차 간소화 방안에 대한, SOFA 제15조 규정 저촉 여부를 귀부에 문의하오니 조속 회신하여 주시기 바랍니다.

첨 부 : 관련 공문 사본 1부. 끝.

상 공 부 장 관

정부공문서 규정 제27조 제2항의 규정에 의하여
통상총괄과장 이 상 [illegible]

042

외 무 부	
접수일시	1984. 10. 23
접수번호	제 035013
주무과	
담당자	
위임근거	

1983 년 월 일까지 처리할것

043

공 란

공 란

공 란

JOINT COMMITTEE
UNDER
THE REPUBLIC OF KOREA AND THE UNITED STATES
STATUS OF FORCES AGREEMENT

29 September 1984

Dear Dr. Hodges,

With regard to your letter of Sep. 20 1984 concerning the request by Trans-Asia Engineering Associates, Inc., a US invited contractor, to contract with the Korea Maritime Port Authority, I would like to inform you that the ROK Joint Committee Representative has no objection to presenting the draft memorandum as an agenda item on the 12 October 1984 Joint Committee meeting for signature, if it has been so agreed by the ROK and US Chairmen of the Commerce Subcommittee.

In principle, however, the US Government, according to paragraph 2(b), Article 15 of the SOFA, should withdraw the designation conferred on a US invited contractor if and when it engages in ROK business activities.

In this connection, it is the view of the ROK Joint Committee Representative that measures should be taken to ensure that no privileges and benefits under SOFA be granted on additional personnel not associated with USFK undertakings. In addition, this particular case should not be quoted in the future as a precedent allowing invited contractors to engage in non USFK-related business activities without loss of SOFA status.

Sincerely,

Yang LEE
ROK Secretary
SOFA Joint Committee

Dr. Carroll B. Hodges
US Secretary
SOFA Joint Committee

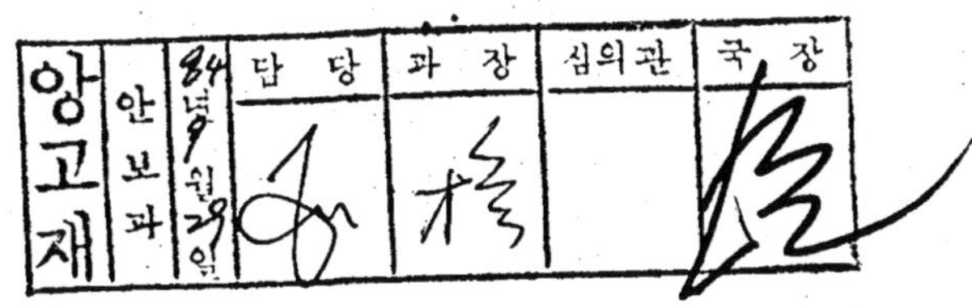

047

공　　　란

MINISTRY OF TRADE AND INDUSTRY.
REPUBLIC OF KOREA
77-6 Saejongro, Chongroku,
Seoul 110, Korea

September 5, 1984

WILFRED J. CURLEY
United States Chairman
Commerce Subcommittee

Dear Mr. Curley:

Thank you for your letter of July 24 regarding the request of Trans-Asia Engineering Associates to participate in the feasibility study for the Third Stage Development of the Port of Incheon.

Of course, it is a well-established principle that the U.S. Government should withdraw invited contractor status from any company that engages in business activity in Korea other than that specified under the terms of the SOFA. As you know, Paragraph I, Article XV of the SOFA states that the business activities of an invited contractor in Korea shall be "solely for the purpose of executing contracts with the U.S. for the benefit of the U.S. Armed Forces."

However, considering the existing precedents approved by the Joint Committee as special cases as well as the current situation of KMPA, all of which pertain immediately and directly to the Government of the Republic of Korea, we are prepared to agree to the participation of Trans-Asia Engineering Associates in the aforementioned feasibility study.

In this connection, we request your office to present the attached documents to the joint committee.

Thank you for your cooperation.

Sincerely yours,

Unsuh Park

PARK Un-Suh
ROK Chairman
Commerce Subcommittee

Enclosure

Incl 2

049

공 란

공 란

공 란

기 안 용 지

분류기호 문서번호	미안 723-	(전화번호)	전결규정 조 항 전결사항
처리기간		장 관	
시행일자	1984.10.		
보존년한			
보조기관 국 장		심의관	협조
과 장			
기안책임자	연상모	안보과	
경 유		발송	통제
수 신	상공부 장관		
참 조	통상진흥 국장		
제 목	시설설계용역 초청 계약자 지정협의 간소화관련 의견회신		

대 : 통총 1314-2257호 (84.10.23)

시설설계용역 초청계약자 지정협의 간소화와 관련 아래와 같이 당부의 의견을 회신합니다.

- 다 음 -

1. SOFA 제15조 제1항, 동조 제2항에 규정된 바와 같이 초청계약 사업에 대한 개별적인 승인절차가 필요한것이 원칙이며, 회계년도내의 포괄지정제로 할 경우 해당 회계년도내의 주된 사업 이외의 기타 초청계약사업에 대해서는 아국정부가 검토, 승인 할수 없게 되므로 SOFA 제15조 규정에 저촉되는 것임.

2. 전례상으로도, 시설설계용역 초청계약자의 지위가 철회된

/계속/

1205-25(2-1)A(갑)
1981. 12. 18 승인

정직 질서 창조

190mm×268mm (인쇄용지 2급 60g/m²)
조 달 청(1,500,000매 인 쇄)

053

적이없고, 비록 같은내용의 승인만이 되풀이되어 한.미
양측에 시간과 인력의 문제를 초래한다 할지라도, 초청
계약자를 승인함에 있어서 초청계약자의 사업참여 타당성
여부검토필요성과 초청계약자에 대한 특권부여의 중요성에
비추어, 초청계약 사업을 개별적으로 승인함이 타당하다고
사료됨. 끝.

1205-25(2-2)(을)
1981. 12. 18 승인

054

190mm×268mm(인쇄용지 2급 60g/m²)
조달청(.,000,000매 인쇄)

27.

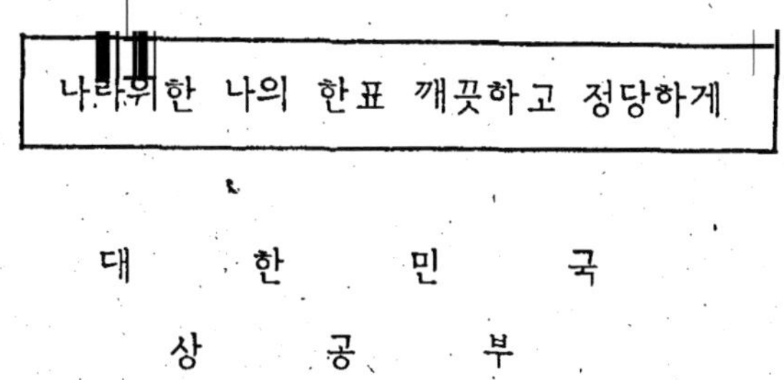
나라위한 나의 한표 깨끗하고 정당하게

대 한 민 국

상 공 부

통 총 28144-212 (720-3513) 1985. 2. 8.

수 신 외무부 장관

참 조 미주국장

제 목 미8군 시설설계용역 초청계약자 지정협의 간소화

1. 미안 723-40798('84. 10. 26) 및 통총 1314-2257 ('84. 10. 23) 관련입니다.

2. 당부는 미측 상무분과위원장의 시설설계용역 초청계약자 지정협의 간소화 요청에 대해 SOFA 규정에 저촉됨을 이유로 불가함을 통보한바 있으나 미측 상무분과위원장은 초청계약자 지정 협의를 회계 년도내의 포괄지정제로 하되 분기별로 계약명, 지정이유, 계약기간을 월별로 초청계약자를 통보할것을 전제로 초청계약자 지정협의 간소화를 재요청하여 왔읍니다.

3. 미8군 시설설계용역은 아국 업체와 초청계약자가 합작 투자한 7개 회사가 전담하고 있는 분야로서 매사업별 초청계약자 지정협의시 특기사항없이 동일회사 및 인원에 대하여 같은 내용의 승인만이 되풀이 협의되어 한미 양측간에 시간과 인력 낭비를 초래한바 미측 상무분과 위원장의 요청을 고려 시설설계용역 초청계약자의 지정협의를 간소화하고자 하니 이에 대한 귀부의 의견을 회시 바랍니다.

첨 부 : 관련 서한 1부. 끝.

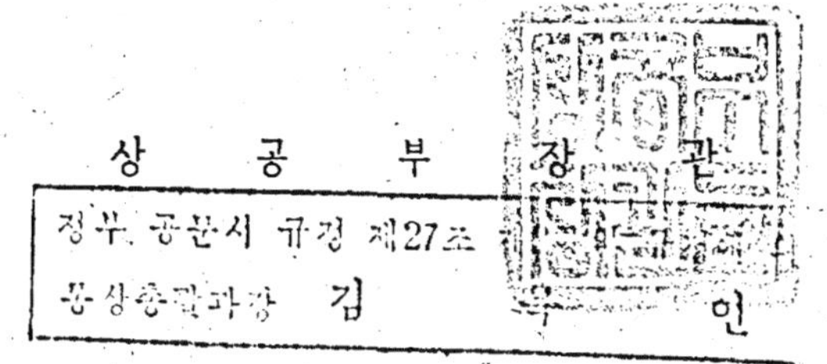
상 공 부 장 관

정부 공문서 규정 제27조
통상총괄과장 김

055

외 무 부		주관	
접수일시	1965. 2. 10 시 분	지시사항	
접수번호	제 04134 호		
주무과			
담당자			
결 재			처리기한 년 월 일까지

056

공　　　　　란

기 안 용 지

분류기호 문서번호	미안 723-	(전화번호)	전결규정 조 항 전결사항
처리기간		장 관	
시행일자	1985.2. .		
보존연한			

보조기관				협조
	국 장	전결	심의관	
	과 장			
		연상모	안보과	

경 유		발신	1985. 2. 25 06596	통제	1985.2.25
수 신	상공부 장관				
참 조	통상진흥 국장				
제 목	미8군 시설설계 용역 초청계약자 지정협의 간소화 관련 의견회신				

대 : 통총 1314-2257(84.10.23)

통총 28144-212호 (85.2.8)

연 : 미안 723-40798호 (84.10.26)

시설설계 용역초청 계약자 지정협의 간소화와 관련 아래와 같이 당부의 의견을 회신합니다.

- 다 음 -

1. SOFA 제 15조 제1항 제2항은 초청계약사업에 대한 개별적인 사전승인절차를 필요로하고 있으며, 이는 초청계약자의 사업참여 타당성 여부를 아국정부가 사전에 검토할 필요가 있기 때문임을 그 취지로 하고

/뒷면 계속/

정서 | 관인 | 발송

1205-25(2-1)A(갑) 1981. 12. 18승인 정직 질서 창조 190㎜×268㎜(인쇄용지 2급 60g/㎡) 조달청(1,500,000매 인쇄)

058

있다고 사료 됨.

2. 따라서, 회계년도 내의 포괄지정제로 할경우 미측이 새로이 제안한바와 같이 매분기별, 매월별 통보 사항이 있다하더라도 해당회계년도 내의 기타 사업에 대해서는 아국 정부가 개별적으로 사전에 검토 승인하는 기회를 상실하는 결과가 되어 규정의 취지에 어긋나는것임.

3. 그러나, 현행의 7개 시설설계 용역 초청계약자의 지정협의 절차가 한미양측 간에 시간과 인력낭비를 불필요 하게 초래하여 이를 간소화할 필요가 있다고 귀부가 판단할 경우, 예외적으로 시설설계 용역분야에서의 초청계약사업과 아국 업체와 초청계약자가 합작투자한 특정 7개회사가 전담하는 경우를 명시적으로 한정하여 미측이 새로이 제의한 회계년도 내의 포괄 지정제 방식을 SOFA 한미상무분과 위원회에서 합의한후 SOFA 한미합동위원회 양측 대표들이 서명하는 합의각서양식으로 채택하여 시행하는 방법이 있을 것으로 사료 됨. 끝.

059

정/리/보/존/문/서/목/록					
기록물종류	문서-일반공문서철		29280	등록일자	2008-08-13
분류번호	729.416	국가코드		주제	
문서철명	SOFA 한.미국 합동위원회 - 상무분과위원회, 1986-87				
생산과	안보과	생산년도	1986 - 1987	보존기간	영구
담당과(그룹)	미주	안보	서가번호	--	
참조분류					
권차명					
내용목차	* 초청계약자 문제, 미군 영내 설치 학교 한국인 등록문제 등				

마/이/크/로/필/름/사/항				
촬영연도	*롤 번호	화일 번호	후레임 번호	보관함 번호

0001

대 한 민 국

상 공 부

통 정 28144 - 691 (503-9445) 1986. 5. 7.

수 신 수신처 참조

제 목 한국 국민의 미군영내의 대학 (초청계약자)에 등록 문제

미군영내에 설치되어 있는 학교 (대학등)에는 SOFA 제15조 제2항 (b)에 의거 원칙적으로 미군과 군속 및 그 가족 그리고 기타 SOFA지위부여자에 한하여 등록할 수 있어, 당부는 한국민의 등록에 대해 미군측에 이의를 제기하였으며 미군측은 별첨서한과 같이 이문제에 관해 협의하기를 희망하여 온 바 이에 관하여 귀부의 의견을 문의하니 별첨서한을 참고하여 귀부의 의견을 제출하여 주시기 바랍니다.

첨 부 : 1. 당부서한 (1986. 4. 24자) 사본 1부.

2. 당부서한 (1986. 1. 21자) 사본 1부.

3. 미군측서한 (1986. 3. 7자) 사본 1부.

4. 미군측서한 (1986. 5. 6자) 사본 1부. - 끝 -

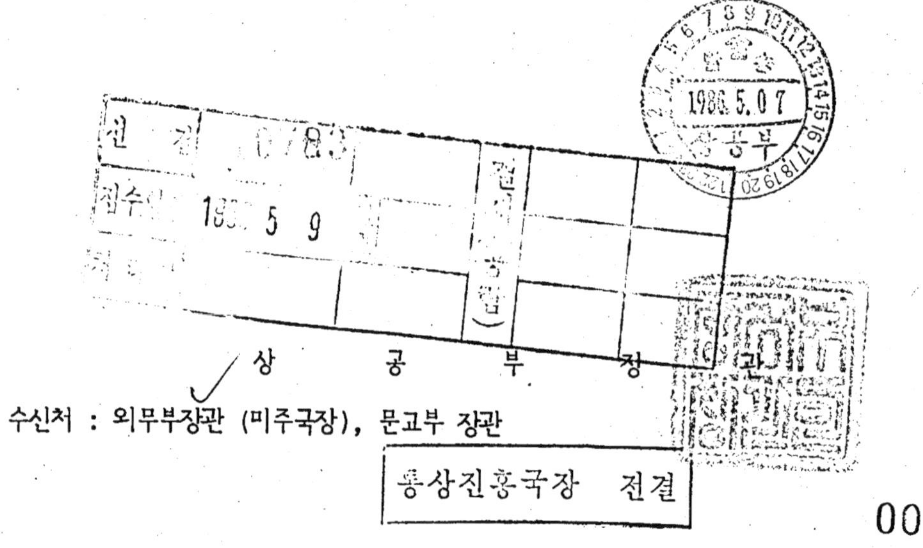

상 공 부 장 관

수신처 : 외무부장관 (미주국장), 문고부 장관

통상진흥국장 전결

0002

MINISTRY OF TRADE AND INDUSTRY
Unified Government Complex
Building No. 3
1 Chungangdong, Kwachun 170-11, Republic of Korea

April 24, 1986

WILFRED J. CURLEY
United States Chairman
Commerce Subcommittee

Dear Mr. Curley:

As you may know, we have been requested by the SOFA Committee, Korean Side, to prepare an agenda for the 158th Korea-U.S. Joint Committee meeting scheduled for May 9, 1986.

However, prior to that meeting, we would like to bring to your attention certain problems concerning the operation of Articles 15 and 16.

1. Operational Problems Involving Article 15

a. It was agreed at the 9th Korea-U.S. Joint Committee meeting on June 5, 1967 that the SOFA Committee should periodically inform the Korean government of the arrival, departure, and place of residence of persons covered by Article 15, Paragraph 4. The U.S. side's failure to comply with this requirement has caused us some difficulties.

b. Article 15, Paragraph 3 stipulates that third country nationals are not entitled to SOFA privileges except insofar as authorized in the Agreed Minutes. Third country nationals who are not so authorized, including those who are not holding permanent U.S. residency rights, are required to report to the Korean Immigration authorities. However, the Ministry of Justice, in whose jurisdiction the Immigration Office lies, has complained to us that third country invited contractor personnel regularly violate this requirement and overstay their legal residence period.

c. U.S. universities operating on USFK premises are entitled to enroll only members of the U.S. military, their dependents, and other SOFA-related personnel. We have nevertheless been informed that Korean nationals regularly register at these universities.

d. It is not possible to award SOFA privileges to Japanese nationals, for example, the NEC Overseas Market Development (an Invited Contractor) under Article 15 Paragraph 1 of SOFA Agreement, but this has been done, in violation of the agreement.

e. The written lists of invited contractors submitted to us have several been found to be inaccurate, thus causing us considerable inconvenience.

2. Operational Problem Involving Article 16

Those persons and companies engaged in military supply should register at the appropriate Korean local government office. The Korean government does not intend to limit the USFK's local procurement. However the Korean government can only permit those who have qualified and who have to make contracts with USFK. USFK personnel should observe Korean law in the light of SOFA Article 7 (respect for local law) and general principle of respect for national soverignty.

Your prompt attention to these matters will be greatly appreciated.

Unsuh Park
Un-Suh Park
Korea Chairman
Commerce Subcommittee

2

0004

MINISTRY OF TRADE AND INDUSTRY
REPUBLIC OF KOREA
77-6 SaeJongro, Chongroku,
Seoul 110, Korea

January 21, 1986

WILFRED J. CURLEY
United States Chairman
Commerce Subcommittee

Dear Mr. Curley:

The Korean government would be grateful if you could inform us how many Korean nationals at U.S. university branches in Korea established for the USFK personnel and their dependents on the basis of invited contractor status.

Your reply by Feburary 5 would be very much appreciated.

Sincerely yours,

Un-Suh Park
Korea Chairman
Commerce Subcommittee

0005

공란

공　　　란

공　　　란

공 란

공 란

공　　란

INVITED CONTRACTOR & TECHNICAL REPRESENTATIVE PERSONNEL DATA REPORT
(Instructions on Reverse)

1. TYPE OF REPORT: ( )ARRIVAL ( )DEPARTURE ( )CHANGE IN DATA

2. CONTRACT NUMBER:______________________ CONTRACT EXPIR DATE:__________

3. COMPANY NAME:____

4. DESCRIPTION OF SERVICE:__________________________________

5. EMPLOYEE'S NAME:____

6. SSN:______________ NATIONALITY:__________ PASSPORT #:____________

7. COMPANY POSITION/TITLE:__________________________________

8. DATE & PLACE OF HIRE:____________________________________

9. ORDINARY RESIDENCE:__________________________(City, State, Country)

10. TRANSPORTATION AGREEMENT WITH COMPANY FOR TRAVEL TO AND FROM KOREA: YES NO (Circle)

11. GS EQUIVALENCY:________________ NUMBER OF DEPENDENTS IN KOREA:________
(Attach rationale if in excess of GS-12) (Complete reverse side if dependents here)

12. DUTY ADDRESS IN KOREA:___________________________________

______________________________ DUTY PHONE:______________

13. HOME ADDRESS IN KOREA:___________________________________

______________________________ HOME PHONE:______________

14. DATE OF ENTRY:______________ PORT OF ENTRY:______________

15. ESTIMATED DATE OF DEPARTURE FROM KOREA:____________________

16. REPORT OF DEPARTURES: DATE OF DEPARTURE:__________________

ID CARD TURNED-IN TO:______________ RCP TURNED-IN TO:______________

17. ____
SIGNATURE OF CONTRACTOR EMPLOYEE DATE

18. ____
SIGNATURE OF USFK RESPONSIBLE OFFICER (RO) DATE

PRINT NAME OF RO:________________________________

UNIT:____

DUTY TELEPHONE:__________________ DEROS:______________

JK FORM XXX

Figure D-1. Front side of JK Form XXX.

INSTRUCTIONS FOR THE USE OF THIS FORM

1. USFK Reg 700-19, USFK Invited Contractors and Technical Representatives, is the regulation that governs the use of this form.

2. Prepare this form in FOUR COPIES:

   a. Send the 1ST and 2ND COPIES to: HQ, USFK
   ACofS, Acquisition Management
   ATTN: ACJ
   APO SF 96301-0010

   b. The USFK Responsible Officer will retain the 3RD COPY.

   c. 4TH COPY will be provided the senior contractor representative in Korea.

3. This form will be completed and forwarded to the above address not later than FIVE WORKDAYS after ARRIVAL, DEPARTURE, and CHANGE IN DATA of a USFK invited contractor or technical representative.

THE FOLLOWING DEPENDENTS ARE ACCOMPANYING THE CONTRACTOR EMPLOYEE IN KOREA:

DEPENDENTS FULL NAME	NATIONALITY	RELATIONSHIP	PORT OF ENTRY	DATE OF ENTR

Figure D-2. Reverse side of JK Form XXX.

REPUBLI— KOREA - UNITED STATES
C——CE SUBCOMMITTEE

31 May 1967

MEMORANDUM FOR: THE JOINT COMMITTEE

1. Subcommittee Members:

Republic of Korea	United States
Mr. SHIM Ui Hwan	COL Floyd R. Waltz, Jr. - J4, USFK
Mr. HAN Byung Il	COL Ralph O. Griffin - J4, USFK
Mr. MOON Ki Sang	COL Lansing H. Myers - USAF
Mr. KIM Chan Dong	LTC Bruce J. Leiser - Eng Section
Mr. RHEE Eun Tak	LTC Nelson W. Hardin - J4, USFK
Mr. LEE Chang Ha	LTC William C. McKinley, Jr. - J5, USFK
Mr. LEE Woong Soo	LCDR Glenn C. Culpepper - USN
Mr. IM Young Duk	MAJ James L. Hicks - USAF
Mr. NAM Koong Chull	Mr. Oliver Kennedy - KPA
Mr. KIM Sae Kwon	Mr. Charles E. Coleman - PACEX
Mr. KIM In Su	Mr. Earl W. Guthrie - USAEDFE
Mr. DOKKO Young	
Mr. MIN Soo Hong	
Mr. KIM Bong Keum	

2. Subject of Recommendation: Procedures for Notification of the Arrival, Departure, and Place of Residence in the Republic of Korea of Persons Covered by Article XV (Invited Contractors), paragraph 4.

3. It is recommended that the US furnish the ROK, in the format attached as Inclosure 1, information on invited contractor employees and their dependents on their initial arrival in the Republic of Korea. Such reports will be provided to the Joint Committee as of the last day of each month, commencing 30 June 1967.

4. It is recommended that the US furnish the ROK, in the format attached as Inclosure 2, information on invited contractor employees and their dependents, on their final departure from the Republic of Korea. Such reports will be provided to the Joint Committee as of the last day of each month, commencing 30 June 1967.

5. It is recommended that the US furnish the ROK, in the format attached as Inclosure 3, any changes of local residential address of invited contractors employees. Such reports will be provided to the Joint Committee as of the last day of each month, commencing 30 June 1967.

9th JC - Incl 8
5 Jun 67

6. It is mutually agreed in the Commerce Subcommittee that in case an employee of an invited contractor in the Republic of Korea elects to remain in Korea after his employment Has been terminated, such information will be provided in lieu of final departure date as specified in paragraph 4 above.

7. It is recommended that a complete list of invited contractor employees and their dependents, in the format attached as Inclosure 1, be provided to the ROK on a quarterly basis, as of 30 June, 30 September, 31 December and 31 March.

8. It is recommended that above reporting procedures be approved.

9. Security classification: Unclassified.

SHIM UI HWAN
Chairman, ROK Commerce Subcommittee

COLONEL FLOYD R. WALTZ, JR.
Chairman, US Commerce Subcommittee

3 Incl
as

APPROVED BY JOINT COMMITTEE
ON 5 JUNE 1967 AT NINTH MEETING

B. O. DAVIS, JR.
Lieutenant General
United States Air Force
United States Representative

YOON HA JONG
Republic of Korea Representative

0014

9th JC-Incl 8
5 Jun 67

ARRIVAL OF INVITED CONTRACTOR EMPLOYEES

초청계약자 고용인의 도착

(Company Name)
회사명

(Local Business Address)
한국 영업소 주소

NAME	NATIONALITY	PRINCIPAL OR DEPENDENT	PASSPORT NO.	PORT OF ENTRY	DATE OF ENTRY	RANK/POSITION	LOCAL ADDRESS
성명	국적 (1)	본인 또는 가족 (2)	여권번호	입국항 (3)	입국일자 (4)	계급과 지위 (5)	한국주소

NOTE (1) - Nationality will be coded as shown.
국적은 다음 기호와 같이 표시한다.
NOTE (2) - Principal or Dependent will be coded as shown.
본인 또는 부양가족은 다음기호로 표시한다.
NOTE (3) - Port of Entry will be coded as shown.
입국항은 다음 기호로 표시한다.
NOTE (4) - Date of Entry will be written as shown.
입국일자는 다음과 같이 표시한다.
NOTE (5) - Rank/Position of employee will be coded in a mutually agreed code not yet determined.
고용인의 계급 및 지위는 아직도 결정은 보지 못했지만 서로 합의된 기호로 표시한다.

276

NATIONALITY CODE 국적기호	PRINCIPAL/ DEPENDENT CODE 본인 및 가족기호	PORT OF ENTRY CODE 입국항 기호	DATE OF ENTRY CODE 입국일자 기호
A - United States 미국인	P - Employee 고용인	Y - Kimpo 김포	Day Month Year 일 월 년
B - Korea 한국인	D - Dependent 가족	X - Inchon 인천	(01 01 66) (1 January 1966 1966년 1월 1일
C - Filipino 필리핀인		W - Osan 오산	
D - Australian 호주인		V - Pusan 부산	

9th JC - Incl 8
5 Jun 67

NATIONALITY CODE 국적기호	PRINCIPAL/ DEPENDENT CODE 본인 및 가족 기호	PORT OF ENTRY CODE 입국항 기호	DATE OF ENTRY CODE 입국일자 기호
E - British 영국인			
F - Chinese 중국인			
G - Japanese 일본인			
I - Ryukyuan 유구인			
J- German 독일인			
K - New Zealand 뉴 질랜드 인			
L - Bolivia 볼리비아인			
M - Canadian 카나다인			

277

9th JC - Incl 8
5 Jun 67

0015

RTURE/TERMINATION OF EMPLOYMENT OF
INVITED CONTRACTOR EMPLOYEES AND DEPENDENTS

초청계약자 고용인의 출국 및 고용계약 완료

(Company Name)

회사명

NAME OF EMPLOYEES & DEPENDENTS

고용자 및 가족의 성명

DEPARTURE DATE OR DATE OF TERMINATION WHEN EMPLOYEE ELECTS TO REMAIN IN KOREA

고용인이 한국에 체재하려고 할때의 해약일자 및 출국일자.

278

1.
2.
3.
4.

9th JC - Incl 8
5 Jun 67

DEPARTURE/TERMINATION OF EMPLOYMENT OF
INVITED CONTRACTOR EMPLOYEES AND DEPENDENTS

초청계약자 고용인의 출국 및 고용계약 완료

(Company Name)

회사명

NAME OF EMPLOYEES & DEPENDENTS

고용자 및 가족의 성명

DEPARTURE DATE OR DATE OF TERMINATION WHEN EMPLOYEE ELECTS TO REMAIN IN KOREA

고용인이 한국에 체재하려고 할때의 해약일자 및 출국일자.

279

1.
2.
3.
4.

9th JC - Incl 8
5 Jun 67

0016

CHANGE OF ADDRESS OF INVITED CONTRACTOR EMPLOYEES
초청계약자 고용인의 주소 변경

(Company Name)
회사명

NAME OF EMPLOYEE
고용자 성명

NEW ADDRESS
새 주소

9th JC - Incl 8
5 Jun 67

280

JOINT COMMITTEE
UNDER
THE REPUBLIC OF KOREA AND THE UNITED STATES
STATUS OF FORCES AGREEMENT

5 June 1967

MEMORANDUM FOR: Chairmen, Facilities and Areas Subcommittee

SUBJECT: Request for Acquisition of Real Estate

1. SOFA provides in Article II, paragraph 2, that the Governments of the United States and the Republic of Korea may agree that facilities and areas or portions thereof shall be returned to the Republic of Korea or that additional facilities and areas may be provided.

2. Pursuant to paragraph 1 above, it is requested that recommendations be presented to the Joint Committee concerning a request for the acquisition of 30.43 acres of non-arable mountainous land located at Kumo-ri, Kunja-myon, Sihung-gun, Kyonggi-do, Korea (Operation Area TAC 3, Site 41). The acquisition is required to formalize use and occupancy of the tactical operational area in support of Battery "B", 7th Missile Battalion (HAWK), 2d Artillery. Because of administrative oversight, acquisition of this acreage was inadvertently omitted during initial acquisition proceedings. However, this real estate has been used by USFK since 1961.

B. O. DAVIS, Jr.
Lieutenant General
United States Air Force
United States Representative
Joint Committee

YOON HA JONG
Republic of Korea Representative
Joint Committee

APPROVED BY JOINT COMMITTEE
ON 5 JUNE 1967 AT NINTH MEETING

9th JC - Incl 9
5 Jun 67

281

0017

1. SOFA 제 15조 제2항(나)에서 명시적으로 규정하고 있는 바와 같이, SOFA 상의 초청계약자가 당초 주한미군과의 계약 사업이 아닌 아국내 타사업 활동에 종사하게 되는 경우는, 원칙적으로 해당업체에 대한 초청계약자 지정을 철회하는 것이 타당함. 이러한 원칙은, 초청계약자의 종사가능 사업범위를 주한 미군과의 계약 이행에만 한정시킨 제 15조 제1항에서도 분명하게 규정되어 있음.

2. 그간 SOFA 합동 위원회에서, 건의 각서 처리 방식을 통해 초청 계약자의 아국내 타사업 활동 종사를 승인해온 전례는, 해당초청 계약자가 아국정부에 즉각적이고 직접적으로 관련되는 아국내에서의 사업활동에 종사하는 경우에 한정해서, 주한미군과의 계약 사업에 투입되는 인원, 자재, 설비와는 완전히 별개의 인원, 자재, 설비를 투입한다는 조건하에, 이를 승인해 준 일종의 특례 조치에 불과함.

0018

- 미 8군 Acq. Management
(Mr. Curley)

비고
사실 가정 X
1월 말 발표

→ sign → 상은 → MCI ——→ 노동조합에 의견 조회

당사자
미8군 해명
기존·선출·33건 추가
요청 이유

→ 업계 설명 통보 → 국장 명의 공문

0019

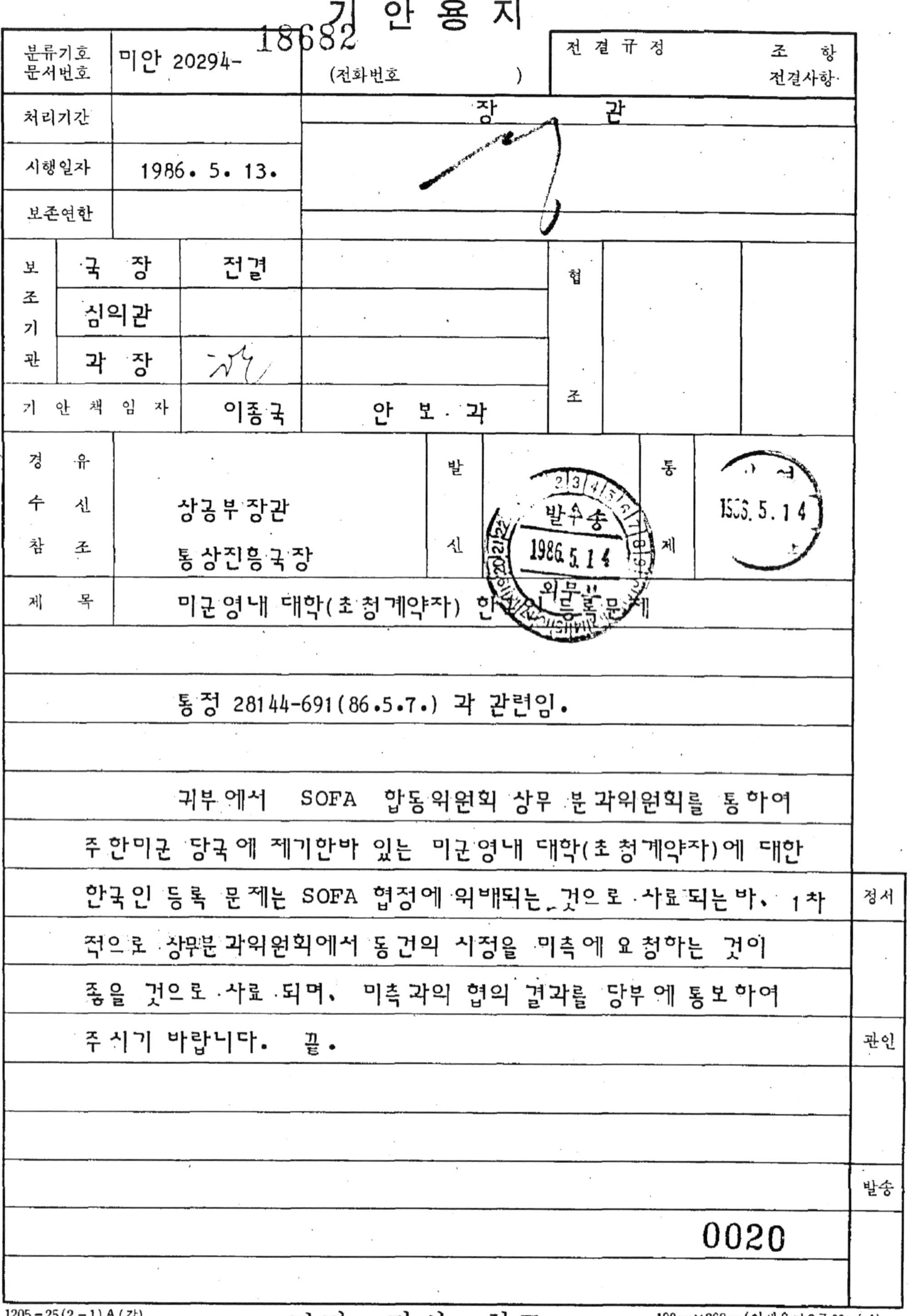

기 안 용 지

분류기호 문서번호	미안 20294- 18682	(전화번호)	전결규정 조 항 전결사항
처리기간		장 관	
시행일자	1986. 5. 13.		
보존연한			

보조기관				협조
	국 장	전결		
	심의관			
	과 장			
기안책임자		이종국	안 보 과	

경 유		발신	발수송 1986.5.14 외무부	통제	1986.5.14
수 신	상공부장관				
참 조	통상진흥국장				
제 목	미군영내 대학(초청계약자) 한국인 등록문제				

통정 28144-691(86.5.7.)과 관련임.

귀부에서 SOFA 합동위원회 상무 분과위원회를 통하여 주한미군 당국에 제기한바 있는 미군영내 대학(초청계약자)에 대한 한국인 등록 문제는 SOFA 협정에 위배되는 것으로 사료되는바, 1차적으로 상무분과위원회에서 동건의 시정을 미측에 요청하는 것이 좋을 것으로 사료되며, 미측과의 협의 결과를 당부에 통보하여 주시기 바랍니다. 끝.

정서 | 관인 | 발송

0020

1205-25(2-1) A(갑) 1981. 12. 18승인

정직 질서 창조

190㎜×268㎜(인쇄용지 2급 60g/㎡) 가 40-41 1985. 8. 7.

기 안 용 지

분류기호 문서번호	미안 20294- 18681 (전화번호)	전결규정 조 항 전결사항
처리기간		장 관
시행일자	1986. 5. 13.	
보존연한		

보조기관			협조
국 장	전 결		
심의관			
과 장	(서명)		
기안책임자	이종국	안 보 과	

경 유 / 수 신 / 참 조	상공부장관, 통상진흥국장	발신	발송 1986. 5. 14 외무부	통제	1986. 5. 14
제 목	SOFA 제15조 운영상 문제점에 대한 의견회보				

통정 28144-692(86.5.7.)와 관련임.

1. 미측이 초청 계약자 입출국및 체류와 관련한 통보에 있어서 SOFA 합동위원회에서 합의된 절차와 양식에 따르지 않고 있다면 SOFA 합동위원회에서 합의된 대로 이행할것을 상무분과 위원회에서 미측에 요청하는 것이 좋을 것으로 사료됩니다.

2. SOFA 합동위원회에서 기 합의된 절차와 양식에 따르는 경우에도 초청계약자의 효과적인 관리에 문제가 있다면 이는 새로운 문제를 제기하는 것이므로 SOFA 합동위원회를 통해 미측에 제기하는 것이 타당할 것으로 사료되는바, 동문제를 미측에 제기할 필요성이 있는지 여부에 대한 귀부의견을 회보하여 주시기 바랍니다.

끝.

정서 / 관인 / 발송

1205-25(2-1)A(갑) 1981. 12. 18승인

정직 질서 창조 0021

190㎜×268㎜(인쇄용지 2급 60g/㎡) 가 40-41 1985. 8. 7.

DISPOSITION FORM

For use of this form, see AR 340-15; the proponent agency is TAGO.

상무분과위
검토 문제

REFERENCE OR OFFICE SYMBOL	SUBJECT
ACJ	Letter to Assistant Minister, MTI

TO	FROM	DATE	CMT 1
SEE DISTRIBUTION	ACJ	28 May 1986 Mr. Watchko/tw/6129	

1. Reference HQ USFK (ACJ) letter dated 23 May 1986 to Dr. Chulsu Kim, Assistant Minister, Ministry of Trade and Industry, copy enclosed.

2. Referenced letter is provided for your information.

3. Point of contact at ACJ for this action is Tom Watchko, 293-6129 or 3221.

Encl

for
WILFRED J. CURLEY
Assistant Chief of Staff
Acquisition Management

THOMAS J. WATCHKO
Procurement Analyst
Acquisition Management

DISTRIBUTION:

DC-SA COMMANDERS
JAJ US Army Korea Contracting Agency
Far East District, Corps of Engineers
AFFES, Korea Area Exchange

TO: ROK SOFA SECRETARIAT
FOR INFORMATION

DC-SA

0022

FORM 2496 PREVIOUS EDITIONS WILL BE USED

HEADQUARTERS, UNITED STATES FORCES, KOREA
APO SAN FRANCISCO 96301-0010

May 23, 1986

REPLY TO
ATTENTION OF:

Assistant Chief of Staff
Acquisition Management

Dr. Chulsu Kim
Assistant Minister
Ministry of Trade and Industry
No. 2 Unified Government Building
1 Chungangdong, Kwachun
Kyunggido 171-11, Korea

Dear Dr. Kim:

This is to keep you informed on events occurring on contract matters between United States Forces Korea (USFK) and the Korea Military Contractors Association (KMCA).

As you know the business relations between KMCA officials and this office have been very good; however, there are disturbing reports that members of the construction division of KMCA are being pressured into unethical practices of collusion in developing their proposals.

This portrays the unfortunate image that the leadership at KMCA is unable to control its members to prevent such practices. In discussion with officials in Washington, D.C., I have been advised to first bring this matter to the attention of the Ministry of Trade and Industry.

Further action within the Republic of Korea government will depend upon the corrective actions taken by KMCA. Since most of KMCA members derive their livelihood from USFK, and USFK depends upon their cooperative contracting support, it will be mutually beneficial for the Ministry of Trade and Industry to give early attention to the problem of collusive contract proposals.

My staff and I are at your disposal if we can assist.

Sincerely,

Wilfred J Curley

WILFRED J. CURLEY
Assistant Chief of Staff
Acquisition Management

Enclosures

Copy Furnished:

Mr. Un-Suh Park
Director General
Bureau of International Trade Promotion

0023

HEADQUARTERS, UNITED STATES FORCES, KOREA

APO SAN FRANCISCO 96301-0010

REPLY TO ATTENTION OF:

May 23, 1986

Assistant Chief of Staff
Acquisition Management

Mr. Kyung Ha Ro
Chairman
Korea Military Contractors Association
Seongji Building, Room 505
43-1, Dohwa 2-dong, Mapo-ku
Seoul, Korea

Dear Mr. Chairman:

The purpose of this letter is to provide you advanced written advice concerning actions being taken by United States Forces Korea (USFK) which will affect both members and nonmembers of the Korea Military Contractors Association (KMCA). Although many discussions, seminars, and briefings pertaining to competition in contracting have been held, I believe this written notice is necessary and appropriate.

As members of KMCA are well aware, the US Congress passed a new law in July 1984 which became effective for USFK in April 1985. During 1985 progressive steps were taken by USFK to convert all purchases and contracts to conform to the new US law, the Competition in Contracting Act of 1984. No matter what you may be told by other sources, this new law limits and restricts our authority to award US government contracts without competition, including awards to contractors in foreign countries.

Officials of the Republic of Korea government have advised USFK that it is the policy of your government to follow and promote competition. US government officials in Washington, D.C. and the Commander of United States Forces Korea have stated emphatically its not a question any longer whether we will compete or not - we will compete - it's the law. If USFK cannot get the supplies and services we need by competitive contracts, we will have to resort to other means of support such as purchasing from US and third-country companies that are willing to compete and using our own USFK personnel for services. If USFK cannot insure construction contracts are competitive, funds allocated to US armed forces in Korea for construction will be curtailed. We are advised this action will be taken no matter what you may hear about planned annual budget allocations.

0024

Enclosure I.

Some of the members of KMCA and nonmembers wanting to do business with USFK have fully cooperated with our USFK contracting offices and are complying with the new competition solicitation and proposal system. Those that have developed their own proposals, independent of other contractors, and winning contract awards, are improving their reputation as professional business firms with high standards of business ethics. However, we have been advised by US government officials that some members of KMCA, especially those involved with construction contracts, are being duped into colluding with each other. It is reported that some members are being coerced by individuals claiming to have influence and inside backing to beat the system and stating it's OK to collude. Members of KMCA who allow their firms to be taken in by persons wanting to collude show signs of weakness, unprofessional behavior, and lack of ethics required to do business with USFK.

All KMCA members should be aware participation in collusion in doing business with USFK will most certainly bring an action of official debarment for periods up to 3 years and longer if required. Information is continually being reported to USFK on such individuals. The fact that a firm may have been given an award erroneously does not mean later termination for default and debarment action will not occur.

There is a misconception that some USFK officials may be tolerant of unethical practices in Korea and that debarment action may not be taken. Your members must be made aware that is false. USFK now has a formal legal system to process reports on firms committing unethical violations and to prohibit those firms from doing contract business with US government contracting offices world-wide. It has taken a long time to develop this procedure in order to insure that all contractors will be treated fairly. In the future, debarment actions will be processed quickly without as much administrative delay.

I earnestly recommend the leadership of KMCA, in coordination with the Minister of Trade and Industry, consider taking firm action to remove KMCA membership entitlement from firms legally found to be guilty of unethical business practices with USFK. It is assumed that the office of the Minister of Trade and Industry will also cancel registration permits of such firms.

It may also be to our mutual benefit for KMCA to develop a new written code of ethnics so new and old members could be reminded of the high ethical standards of professional conduct and reputation required of KMCA members. Many associations have developed such a code with good results.

0025

Since the primary business of KMCA and livelihood of its members depends upon USFK, your understanding, cooperation, and leadership are solicited. If we can be of any assistance in this endeavor, please contact my office.

Sincerely,

WILFRED J. CURLEY
Assistant Chief of Staff
Acquisition Management

0026

FY85 CONTRACT SUPPORT TO USFK

	KCA		FED		KOAX		1ST SIG		DET 28		TOTALS	
$25K & Over	Number	Dollars	Number	Dollars	Number	Dollars	Number	Dollars	Number	Dollars	Number	Dollars
SUPPLY	31	1,996,624			1	56,846			17	15,800,000	49	17,853,470
SERVICE	65	10,732,366			7	4,971,720	13	43,094,000			85	58,798,086
CONSTRUCTION	169	36,793,880	112	153,319,387	8	5,509,005					289	195,622,272
A-E			465	20,923,692							465	20,923,692
NAF	3,123	7,652,183									3,123	7,652,183
GBL's	36,395	4,531,586									36,395	4,531,586
MODs & ORDERS	3,020	85,968,640	704	24,848,637	24	78,052			263	6,100,000	4,011	116,995,329
UTILITIES & SUBSISTENCE	143	36,520,560									143	36,520,560
LESS THAN $25K	47,208	24,444,184	616	490,451	186	667,694			46	200,000	48,056	25,802,329
TOTALS:	90,154	$208,640,023	1,897	$199,582,167	226	$11,283,317	13	$43,094,000	326	$22,100,000	92,616	$484,699,507
HEAD OF CONTRACTING ACTIVITY	COMMANDER, EUSA		CHIEF OF ENGINEERS		COMMANDER, AAFES-PACIFIC		COMMANDER, US ARMY INFORMATION SYSTEMS COMMAND (USAISC)		HEADQUARTERS AFLC (AFLC/PM) DIRECTOR OF CONTRACTING			

0027

Enclosure 2

공 란

기 안 용 지

분류기호 문서번호	미안 20294- 25941	(전화번호)	전결규정 조 항 전결사항
처리기간		장 관	
시행일자	1986. 7. 2.	(서명)	
보존연한			

보조기관	과 장	전 결	협조
기 안 책 임 자	황준국	안 보 과	

경 유 수 신 참 조	수신처 참조	발신	발송 1986.7.02 외무부	통제	검열 1986.7.02 통제관

제 목	주한미군 초청 계약자 명단 송부

SOFA 제15조 제4항 및 합동위원회 제9차 회의에서 합의된 절차에 따라 주한미군 당국이 통보하여온 86.5.31. 현재 주한미군 초청 계약자 명단을 별첨 송부하오니 협정및 관계 합의 사항이 철저히 이행되고 있는지 여부를 검토하여 주시기 바랍니다.

첨부 : 동 명단 각 1부. 끝.

수신처 : 상공부장관(5부), 재무부장관(1부)
법무부장관(1부), 교통부장관(1부)
국세청장 (1부), 관세청장(1부).

정서 / 관인 / 발송

0029

1205-25(2-1)A(갑)
1981. 12. 18승인

정직 질서 창조

190mm×268mm(인쇄용지 2급 60g/㎡)
가 33 - 41 1985. 2. 6.

대 한 민 국

상 공 부

통 정 28144 -1273 (503-9445) 1986. 8. 12.

수 신 수신처 참조

제 목 미군영내에 설치된 학교(대학등)에 한국인의 등록에 관한 문제

1. 학무 25210 - 561 ('86. 6. 22) 및 미안 20294 - 18682 ('86. 5. 13)의 관련입니다.

2. 당부에서는 미군영내에 설치된 학교(대학 등)에 한국인이 등록하고 있는 것은 SOFA 제 15조에 의거 SOFA지위 부여자의 자질향상을 위한 목적으로 초청계약자 지위로 미군영내에 설치된 학교의 설치 의도에 벗어나고 있어 관련부처의 의견을 받아 미군측에 그 운영에 있어 시정을 요구한 바 있읍니다. 이에 미군측은 별첨서한과 같이 회신하여 왔기에 이를 송부하니 귀부의 의견을 통보합니다.

첨 부 : 미군측 관련서한 사본 1부. = 끝 =

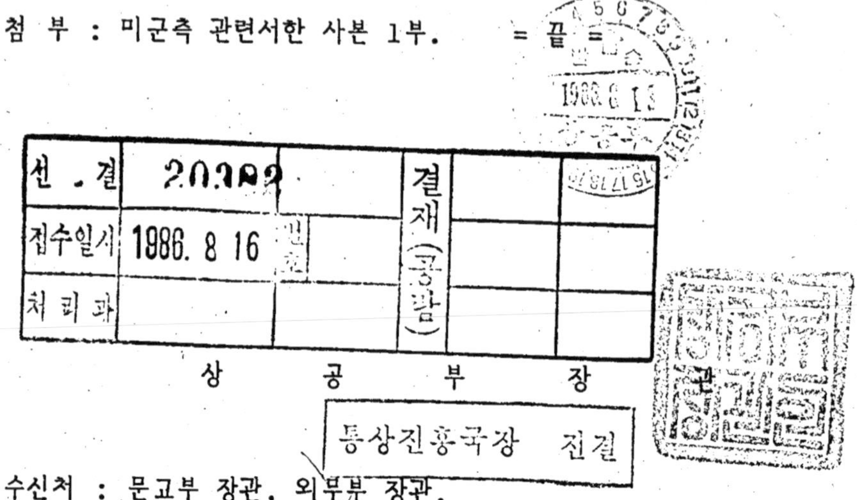

선 . 결	20382		결재(공람)		
접수일시	1986. 8 16				
처 리 과					

상 공 부 장 관

통상진흥국장 전결

수신처 : 문교부 장관, 외무부 장관.

0030

공 란

기 안 용 지

분류기호 문서번호	미안 20294- 553 (전화번호)	전결규정 조 항 전결사항
처리기간		장 관
시행일자	1986. 8. 18.	
보존연한		

보조기관			협조
국 장	전결		
심의관			
과 장			
기안책임자	한성환	안 보 과	

경 유		발신	통제
수 신	상공부 장관		
참 조	통상진흥국장		
제 목	미군영내에 설치된 학교에 한국인의 등록에 관한 문제		

통정 28144-1273과 관련입니다.

1. 대호 미국영내에 설치된 학교에의 한국인 등록 문제와 관련하여 한미 관계관간의 협의를 갖자는 미측의 제의를 받아드리는 것은 무방할 것으로 사료 됩니다.

2. 다만 미측과의 협의에 앞서 국방부등 관계 부처간의 충분한 사전협의를 가진후 의제별 아측입장을 결정하는 것이 필요한 것으로 사료됩니다. 끝.

정서 | 관인 | 발송

0032

1205-25(2-1)A(갑) 1981. 12. 18승인

정직 질서 창조

190mm×268mm(인쇄용지 2급 60g/㎡) 가 33-41 1985. 2. 6.

기 안 용 지

분류기호 문서번호	미안 20294- 037168 (전화: 720-2239)	시 행 상 특별취급	
보존기간	영구·준영구. 10. 5. 3. 1.	장 관	
수 신 처 보존기간			
시행일자	1986. 9. 22.		
보조기관 국 장	전 결	협조기관	문 서 통 제
심의관			
과 장			
기안책임자	손성환		발 송 인
경 유 수 신 참 조	상공부장관 통상진흥국장(SOFA 합동위 상무분과위원장)	발신명의	
제 목	주한 미군 초청계약자의 불법 활동 통보		

1. 법무부는 별첨과 같이 주한미군 초청계약자인 TV Guide Publications, LTD. 의 대표가 국내에서 SOFA 협정에 위배되는 영리활동을 하고 있음을 지적, 이를 시정토록 조치하여 줄것을 요청하여 왔는바, 당부는 SOFA 합동위원회를 통하여 미측에 이에대한 적절한 조사 및 시정을 요청하였읍니다.

2. 귀부에서도 상무 분과위원회에서 이의 시정을 미측에 요청하여 주시고 그 결과를 당부에 통보하여 주시기 바랍니다. 0033

1505-25(2-1) 일(1)갑
85. 9. 9. 승인

190㎜×268㎜ 인쇄용지 2급 60g/㎡
가 40-41·1985. 10. 29.

첨 부 : 1. 법무부 공문 사본 1부. 끝.

0034

법 무 부

체류 23630- 11041 (503-7102) 1986. 9.4

수신 외무부장관 (1년)

참조 안보과장

제목 주한미군 초청계약자 불법활동

아래 외국인은 주한미군 초청계약회사에 근무중인자로서 다음과 같이 입국목적에 위배된 활동을 한 사실이 있어 통보하오니 미군당국에 동인의 불법활동을 단속하여 주도록 요청하여 주시기 바랍니다.

가. 인적사항

국 적: 미 국

성 명: KADAGIAN, RAYMOND JOHN (남)

생년월일: '37.5.27

주 소: 서울 용산구 동부이촌동 30-116, 현대(아)23-403

소 속:

ID 카드번호: HT 99175

나. 불법활동내용

○ 동인은 초청계약업체인 TV GUIDE PUBLICATIONS LTD. 의 부 발행인으로서 83.12.16 부터 미군당국과 계약에 의해 KORUS (주한미군 및 군속등을 대상으로 배포되는 신문)를 발행, " PACIFIC STARS & STRIPES "에 납품하고 있는 자인바, 동인은 85년 5월부터 현재까지 TATTLER(사단법인 서울클럽 회보)를 매월 2,000여부씩 제작, 서울클럽에 납품하면서 그동안 제작비조로 매월 약 250만원씩 받아 왔으며,

○ 81.11.1 부터 현재까지 미군당국과 별도의 계약을 체결함이 없이 TV GUIDE (월간잡지)를 매월 75,000여부씩 발행하면서 거액의 광고수수료를 취하는 등 영리활동을 하였고,

0035

(ㅈ-1)

체류 23630- (503-7102) 1986. 9.4

o 84년 6월부터 현재까지 미국인 HENDERSON, NANCY E.를 동 회사에 불법고용하였음. 끝.

법 무 부 장 관

선 결	체류심사과장	결재	결		
접수일시	1986. 9 6	번호 22313	(공람)		
처 리 과					

(ㅈ-ㅈ)

0036

공 란

공　　란

공 란

공 란

공 란

공 란

공　　　란

CONTENTS

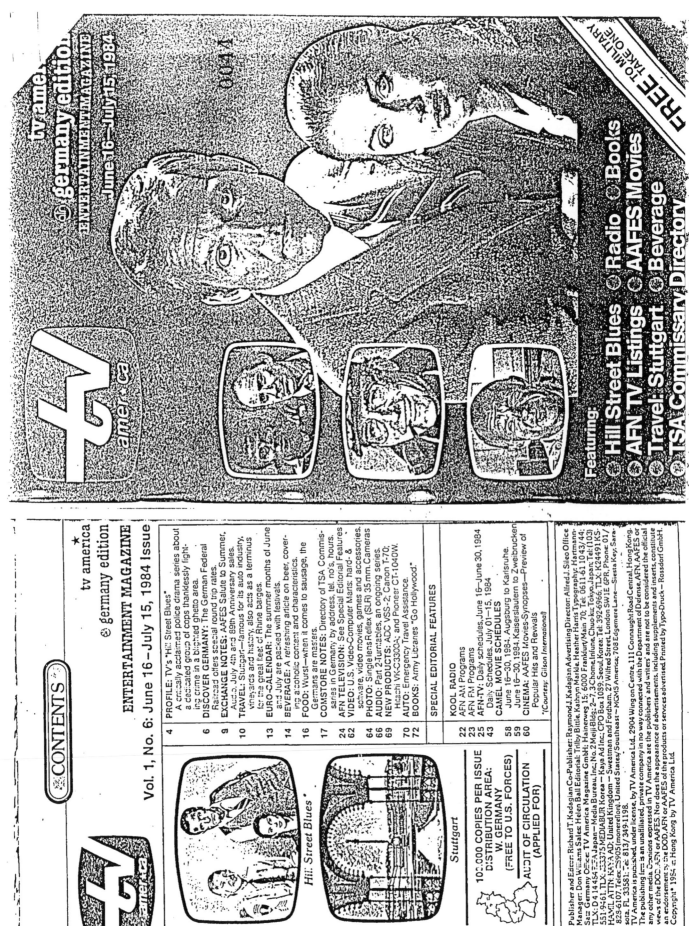

tv america ★
germany edition
ENTERTAINMENT MAGAZINE
Vol. 1, No. 6: June 16–July 15, 1984 Issue

Hill Street Blues*

Stuttgart

*(Courtesy: Gilson International)

100,000 COPIES PER ISSUE
DISTRIBUTION AREA:
W. GERMANY
(FREE TO U.S. FORCES)

AUDIT OF CIRCULATION
(APPLIED FOR)

Publisher and Editor: Richard T. Kadagian Co-Publisher: Raymond J. Kadagian Advertising Director: Alfred J. Sileo Office Manager: Don Williams Sales: Helen Ball Editorial: Trilby Bittle, Kathryn Markle, Heather Harris Typography: Hartmann-Satz Germany Office: TV America Magazine GmbH; Hainerweg 15; 6000 Frankfurt/Main 70; Tel: 0611-61 10 43/44; TLX: D 4 14 454 ... Japan—Media Bureau, Inc; No. 2 Meiji-Bldg; 2-7, 3 Chome, Infune, Chuo-ku; Tokyo, Japan; Tel: (103) 551-9461, TLX: ...375 MEDIABUR Korea—Kaya Ad Inc; CPO Box 1089; Seoul, Korea; Tel: 392-6966; TLX: K24491 KS-HAMIL ATTN: KAYA AD; United Kingdom—Sweatman and Fordham, 27 Wilfred Street, London SW1E 6PR, Phone: 01/828-6107, Telex: ...905 (monereflon). United States/Southeast—MGMS America; 708 Edgemere Lane—Siesta Key, Sarasota, FL 33581; Tel: 813/349-1198.
TV America is published, under license, by TV America Ltd., 2904 Wing on Centre, 111 Connaught Road Central, Hong Kong. The publishing firm is an unaffiliated, private company in no way connected with the Department of Defense, AFN, AAFES or any other media. Opinions expressed in TV America are the publishers' and writers' and are not to be considered the official views of the DOD, AFN or AAFES. Nor does the appearance of advertisements, including supplements and inserts, constitute an endorsement by the DOD, AFN or AAFES of the products or services advertised. Printed by Typo-Druck—Rossdorf GmbH.

"6"

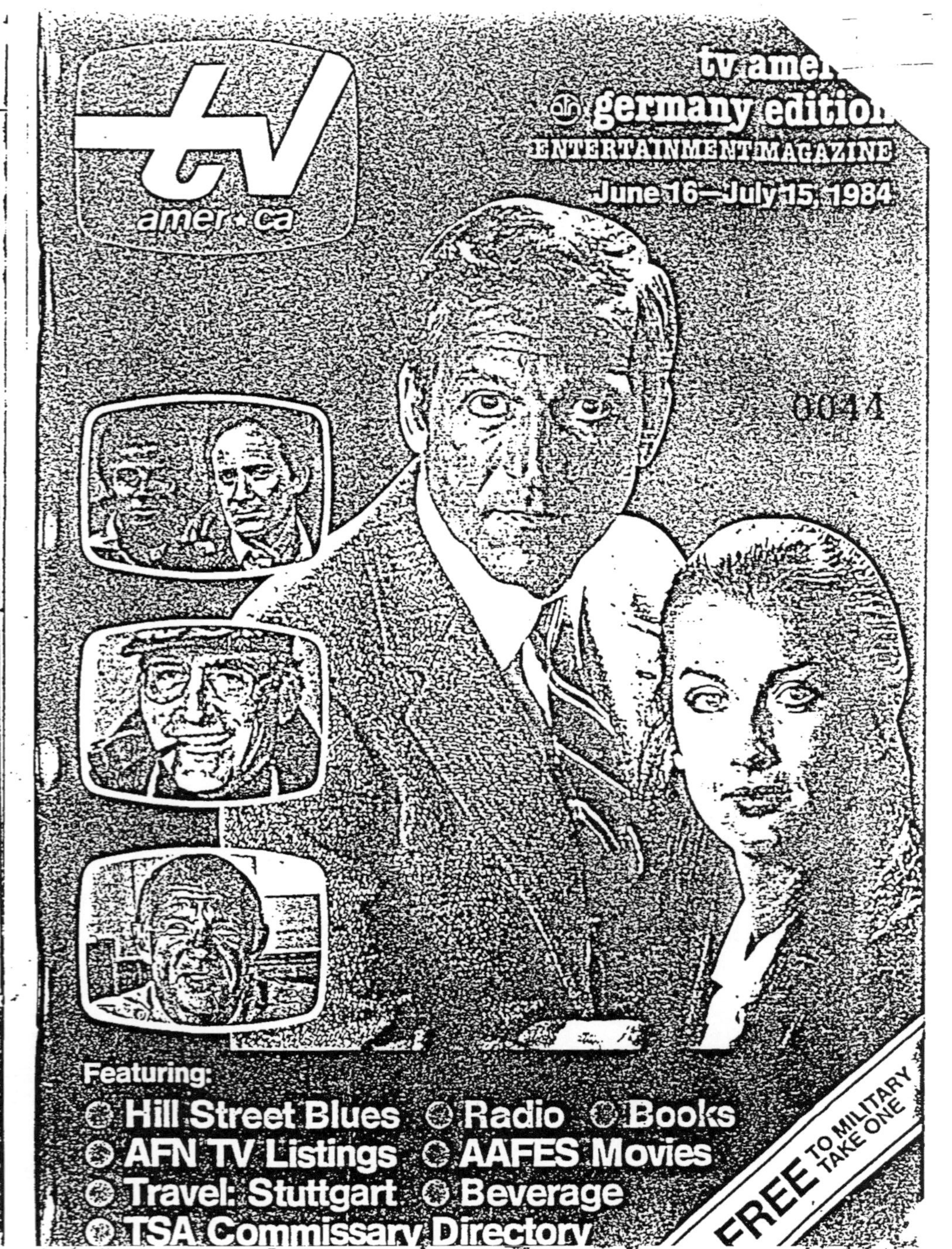

CONTENTS

tv guide★korea

FM afkn AM
korea★tv guide®
ENTERTAINMENT MAGAZINE
Vol. 6, No.10: October 1—31 1986 Issue

Donna Mills

Travel USA

40,000 COPIES MONTHLY
Distribution and
Audit of Circulation by
Pacific Stars and Stripes

KOREA/TV GUIDE IS A PRIVATE COMMERCIAL COMPANY UNAFFILATED WITH AFKN, KOAX OR DOD.

Publisher: Richard T. Kadagian Production Coordinator: Hwang Eun Sook Production Staff: Jang Seon Gwang, Baek Nam Joo KOREA LIAISON OFFICE: TV Guide Publications, Ltd. Yongsan P.O. Box 1 Seoul 140, Korea; TEL: 712-6976/9734 TLX: K25249 BHDEVC
ADVERTISING OFFICES:
•Korea—Kaya Ad Inc. CPO Box 1089, Seoul, Korea; TEL: 719-6906, 6907, 9813 FAX: (822) 719-9816 TLX: K32144 KAYAAD Seoul.
•Japan—Media Bureau, Inc. No. 2 Meiji-Bldg, 2-7, 3-Chome Irifune, Chuo-ku, Tokyo, Japan; TEL: (103) 551-9461, TLX: J33375 MEDIABUR.
•Hong Kong—Int'l Media Representatives, Ltd. 7th Fl., SPA Centre, 53-55 Lockhart Rd., Wanchai, Hong Kong TEL: 5-8611377 TLX: 84823 IMR HX
•United States—The N. DeFilippes Corp., 383 Fifth Avenue, 4th Fl., New York N.Y. 10016. TEL: (212) 684-7557, TLX: 236869 (DEFUR).
•Europe—Markad Communications Inc. Schweinfurter Weg 80, 6 Frankfurt/Main 70 W. Germany; TEL: 069-682060, TLX: 414484 (TVA-D).
Korea/TV GUIDE is published by TV Guide Publications, Ltd., 2904 Wing on Centre, 111 Connaught Road Central, Hong Kong. Opinions expressed in Korea/TV GUIDE are the publishers and writers and are not considered the official views of the DOD, AFKN or KOAX. Nor does the appearance of advertisements, including supplements and inserts, constitute an endorsement by the DOD, AFKN or KOAX of the products or services advertised. Printed by Samhwa Printing Co., Ltd. Seoul, Korea Copyright® 1986 in Hong Kong by TV Guide Publications Ltd. All rights reserved.

기 안 용 지

분류기호 문서번호	미안 20294- 40085 (전화: 720-2239)	시행상 특별취급	
보존기간	영구·준영구. 10. 5. 3. 1.	장 관	
수신처 보존기간			
시행일자	1986. 10. 15.		
보조기관	과 장 / 전 결	협조기관	문서통제 (검열 1986.10. 21 통제관)
기안책임자	손성환		발송인 (발송 1986.10.21 외무부)
경유 수신 참조	수신처 참조	발신명의	
제 목	주한미군 초청 계약자 명단 송부		

SOFA 제 15조 제 4항 및 합동위원회 제 9차 회의에서 합의된 절차에 따라 주한미군 당국이 통보하여온 86.6.31.현재 주한 미군 초청계약자 명단을 별첨 송부하오니 협정 및 관계 합의 사항이 철저히 이행되고 있는지 여부를 검토하여 주시기 바랍니다.

첨 부 : 동 명단 각 1부. 끝.

수신처 : 상공부장관 (2부), 재무부장관 (1부), 법무부장관 (1부), 교통부장관 (1부), 국세청장 (1부), 관세청장 (1부)

0046

1505-25(2-1) 일(1)갑
85. 9. 9. 승인

190㎜×268㎜ 인쇄용지 2급 60g/㎡
가 40-41·1985. 10. 29.

MINISTRY OF TRADE AND INDUSTRY
Kwachon, Kyongki-do 171-11
Republic of Korea

October 16, 1986

Wilfred J. Curley
United States Chairman
Commerce Subcommittee

Dear Mr. Curley:

Subject: Activities in Violation of SOFA Regulations concerning USFK Invited Contractors

This is to notify you that the following person is working in Korea under the Invited Contractor Status and has committed violations against SOFA agreement Article 15, Para 2, as below and we request you to take prompt action on this matter.

Nationality:	USA
Name:	Kadagian, Raymond John (M)
Date of Birth:	May 27, 1937
Address:	Ah 23-403 Hyundai Apt., 30-116, Dongbu-Ichondong, Yongsanku, Seoul, Korea
ID Card No:	HT99175

1. Mr. Kadagian is a co-publisher for TV Guide Publications, Ltd. which is an invited contractor. He has been publishing "Korus" (a newspaper for USFK personnel and civilians in the US compounds) and has supplied it to the Pacific Stars and Stripes since December 16, 1983.

2. Since May 1985, he has been printing 2,000 copies each month of the "TATTLER" (The Seoul Club Circulars) which were supplied the Seoul Club, for which he received around W2,500,000. each month as a printing fee.

3. Since November 1, 1981, he has been selling advertising in the TV Guide (a monthly Magazine), printing 75,000 copies each month without permission, which constitutes operating a business for profit.

4. He has employed Ms. Nancy E. Henderson, US Citizen, in violation of the regulation, since June 1985.

Sincerely yours,

Un-Suh Park
Republic of Korea Chairman
Commerce Subcommittee

"A"

Encl 1

0047

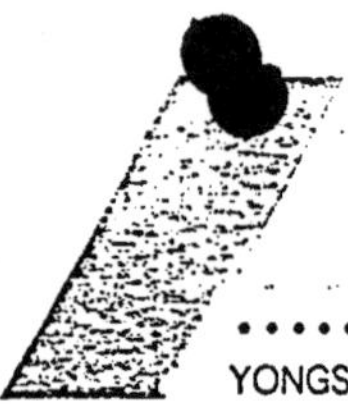

TV GUIDE PUBLICATIONS, LTD.

YONGSAN P.O. BOX 1 • SEOUL 140, KOREA

Mr. Patrick Cox
USAKCA
APO SF 96301

Sept. 22, 1986

Dear Mr. Cox:

Subject: SOFA Committe Inquiry.

RE: September 23, 1986 meeting held at KCA, 2:00 P.M. whereby following personel attended.

Mr. Patrick Cox
Mr. James Groner
Mr. Pak Chung Kil

1. TVGPLtd is not publishing "Seoul Club Monthly Tattler". Company is only doing production work and printing for 2,000 copies of this private clubs in house 24-32 page booklet.

2. I've informed Seoul Club of possible MCI violation publishing monthly magazine. Seoul Club has already been informed by MCI to submit registration paper work for publishing monthly booklet.

3. TVGPLtd receives monthly fee from SCMT to include V.A.T., in turn TVGPLtd remits VAT to Korean authorities on quarterly basis. Balance of income derived from SCMT is booked into TVGPLtd monthly income statement for year end Korean Income Tax preparation, tax's are paid accordingly before May of past tax year.

As mentioned in the meeting competition will probably write additional letters because of the newly published "Korea Traveler" (copy enclosed) which is not a TVGPLtd property.

Reference, R.J. Kadagian TVGPLtd involvement. Effective today, I am starting to withdraw my name from any of the TVGPLtd properties by hiring a Korean local agent. Estimate this procedure will take sixty to ninety days. This action should avoid future competitors letter writing to MCI.

Any other information required, please don't hesitate to call.

Yours truly,

Raymond J. Kadagian

Raymond J. Kadagian
Publisher/KORUS

encl.: Seoul Club Monthly Tattler
Korea Traveler

cc: RTK/fft
TVGPLtd/hong kong

0048

Encl 2

공 란

대 한 민 국

상 공 부

통 정 28144 - 1787 (503-9445) 1986. 11. 1.

수 신 수신처 참조

제 목 초청계약자 불법활동 통보에 대한 회신

1. 미안 20294 - 037168 (86. 9. 23)의 관련입니다.

2. 위 호로 통보된 주한미군의 초청계약자 (TV Guide Publications LTD.)의 SOFA협정에 위배되는 영리활동에 대해 SOFA협정에 위배되는 영리활동에 대해 SOFA상무분과위원회를 통해서 이의 시정을 요청한바, MR. Richard T. Kadagian (Publisher/TV Guide Publications, LTD.)는 별첨과 같이 SOFA위반사실을 부인하여 왔음을 통보합니다. (미측 SOFA상무분과위원장의 서한은 추후통보 예정임)

첨 부 : 관련서한 1부. 끝.

상 공 부 장 관

통상정책과장 전결

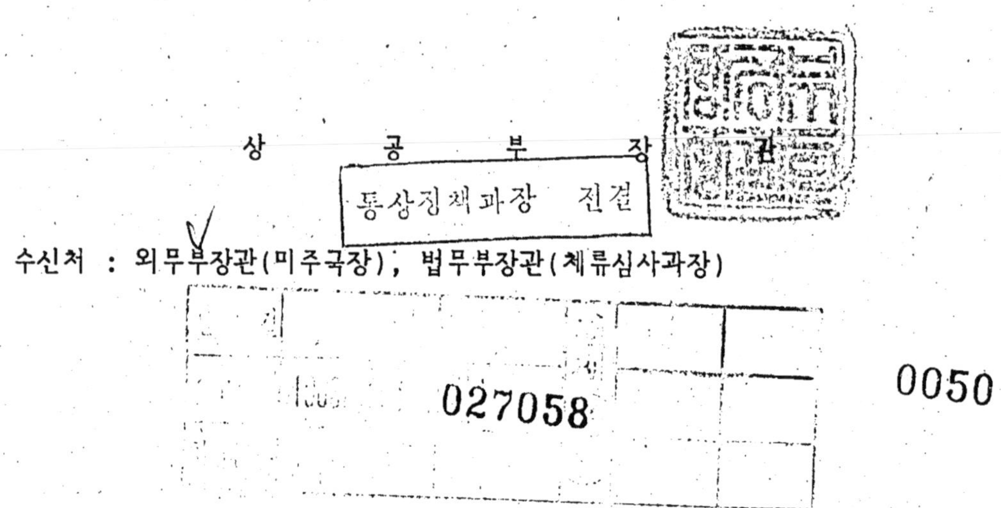

수신처 : 외무부장관(미주국장), 법무부장관(체류심사과장)

027058

0050

공 란

HEADQUARTERS, UNITED STATES FORCES, KOREA
APO SAN FRANCISCO 96301-0010

REPLY TO
ATTENTION OF:

ACJ

12 September 1986

SUBJECT: Invited Contractor Listing

U.S. SOFA Secretary
ATTN: DC-SA
APO SF 96301

1. Reference USFK Listing of Invited Contractors as of June 30, 1986.

2. Information contained in the above reference is still current and no changes have been occurred during the months of July and August; therefore, this office will not publish Invited Contractor Listings for the months of July and August 1986.

3. Request your office advise the Republic of Korea Government on this matter.

for
WILFRED J. CURLEY
Assistant Chief of Staff
Acquisition Management

0052

MINISTRY OF COMMERCE AND INDUSTRY
UNIFIED GOVERNMENT BUILDING · SEOUL

October 27, 1983

RECEIVED
31 OCT 1983

JAMES F. BEATTY
Colonel, USAF
United States Chairman
Commerce Subcommittee

Dear Mr. Chairman:

Subject: Designation of US Invited Contractor Under Article XV, Status of Forces Agreement

1. Reference:

a. Paragraph 2, Article XV, Status of Forces Agreement.

b. Company Name and Local Address:

TV Guide Publications, Ltd., 40-1 Sin Kye-Dong, Yongsan-Ku, Seoul, Korea

c. U.S. Commerce Subcommittee Memorandum of Consultation dated October 27, 1983 subject as above, pertaining to awarding a licensing agreement to publish KORUS, a magazine published in the interest of personnel within USFK. Negotiations are being conducted with TV Guide Publications, Ltd., a company incorporated in Hong Kong. The proposed licensing agreement will be USAKCA-84-C-01.

2. The US Memorandum, Reference 1(c) above, has been reviewed and the government of the Republic of Korea understands the KORUS is an American "Cultural-Style" magazine directed toward contemporary tastes and habits of US service members, and has no objection to the local advertising in this instance.

Hahn-Choon LEE
ROK Chairman
Commerce Subcommittee

Encl 3

0053

HEADQUARTERS, UNITED STATES FORCES, KOREA
APO SAN FRANCISCO 96301-0010

REPLY TO
ATTENTION OF:

PAJ-CI 21 October 1986

SUBJECT: SOFA Committee Inquiry

U.S. Secretary
SOFA Joint Committee
APO San Francisco 96301

1. We regret the delay in responding to your inquiry regarding Ray Kadagian's SOFA status as an invited contractor.

2. The KORUS magazine contract was awarded to Mr. Kadagian in November 1983 following proper solicitation and bidding through U.S. Army Korea Contracting Agency. We have asked their representative, Perry Hicks, to clarify the situation. His response and supporting documents are attached.

3. Mr. Kadagian assures us that he has established separate accounts for each company and is not comingling the personnel, as he was instucted in November 1983. His records have been scrutinized and approved by Korean government officials as recently as last month following similar accusations by one of his competitors.

4. We are confident this will satisfy the SOFA Committee that all is in order; however, we are also aware that Mr. Kadagian's competitors may continue to make allegations in their attempt to damage his business reputation.

Shirley R. Polomsky
SHIRLEY R. POLOMSKY
Lt Col, USAF
Acting Public Affairs Officer

3 Enclosures
1. Ltr, USAKCA, 24 Sep 86
2. Ltr, MCI 27, Oct 83
3. Ltr, TV Guide Pub., 22 Sep 86

0054

DEPARTMENT OF THE ARMY
UNITED STATES ARMY KOREA CONTRACTING AGENCY
APO SAN FRANCISCO 96301-0062

EAKC-CS

24 September 1986

SUBJECT: SOFA Committee Inquiry

Commander
United States Forces, Korea
ATTN: PAJ
APO 96301-0010

1. Reference letter from Joint Committee under the Republic of Korea and the United States Status of Forces Agreement dtd September 15 1986 (Encl 1), regarding SOFA violation by TV Guide Publications, Ltd. a meeting was convened around 1400, 22 Sep 86 and concluded as stated in TV Guide Publications, Ltd. letter dtd 22 Sep 86 (Encl 2).

2. For additional information, at the time of award of KORUS Magazine in Nov 83, it was known to all parties concerned that Ray Kadagian was affiliated with TV Guide Publications, Ltd. and SOFA Committee approved his Invited Contractor Status (Encl 3). It was emphasized to Mr. Kadagian that he should set up separate accounts for each company and also not to comingle the personnel.

3. At the meeting held on 22 Sep 86 Mr. Kadagian indicated that he is taking all necessary action to relinquish his involvement with TV Guide, which would automatically curtail his relationship with Seoul Club. This action will take approximately 60 to 90 days to complete legal action and transfer.

4. For any other inquiries or assistance on this matter, please call Mr. Groner or Mr. Cox at Yongsan 7017 or 6267.

FOR THE COMMANDER:

3 Encls

PERRY HICKS
Chief, ASD

0055

TV GUIDE PUBLICATIONS, LTD. 정책과 연

YONGSAN P.O. BOX 1 • SEOUL 140, KOREA

To: Mr. Wilfred J. Curley
U.S. Chairman/Commerce Committee
HQ., U.S. Forces Korea
APO San Francisco 96301-0010

Oct 24, 1986

To: Mr. Un-Suh Park
R.O.K. Chairman/Commerce Committee
Ministry of Trade & Industry
Kwachon, Kyongki-do 171-11
Korea

To: Lt. Col. Shirley R. Polomsky, USAF
Acting Public Affairs Officer
HQ., U.S. Forces Korea
APO San Francisco 96301-0010

Fm: Mr. Richard T. Kadagian
Publisher/TV Guide Publications, Ltd. (TVGP Ltd)
29th Floor, Wing On Central
Hong Kong

SUBJECT: Raymond J. Kadagian (RJK)
(Alleged violations to SOFA regulations)

RE: Mr. Un-Suh Park's letter of Oct. 16, 1986 (Exhibit "A")

I wish to comment on all four alleged violations as stated in Mr. Park's letter:

POINT 1: Mr. R. J. Kadagian is a co-director in TVGP Ltd.; his corporate title is co-publisher... a formal, honorary designation imposed by the corporation. As an extension of TVGP Ltd publishing activities, his name has appeared in our publications as co-publisher, whether or not he functioned as co-publisher. For example, Mr. RJK was routinely assigned the role of co-publisher of TV America magazine (see Exhibit "B"), a publication in W. Germany, despite the fact he never functioned in this (title) capacity.

Similarly, with TV Guide/Korea and TV Guide/Okinawa, Mr. RJK's name has appeared in the masthead as co-publisher. His name was listed in both books before the KORUS contract was awarded. And again, in a perfunctory manner-with negligence? On my part-his name continued to appear in both books after the KORUS contract was awarded.

Since this alleged violation has been brought to my attention, Mr. RJK's name/title has been removed from the masthead in addition to the cessation of activities associated with co-publishing.

0056

TV GUIDE PUBLICATIONS, LTD.

YONGSAN P.O. BOX 1 • SEOUL 140, KOREA

POINT 2: Regarding the "TATTLER," a private/member's only,in-house publication of the Seoul Club, please be advised that Mr. RJK neither performed nor acted in the capacity of publisher and/or co-publisher.

In fact, TVGP Ltd assumed this job as the production house for the Seoul Club, the de fecto publisher. In this capacity, TVGP Ltd provided publication services (typesetting/layouts) which included printing the finished product. As such, there has been no co-mingling of revenue, and local R.O.K. taxes have been paid.

I have asked the management of the Seoul Club to corroborate the above in writing. And all addressees, of this communique, should be receiving a copy.

POINT 3: With respect to the allegation that Mr. RJK has been selling advertising in TV Guide, please be advised that this assertion is incorrect.

Our advertising representative, in the Korea market is KAYA Ad. Inc. (See Exhibit "C"). As such Kaya solicits advertising for both TV Guide publications. Again, there is no co-mingling of funds and local taxes are duly paid.

POINT 4: TVGP Ltd. and not Mr. RJK, hired Mrs. Henderson as a part-time free lance writer for the TV Guide Publications. As such, Ms. Henderson neither worked for or on KORUS.

And since Ms. Henderson had no connection with KORUS, I don't understand how this situation constitutes a breach of (SOFA) contract?

In summation, I should like to say the following:

a. Mr. Raymond J. Kadagian has disassociated himself from those activities construed to be violations of SOFA regulations.

b. There are certain "competitive" firms/individuals who have attempted to discredit TVGP Ltd and Mr. RJK-in credibility and reputation-by circulating false, malicious and libelous accusations.

Our detractors hope that by undermining us, in a pernicious campaign to villify, that they'll be in a position to receive the KORUS contract. I trust all recipients of this letter will not be led astray by their duplicity.

Lastly, I should like to close on this note: For the past three years on KORUS we have rendered services and performed in good faith. If there have been violations, real or imaginary, I'm sure they could be resolved in an amicable manner.

Thank you,

Richard T. Kadagian

0057

공　　　　　란

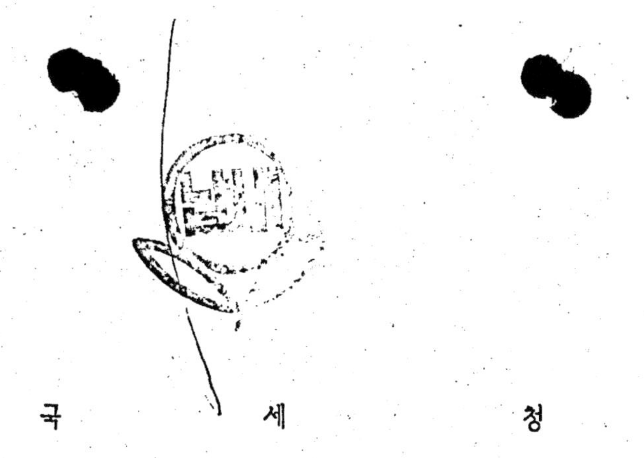

국 세 청

국이 22630-200 720-4793 86. 10. 28.

수신 외무부 장관

참조 미주 국장

제목 초청계약자의 소재지 확인

SOFA 협정 제15조 규정에 의한 초청계약자의 명단을 활용함에 있어 이들의 소재지가 필요하오니 85. 12. 31 이후 국내에 거주하는 초청계약자의 소재지를 통보해 주시기 바랍니다. 끝.

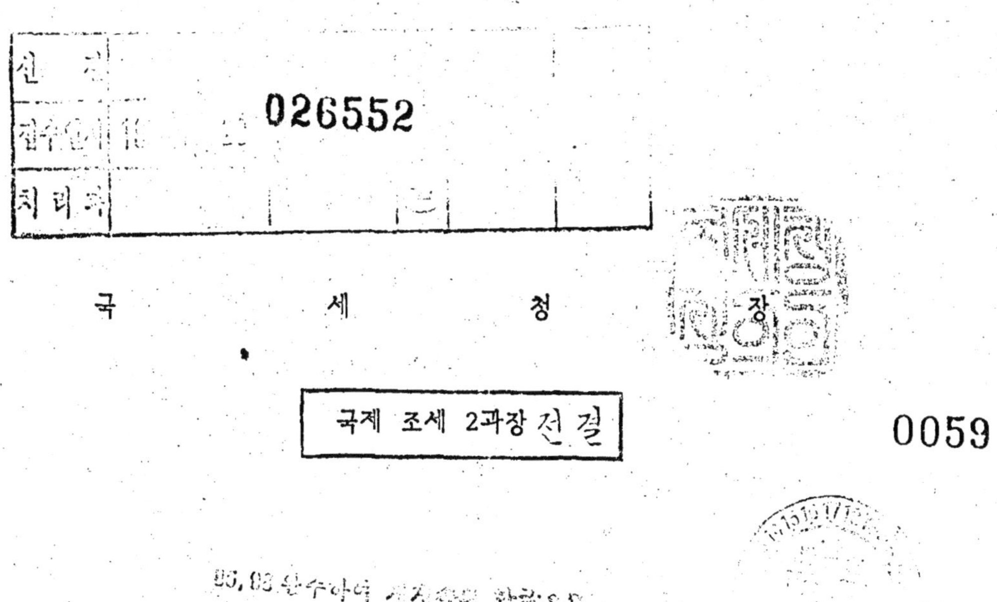

026552

국 세 청

국제 조세 2과장 전결

0059

공　　란

공　　　란

SEOUL CLUB

October 27, 1986

Mr. Un-Suh Park
R.O.K. Chairman/Commerce Committee
Ministry of Trade & Industry
Kwachon, Kyongki-do 171-11
Korea

SUBJECT: Raymond J. Kadagian (RJK)
(Alleged violations to SOFA regulations)

RE: Mr. Un-Suh Park's letter of Oct. 16, 1986
Point 2

The "TATTLER" is a monthly publication of the Seoul Club; this inhouse magazine is provided, free-of-charge, to members of the Seoul Club.

The Seoul Club is, and has been since inception, the sole publisher of the magazine. We creat and prepare all editorial and advertising material for each monthly issue.

TV Guide Publications, Ltd. acts as our production supplier providing typography, color separations, design and other elements necessary to produce the finished product which includes printing.

Our agreement is with TVGP Ltd., and not with Mr. Raymond J. Kadagian per se.

TVGP Ltd. invoices us; the Seoul Club pays TVGP Ltd. with VAT. To the best of my knowledge, TVGP Ltd. discharges its tax obligations.

I trust this clarifies the record.

Respectfully yours,

C. V. Crump

C. Vincent Crump, CCM
General Manager

0062

208, Jangchoong-dong 2-ka, Chung-ku, Seoul, Korea.
Telephone 253 7900, 253 0943. CPO Box 1589, Seoul. Cables SOCLUB SEOUL.

기 안 용 지

분류기호 문서번호	미안20294- 42669)	시 행 상 특별취급	
보존기간	영구·준영구. 10. 5. 3. 1.	장 관	
수 신 처 보존기간			
시행일자	1986.10.29.		

보조기관	과 장	전 결	협조기관		문서통제
기안책임자	손성환				발 송 인

경 유 수 신 참 조	수신처 참조	발신명의	
제 목	주한미군 초청계약자 명단 송부		

SOFA 제 15조 제 4항 및 합동위원회 제 9차 회의에서 합의된 절차에 따라 주한미군 당국이 통보하여온 86.9.31. 현재 주한미군 초청계약자 명단을 별첨 송부하오니 협정 및 관계 합의사항이 철저히 이행되고 있는지 여부를 검토하여 주시기 바랍니다.

첨 부 : 동 명단 각 1부. 끝.

수신처 : 상공부장관(3부), 재무부장관(1부), 법무부장관(1부), 고통부장관(1부), 국세청장(1부), 관세청장(1부)

0063

1505-25(2-1) 일(1)갑
85. 9. 9. 승인

190㎜×268㎜ 인쇄용지 2급 60g/㎡
가 40-41 · 1985. 10. 29.

대 한 민 국

상 공 부

통정 28144-1805 (503-9445) 1986. 11. 7.

수신 수신처참조

제목 초청계약자 불법활동 통보에 대한 회신

1. 미안 20294-03768('86.9.23) 및 통정 28144-1787 ('86.11.1)의 관련입니다.

2. Seoul Club General Manager C. Vincent Crump, CCM 으로부터 별첨과 같이 서한을 보내온바, 송부하니 업무에 참고하시기 바랍니다.

첨부 : 관련서한 1부. 끝.

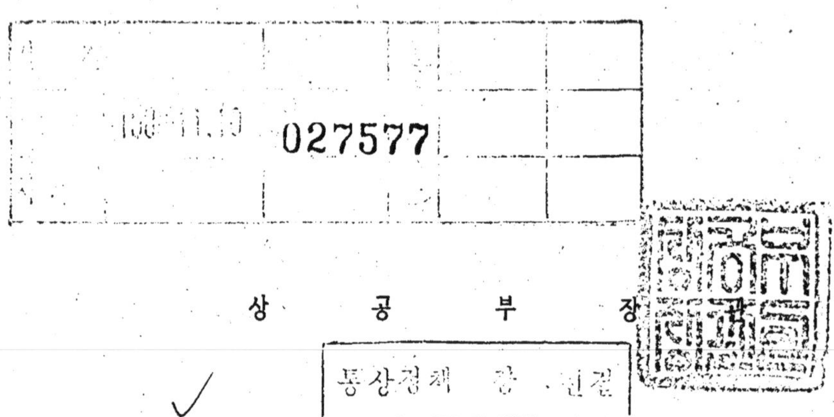
027577

상 공 부 장 관

통상정책 장 ...

수신처 : 외무부장관 (미주국장), 법무부장관 (체류심사과장)

0064

3/17

JOINT UNITED STATES MILITARY ASSISTANCE GROUP-KOREA
APO SAN FRANCISCO 96302-0187

REPLY TO ATTENTION OF:

MKOP-P 13 November 1986

SUBJECT: Request for SOFA Privileges

Ministry of Foreign Affairs
American Affairs Bureau
Security Division (Mr. HAN, Tae Kyu)
Seoul, Korea

1. Request approval be granted to the following personnel to allow them logistic support while residing in Korea. All sponsors are employed by United Technologies, Pratt and Whitney. This approval would improve efficiency and expedite accomplishment of their duties.

a. William S. Dees and Sylvia (Wife)

b. Francis G. Banks and Roberta (Wife)

c. Marvin G. Spallina and Francis (Wife)

d. Gary Nelson and Gloria (Wife)

e. Hal Hutchinson and Pauline (Wife)

2. Each is working with Samsung-United Aerospace (SUA) on a joint venture that was established under the laws of the Republic of Korea with the specific objective to provide F100 engine depot maintenance and item repair support for the U.S. Air Force and their foreign military sales customers in the Pacific area. As prime contractor to the U.S. Air Force, SUA shall be responsible for program coordination between the U.S. Air Force and their customers, administrating the contract and assuring it's successful performance within SUA and their subcontractors. In meeting this responsibility, SUA shall retain skilled U.S. nationals. These U.S. nationals shall provide technical assistance in the areas of management, contracting, pricing, cost accounting, logistics, maintenance and engineering.

3. Each person listed is working the Peace Bridge I program, Case KS-D-SFJ (Depot Overhaul Services). The contract is scheduled for a 28 month period.

0065

4. Support requested is as follows:

a. Commissary

b. Class VI

c. Post Exchange

d. SOFA driver's license

e. SOFA vehicle registration and license plates

f. Military Postal Service (APO)

g. Purchase of petroleum, oil and lubrication (PO2) on a reimbursable basis

h. Personal legal assistance

i. Pet and firearms registration and control

j. Use of credit unions and banking facilities

k. Medical and dental care on a reimbursable basis

l. Mortuary service, on a reimbursable basis

m. BOQ space, if available, on a reimbursable basis

n. Transient BOQ space, if available, on a reimburseable basis

o. Dependent schooling on a tuition reimbursable basis

p. Transportation, as available, on a reimbursable basis

q. Use of social facilities

5. Once decision is reached, please advise HQ JUSMAG-K/MKOP-P, APO San Francisco 96302. JUSMAG-K will be the sponsoring activity.

6. Thank you for your consideration of this matter.

FOR THE CHIEF:

Paul Marsh Jr.

PAUL MARSH JR.
Colonel, USAF
Chief of Staff

0066

공　　란

공 란

대 한 민 국

상 공 부

통 정 28144 1869 (503-9445) 1986. 11. 20.

수 신 수신처 참조

제 목 주한미군 초청계약자에 관한 자료통보절차 이행촉구

SOFA 제15조 제4항에 의거 초청계약자의 입국.출국.주소지 변경등의 자료를 1967. 6. 5개최된 제9차 합동회의에서 합의된 통보절차에 따라 이행하여줄 것을 별첨과 같이 요청하였음을 통보합니다.

첨 부 : 관련서한 1부. 끝.

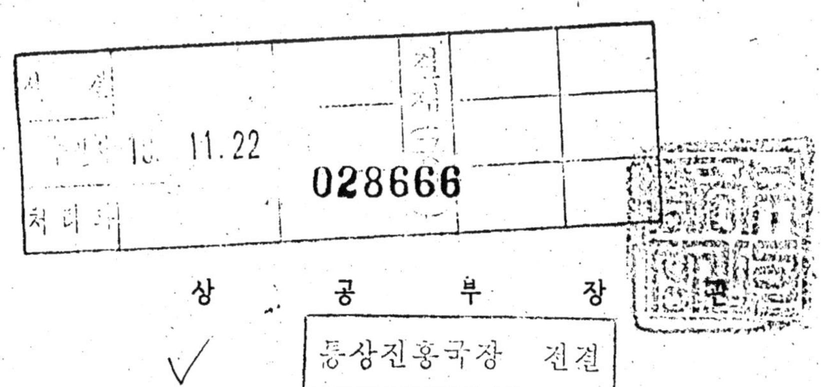

상 공 부 장 관

통상진흥국장 전결

수신처 : 외무부장관(미주국장), 법무부장관(체류심사과장), 국세청장(국세조세2과장)

0069

MINISTRY OF TRADE AND INDUSTRY

Kwachon, Kyongki-do 171-11

Republic of Korea

November 12, 1986

Wilfred J. Curley
United States Chairman
Commerce Subcommittee

Dear Mr. Curley:

Subject: Request for Updated Data on Invited Contractor Employees and Dependents

In accordance with the memorandum approved at the 9th joint meeting on June 5, 1967, I hereby request that you supply this office with relevant data regarding invited contractors and their employees.

As you know, all foreign residents in Korea are, in principle, required to register with the administrative authorities of the area in which they reside. Employees of invited contractors and their employees are exempted from this requirement and are instead covered under the provisions of Article 15, Paragraph 4, of SOFA Agreement.

We need to receive a monthly report containing the following information on invited contractor employees and their dependents status. This report should list the changes in status that have taken place during the current month, and it should be prepared and submitted to us at the end of each month:

1) the date of their arrival in Korea

2) the date of their departure from Korea

3) their local address, and any changes of address

4) information about people who plan to stay in Korea after their period of employment is over

In addition, a complete and updated list of all invited contractors and their dependents should be provided on a quarterly basis at the end of March, June, September, and December.

Failure to provide these data in the case of individual employees could prejudice the legal residency status of those employees in the Republic of Korea and possibly entail unnecessary delays and complications affecting both them and their employers.

In view of these considerations, I trust that we may count upon your full cooperation in this important matter.

Sincerely yours,

Un-Suh Park

0070

Un-Suh Park
Republic of Korea Chairman
Commerc[illegible]committee

0025

법 무 부

체류 23630- 5012 (503-7101) 1987.4.8

수신 수신처참조 (1년)

제목 주한미군 초청계약자 명단 통보에 관한 업무협조

SOFA 제15조 4항 및 합동위원회 제9차 회의에서 합의된 절차에 의하면 주한미군 초청계약자의 고용원 및 그 가족의 총명단을 매분기말 대한민국 당국에 통보토록 되어있으며, 신규입국자, 완전출국자 및 국내체류지 변경자 명단은 매월말 현재 미군당국이 작성, 대한민국 당국에 통보하도록 되어 있으나 그 이행이 잘되지 않고 있는바, 주한미군 당국에 이의 시정을 촉구하여 주시기 바랍니다. 끝.

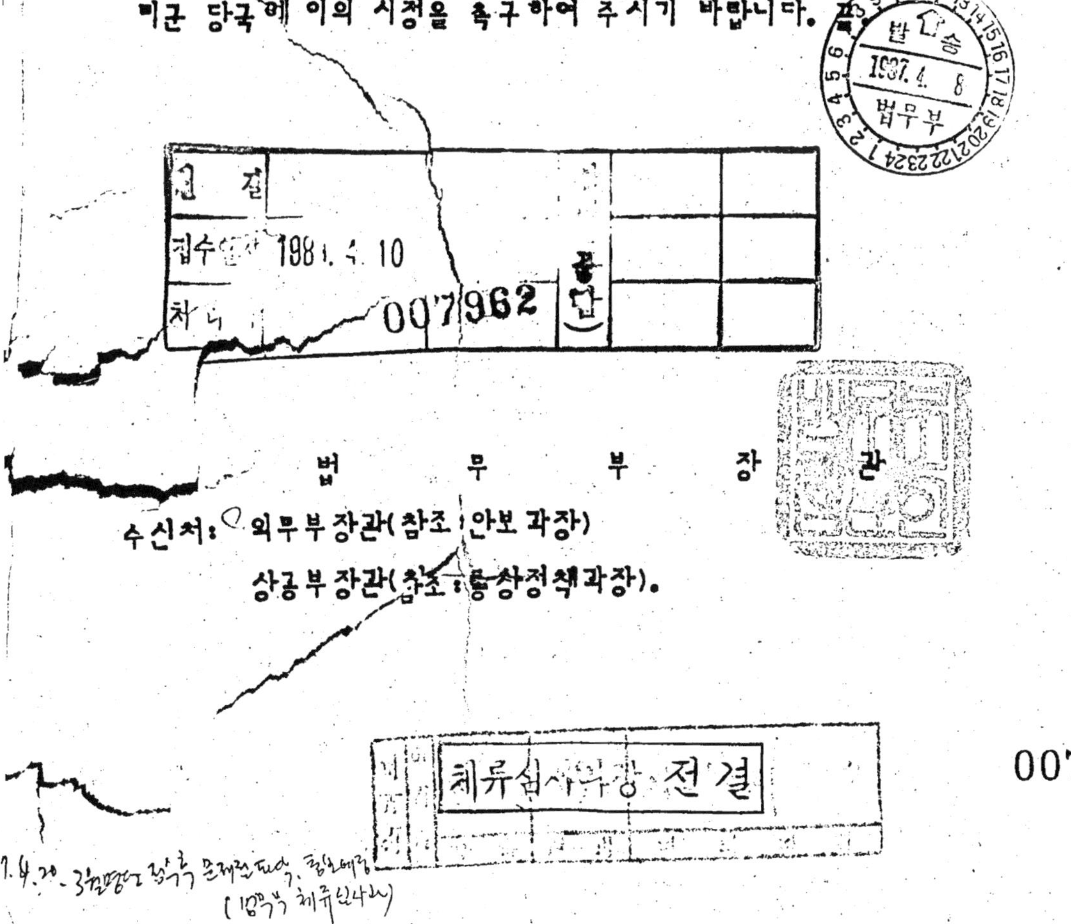
접수 1987.4.10
007962

법무부장관

수신처: 외무부장관(참조: 안보과장)
상공부장관(참조: 통상정책과장).

체류심사과장 전결

0071

법 무 부

체류 23630- (503-7101) 1987.4.9

수신 수신처참조 (경유)

제목 주한미군 초청계약자 명단 통보에 관한 업무협조

(SOFA) 제15조 4항 및 합동위원회 제9차 회의에서 합의된 절차에 의하면 주한미군 초청계약자의 고용원 및 그 가족의 총명단을 매월 1회 대한민국 당국에 통보토록 되어있으며, 신규입국자, 완전출국자 및 국내체류지 변경자 명단은 매월말 단위 미군당국이 작성, 대한민국 당국에 통보하도록 되어 있으나 그 이행이 잘되지 않고 있는바, 주한미군 당국에 이의 시정을 촉구하여 주시기 바랍니다. 끝.

법 무 부 장 관

접수	1987.4.10

수신처: 외무부장관(참조: 안보과장)
상공부장관(참조: 통상진흥과장).

안보과	과장	담당	처리지침

0071

0072

정 리 보 존 문 서 목 록

기록물종류	일반공문서철	등록번호	29302	등록일자	2008-08-18
분류번호	729.417	국가코드		보존기간	영구
명 칭	SOFA 한.미국 합동위원회 - 교통분과위원회, 1990-91				
생 산 과	안보정책과	생산년도	1990~1991	담당그룹	
내용목차					

0001

R

- 외무부 수신.

사람마다 인구조사 집집마다 주택조사

내 무 부

외사 02666-001688 (313-0848) 90. 10. 29.

치안본부 외사2과

수신 수신처 참조

제목 업무협조의뢰

주한 외국인 소유차량 운행에 따른 문제점을 별첨과 같이 통보하오니 업무에 참고하시고 불법 외국인차량 관리에 적극 협조하여 주시기 바랍니다.

첨부 : 주한 외국인 소유차량 운행에 따른 문제점 1부. 끝.

30402

내 무 부 장

외사관리관 전결

수신처 : 7120, 34.

0002

90. 10.

駐韓 外國人 所有車輛 運行에 따른 問題點

治 安 本 部

0003

目　　次

0004

駐韓 外國人 所有 車輛 運行에 따른 問題點

背 景

國內에 運行中인 外國人 所有車輛이 無登錄 및 不正 番號板 附着 不法 運行하고 外交官車, 美軍用車等이 交通法規를 違反하는 事例가 頻發하고 있어, 이에 對한 團束을 强化, 國法秩序 確立이 必要한 實情임.

現況 및 問題點

〈現 況〉 90. 8.30 現在

區 分	臺 數	登 錄 處	備 考
計	8,276		
外 交 官 車	876	外 務 部	
S O F A · 車	6,546	市.道知事	
페리號, 일시반입車	854	釜山市廳	

〈問題點〉

○ 駐韓 外交官 車輛의 交通法規 違反은 國際 慣例에 의하여 處罰하지 않는점을 惡用, 違反事例 頻發

0005

※ 駐韓 外交官, SOFA車輛의 交通法規 違反은 報告事項만 記錄, 關係機關 또는 所屬機關에 通報토록 되어있어 團束의 實效性이 없음.

○ 無登錄 또는 不正 番號板 附着車輛은 交通事故 調査中에 밝혀지는 경우 이외는 識別 困難하며, 즉시 照會 困難

<主要 違反 事例>

- SOFA 車輛을 內國人에게 賣渡한 경우, 登錄치 않고 內國人이 SOFA車輛 番號板를 그대로 附着, 運行하고 있으며

- 外國에서 購入한 車輛을 國內에 搬入한 경우, 登錄치 않고 外國 番號板 그대로 附着 運行하는 事例가 있으며,

- 特히 內國人인 경우에도 外國에서 사용하던 車輛을 이사짐 일부로 通關 搬入, 외국 番號板를 그대로 附着 運行하는 事例도 있음

○ 外國人들의 國內 交通法規 및 地理未熟等으로 인한 交通法規 違反 事例 頻發하고 있으나, 外國人 車輛에 對한 團束 實積은 全無한 實情임

※ 外國人 優待風潮 및 團束警察官의 外國語 구사能力 不足으로, 團束을 忌避하는 傾向이 있으며, 또한 團束이 外交上 問題로 飛火되는 것을 憂慮, 團束을 忌避하고 있는 實情임

○ 外交官等의 車輛 交通事故는 "領事關係에 관한 비엔나 協約(77.4.15)"에 依據 民事上. 刑事上 裁判 管轄圈이 없으므로 調査(任意)는 할수 있으나 刑事處罰은 不可

※ 民事上 辨償責任은 있으나 잘 履行되지 않고 있음.

○ 外交官 車輛等의 交通事故 發生時 韓國政府가 적당한 措置를 취하지 못하여 被害者들로부터 怨聲을 사고 있는 實情임

0006

對策

○ 持續的이고 段階的인 團束 强化로 法規 違反事例 根絶 (交通指導課)

- 段階別 團束 方向
  . 1 段階 : 弘報, 啓導
  . 2 段階 : 外國 公館 通報
  . 3 段階 : 言論 誘導
  . 4 段階 : 所管 部處別로 團束
- 外國人 住居. 職場 密集地域에 外國語에 能한 交通 團束要員 配置 活用
- 團束警察官에 對하여 持續的인 教育 實施

○ 效率的인 團束이 可能토록 根據 法規 一部 改正(交通團束 處理指針等) 토록 關係部處에 通報

- 內國人이 外國公館에 雇傭되었을 경우일지라도 內國人과 同等하게 取扱 (現在 外交官에 준해 處理하고 있음 : 交通團束 處理指針 第2章 2〈라〉)
- 모든 法規 違反 行爲에 對해 摘發 報告書를 發付하고, 法規 違反 事項을 所屬機關에 月 1回 일괄 通報

○ 外務部, 交通部等 所管 部處와 有機的인 協調體制 維持로 效率的인 團束 實施
- 登錄車輛인지 與否를 즉시 照會 可能토록 일괄 電算入力 方案 講究
- 所管 部處別로 不法車輛 團束 制度化

○ 交通事故 發生時 內國人이 適正한 報償을 받을수 있도록 保險要件 强化等 制度的 裝置를 마련토록 誘導

0007

1. 외국인 차량에 대한 각국의 단속 실태

<미 국>

0. 외교관(영사, 준외, 국제 기구 포함) 차량

- 모든 법규 위반 행위에 대해 적발 보고서를 발부하되 주차위반의 경우는 선처를 요망하는 공한이 있으면 불문에 처하고 기타 신호 위반 등 운행간 위반 행위에 대하여는 예외없이 벌금을 징수

- 교통소통에 지장을 초래하는 곳에 불법 주차한 외교관의 차량은 교통에 방해가 되지않는 곳까지 강제 견인

- 외교관의 음주운전을 적발하면 그자리에 정차시키고 가족이나 친지에게 연락하여 대리운전케 하거나 택시를 타고 귀가하거나 경찰서에 대기하였다가 술이 깬 뒤에 운전하는 방안 중 택일케 함

- 차량번호판에는 D-plate (외교관), C-plate (영사, 직원), S-plate (동 기관의 고용원) 등 3종이 있으며, 이중 S-plate 의 경우는 일반 미국인과 동등하게 취급함

0. 일반 외국인 차량

- 내국인의 법규 위반시와 동일한 요령으로 처리

0. 무등록 및 부정번호판 등 단속

- 무등록 차량을 발견하면 경찰서에 압류하고 적법한 등록 서류를 게시한후 찾아가도록 함

5

0008

- 미국은 등록 거래상을 통해서만 차량을 공급하고 있어 무등록 차량은 없으며, 폐차 기간 경과, 자동차세 미납 등의 경우는 벌금형에 처함

- 차량의 적법 등록 여부는 순찰차에 장착된 컴퓨터 터미널에 의한 조회, 교통법규 위반 및 사고 차량에 대한 등록증 제시요구 등을 통해 확인

- 교통법규 위반으로 여러번 스티커를 발부받고 벌금을 납부하지 않은 차량을 발견하면 바퀴에 족쇄(Denver Boot)를 채워 벌금납부를 강제함

<일 본>

0. 외교관 차량에 대해서는 "영사관계에 관한 비엔나협약"을 존중하는 뜻에서 예우, 통상 교통법규 위반시 단속하지 않고 있으며,

0. 불법 주차의 경우, 주차위반 스티카는 부착하되, 범칙금은 납부하지 않으며, 출두하지 않는것으로 양해하고 있음
   - 견인되었을 경우에는 견인비를 납부하여야 함

<영 국>

0. 스티카는 발부해도 범칙금은 납부안해도 됨

<싱가포르 및 동남아제국>

0. 위반사항은 정차시켜 주의만 줌

6

0003

2. 관 계 법 령

< 한 · 미 행정협정 >

제22조(형사재판권) 1. 본건의 규정에 따를 것을 조건으로,

(가) 합중국 군 당국은 합중국 군대의 구성원, 군속 및 그들의 가족에 대하여 합중국 법령이 부여한 모든 형사재판권 및 징계권을 대한민국 안에서 행사할 권리를 가진다.

(나) 대한민국 당국은 합중국 군대의 구성원, 군속 및 그들의 가족에 대하여 대한민국 영역안에서 범한 범죄로서 대한민국 법령에 의하여 처벌할 수 있는 범죄에 관하여 재판권을 가진다

3. 재판권을 행사할 권리가 경합하는 경우에는 다음의 규정이 적용된다

(가) 합중국 군 당국은 다음의 범죄에 관하여는 합중국 군대의 구성원이나 군속 및 그들의 가족에 대하여 재판권을 행사할 제1차적 권리를 가진다

(1) 오로지 합중국의 재산이나 안전에 대한 범죄 또는 오로지 합중국 군대의 타 구성원이나 군속 또는 그들의 가족의 신체나 재산에 대한 범죄,

(2) 공무집행중의 작위 또는 부작위에 의한 범죄

(나) 기타의 범죄에 관하여는 대한민국 당국이 재판권을 행사할 제1차적권리를 가진다

(다) 제1차적 권리를 가지는 국가가 재판권을 행사하지 아니하기로 결정한 때에는 가능한 한 신속히 타방 국가당국에 그 뜻을 통고하여야 한다. 제1차적 권리를 가지는 국가의 당국은 타방국가의 이러한 권리포기를 특히 중요하다고 인정하는 경우에

7

0010

있어서 그 타방국가의 당국으로 부터 그 권리포기의 요청이 있으면 그 요청에 대하여 호의적 고려를 하여야 한다

제24조(차량과 운전면허) 1. 대한민국은 합중국이나 그 하부 행정 기관이 합중국 군대의 구성원, 군속 및 그들의 가족에 대하여 발급한 운전허가증이나 운전면허증 또는 군의 운전허가증을 운전시험 또는 수수료를 과하지 아니하고 유효한 것으로 승인한다

2. 합중국 군대 및 군속의 공용차량은 명확한 번호표 또는 이를 용이하게 식별할 수 있는 개별적인 기호를 붙어야 한다

3. 대한민국 정부는 합중국 군대의 구성원, 군속 또는 그들의 가족의 사용차량을 면허하고 등록한다. 이러한 차량소유자의 성명 및 동 차량의 면허와 등록을 시행함에 있어서 대한민국 법령의 요구하는 기타 관계자료는 합중국 정부 직원이 합동 위원회를 통하여 대한민국 정부에 이를 제공한다.

< 영사관계에 관한 비엔나 협약 >

제 2 절 직업영사관원과 기타의 영사기관원에 관한 편의, 특권 및 면제

제40조(영사관원의 보호) 접수국은 상당한 경의로써 영사관원을 대우하여야 하며 또한 영사관원의 신체자유 또는 위엄에 대한 침해를 방지하기 위한 모든 적절한 조치를 취하여야 한다

제41조(영사관원의 신체의 불가침) 1. 영사관원은 중대한 범죄의 경우에 권한있는 사법당국에 의한 결정에 따르는 것을 제외하고 재판에 회부되기전에 체포되거나 또는 구속되지 아니한다

2. 본조1항에 명시된 경우를 제외하고 영사관원은 구금되지 아니하며 또는 그의 신체의 자유에 대한 기타 어떠한 형태의 제한도 받지 아니한다. 다만, 확정적 효력을 가진 사법상의 결정을 집행하는 경우는 제외된다

제43조(관할권으로 부터의 면제) 1. 영사관원과 사무직원은 영사직무의 수행중에 행한 행위에 대하여 접수국의 사법 또는 행정당국의 관할권에 복종할 의무를 지지 아니한다

2. 다만, 본조1항의 규정은 다음과 같은 민사소송에 관하여 적용되지 아니한다

(a)영사관원 또는 사무직원이 체결한 계약으로서 그가 파견국의 대리인으로서 명시적으로 또는 묵시적으로 체결하지아니한 계약으로부터 제기되는 민사소송

(b)접수국내의 차량, 선박 또는 항공기에 의한 사고로 부터 발생하는 손해에 대하여 제 3자가 제기하는 민사소송

<한·일간 운항하는 훼리편으로 일시 수출입하는 차량에 관한 통관요령>

제 1 장 총 칙

제1조(목적) 이 요령은 한·일간을 왕래하는 훼리편으로 우리나라에 일시 입국하는 자가 입국할때 훼리편으로 수송하여온 자가용 승용자동차와 훼리편으로 수출입 물품을 운송하기 위한 특수차량을 관세법 시행규칙 제23조, 제29조에 의거 일시 수출입하는데 따르는 통관절차 및 사후관리 등을 효율적으로 운영하기 위하여 필요한 사항을 규정함을 목적으로 한다

9

0012

제 2 장 일시수입차량

제6조(수입면허 조건) ①이 요령에 의하여 승용차를 일시 수입할 수 있는자는 다음에 해당하는 자에 한한다

1. 우리나라에 주거를 두지 아니한 자로서 일시 우리나라에 체류할 예정으로 입국하는자
2. 국제운전면허증 또는 우리나라의 권한있는 관서가 발행한 운전 면허증을 소지한 자
3. 한·일간 운항하는 훼리편에 의하여 승용차와 동시에 입국하는자

②이 요령에 의하여 일시 수입할 수 있는 승용차는 다음에 해당하는 것에 한한다.

1. 한·일간 운항하는 훼리편에 의하여 수송되어 온 승용차일 것
2. 이 요령에 의하여 일시 수입되었다가 수출된 승용차로서 당해 수출면허일로부터 1월이 경과한 승용 차일것
3. 우리나라에 승용차를 일시 수입하였다가 출국한 자가 출국일로 부터 1월이 경과한 승용차일 것

제12조(재수출 기간) ①일시 수입한 승용차는 수입면허일로 부터 30일내에 수입자가 출국하기 전에 재 수출하여야 하며 이를 양도 하거나 대여할 수 없다. 다만, 다음 각호의 1에 해당하는 경우에는 30일 범위안에서 그 기간 만료전에 세관장의승인을 받아 지정한 기간을 영장 할 수 있다.

1. 여행기간이 연장되었음이 사증에 의하여 확인될 때
2. 천재지변, 도난, 교통사고, 질병 등 불가항력에 의하여 재수출할 수 없을때

제14조(관계기관에 대한 통보) 일시 수입된 차량을 기간내에 재수출 하지 아니할 경우에는 세관장은 내무부장관 및 교통부장관에게 즉시 통보하여야 한다

제15조(위반 차량에 대한 조치) ①교통부장관은 기간내에 재수출되지 아니한 차량에 대하여는 운행을 정지한다.

②내무부장관은 재수출기간 경과한 차량을 발견한 때에는 즉시 관할 세관장에게 인계한다.

<교통단속 처리지침>

제 2 장 차량단속 요령

1. 일반 차량

2. 군용, 관용, 외교관용 차량

가. 한국 군용차량

위반사항을 발견시는 보고내용(위반일시, 장소, 차량번호, 소속 및 위반내용, 이하 보고사항이라 한다)을 별표 제2호 서식에 의거 경찰서장에게 보고하며, 경찰서장은 진기 서식에 의거 경찰국장에게 보고하고, 경찰국장은 보고된 사항을 취합하여 소속 부대장에게 통보한다

나. 미군용 차량

미군인이 미군용 또는 자가용 차량등을 운전할 경우에는 전항과 같이 한다

단, 한국 민간인 운전자의 법규위반은 일반운전자와 동일하게 조치하고 전항과 같이 보고 통보할 수 있다

11

0014

라. 외교관용 차량

(1)교통법규 위반

①주한 외교관(준외교, 영사, 국제기구 포함) 차량의
교통법규위반은 국제관례에 의하여 처벌하지 않고
다음과 같은 요령으로 처리한다

- 외교관 및 그 가족이 동승하고 운행하는 차량의 교통
법규위반은 보고사항만 기록하여 관계기관에 통보한다
- 외교관차량을 한국인 운전자가 단독 운행할때의 교통
법규위반은 소속기관에 고용되었을 경우에만 전항과
같이 처리한다

②SOFA 차량

- 미국인, 군속, 그 가족이 운행하는 차량의 교통법규
위반은 보고사항만 소속기관에 통보한다
- SOFA 차량을 한국인 운전자가 단독 운행할때의 교통
법규 위반은 일반운전자와 동일하게 처리한다
- 일반 외국인이 자가용 차량을 운행할때의 교통법규
위반도 위와같다. 다만 국제운전면허증을 소지하고
운행타가 교통법규 위반시는 출석 지시서를 발급하여
즉결재판에 회부한다

(2)행정사항

①외교관차량에 대하여는 국제예우에 어긋남이 없이 정중히
처리한다. (특히 외교관이 동승한 경우는 확인 즉시
발차 조치)

②위반차량을 정지시켜도 정차하지 않을때는 무리하게 정차시키지 말고 차량번호를 확인하여 보고내용을 기록하여 조치한다

③관계기관 통보는 서장이 경찰국장에게 보고하고, 경찰국장은 치안본부장에게 보고한다

(3)주한 외교관차량 등록

구 분	등 록 처	번 호 판
외 교 관 용	외 무 부	외교 - 다갈색지 백색문자
영 사 용	"	영사 - "
준외교관용	"	준외 - 백색지 다갈색문자
국제기구용	"	국제 - 청색지 백색문자
SOFA 차 량	시도지사	Ⓢ - 녹색지 백색문자

※ 외 교 : 대사관의 외교직 직원의 차량(대사, 공사, 참사 서기관)

준 외 : 대사관의 행정직, 기능직 직원의 차량

영 사 : 영사관 직원의 차량

국 제 : 국제연합 및 전문기구의 차량(외교관 대우)

(4)등록에 대한 법적근거

0. 외교관용

대한민국에 주재하는 외국공관 및 공관원의 차량에 관한 규칙(외무부 규칙) : 외교관 차량번호, 소속확인은 외무부 특진과

13

0016

(5)외교관등 차량의 교통사고는 "영사관계에 관한 비엔나협약 (77.4.15)"에 의거 민사상, 형사상 재판 관할권이 있으므로 조사(임의)는 할 수 있으나 형사처벌은 불가하다

마. 외국인(일반인) 운전 차량단속

자가용 번호판을 부착한 차량을 외국 국적의 일반인이 운전중 교통법규를 위반한 때는 한국인 운전자와 동일하게 조치한다

바. 법규위반, 사고야기 도주차량 단속

법규위반이나 사고야기를 하고 도주하는 차량은 소속 여하를 막론하고 이를 추격하여 검거하거나 수배하여 검거케 한다

사. 외국국적의 일반인 운전자에 대하여는 운전면허 행정처분 및 사법처분을 과하도록 하고 외국군인 차량은 미 헌병대에 연락하여 합동으로 조사 처리할 것이며 외교관용 차량은 보고 사항만 기록하여 보고한다.

분류기호 문서번호	특전20162-29	협조문용지 ( )	결재	담 당	과 장	의전관
시행일자	1991. 3. 25.					
수 신	미주국장	발 신	의 전 장		(서 명)	
제 목	국제여객 공항이용료 징수 협의					

교통부는 항공시설 관리 규칙 제12조 제4항 제5호의 규정을 별첨과 같이 개정할 예정임을 통보하면서, 동 규정의 개정으로 대한민국에 주둔하는 국제연합군 소속의 군인 및 군무원이 국제여객 공항 이용료 면제대상에서 제외될 경우 한미행정 협정등과 관련하여 문제점이 없는지 여부를 문의해온 바, 이에 대한 귀국의 의견을 당실로 조속 회시해 주시기 바랍니다.

첨 부 : 1. 관련 공한 1부.

2. 항공시설 관리규칙 개정안 1부. 끝.

0018

교 통 부

항정 33200-600 392-9505 1991.1.17.

수신 외무부장관

참조 미주국장

제목 국제여객공항이용료 징수 협의

1. 우리부에서는 항공법 제47조와 한국공항관리공단법 제18조의 규정 및 항공시설관리규칙 (교통부령)에 의거하여 국제공항을 이용하는 여객에 대하여 국제여객공항이용료 (1인당 6,000원)를 징수하고 있습니다.

2. 항공시설관리규칙 제12조 제4항 제5호의 규정을 별첨과 같이 개정하여 외교관 여권 소지자와 대한민국에 주둔하는 국제연합군 소속의 군인 및 군무원을 국제여객공항이용료 면제대상에서 제외할 경우 한미 행정협정등과 관련하여 문제점이 없는지 귀부의검토 의견을 회시하여 주시기 바랍니다.

첨부 항공시설관리규칙 개정안 1부 끝.

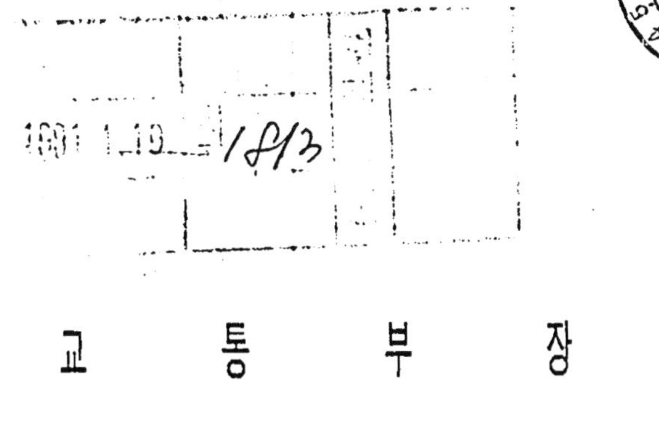

교 통 부 장

0019

항공시설관리규칙 개정안

현 행	개 정 안	사 유
제12조(착륙료등)		
①-③ (생략)	① - ③ (현행과 같음)	
④ 다음의 경우에는 착륙료, 항공보안시설이용료, 정류료, 격납고사용료, 조명료, 주차장 사용료, 국제여객공항이용료, 계류장 사용료와 환송대, 입장료를 면제할 수 있다	④ (현행과 같음)	
1 - 4 (생략)	1 - 4 (현행과 같음)	
5. 외교관여권소지자와 2세미만의 소아 또는 대한민국에 주둔하는 국제연합군 소속의 군인, 군무원과 우리나라를 통과하는 여객이 공항의 폐쇄 또는 기상관계로 인하여 항고기의 출발이 지연되거나 다른항공기와의 접속이 불가능하여 부득이 공항 보세구역을 벗어나는 여객에 대한 국제여객공항이용료	5. 2세미만의 소아 및 --	공항이용료 부과 형평 유지

0020

협조문용지

분류기호 문서번호	미안 01225-15	(전화 : 720-2324)	결재	담 당	과 장	심의관
시행일자	1991. 3 . 27.			김인철		
수 신	의전장	발 신	미 주 국 장 (서명)			
제 목	주한미군 공항이용료 징수					

대 : 의전 20162-29 (91.3.25)

1. 주한미군은 수송시설 및 기관을 포함한 아국 정부 또는 지방행정 기관이 소유, 관리, 규제하는 공공용역을 국내 어느 타 이용자에게 부여된 것보다 불리하지 아니한 우선권, 조건 및 사용료나 요금으로 사용할 권리가 있읍니다. (SOFA 第6조)

2. 따라서 국내에서 일반적으로 통용되는 공항 사용료를 주한미군에 부과하는 것은 법적으로 문제점이 없는 것으로 사료됩니다.

3. 다만, 현행 공공용역 요금 변경에 대해서는 관련 SOFA 분과위에서 사전에 협의되어야 하는바(동조 합의 의사록 제1), 교통부와 주한미군간의 사전 협의를 거친후 공항 이용료에 관한 국내법 개정을 검토하는 것이 바람직한 것으로 판단됩니다.

/ 계 속 /

0021

4. 아울러 주한 유엔군 및 주한 미군은 상이한 법인격인 바, 주한 유엔군의 공항 이용료 면제를 규정하는 현행법이 주한미군의 공항 이용료 면제근거가 될 수 없음을 참고하시기 바랍니다. 끝.

0022

공　　　란

공 란

공 란

공 란

공 란

공 란

공 란

REGULATIONS OF MANAGEMENT OF AVIATION FACILITIES

(Ministry of Transportation Order #335)

(18 July 1969)

(EXCERPTS)

(4) The following passengers may be exempted from payment of the airport service charge:

5. Persons who are in possession of diplomatic passport; infants who are under two years old; and the servicemembers and civilian components of the United Nations forces stationed in the Republic of Korea.

o With the current regulation USFK cannot be exempted.

o ~~it can be amended~~ as accorded ~~in the J/C~~. → it has been.

o also in that case (if we strictly follow the commitments of MOT) persons on leave and ordinary DOD personnel cannot be exempted because they are not included in the committed scope.

o this may raise interpretation of Article I, of which we cannot help but try to minimize the extent of SOFA status personnel

- review your E/D list. (6th and 14th J/C)
inv. Con. 7th 67 771-80.

o Article VIII doesnot provision for exempt it provisions visa exempt (registration)

- visa can be a identifying point.

X provisions exempt to vehicles.

VI will be applicated and then it can override the J/C commitment

So, 1. pursue amendment (1974 9 5765-6 3)

2. negotiate scope to be amended

3. follow the current practice (superlegal, benefit).

0030

ENCL 3

항공시설관리규칙 〔 1969. 7.18 교통부령제 335 호 한글화 〕

교통부령 제 352 호 1969. 9.15개정	교통부령 제 444 호 1973. 4.24개정
교통부령 제 470 호 1974. 1.21	교통부령 제 523 호 1976. 1.14
교통부령 제 547 호 1976.12.27	교통부령 제 578 호 1977. 8.12
교통부령 제 590 호 1978. 3. 6	교통부령 제 665 호 1980. 6.20
교통부령 제 703 호 1981. 4.30	교통부령 제 730 호 1982. 1.29
교통부령 제 748 호 1982.11.23	교통부령 제 761 호 1983. 4.29
교통부령 제 788 호 1984. 7.11	교통부령 제 846 호 1986.12.22
교통부령 제 873 호 1988. 1. 6	교통부령 제 883 호 1988. 5.18
	교통부령 제 920 호 1990. 2. 1

제 1 조(목적) 이 규칙은 항공시설의 관리와 규제를 행함으로써 항공시설을 능률적으로 운영하고 그 질서를 유지하기 위하여 필요한 사항을 정함을 목적으로 한다.

제 2 조(정의) 이 규칙에서 "항공시설"이라함은 교통부 및 국제공항관리공단법에 의한 국제공항관리공단(이하 "공단"이라 한다)이 관리 운영하는 비행장(국제공항을 포함한다. 이하 같다)의 여객청사, 화물청사, 활주로, 계류장, 주차장, 관제통신 및 항공보안시설과 그 부대시설 및 지원시설을 말한다.
〈개정 76.1.19 교통령 523, 전문개정 80.6.20 교통령 665〉

제 3 조(적용제외) 항공시설을 군용항공기가 이용하는 경우에는 제 4 조, 제 5 조, 제 7 조 내지 제 9 조, 제 12 조 내지 제 18 조, 제 23 조 내지 제 25 조, 제 27 조의 규정은 이를 적용하지 아니한다.

제 4 조(입장의 제한) ①비행장에 입장하고자 하는 자는 비행장 입구에서 입장표의 교부를 받아야 한다.
다만, 다음 각 호의 1에 해당하는 자는 예외로 한다〈개정84.7.11 교통령 788〉
1. 항공기 승무원 및 여객
2. 비행장 근무하는 자로서 비행장장(국제공항장을 포함한다. 이하같다)이 발행하는 입장증을 가진 자.
3. 비행장장이 특히 허가한 자.

1-3-1

〈추2〉

0031

④다음의 경우에는 착륙료, 항공보안시설이용료, 정류료, 고사용료, 조명료, 주차장사용료, 국제여객공항이용료, 계류장사용료와 환송대 입장료를 면제할 수 있다.

<개정 76.1.19 교통령 523, 76.12.27 교통령 547, 81.4.30 교통령 703>

1. 이륙후 1시간 이내에 부득이한 사유로 이륙한 비행장에 다시 발착하거나 부득이한 사유로 어느 비행장에 불시착하거나 불시착후 최초로 이륙하는 경우

2. 외교상의 목적 또는 공용에 사용되는 항공기와 시험비행 또는 교육법 제109 조의 규정에 의한 대학이나 이와 동등 이상의 교육기관에서 실시하는 조종훈련을 위한 항공기의 착륙 및 이륙의 경우<개정 84.7.11 교통령 788>

3. 행정상의 필요에 의하여 명하여진 착륙 및 이륙의 경우

4. 외교상의 목적으로 사용되는 자동차와 비행장내에 소재하는 행정기관 소속의 자동차의 주차장사용료 및 계류장사용료.

5. 외교관여권소지자와 2세미만의 소아 또는 대한민국에 주둔하는 국제연합군 소속의 군인, 군무원과 우리나라를 통과하는 여객이 공항의 폐쇄 또는 기상관계로 인하여 항공기의 출발이 지연되거나 다른 항공기와의 접속이 불가능하여 부득이 공항보세구역을 벗어나는 여객에 대한 국제여객공항이용료<개정 81.4.30 교통령 703>

6. 6세 미만에 대한 환송대 입장료

7. 항공시설의 건설, 개량, 보수 및 유지를 위하여 출입하는 차량 및 장비에 대한 주차장사용료 및 계류장 사용료<신설 81.4.30 교통령 703>.

⑤입장권의 개찰후 일기의 불순 기타 부득이한 사유로 항공기가 이륙 또는 착륙하지 못하여 결항된 경우에 있어서 입장료 환불 요건이 있을 때에는 당해 비행장장 또는 공단이사장은 결항을 확인한 후 입장료의 전액을 환불할 수 있다<개정 80.6.20 교통령 665>.

⑥국제여객공항이용료는 탑승절차를 취할 때에 당해 항공운송사업자를 거쳐 비행장장 또는 공단이사장에게 납부하여야 한다<개정 80.6.20 교통령 665>.

⑦특별대합실사용료는 당해 항공기가 결항한 때에는 이를 징수하지 아니한다<개정 80.6.20 교통령 665>

1-3-5 <주2>

0032

공 란

<table>
<tr><td colspan="6">정/리/보/존/문/서/목/록</td></tr>
<tr><td rowspan="2">기록물종류</td><td rowspan="2">문서-일반공문서철</td><td rowspan="2">등록번호</td><td>519</td><td rowspan="2">등록일자</td><td rowspan="2"></td></tr>
<tr><td>3121</td></tr>
<tr><td>분류번호</td><td>729.417</td><td>국가코드</td><td></td><td>주제</td><td></td></tr>
<tr><td>문서철명</td><td colspan="5">SOFA 한.미국 합동위원회 교통분과위원회, 1968-69</td></tr>
<tr><td>생산과</td><td>안보담당관실</td><td>생산년도</td><td>1968 - 1969</td><td>보존기간</td><td>영구</td></tr>
<tr><td>담당과(그룹)</td><td>미주</td><td>안보</td><td>서가번호</td><td colspan="2">--</td></tr>
<tr><td>참조분류</td><td colspan="5"></td></tr>
<tr><td>권차명</td><td colspan="5"></td></tr>
<tr><td>내용목차</td><td colspan="5"></td></tr>
</table>

<table>
<tr><td colspan="5">마/이/크/로/필/름/사/항</td></tr>
<tr><td>촬영연도</td><td>*롤 번호</td><td>화일 번호</td><td>후레임 번호</td><td>보관함 번호</td></tr>
<tr><td></td><td>Re-07-09</td><td>03</td><td>1-88</td><td></td></tr>
</table>

결 번

넘버링 오류

외 무 부

종 별

발신전보

번 호 : WJA-0963 일 시 : 071140

수 신 : 주일대사

발 신 : 장 관

1. 미일군대지위협정 (Status of Forces Agreement) 제10조 1항에 의하면 일본은 미국이 미국군대구성원, 군속또는 그들의 가족에게 발행한 운전면허, 또는 군대운전허가를 운전시험이나 수수료를 받지않고 유효한것으로 수락한다고 규정하고 있음.

2. 귀하는 이조항에 관련하여 아래사항을 조사하여 지급 보고바람.

가. 일본이 상기 미국의 운전면허 또는 군대운전허가를 수락하는 방법에 있어 미국의 원면허를 그대로 수락하는지 또는 일본어로 된 번역문을 첨부케 하는지 또는 유효한 미국의 면허를 일단 접수하고 새로운 일본면허를 발급하는지 여부.

나. 주일미군 당국은 군속 또는 그들의 가족이 개인사유차량을 군사시설 밖에서 운전하는 경우에도 운전면허를 발급하는 권한이 있는지 여부. (미이)

북미2	앙 고 재	담 당	과 장	국 장

3

발신시간 :

최종결재	
지 참 자	

접 수	담 당	주 무	과 장
7/12			

외 무 부

발신전보

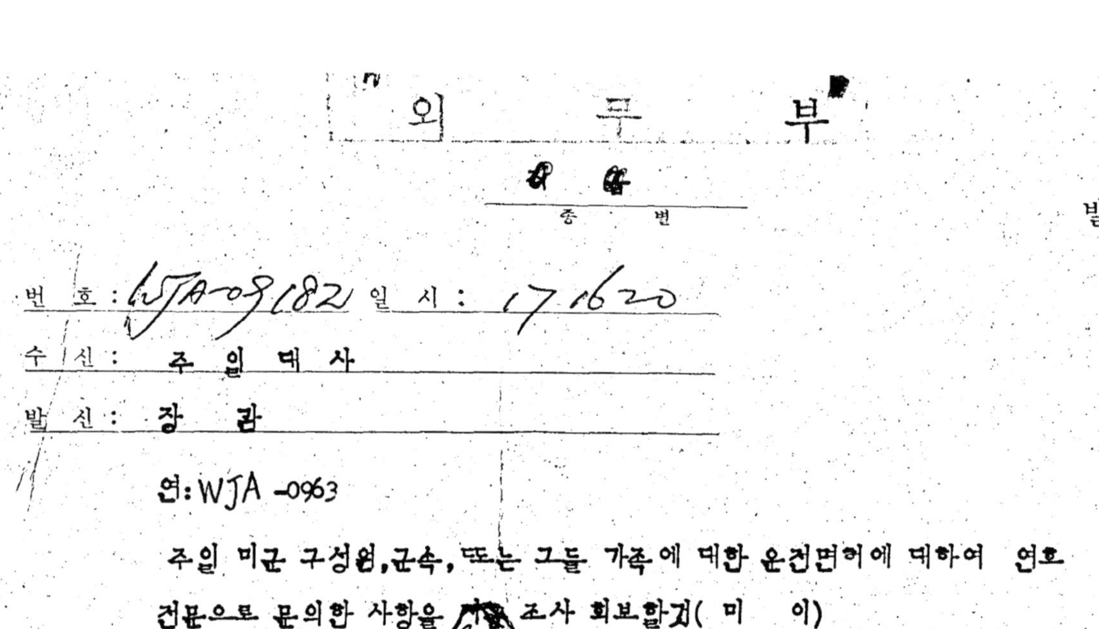

번 호 : WJA-09182 일 시 : 171620

수 신 : 주 일 대 사

발 신 : 장 관

연: WJA-0963

주일 미군 구성원, 군속, 또는 그들 가족에 대한 운전면허에 대하여 연호 전문으로 문의한 사항을 조속 조사 회보할것 (미 이)

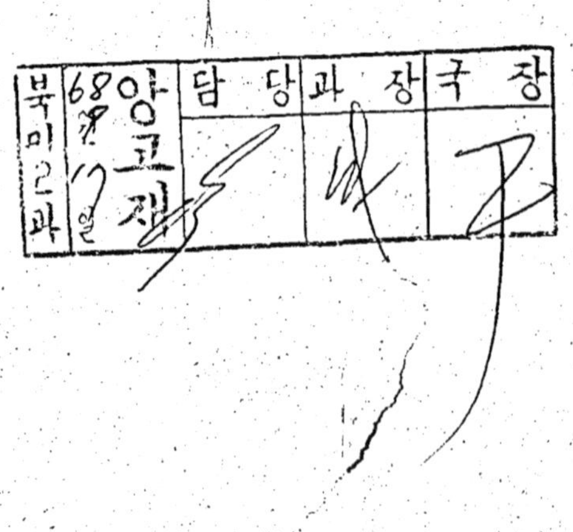

북미2과	68	양고제	담 당	과 장	국 장

발신시간:

최종결재	
지 참 자	

접 수	담 당	주 무	과 장

기 안 용 지

분류기호 문서번호	미이723-	(전화번호)	전결규정 조 항 국 장 전결사항
처리기한		기 안 자	결 재 자
시행일자		북미제2과 김순대	
보존년한		68. 10. 31.	
보조기관	북미2과장		
협 조			
경유 수신 참조	교통부 장관		
제 목	미군초청계약자의 사유차량의 면허및 등록		

1. 한.미군대지위협정에 의하여 설치된 합동위원회 예비실무자회의 제 2차회의(67.1.19개최)에서 교통분과위원회에 대하여 주한미군초청계약자의 사유차량의 면허및 등록에 관한 절차를 제정하도록하는 과제를 부여한바 있읍니다.

2. 그동안 합동위원회 한.미양측간사간의 이에 관한 많은 의견교환을 거쳐 별첨과같은 절차안을 작성하여 이것을 오는 11월 7일 합동위원회 제 32차회의에 제출코자 하오니 검토하시고 이에 대한 수락여부를 당부에 통보하여 주시기 바랍니다. 끝.

첨부 : 동 절차안 1부

공통서식 1-2-1 (갑) (18절지)

외 무 부

미이723- 1968. 10. 31.

수신 : 교통부 장관

제목 : 미군초청계약자의 사유차량의 면허및 등록

1. 한.미군대지위협정에 의하여 설치된 합동위원회 예비실무자회의 제 2차회의 (67. 1. 19)에서 교통분과위원회에 대하여 주한미군초청계약자의 사유차량의 면허및 등록에 관한 절차를 제정하도록하는 과제를 부여한바 있읍니다.

2. 그동안 합동위원회 한.미양측간의 이에 관한 많은의견교환을 거쳐 별첨과같은 절차안을 작성하여 이것을 오는 11월7일 합동위원회 제 32차회의에 제출코자 하오니 검토하시고 이에 대한 수락여부를 당부에 통보하여 주시기 바랍니다. 끝.

첨부 : 동 절차안 1부

외 무 부 장 관

6

증산 수출 건설

교 통 부

기술 1547.3-73(구내55) 1968, 11, 7

수신 외무부장관

제목 미군초청 계약자 사유자동차의 면허 및 등록

1. 미이723-28717(68, 10, 31)에 대한 회신 입니다.

2. 본건에 관하여는 미군초청 계약자의 사유차량의 면허 및 등록 제6항중 "차량등록에 필요한 수수료는 면허감찰과 봉인이 차량에 부착되었을 때 대한민국 당국에 납부 한다" 를" 차량의 등록에 필요한 수수료는 한국 법령에 따라 등록 신청시에 대한민국당국에 납부하여야 한다." 로 정정 할것을 조건으로 수락 합니다.

1968.11.7
39572
1968.11.7
교통부

교 통 부 장 관

세입살림 나라살림
저축으로 부강하

북미2과

내 무 부

교통 2039-625　　1969. 2. 5.

수신 외무부장관

참조 구미국장

제목 주한 미군 초청계약자의 운전면허 사무처리에 대한 질의

1. 68.11.7. 한미합동위원회 제32차 회의에서 한미합동위원회 교통분과 위원회 건의사항중 합의 채택된 내용중 아래사항에 관한 유권적인 해석을 하여 주시기 바랍니다.

2. 질의내용

주한 미 제8군 사령부에 예속되어 있는 초청계약자가 소지한 운전면허는 그 대부분이 입국당시에 소지하였든 운전면허로서 장기체한으로 안하여 그유효기간이 경과 되어 미제 8군 사령부에서 발급한 운전면허를 소지하고 있는바 이들에게 미제8군 사령부에서 발급한 운전면허가 양국 합의된 내용중 "본국정부의 관계당국이나 정부의 정치적 기관이 발급한 유효운전면허"로서의 효력을 인정할수 있는지의 여부. 끝

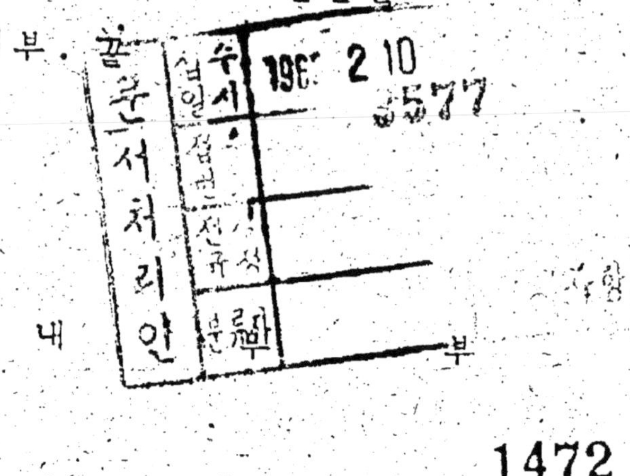

내 무 부 장 관

1472

1244 237

기 안 용 지

분류기호 문서번호	미이723-	(전화번호)	전결규정 조 항 국 장 전결사항
처리기한		기 안 자	결 재 자
시행일자		북미2과 오 명 두 69. 2. 11.	
보존년한			
보조기관	북미2과장		
협 조			
경유 수신 참조	내무부장관	통제	발송
제 목	주한미군 초청계약자의 운전면허사무처리에 대한 질의응신		

1. 귀 교통 2039 - 625(69.2.5)에 대한 응신입니다.

2. 주한미군 사령관이 비군인에 대하여 신규로 비군용 차량 운전 면허를 발급하는 권한 유무에 관하여는 상금 한.미간에 이견이 있어 합의된 해석이 존재하지 않습니다.

3. 그러나 장기 체류자에 관하여는 면허증의 갱신이 사실상 불가능하며, 본시 면허증의정기 갱신제도가 면허 취소 사유 유무를 확인하는데 목적이 있고 또 일단 취득한 운전 기술은 소실되는 성질의것이 아니므로 주한 미군사령관이 기한이 경과한 면허증을 근거로 약식 면허증을 발급하는것은 이를 인정하여도 무방할것으로 사료됩니다.

공통서식 1-2-1 (갑)
(1967. 4. 4. 승인)

(18절지) (2급인쇄용지74g/m²)
(조달청)(300,000매 인쇄)

/ 계속 /

특히 본건에 있어서는 한국 면허증을 취득할때까지의 1개월간의 경과조치이고, ~~한국 내에서 면허 취소 사유가 발생한 경우에는 면허증 발급을 거부하므로서~~ 또한 필요에 따라 통제가 가능하므로 현실적으로 아무런 무리가 없을것이므로, 귀 질의의 경우, 한.미간에 합의된 "유효한 운전 면허"로 간주하여 무방할것으로 사료됩니다.

끝.

10

외 무 부

미이723- 1969. 2. 11.

수신 : 내무부장관

제목 : 주한미군 초청계약자의 운전 면허 사무처리에 대한 질의 응신

1. 귀 그룡 2039 - 625 (69.2.5) 에 대한 응신입니다.

2. 주한미군 사령관이 비군인에 대하여 신규로 비군용 차량 운전 면허를 발급하는 권한 유무에 관하여는 상금 한.미 간에 이견이 있어, 합의된 해석이 존재하지 않습니다.

3. 그러나 장기 체류자에 관하여는 면허증의 갱신이 사실상 불가능하며, 본시 면허증의 정기 갱신제도가 면허 취소 사유 유무를 확인하는데 목적이 있고 또 일단 취득한 운전 기술은 소실되는 성질의 것이 아니므로 주한 미군 사령관이 기한이 경과한 면허증을 근거로 약식 면허증을 발급하는것은 이를 인정 하여도 무방할것으로 사료됩니다.

특히 본건에 있어서는 한국 면허증을 취득할때까지의 1개월 간의 경과조치이고, 또한 필요에 따라 통제가 가능하므로

11

현실적으로 아무런 무리가 없을것이므로, 귀 질의의 경우, 한.미간에 합의된 "유효한 운전 면허"로 간주하여 무방할 것으로 사료됩니다. 끝.

외 무 부 장 관

12

협 조 전

응신기일

분류기호 미이 - 79　　제목 국무회의보고 안건과 대한 의견

수신 법무관　　발신일자 1969. 2. 12. (협조제의)

(발신명의) 북미2과장

(제1의견)

교통부 장관이 제출하는 " 주한 외국인 차량 매매 알선 업소 지정에 관한 보고 " 에 대하여 별지와 같은 당과 의견을 송부하오니 참조 하시기 바랍니다.

첨부 : 의견서 1통. 끝.

(제2의견)

공통서식 1—23
(1967.4.4.승인)

(18절 지)(신문용지)
(조달청)(150,000매 인쇄)

13

주한외국인 차량 매매 알선 업소 지정에 관한보고

(국무회의 보고사항, 교통부장관 제출)에 대한 의견

(북미 2과)

군인, 군속, 초청계약자및 그가족 사유차량 관계

1. 참고 사항

가. 군인, 군속및 그가족, 초청계약자및 그 가족의 사유차량은 한.미군대지위협정 제 9조 3항 및 제 15조 3항 규정에 의하여 면세 도입된것임.

나. 동 제 15조 6항은 면세 도입한 물자는 상호 합의된 조건에 의하여 한.미양 당국이 승인하는 경우를 제외하고는 면세 수입 특권을 향유하지 않는자에 처분할수 없다고 규정하고 있으며, 동 규정에 의거하여 한.미합동위원회는 67. 6. 22. 개최된 제10차 회의에서 처분 절차를 제정한바 있음.

다. 군대지위협정상으로는 자동차도 한.미양당국의 승인이 있는경우 국내 처분이 불가능 한것은 아니다. 이들 차량의 통관면장에는 국내 처분 불허의 취지를 명시하고 있으며, 또 자동차 공업보호법의 취지와 공업및 상역정책상의 문제로 종전 국내 처분을 일체 불허

14

923.9-13

한다는 일반 방침을 견지하여 왔음.

2. 문제점

가. 동 보고 문건은 미 군인, 군속, 초청계약자및 그들의 가족이 사유하는차량의 국내 처분이 가능한듯한 인상을 주고 있는바, 전기 현 방침이 지적되어야 할 것이며, 동 방침의 변경이 필요한 경우에는 별도로 정책수정 여부의 기본적 검토가 별도로 이루어져야 할것임.

나. 본안은 외국인 차량 인수기관을 지정한다는 취지인바, 지적될 장점이 있는 반면, 사유재산의 자유처분권을 제한하는 결과를 초택하고, 또 특정 중간 이득기관을 지정하므로 인한 폐단으로 대외적인 인상이 좋지 못할 가능성이 있다는 점이 고려되여야 할 것임.

15

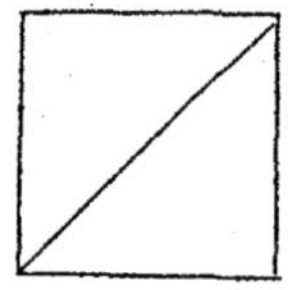

의안번호	제 호
접 수 년 월 일	1969. . . (제 회)

보고사항

주한외국인차량매매알선업소지정에관한보고

제 출 자	국무위원 강 서 룡 (교통부장관)
제출년월일	1969. 2. .

16

1. 보고주문

주한외국인차량이 부당한 가격으로 매매됨을 억제하고 위법적으로 양도되어 등록문제로 사회적 물의를 일으키는 일이 없도록 공신력있는 외국인차량매매알선업소를 주요도시에 지정하여 매매후의 하자담보책임을 지움으로써 선의의 매수자를 보호하고 아울러 부당한 외화유출과 세금포탈을 방지하여 국고수입을 증대케 한다.

2. 보고이유

가. 한미협정에 의하여 주한외국인의 사유차량을 우리나라 법령에 따라 등록하게 됨을 계기로 외국인 차량이 부당한 가격으로 매매됨을 억제하고

나. 위법적으로 양도되어 등록에 따른 절차문제로 물의를 일으켜 한미간의 친선과 국제적인 체면을 손상케 하는 예가 없도록 하고,

-시-

117

다. 공신력있는 업소로 하여금 자동차매매에 따른 하자담보책임제도를 확립함으로써 불법거래로 야기되는 선의의 매수자들에 대한 피해를 막고,

라. 부당한 거래로 인한 외화유출을 방지하고 세원을 포착하여 국고수입을 증대케 한다.

3. 주요골자

가. 전국주요도시 (서울, 인천, 대구, 부산)에 주한외국인자동차매매알선업소를 교통부장관이 지정한다.

나. 알선의 대상차량은 주한외국인이 소유하고있는 자동차 (외교관및 준외교관차량포함)로서 내국인에게 양도허용된 차량을 대상으로 한다.

다. 알선업소의 업무는 자동차매매에 따른 하자담보책임을 지는 동시에 자동차등록에 관련된 절차이행을 위한 업무를 대행할수 있다

130

라. 주한외국인자동차를 내국인 명의로 등록코자할 경우에는 알선업소의 하자담보책임증명서를 첨부하여야 한다

만일 이를 첨부하지못할 경우에는 재산총액 2천만원이상 소유자의 연대보증서를 첨부하여야 한다. 瑕疵擔保責任證明書

4. 참고사항

가. 주한외국인차량매매알선업소의 지정문제는 금년도의 당부 주요사업계획으로 채택하여 대통령각하 연두순시시에 보고드린 사항임

나. 알선업소의 주요업무내용 (별첨)

다. 외국인 소유차량 현황 (별첨)

19

알선업소의 주요업무내용

1. 주한외국인차량의 내국인에 대한 매매알선

가. 매매차량 전시

나. 매매업무에 관한 편의제공

다. 정당한 가격조성

2. 차량등록, 검사, 통관업무대행 (위임장에 의하여)

3. 매매후의 하자보증

4. 차량의 보관관리

외국인 소유 차량 현황

구 분	차량대수	비 고
외교및 준외교관차	1,200	
군인 군속 가족차	2,000	
초청 계약 자차	500	
일반 외국인차	1,200	면세수입 200대 과세 " 1,000대
계	4,900	

21

교 통 부

기술 1547.3-544 (구내55) 1969.3.17

수신 수신처참조

제목 군납용 택시 운행의 합리화에 관한 통보

서울특별시 종로구 안국동 163 국제관광공사(용재 김일환) 및 서울특별시 중구충무로4가 152의 1 해강산업주식회사(대표 임병주) 소속 군납용택시에 관하여 별첨과 같이 조치 하였기 이를 통보하니 업무에 참고하기 바랍니다.

첨부 안 1공문사본 1부. 끝.

교 통 부 장 관

수신처 : 외무부,내무부,상공부

22

미2과

교 통 부

기술 1547.3- (구내55) 1969,3,17

수신 수신처참조

제목 군납용택시 운행의 합리화에 관한 지시

1. 서울특별시 종로구 안국동 163 국제관광공사 총재 김일환과 서울특별시 충무로 4가 152의 1 해강산업주식회사 대표 임병주로 부터 당사에서 운행하고 있는 군납용택시의 검사는 미8군 차량관리 규정과 한국법령에 의하여 이중적으로 규제를 받고 있으므로써 용역업무에의 지장과 외화획득에의 손실을 초래하고 있으니 SOFA에 따른(한미협정 제9조 제13조, 제14조, 제24조)합리적인 조치를 요망한다는 요지의 건의서가 당부에 제출되었기 다음과 같이 지시하니 업무에 차질이 없도록 할것.

2. 국제관광공사 및 해강산업주식회사 명의로 등록된 자동차중 자동차 등록원부 및 검사증상에 "이차량의 소유권은 미국정부에 있음" 하고 기재된 자동차의 검사는 미8군 차량관리 규정에 의하여 시행한 검사로서 인정토록 한다. 끝.

교 통 부 장 관

수신처 : 나 1,2,3,4,7,8,9,10

23

JOINT COMMITTEE
UNDER
THE REPUBLIC OF KOREA AND THE UNITED STATES
STATUS OF FORCES AGREEMENT

2 April 1969

Dear Mr. Kang:

I want to take this opportunity to congratulate you on your return to your former post as the Director of the Bureau of Civil Aviation of the Ministry of Transportation. I would also like to welcome you back again as a member of the Republic of Korea - United States Status of Forces Agreement Joint Committee.

The United States military authorities in Korea appreciate the close and friendly coöperation that they have received from the Republic of Korea authorities in the Ministry of Transportation and at the Kimpo International Air Port. The United States military authorities recognize that commercial flights into and out of Kimpo are under the jurisdiction of the Republic of Korea Government authorities, but they want to take this opportunity to point out the special status of the non-commercial, military flights, made under direct contract with the United States Department of Defense.

The United States Department of Defense contracts with American airlines to transport United States military personnel from the United States to Korea at the beginning of their tour of duty, and back to the United States after their tour in the Republic of Korea is completed. These Department of Defense air transport contracts are in accordance with the provisions of the United States - Republic of Korea Mutual Defense Treaty and the Status of Forces Agreement.

Most of the Department of Defense military contract flights between the United States and Korea are flown by planes of the Northwest Airlines, which is the only American airline with regularly scheduled service into Korea. Other American airline companies, however, fly Department of Defense military contract flights into Korea, including Pan American World Airways, Braniff, and others. At the direction of United States Government authorities, the Northwest Airlines has been performing the servicing on all United States Department of Defense contract charter flights into Korea, both for its own Northwest planes and for those of other American airlines under United States Government charter.

It has come to the attention of United States military authorities that Republic of Korea officials operating the Kimpo International Air Port may be contemplating that United States Department of Defense military

24

contract planes, other than Northwest Airlines contract planes, should be serviced by a private Korean company. It is our desire to inform appropriate officials of the Government of the Republic of Korea that the United States Government plans to continue to have its military contract flights into Korea serviced by the Northwest Airlines. In accordance with the provisions of the United States - Republic of Korea Status of Forces Agreement, this servicing, as part of the Department of Defense contract with American airlines, is not subject to taxation by the Government of the Republic of Korea.

I will be most happy to discuss this subject, or others as you desire, with you at any time convenient with you.

Sincerely,

M. R. MASSIE
CAPT USN
Alternate United States Representative

Mr. KANG Ho Yun
Director
Bureau of Aviation
Ministry of Transportation
Seoul, Korea

2

75-4281 交通部 安全計課 Hong.

69. 6. 2.자 (미측교통분위장의 한국측 교통분위장 앞 서한)

1. 수주전부터 서울시 차량등록과장은 주한미군의 사유차량중 백.적색차량에 대한 등록을 거부

2. 1963. 10. 20.자 한국자동차 안전법규는 백.적색 차량의 개인소유를 금지

3. SOFA 규정상 명문화된 조항이 없을뿐더러 교섭회의나 분과위 또는 합동위원회 회의에서 한국측은 하등 사유차량 색갈에 관한 언급이 없었다.

4. 1968. 11.부터 주한미군 사유차량의 등록이 시작된 이래 백색-187대, 적색 - 126대의 차량이 등록됨.

5. 미측은 등록된 사유차량이외에 이미 도입되어온 백.적색 사유차량에 대해서는 조속한 시일내에 한.미양측의 합의절차로서 등록될수 있도록 협조 요망.

※ 赤. 白色 未登錄車輛 36台 大部分 赤色

69. 7. 22. 7.24
교통부 항공국 공역과장에게 동건 추진사항 問議
한.미 관계 실무자 회의를 개최하여 解決方法을 강구할 것임.
最終的으로 双方合意가 어려울 경우 SOFA를 통한 해결모색.

69. 7. 29 교통부 공역과장, 교통분위(한.미)를 소집하여 이미 ... 導入 또는 登錄된 白.赤色 車輛에 대해서는 登錄許可하는 方向으로

69.7.7자 (미측교통분위장의 한국측 교통분위장 앞 서한)

1. SOFA 교섭단계에서나 그후 사유차량등록신청 절차를 규제한 28차 합동회의에서 차량도색에 관한 언급은 없었고

2. 처음으로 이 문제가 야기된것이 69년 봄 부터

3. 한국의 교통안전법규가 SOFA 및 관계 합동위원회의 합의사항과 배치되어 있다면 한국정부는 SOFA 협정 제29조 2항에 의거해서 본국제적 협정과의 일치성을 기하기 위해 관계국내법을 수정할 책임이 있음을 제시한다.

4. 이러한 제한규정을 주한미군구성원에 효과적으로 부과하기에 앞서 보다 충분하고 완전한 고려가 있어야 할것으로 보인다.

5. 차량도색으로 인한 등록거부는 SOFA 와 합동위의 합의된 절차에 위배되는것으로 이는 전단적인 것이며 또한 부당한 법규 적용제한이 된다.

6. 이미 도입되어 미등록중인 사유차량 가운데는 백.적 도색이 있으며 그중 일부는 한국내에서 현지 구매된 것으로 대행업자는 하등 차량도색에 관한 사전 지식을 준바도 없다.

217

USFK EJ

2 June 1969

Mr. KANG Ho Ryun
Chairman, ROK Component
Transportation Subcommittee
Seoul, Korea

RECORD, IRO, J-5

Dear Mr. Kang:

A problem has arisen in the registration of privately owned vehicles of United States Forces, Korea (USFK) personnel which, I believe, should be brought to your attention. It concerns the color of the vehicles being registered.

Several weeks ago the Chief of Registration at Seoul City Hall began refusing to register the privately owned automobiles of USFK personnel if these vehicles were painted red or white. He stated that the Republic of Korea Auto Safety Code of 20 October 1963 forbade such colored vehicles to private individuals because these colors were reserved for emergency vehicles.

Unfortunately, this information was not included in the licensing and registration procedures for such vehicles approved on 3 July 1968 at the 23th Meeting of the Joint Committee under the Republic of Korea and the United States Status of Forces Agreement. Nor, indeed, was it ever discussed by the ROK members of the Transportation Subcommittee at any of the negotiating sessions during 1967 and 1968, or by the ROK SOFA negotiators during the negotiation of Article XXIV during the years 1964-66.

Registration began in November 1968. Since then, the ROK Government has registered 126 red vehicles and 187 white vehicles privately owned by USFK personnel without raising any objections to the color.

20

Mr. KANG 2 June 1969

I earnestly solicit your help to permit those vehicles already in-country to be registered in accordance with approved US-ROK Government procedures as soon as possible. Refusal to register these automobiles would cause unnecessary hardship and expense to personnel who are serving with USFK for the mutual defense of the Republic of Korea.

Sincerely,

C. G. COLLINS
Colonel, USA
Chairman, US Component
Transportation Subcommittee

Copies furnished:
JAJ
J-1
J-3
J-4
EAPM
EATR

29

RED AND WHITE VEHICLES REGISTERED IN KOREA

AREA	RED	WHITE
ASCOM	29	29
PUSAN	1	2
SEOUL	76	142
TAEGU	20	13
KANGWON	0	1
TOTAL	126	187

LTC MOSSMORE

LTC [illegible]
3076

70

CIVIL AVIATION BUREAU
MINISTRY OF TRANSPORTATION
REPUBLIC OF KOREA
SEOUL, KOREA

Mr. C. G. Collins
Colonel, USA
Chairman, US Component
Transportation Subcommittee

21 June, 1969

Dear Mr. Collins:

Reference your letter of 2 June 1969 concerning the color of privately owned vehicles of United States Forces, Korea personnel, which are registered to the Korea authorities concerned.

On facing the requirement to be met in the registration of colored vehicles, I took counsel with government officials of the Land Transportation Bureau, MOT and Seoul City Hall in charge of the registration of automobiles in Korea.

They stated that the color of early-registered 126 red vehicles and 187 white ones privately owned by USFK personnel were neither pure red nor white.

According to the Article 46, the Republic of Korea Safety Code of 20 October 1963, both pure red and white colored vehicles are forbaded to private individuals except emergency vehicles.

I request you, therefore, to advise USFK personnel not to bring such colored automobiles in Korea as far as possible so that any objections to the color will not be further arisen.

Your special consideration and positive assistance on this matter will be highly appreciated.

Sincerely yours,

Ho Ryun Kang
Director
Chairman, ROK Component
Transportation Subcommittee

Enclosure: Color Table

71

HEADQUARTERS, UNITED STATES FORCES, KOREA
APO SAN FRANCISCO 96301

USFK EJ

JUL 17 1969

Mr. KANG, Ho Ryun
Chairman, ROK Component
Transportation Subcommittee
Seoul, Korea

Dear Mr. Kang:

In reply to your letter of 21 June 1969, I would like to further explore several aspects concerning the registration of privately owned vehicles by US personnel serving in the Republic of Korea under the US-ROK Mutual Defense Treaty. I believe this problem should be considered from these points of view to assist in reaching an appropriate solution to the problem relating to red and white vehicles.

As I know you well appreciate, United States personnel presently serving in Korea in our mutual defense interests are subject to the US-ROK Status of Forces Agreement. This valid and effective international agreement provides in paragraph 3 of Article XXIV that "The Government of the Republic of Korea will license and register those vehicles privately owned by members of the United States armed forces, the civilian component or dependents." The subject of the colors of the vehicles was not raised by officials of the Government of the ROK during the negotiations of Article XXIV during the years 1964-1966, or in the Joint Committee and Subcommittee negotiations on procedures for registration and licensing of such vehicles in 1967 and 1968. At the 28th US-ROK Joint Committee of 3 July 1968, both the US and the ROK Representatives approved the application form for registration of privately owned vehicles which provides for designation of the color of the vehicle to be registered.

The first time the question of the color of such USFK vehicles was raised was in the Spring of 1969, when Seoul City authorities began refusing to register USFK privately owned vehicles if such vehicles were painted red or white. It is our belief that the rights of US personnel who are denied vehicle registration because of the color of their cars are being subject to arbitrary and unwarranted derogation, contrary to the interest of the US-ROK SOFA and approved Joint Committee procedures. May I

32

suggest that if Article 46 of the Republic of Korea Safety Code of 20 October 1963 is in conflict with the Status of Forces Agreement and related US-ROK Joint Committee Agreements then it may be incumbent upon the Government of the Republic of Korea to amend its local laws to establish conformance with these international agreements, in accordance with paragraph 2 of SOFA Article XXIX.

In your letter you state that USFK personnel be advised not to bring such colored automobiles into Korea, which raises a point that requires further amplification. Several of the US personnel with automobiles of one or the other of the proscribed colors purchased their automobiles in Korea from Korean firms, which did not advise them against buying an automobile of such a color or of the possibility that they would not be allowed to register the automobile once they had accepted delivery. It appears, therefore, that there are several areas that require full and complete consideration before our two governments could effectively impose this restriction on USFK personnel.

I will certainly appreciate your special consideration of the points I have presented in amplification of what we feel to be the proper and legal resolution of this problem. I earnestly solicit your further assistance in resolving this matter in order to maintain the effectiveness of the Status of Forces Agreement and to continue the excellent relationships between the American and Korean personnel in affairs of mutual interest.

Sincerely,

C. G. COLLINS
Colonel, USA
Chairman US Component
Transportation Subcommittee

2

33

서 울 특 별 시

차량 1547.11— 3KK·　　　　　　　　— 69. 7. 22.

수신　용산구 북한남동 687의14　　윌리암 B. 맥마혼 William B. MacMahon

제목　을종 정기점검정비 미필자동차에 대한 정비명령

1. 다음자동차는 도로운송 차량법 제43조의2의 규정에 의한 을종정기점검정비를 지정기일내에 시행치 아니하였으므로 동법 제67조의 규정에 의한 벌칙을 필하시고 (집행필증 69.7월31일 까지 을종 정기점검정비를 시행하기 바랍니다.

2. 지정 기일내에 을종 정기점검정비를 시행치 않을시는 동법 제43조의7의 2 항에 의거 사용정지 처분할것을 첨언합니다.

3. 을종 정기점검 정비미필 차량

등록번호	계속검사 유효기간	을종정기점검정비시행일
서자 4 - 8018	68.12.14 ~ 69.12.13	69. 6. 13 경

서 울 특 별 시

Recd.
24 July '69

34

서 울 특 별 시

차량 1547.11- 69. 7. 23.

수신 미8군영내 건물510호. 마스 회사

제목 음송 정기점검정비 미필자동차에 대한 정비명령

1. 다음자동차는 도로운송 차량법 제43조의2의 규정에 의한 음송정기점검정비를 지정기일내에 시행치 아니하였으므로 동법 제67조의 규정에 의한 벌칙을 면하시고 (집행필증 69.9월 2일 까지 음송 정기점검정비를 시행하기 바랍니다.

2. 지정 기일내에 음송 정기점검정비를 시행치 않을시는 동법 제43조의7의 2항에 의거 사용정지 처분할것을 첨언합니다.

3. 음송 정기점검 정비미필 차량

	등록번호	계속검사 유효기간	음송정기점검정비시행일
서자	4-8022 (버나드부룩스)	68.12.17~69.12.16	69.6.15
	4-8028 (존 티그린)	68.12.19~69.12.18	69.6.18
	4-8031 (유인 W 모폿트)	68.12.21~69.12.20	69.6.20
	4-8032 (하버트 파튼)	68.12.21~69.12.20	69.6.20
	4-8037 (룩스 버트커드)	68.12.26~69.12.25	69.6.25
	4-8041 (윌리암 이안드 메셔커)	68.12.27~69.12.26	69.6.26
	4-8044 (보어 헤스터)	68.12.28~69.12.2[illegible]	[illegible] 6.27
	4-8050 (윌리암 세인트폭스)	68.12.30~69.12.[illegible]	[illegible] 6.28 끝

서 울 특 별 시

354

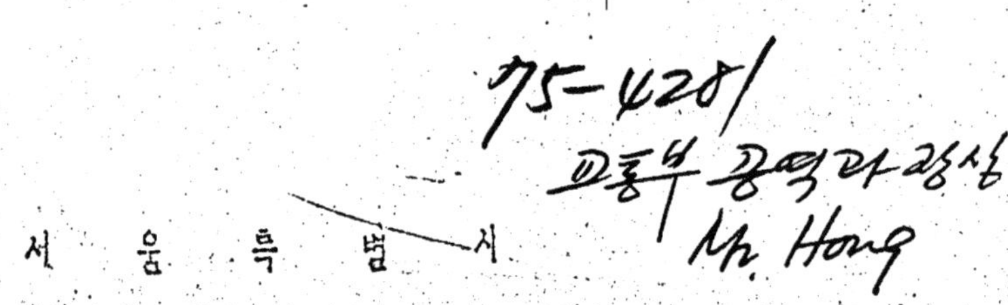

서 울 특 별 시

차량 1547.11— 69. 7. 23.

수신 용산구 이태원 아케트너 <아드리안 윌슨 마쏘씨에르>

제목 운송 정기점검정비 미필자동차에 대한 정비명령

1. 다음자동차는 도로운송 차량법 제43조의2의 규정에 의한 운송정기 점검정비를 지정기일내에 시행치 아니하였으므로 동법 제67조의 규정에 의한 벌칙을 면하시고 (접대필증) 69. 8월 2일까지 운송 정기점검정비를 시행하기 바랍니다.

2. 지정 기일내에 운송 정기점검정비를 시행치 않을시는 동법 제43조의7의 2항에 의거 사용정지 처분할것을 첨언합니다.

3. 운송 정기점검 정비미필 차량

등록번호	계속검사 유도기간	운송정기점검정비시행일
서라 4-8004	68.12.27 - 69.12.26	69. 6. 26

8,100

서 울 특 별 시

1969. 7. 23 서울특별시

36

◎ 招請契約者 私有車輛 安全檢査

(69. 7. 30 교통부 항공국 공역과 Mr. Hong에 확인 한)

1. 69. 7. 29 교통부 공역과에서 한미 交通分委를 召集하여 私有차량中 赤色車輛 登錄 문제를 協議時에 本件 招請契約者 私有車輛에 대한 安全檢査 有効期間에 관해서도 論議됨. 現行 SOFA協定에 따른 32次 合同委의 節次는 年 一回의 安全檢査를 하도록 規制하고 있음. 國內法(道路運送차량法)은 年一回의 安全검사 以外에 6個月 定期검사로 되어 있어 前記 節次中 一部改正(4條) 문제가 協議됨.

2. 施行節次中 一部改正에 따른 잠정적 措置 문제를 具體化 하기 爲해 69. 7. 31에 교통分委 再會合하기로.

◎ (北美二課長 — Mr. Kinney 通話內容)
69. 7. 31. 09:30

1. Gen. Smith는 SOFA 協定 不履行을 지적하여 韓國政府에 抗議 각서 提出 준비中이라고

2. 交通分委의 會合이 今日 午后 있을 予定이니 同會合結果가 있을 때까지 기다려 보기로 諒解.

◎ (교통부 공역과 Mr. 洪에게 再확인, 69. 7. 31. 10:30)

1. 今日 會합에서 서울市當局과 결탁하여 잠정적 措置에 관한 結末을 볼 것을 종용함. (과태료 및 운행정지 처분 철회)

2. 교통부 육운국은 서울市와 事前에 協議할 것이라 함

37

주한미군 초청계약자 사유차량검사의 문제점

문제점:

1. 1968. 11.7에 개최된 한.미군대지위협정에 따른 제32차 한.미합동회의에서는 주한미군 초청계약자의 사유차량에 대한 등록, 검사절차를 규제승인한바 있으며, 동시행절차에 따라서 현재 초청계약자의 사유차량은 년 1회의 안전검사를 받고있음. (한국의 차량검사 시설에서)

2. 그러나 차량검사 업무 담당 기관인 서울특별시 당국(차량과)은 국내법(도로운송 차량법)을 적용하여 상기 사유차량들에 대하여 년 1회의 안전검사 이외에 6개월마다 1회의 윤종정기검사를 요구하고 있음.

3. 서울특별시 당국은 상기 초청계약자 사유차량이 6개월 검사를 미필하였다하여 과태료(3000원)를 부과하는 한편 차량운행 정지처분 통고까지 한바 있음.

4. 이에 대하여 한.미군대지위협정 합동위원회의 미측 수석대표는 한국정부에 대하여 항의각서를 제출할 준비를 하고 있음.

해결방안:

1. 69. 7. 29. 한.미군대지위협정 교통분과위원회는 회의를 소집하여

350

023.9-14

문제해결방안을 논의했으나 합의점에 도달하지 못하여,

2. 69. 7. 31. 13:00시에 한.미교통분과위원회는 재회합하여 전기 사유차량 등록검사절차의 일부 수정 문제와 이에 따른 잠정적 조치문제를 협의케 될것이라 함. (관계부처: 교통부 항공국, 육운국, 내무부 및 서울특별시 차량과 참석)

3. 전기 문제가 한.미정부간의 문제로 대두되기전에 우선 서울시 당국이 전기 사유차량에 대한 검사 미필과태료 부과와 운행정지 처분을 하지 않도록 조치 함이 시급 함.

39

It was confirmed that no instructions to extinguish major seacoast navigation lights were given by the Ministry of Transportation or any other Korean Government agencies.

It is understood that advance notification of any changes in established navigation aids is being done in compliance with not only the provisions of the SOFA but also the requirements of international law.

Necessary steps will be taken in order to prevent any potential maritime disasters in the future should there be such actions as affecting the safety of United States ships. It is requested that details of information be given by the U.S. military authorities if there are any misconduct, indicating particular time and place or area where navigation lights are affected.

40

The US Representative has received a report(s) that the ROKG Ministry of Transportation has taken steps to extinguish major seacoast navigation lights maintained by the ROKG in its territorial waters. Under International law these lights are required to support the safety of ships traversing navigable waters.

The US Representative invites the attention of the ROKG Representative to paragraph 2 of Article XII of the SOFA which provides that before any changes are made in established navigation aids the authorities of the other Government shall be notified in advance.

While we appreciate the reasons for this action it is essential for the safety of United States ships that we be apprised in advance of any navigational aid changes.

It is requested that you take steps to ascertain the facts concerning this report and advise the US Representative. If the report is factually correct it is further requested that the appropriate agency of the ROKG provide adequate notification of these changes to Commander Naval Forces Korea.

4

공 란

공 란

공 란

공 란

공 란

공　　란

공　　　란

공 란

공 란

공 란

공 란

공 란

공 란

공 란

공 란

공 란

공 란

공 란

공 란

공 란

공 란

공　　란

공 란

공　　란

공 란

공　　　란

공 란

공 란

공　　　란

공 란

공 란

공 란

공 란

공 란

공 란

공　란

공 란

공 란

공　　란

공 란

공 란

공　　　　란

공 란

공 란

공 란

공 란

공 란

공　　　란

분류번호	729.417 1970-73	등록번호	520	보존기간	영구Z
기능명칭	SOFA 한미 합동위원회 교통분과 위원회, 1970-73.				
생 산 과	안보담당관실		생산년도	1973.	

주; 1. 1970년
2. 1971-'72년
3. 1973년

	M/F No.	

1. 1970

1

KOREA HIGHWAY CORPORATION
SEOUL, KOREA

March 24, 1970

Col. James L. Melloh
Provost Marshal
Eighth U.S. Army
APO 96301 U.S. Forces Korea

Re: Cancellation of Toll Exemption for Undercover Vehicles

Dear Col. Melloh:

₩63,000원

With regard to the subject, we regret to inform you that forty five (45) undercover vehicles operating under your control will be collected toll on Expressway which have been free from. 80+

The ministry of Construction advised us recently that even U.S. military vehicles, when they fasten themselves civilian identification numbers, have to get a prior permission for toll exemption from the minister in accordance with Article 6, Paragraph 4, of Enforcement Decree for Law of Toll Road.

Accordingly, we decided that toll exemption for the above-mentioned undercover vehicles (CID 4-number vehicles) will be cancelled effective from April 1, 1970.

It would be much appreciated, therefore, if you would advise this effect to the personnel concerned.

With the confidence that this matter will be given the most prompt attention and looking forward to your full cooperation and I remain,

Sincerely yours,

Pil Eun HUH
President

VICE PRES.
GEN. LEE
AUDITOR.

건설부 도로계획과
양궁환 과장
73-1639 -8371

2

도로공사 72-7306-09.

기 안 용 지

분류기호 문서번호	미이723-	(전화번호)	전결규정 조 항 전결사항
처리기한		기 안 자	결 재 자
시행일자		북미 2과 박양천	
보존년한		70. 5. 11.	국 장
보조기관	과 장		
협 조			
경유 수신 참조	건설부장관, 도로공사사장	통제	1970. 5. 12 외무부 정서
제 목	위장 남버를 부착한 미군 차량의 통행료 면제.		

1. 최근 도로공사는 미군 헌병 참모 앞 서한에서 위장 남버를 부착한 미군 차량의 통행료 면제는 귀하의 사전 허가를 요함을 지적하고 4월 1일 부터 동 미군 차량에 대한 통행료를 징수하고 있다고 하는바, 여사한 조처는 한.미 군대지위협정 제 10조 2항의 " ..... 합중국 정부 보유 차량 및 합중국 군대의 구성원 군속 및 그들의 가족은 합중국 군대가 사용하고 있는 시설과 구역에 출입하고 이들 시설과 구역간을 이동하고 또한 이러한 시설과 구역 및 대한민국의 항구 또는 비행장 간을 이동할수 있다. 합중국 군용 차량의 시설과 구역에의 출입 및 이들 시설과 구역간의 이동에는 도로 사용료 및 기타의 과징금을 과하지 아니한다"는 규정에 저촉되오니 필요한 시정 조처를 취하시기 바랍니다. 3

공통서식 1—2—1 (갑)
1967. 4. 4. 승인

(18절지) 2급인쇄용지 70g/m²
(조달청) (500,000매 인쇄)

2. 조약의 해석 및 체결권은 외무부 직제 제7조에 의거 당부 조약과가 "조약 기타 국제 협정의 심사 체결과 비준 및 해석에 관한 사항을 분장" 하게 되어 있음을 참고로 첨언 합니다.

3. 국가간의 조약을 이행하지 않을 경우에는 국가의 배상 책임이 제기될 가능성이 있아오니 상기 협정 적용에 착오가 없도록 신중을 기하여 주시기 바랍니다. 끝.

0091

4

외 무 부

미이 723 - 70. 5. 12.

수신 : 건설부 장관, 도로공사 사장

제목 : 위장 남버를 부착한 미군 차량의 통행료 면제.

1. 최근 도로공사는 미군 헌병참모 앞 서한에서 위장 남버를 부착한 미군 차량의 통행료 면제는 귀하의 사전 허가를 요함을 지적하고 4월 1일 부터 동 미군 차량에 대한 통행료를 징수하고 있다고 하는바, 여사한 조치는 한.미 군대지위협정 제 10조 2항의 " ..... 합중국 정부 보유 차량 및 합중국 군대의 구성원, 군속 및 그들의 가족은 합중국 군대가 사용하고 있는 시설과 구역에 출입하고 이들 시설과 구역간을 이동하고 또한 이러한 시설과 구역 및 대한민국의 항구 또는 비행장 간을 이동할수 있다. 합중국 군용 차량의 시설과 구역에의 출입 및 이들 시설과 구역간의 이동에는 도로 사용료 및 기타의 과징금을 과하지 아니한다" 는 규정에 저촉되오니 필요한 시정 조치를 취하시기 바랍니다.

2. 조약의 해석 및 체결권은 외무부 직제 제 7조에 의거 당부 조약과가 "조약 기타 국제 협정의 심사체결과 비준 및 해석에 관한 사항을 분장" 하게 되어 있음을 참고로 첨언 합니다.

3. 국가간의 조약을 이행하지 않을 경우에는 국가의 배상 책임이 제기될 가능성이 있아오니 상기 협정 적용에 착오가 없도록

5

신중을 기하여 주시기 바랍니다. 끝.

외 무 부 장 관

6.

JOINT COMMITTEE
UNDER
THE REPUBLIC OF KOREA AND THE UNITED STATES
STATUS OF FORCES AGREEMENT

USFK EJ 5 June 1970

Mr. KIM, Hyun Kun
US-ROK Joint Committee (SOFA)
ROK Secretary

Dear Mr. KIM,

Over the past month several conversations were held by Lt Col Roy J. Connor of this office with yourself and your predecessor, Mr. ROH, Jae Won on the subject of undercover vehicles of the US military police and investigation units in Korea. In a change to previous practice effective 1 April 1970, the Ministry of Construction directed operators at the gates of the toll highways to collect tolls from any vehicle that displayed a standard Korean license plate, regardless of the fact that it might in actuality be a US military vehicle. It has long been an established fact under SOFA that military vehicles are to be afforded access to the highways of the Republic of Korea without payment of toll.

We have been well aware of the problem of identification in the present instance. The undercover vehicles are not painted in standard military colors, have no organizational markings, carry a civilian license plate and are driven by an individual in civilian clothes. We do appreciate that the presentation of proper police credentials by the individual does not necessarily certify that the vehicle he is driving is a US military vehicle.

In an attempt to provide a solution to this problem, this office has contacted the various US military police and investigative units in Korea who have been affected by the ruling and have expressed their concern to the SOFA Secretariat.

The only organization that has responded to date has been the office of the Provost Marshal, 8th US Army. Inclosed in this letter is the listing of 90 license numbers, in 70 copies, assigned to the

7

undercover vehicles of the various units of the 8th US Army. If your office will provide these to the appropriate offices in the Ministry of Construction, as agreed to in conversations on this subject, this should provide the answer to the problem of identification for the vehicles of these units.

As other units respond, or as changes to this list occur, we will provide updated listings in order that legal access be provided for those military vehicles authorized toll free use of the highways.

Robert A. Kinney

1 Incl

ROBERT A. KINNEY
US-ROK Joint Committee (SOFA)
U. S. Secretary

8

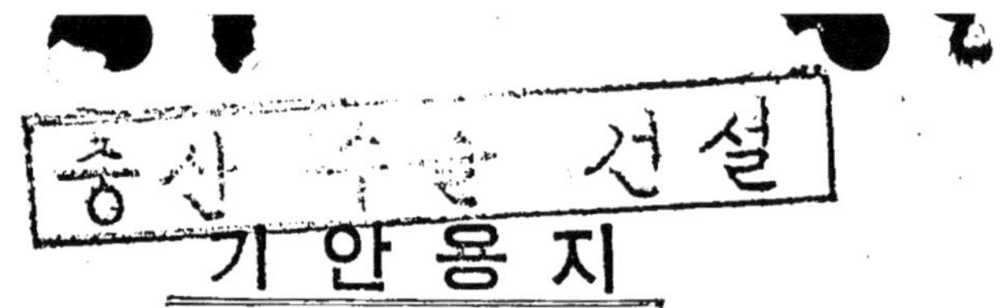

기안용지

분류기호 문서번호	미이723	(전화번호)	전결규정 조 항 전결사항
처리기한		기안자	결재자
시행일자		북미2과 박양천	
보존년한		70. 6. 12.	국장
보조기관	과장		
협조			
경유 수신 참조	건설부 장관 도로운영과장	통제 1970. 6. 13	발송 1970. 6. 13 11735
제목	위장 남버를 부착한 미군 차량 List 송부.		

참조 : 미이 723-9318 (70. 5. 11.)

1. 위장 남버를 부착한 미군 수사용 차량 List 를 별첨 송부합니다.

2. 동 위장 남버를 부착한 미군 차량도 한.미 군대지위협정 제 10 조 2항에 따라 도로 사용료등 일체의 과징금을 부과할수 없는 것임을 양지하시기 바랍니다.

첨부 : 8군 헌병대 소속 차량 90 대의 차량번호 69 매. 끝.

9

공통서식 1—2—1 (갑) 1967. 4. 4. 승인 (18절지) 2급인쇄용지 70g/m²) (5)0,000매 인쇄)

절세로 자립경제

외 무 부

미이 723-　　　　　　　　　　　　70. 6. 13.

수신 : 건설부 장관

참조 : 도로운영과장

제목 : 위장 남버를 부착한 미군 차량 List 송부.

1. 위장 남버를 부착한 미군 수사용 차량 List 를 별첨 송부합니다.

2. 동 위장 남버를 부착한 미군 차량도 한.미 군대지위협정 제 10조 2항에 따라 도로 사용료등 일체의 과징금을 부과할수 없는 것임을 양지하시기 바랍니다.

첨부 : 8군 헌병대 소속 차량 90대의 차량번호 69매. 끝.

외 무 부 장 관

10

OSI DISTRICT 45 VEHICLES

VEHICLE NR	NOMENCLATURE	LICENSE	LOCATION
65B9566	Jeep, 2 dr	4-8671	4506 (Osan)
68B7350	Ford Sedan, 4 dr, Green	4-8670	4506 (Osan)
68B7371	Ford Sedan, 4 dr, Green	4-8669	4506 (Osan)
65B8912	Jeep, 2dr	4-8665	4506 (Osan)
65B9568	Jeep, 2 dr	4-8668	4506 (Osan)
69B5763	Toyota, 2 dr, green	4-8763	4504 (Taegu)
69B5764	Toyota, 2 dr, green	4-8764	4503 (Kwangju)
65B9565	Jeep, 2 dr, gray	4-8756	4502 (Kunsan)
69B5765	Toyota, 2 dr, green	4-8765	4502 (Kunsan)
68B7292	Ford Sedan, 4 dr, white	4-8752	45 (Seoul)
69B5762	Toyota, 2 dr, Green	4-8762	45 (Seoul)
68B7293	Ford Sedan, 4 dr, white	4-8753	45 (Seoul)
64B810	Ford Station wagon, yellow	4-8757	45 (Seoul)
68B7345	Ford, 4 dr, green	4-8754	45 (Seoul)
65B9567	Jeep, 2 dr, white	4-8666	45 (Seoul)
64B4281	Scout, 2 dr, blue	4-8760	45 (Seoul)
69B5761	Toyota, 2 dr, green	4-8761	45 (Seoul)
68B7291	Ford Sedan, 4 dr, black	4-8751	45 (Seoul)
68B37	Jeep, 2 dr, green	4-8755	45 (Seoul)
64B6734	Datsun, 4 dr, blue	4-8759	45 (Seoul)

20

11

Organization	Numbers of Plates	Details					
523d CID	8 sets	Seoul Ja:	4-8901	4-8910	4-8924	4-8930	4-8935
			4-8960	4-8906	4-8919		
2d CID	14 sets	Seoul Ja:	4-8902	4-8903	4-8904	4-8908	4-8911
			4-8912	4-8915	4-8916	4-8918	4-8921
			4-8928	4-8931	4-8933	4-8925	4-8926
		Kyonggi Ja:	4-8650	4-8621			
2d DIV CID	9 sets	Kyonggi Ja:	4-8603	4-8610	4-8611	4-8616	4-8620
			4-8623	4-8629	4-8634	4-8652	
		Seoul Ja:	4-8961				
7th DIV CID	8 sets	Kyonggi Ja:	4-8606	4-8608	4-8615	4-8627	4-8636
			4-8639	4-8642	4-8647		
19th CID	20 sets	Seoul Ja:	4-8959				
		Kyonggi Ja:	4-8602	4-8604	4-8607	4-8613	4-8614
			4-8619	4-8625	4-8628	4-4630	4-8632
			4-8633	4-8637	4-8641	4-8643	4-8645
			4-8646	4-8648	4-8649	4-8654	4-8659
7th CID	16 sets	Seoul Ja:	4-8956	4-8957	4-8958		
		Kyonggi Ja:	4-8601	4-8609	4-8612	4-8618	4-8622
			4-8626	4-8631	4-8635	4-8638	4-8640
			4-8644	4-8651	4-8653		
65th CID	10 sets	Kyongbuk Ja:	4-8002	4-8003	4-8004	4-8005	4-8006
			4-8007				
		Pusan Ja:	4-8216	4-8226	4-8236	4-8246	

12

JOINT COMMITTEE
UNDER
THE REPUBLIC OF KOREA AND THE UNITED STATES
STATUS OF FORCES AGREEMENT

USFK EJ 15 June 1970

Mr. KIM, HyungKun
US-ROK Joint Committee
ROK Secretary

Dear Mr. KIM,

Last week I brought two sets of vehicle listings to your office for undercover vehicles of the US Air Force, OSI and 8th US Army, Provost Marshall to be forwarded to the Ministry of Construction. This was to facilitate the toll free use by these US military vehicles of the toll highways of Korea.

I have since been advised by the office of the Provost Marshall that the Korean Highway corporation has agreed with them to issue special administrative passes to each license number listed. This pass will be shown by the vehicle driver to the toll gate attendants to secure toll free entry to the highways.

If your office would therefore forward copies of the vehicle listings direct to the Korean Highway Corporation, this will facilitate the issuance of these passes by their offices.

I believe that we may both take pleasure in these developments which demonstrate again the effective cooperation which continues among the agencies of our respective governments in the solution of our common problems.

Respectfully,

Robert A. Kinney

ROBERT A. KINNEY
US-ROK Joint Committee
US Secretary

13

2.1971-72년

기 안 용 지

분류기호 문서번호	미이 723 -	(전화번호)	전결규정 조 항 국장 전결사항
처리기간			
시행일자	71. 6. 5.	장 관	
보존년한			

보조기관	외무부	구미국장		협조
		북미 2과장		
기안책임자		주 사	박양천	

경 유		발신	
수 신	교통부장관		No. 10219 1971 6. 8 외무부
참 조	종합수송관		검열 1971. 6. 8 통제관
제 목	차량 등록에 관한 한.미 각서 교환		

1. 주한 미군을 위하여 한국에 주재하는 미국 적십자사, United Service Organization, United Seamen's Service Center, Bank of America 소속 차량은 임의의 "면허 감찰" 을 부착, 운행하고 있었으므로 이를 규제하기 위하여 한.미 군대지위협정 합동위원회 제 62차 회의는 양국 대표 간의 각서 교환을 통하여 여사한 차량의 등록 면허는 제 28차 합동위 (68. 7. 3.) 에서 합의한바 있는 주한 미군 요원 사유차량 면허 및 등록 절차에 따르며, 한국 정부가 발행하는 "면허 감찰" 을 부착키로 합의 하였읍니다.

2. 상기 등록 절차 시행기관에 통고하여 필요한 조치를 취하도록 하여주시고 아울러 상기 차량중 임의의 "면허 감찰" 을 부착, 운행하는 차량에 대하여는 의법조치 하시기 바랍니다.

첨부 : 회의록 1부. (90, 91 페이지 참조) 끝.

정서 / 관인 / 발송

공통서식 1-2 (갑)
1967. 4. 4 승인

190mm×268mm 중질지 70g/m²
조달청 1000,000매 인쇄)

15

외 무 부

미이 723 - 71. 6. 7.

수신 : 교통부장관

참조 : 종합수송관

제목 : 차량 등록에 관한 한.미 각서 교환

1. 주한 미군을 위하여 한국에 주재하는 미국 적십자사, United Service Organization, United Seamen's Service Center, Bank of America 소속 차량은 임의의 "면허 감찰" 을 부착, 운행하고 있었으므로 이를 규제하기 위하여 한.미 군대지위협정 합동위원회 제 62차 회의는 양국 대표 간의 각서 교환을 통하여 여사한 차량의 등록 면허는 제 28차 합동위 (68. 7. 3.) 에서 합의한바 있는 주한 미군 요원 사유차량 면허 및 등록 절차에 따르며, 한국 정부가 발행하는 "면허 감찰" 을 부착키로 합의 하였읍니다.

2. 상기 등록 절차 시행기관에 통고하여 필요한 조치를 취하도록 하여주시고 아울러 상기 차량중 임의의 "면허 감찰"을 부착, 운행하는 차량에 대하여는 위법조치 하시기 바랍니다.

첨부 : 회의록 1부. (90, 91 페이지 참조) 끝.

외 무 부 장 관

16

問題点:

① 会員 자격.

② License 및 Registration 問題.

③ Aircraft 所有者. 및 civilian or military craft.

④ 同 club의 운영. 一부의 [illegible] 下部

⑤ NAFIO integral part

⑥ SOFA 13조 特技 해석.

⑦ [illegible]자격.

⑧ [illegible]

1341

1572 외 무

17

* 美側에 資料[illegible]請 (12.1)
* 美側에 再次 資料要請. (72.1.20)
(一次要請에서 General Data 接受 하였으나 不充分.)
* 三次資料要求 (2.4)

교 통 부

항운1554 - 1887 1971.11.18

수신 외무부장관

제목 S O F A 제13조 해석에 관한 질의

1. 현행항공법제103조 (외국항공기의 국내 사용)에 의하면 " 외국의 국적을 가진 항공기는 대한민국 내의 각지간에서 항공의 용에 공하여서는 아니된다. 다만 교통부장관의 허가를 얻은 경우에는 예외로 한다"로 규정되어 있으나 주한미8군 Flying club 에서는 항공법에 의한 소정절차를 취함이 없이 미국국적을 가진항공기 (N 번호) 로 국내비행을 가끔하고 있는바

2. 동 Flying club 측에서는 동 Club 항공기의 운항은 제13조에 따른 특전및 면제규정의 대상이 된다는 견해를 가지고 있으니, 동 Club 항공기 운항이 SOFA 제13조의 규정을 받아 항공법의 규제 대상에서 제외되는 여부를 판시하여 주시기 바랍니다. 끝.

교 통 부 장 관

외 무 부	
접수 일시	197 20 NOV 71 10 : 01
접수 번호	제 46719
주무과	
담당자	
처리 기일	

EIGHTH U.S. ARMY FLYING CLUB
c/o 55th Aviation Company (A)
APO San Francisco 96301

13 September 1971

GENERAL:

The Eighth US Army Flying Club is a nonappropriated sundry fund activity established under the provisions of AR 28-95.

The primary mission of the Club is to furnish flight instruction to eligible personnel at nominal cost.

The organization is self supporting, receives no grants or monies from outside sources, and all monies received are used entirely for the operation and maintenance of the Club.

The governing and policy-making aspect of the Club is performed by a Board of Governors consisting of a President, Vice President, Operations Officer, Maintenance Officer, Safety Officer, Secretary, Custodian, and four members at large. The Board members are elected by a meeting of the general membership twice yearly and serve for a term of six months.

The Club membership normally exceeds 100 members. Student training accounts for approximately 90% of the total flying hours.

1. ELIGIBILITY:

a. All members of the Armed Forces.
b. Department of the Army Civilians (DAC).
c. Retired personnel of the Armed Forces.
d. Members of the Armed Forces Active Reserve.
e. Members of the State Department.
f. Department of Defense Civilians.
g. Invited Contractors.
h. Other civilians and personnel authorized foreign exchange privileges (accepted on a case-by-case basis, with the approval of CG, EUSA).

Note: Legitimate dependents of above listed personnel are eligible for membership.

19

2. FEES AND PROCEDURES:

a. A new member is required to pay a $25 initiation fee in order to join the Club. Due to a reciprocal agreement among service-connected clubs, providing a member has paid all bills and fees, he will receive a "letter of good standing" upon departure from Korea. This letter will enable him to join another service-connected club without payment of an additional initiation fee.

b. A deposit of $50 will be charged to all members and must accompany the application for membership. The deposit will be refunded on departure or termination.

c. Dues are $8 per month, payable on the first of each month with a ten-day period of grace.

d. The Club has seven aircraft: One L-16 Aeronca Champ and four Cessna 150's primarily for student training; one Cessna 180 and one L-5 Stinson for use on cross-country flying by private or higher rated pilots. The rates including gas and oil are as follows:

L-16	$ 6 per hour
Cessna 150	$ 8 per hour
Cessna 180	$10 per hour.

3. INSTRUCTION:

a. The cost per hour for an instructor in all Club aircraft is $5. For example, the cost of one hour dual instruction in a Cessna 150 would be $13. The flight instructor is paid directly by the member. All instruction fees and aircraft costs are payable upon the termination of the flight.

b. The Club is open seven days a week, 0800 hours to sunset, with instructors available. Local flights may be scheduled two weeks in advance. Cross-country flights may be scheduled up to three months in advance.

4. AIRCRAFT INFORMATION:

The Club has one full-time A&P mechanic and one mechanic assistant. All maintenance, gas and oil are the responsibility of the Club except on extended cross-country flights out of country.

2

120

5. JOINING THE EIGHTH ARMY FLYING CLUB AND REQUIREMENTS FOR A PRIVATE PILOT'S LICENSE:

a. A new member will complete an application form and pay the initiation fee of $25 plus the $50 deposit and the $8 dues at the time of the application. The membership card will be furnished after the Board of Governors approve the application for membership. As soon as a new member has paid the above mentioned fees, he may schedule his first flight, called the orientation flight.

b. Dues are not prorated according to the day a new member joins due to the fact that no dues are collected during the month in which the member departs.

c. Federal Aviation Administration (FAA) regulations specify that a minimum of 40 hours are necessary before applying for a private pilot license. However, there is no guarantee that a member will become a rated pilot in this minimum time. The average student usually has logged between 50 to 60 hours before going for his flight check. Of the minimum 40 hours, a student must have 20 hours of solo flight time to include a minimum of 10 hours solo cross-country time.

d. All instruction is given in phases of dual and solo periods. An individual usually makes his first solo flight between 8 and 15 hours.

e. An estimated cost of obtaining a private pilot's license in the Club is approximately $500 for the aircraft and instructor. This compares very favorably with the $800 to $1,000 cost of the same instruction from civilian sources. The time element depends upon such factors as number of hours flown per week, individual capacity to absorb instruction, weather conditions, and aircraft availability. Usually allow from three to six months to complete the program.

THIS IS YOUR INVITATION TO COME TO THE CLUB. INSPECT OUR NEW FACILITIES, AND START A NEW AND REWARDING HOBBY. SEE YOU AT THE CLUB HOUSE LOCATED ON K-16 AIRFIELD (SEOUL EAST). THERE IS A FREE US ARMY BUS BETWEEN YONGSAN TERMINAL AND K-16 ABOUT EVERY TWO HOURS DAILY.

1 Incl
Private Pilot Course Outline

ROBERT J. KRIWANEK
Colonel, MPC
President

PRIVATE PILOT COURSE OUTLINE

PHASE I	Orientation and basic maneuvers; straight and level, climbs, glides, turns, slow flight, stalls, ground reference maneuvers, simulated emergency situations. References: FAR's Part 1, 61, 91 and 430; Kershner's Student Pilot Manual; AC 00-6 Aviation Weather; AC61-23 Private Pilot's Handbook of Aeronautical Knowledge.
PHASE II	Pre-solo take-offs and landings including power-off full stall landings; power approaches; cross-wind take-offs and landings and proper patterns for all approaches.
PREREQUISITES for PHASE III	Class III medical and pre-solo written test passed. Radio telephone permit required for CONUS flights.
PHASE III	Three supervised solo periods in the traffic pattern.
PHASE IV	Three unsupervised solo periods to include take-offs and landings and review of basic airwork.
PREREQUISITES for PHASE V	Proper use of the Airman's Information Manual, compass errors, omninavigation orientation, short and soft field take-offs and landings (see Kershner's Manual), aeronautical chart and symbol familiarization, radio frequency utilization and computer and plotter use, cruising altitudes and FAR's.
PHASE V	Dual cross-country flying; pilotage, dead reckoning and omninavigation including traffic patterns, fuel consumption, figuring ETA's and inflight emergencies.
PHASE VI	Solo cross-country flying; 10 hours required, one trip to include a leg at least 100 miles from point of departure.
PREREQUISITES for PHASE VII	Private pilot written test passed 70%.
PHASE VII	Review and preparation for private check ride including a review of all private pilot maneuvers required by FAR 91.
PHASE VIII	PRIVATE PILOT CHECK RIDE.

Incl 1

ARMY REGULATION No. 28-95

HEADQUARTERS
DEPARTMENT OF THE ARMY
WASHINGTON, D.C., 15 October 1968

WELFARE, RECREATION, AND MORALE
ARMY FLYING CLUB PROGRAM

Section I. GENERAL

1. Purpose and mission. This regulation authorizes the establishment of Army Flying Clubs and sets forth basic policies and procedures under which these clubs will function. This program will be conducted solely as an off-duty, voluntary participation program in the interest of welfare, recreation, and morale.

2. Scope. These policies and procedures are applicable in continental United States and Alaska. Other oversea commanders will be guided by this regulation and policies established by commanders of unified commands. Where conflicts exist, the policies of the unified commander will govern.

Section II. BASIC OPERATIONAL PRINCIPLES

3. Establishment. *a.* Army Flying Clubs may be established at installation level and operated as sundry fund activities on a self-supporting basis under the provisions of AR 230-5. These funds are Government instrumentalities and are entitled to limited assistance as stipulated in AR 210-55 and AR 420-80, including hangaring and/or tying down of aircraft at installations when adequate facilities and space are available.

b. Clubs will be organized under a constitution and bylaws which provide for their operation and dissolution in accordance with this regulation and other applicable regulations.

c. Local policies and regulations may be issued to insure that clubs operate smoothly, efficiently, and properly, provided the policies are consistent with this regulation and other applicable regulations.

d. Flying clubs established as private associations under the provisions of paragraph 1-2*c*, AR 230-5, do not fall within the purview of this regulation.

4. Membership. Membership will be voluntary and composed predominately of military personnel. Membership may be extended to the following categories of personnel subject to such further

---

*This regulation supersedes AR 28-95, 2 July 1964, including Change 1; letter, AGPN(M) (1 Dec 64) 4 December 1964, subject: Army Flying Club Program; letter, AGMS-A(M) (24 Jan 67), 2 February 1967, subject: Administration and Operation of Army Flying Clubs; DA message 844742, 21 December 1967, and rescinds Reports Control Symbol CAB-1001.

restrictions as may be prescribed by installation commanders:

a. Active membership will be extended to military personnel on active duty.

b. Associate membership may be extended to—

(1) Retired military personnel.

(2) Adult dependents (16 years or older) of active duty military personnel.

(3) Civilian employees of Department of Defense paid from appropriated or nonappropriated funds.

(4) Members of the Armed Forces Reserve Components.

(5) Allied military personnel stationed in CONUS under the foreign student exchange program for a period greater than 90 days. Participation by allied military personnel is contingent upon—

(*a*) Sufficient fluency in the English language to assure effective air-ground communications and safe operation of aircraft (para 6*b* (1) (*g*) and (2) are applicable).

(*b*) Favorable recommendation by installation and major Army commanders of application submitted by each individual concerned. Individuals will include in their applications a signed and witnessed statement, prepared by the local staff judge advocate, relieving the flying club concerned and the United States Government of any liability or responsibility in the event of accidental injury or death of the applicant while participating in flying club activities.

(*c*) Specific approval, in each case, by The Adjutant General, Department of the Army, and the foreign government concerned.

5. Flight participation. The following individuals are authorized as passengers aboard Army Flying Club planes:

a. Active and associate members as defined in paragraph 4.

b. Dependents of active and associate members when the club plane is piloted by the sponsor member.

c. Other passengers are not authorized, except for persons whose official duties require them to be passengers, such as FAA inspectors, and civilian instructors hired by the local flying club.

6. Responsibility. *a.* Major Army field commands and The Surgeon General will—

(1) Assure that, where feasible, clubs are established at locations where the maximum number of interested personnel may participate. For this purpose, the establishment of flying clubs on a regional basis to cover all posts, camps, and stations located within a designated area is authorized.

(2) Allocate airplanes made available by the Department of the Army in a manner designed to meet the above requirements.

(3) Exercise control over all phases of this program.

(4) Notify The Adjutant General, ATTN: AGMS, Department of the Army, when airplanes allocated pursuant to (2) above and club-owned aircraft become excess to major command requirements (exempt report, para 7-2*a*, AR 335-15).

(5) Notify The Adjutant General, ATTN: AGMS, Department of the Army, when airplanes owned by or on loan to a club are transferred between flying clubs within the major command, and of other disposition (exempt report, para 7-2*o*, AR 335-15).

b. Installation commanders assigned the responsibility for flying clubs will—

(1) Supervise operations and administration to insure—

(*a*) That flight records reflect the names of passengers and are retained for a minimum period of 12 months for review by appropriate officials.

(*b*) That a custodian and board of governors are elected or appointed from the active membership.

(*c*) That an officer who is a rated pilot is appointed as club advisor to assist the club board of governors and custodian.

(*d*) That effective air and ground safety programs are followed.

(*e*) That clubs operate in an economical, efficient, and businesslike manner and are solvent at all times.

(*f*) That a reasonable radius of operations from the home field is established for the various club-operated aircraft. In establishing such boundaries, consideration will be given to terrain, type of aircraft, cruising range, population density, and the ability of the club to finance major repairs in commercial facilities or to defray shipping and transportation costs back to parent

24

installation if aircraft is not to be repaired at point of breakdown.

(*g*) Appropriate operational and administrative procedures are established and followed to insure maximum safety of flight. Cross-country flight plans will be filed with FAA or a military flight facility. Local flight plans will be filed and monitored at the home installation until the aircraft is returned. The rules and regulations of the FAA should be supplemented if required, based on flying experience available within the club.

(2) Assure that all personnel who fly or maintain airplanes belonging to or on loan to the clubs are appropriately licensed by the FAA and that all flying clubs maintain an up-to-date roster of club pilots showing their proficiency and physical flight qualifications.

(3) Provide equitable opportunity for all eligible personnel to take part in flying club activities.

(4) Notify The Adjutant General, ATTN: AGMS, Department of the Army, of the establishment or dissolution of flying clubs within their command (exempt report, para 7-2*o*, AR 335-15).

7. Property. *a. Club-owned.*

(1) Acquisition through procurement, contributions and donations will be made in accordance with AR 230-5.

(2) Classification and accountability will be in accordance with AR 230-65.

(3) Disposition will be in accordance with AR 230-60 as authorized by The Adjutant General, ATTN: AGMS, Department of the Army, after such aircraft has been determined excess to all Army Flying Clubs.

b. Government-loaned.

(1) Aircraft determined to be excess to requirements of the established Army supply program will be made available to major commands on a nonreimbursable basis. Planes will be moved from their present location at no expense to the Government.

(2) At installation level, these airplanes will be reflected in TDA as prescribed in AR 310-49 and accounted for in accordance with procedures specified in AR 735-35, and will be loaned to established flying clubs as Government-owned portable equipment.

(3) Title to this property will remain with the Government, but airplanes will be licensed by the FAA.

(4) Disposition. Aircraft determined to be excess to The Adjutant General, ATTN: AGMS, Department of the Army will be turned in to the installation supply officer for processing in accordance with AR 755-1, or, if authorized in writing by the installation supply officer, may be turned in to the nearest property disposal officer.

c. Station property officers may request surplus aircraft from the appropriate General Services Administration Regional Office. Any aircraft received through this source will be accounted for in the same manner as aircraft loaned to flying clubs.

8. Supply and maintenance. *a.* After an aircraft is transferred to the installation supply officer for assignment to flying clubs, maintenance and repair will become the responsibility of the individual flying club. Repair parts may be obtained by purchase from commercial sources, or by purchase through a property disposal sales office, at no cost to the Government, in the same manner as authorized the general public, or by transfer from a property disposal officer as authorized by AR 755-21.

b. Communications, electronic navigation equipment, and their respective repair parts, determined to be excess to the Department of the Army supply program requirements may, upon approval of the installation commander, be transferred to flying clubs when considered necessary in the interest of safety. Such items will be furnished to the flying clubs on a reimbursable basis and Army accountability will be dropped at the time of transfer.

9. Petroleum products. Procedures for procurement of petroleum products for Army Flying Clubs will be in accordance with AR 210-58.

Section III. SPECIFIC OPERATIONAL PRINCIPLES

10. Federal Aviation Administration. All airplanes utilized by Army Flying Clubs and all personnel flying, maintaining, giving, or undergoing instructions will be appropriately certified by the FAA. Installation commanders are responsible to insure that Federal Aviation Regulations in parts 61– and 91– will be strictly adhered to by club members.

11. **Pilot/Operator Aircraft Accident Report, General Aviation Aircraft, RCS DOT–1001.** Accidents incident to flight involving fatality, serious injury and/or damage exceeding $300 will be reported to the National Transportation Safety Board in accordance with part 320, National Transportation Safety Board Regulations. One additional copy will be prepared and forwarded to The Adjutant General, ATTN: AGMS, Department of the Army, Washington, D.C. 20315.

12. **Insurance.** Insurance coverage of all aircraft owned or leased by Army Flying Clubs or Government aircraft on loan to Army Flying Clubs will be in accordance with AR 230–8.

13. **Administration.** Administration of Army Flying Club sundry funds will be in accordance with applicable provisions of AR 230–60 and AR 230–65.

The proponent agency of this regulation is The Adjutant General's Office. Users are invited to send comments and suggested improvements to The Adjutant General, ATTN: AGMS, Department of the Army, Washington, D.C. 20315.

By Order of the Secretary of the Army:

W. C. WESTMORELAND,
General, United States Army,
Chief of Staff.

Official:
KENNETH G. WICKHAM,
Major General, United States Army,
The Adjutant General.

Distribution:
To be distributed in accordance with DA Form 12–9 requirements for AR, Welfare, Recreation and Morale:
Active Army: C (Quan Rqr Block No. 58).
ARNG: D (Quan Rqr Block No. 59).
USAR: C (Quan Rqr Block No. 58).

U.S. GOVERNMENT PRINTING OFFICE: 1968

공 란

EIGHTH U.S. ARMY FLYING CLUB
c/o 55th Aviation Company (A)
APO San Francisco 96301

13 September 1971

GENERAL:

The Eighth US Army Flying Club is a nonappropriated sundry fund activity established under the provisions of AR 28-95.

The primary mission of the Club is to furnish flight instruction to eligible personnel at nominal cost.

The organization is self supporting, receives no grants or monies from outside sources, and all monies received are used entirely for the operation and maintenance of the Club.

The governing and policy-making aspect of the Club is performed by a Board of Governors consisting of a President, Vice President, Operations Officer, Maintenance Officer, Safety Officer, Secretary, Custodian, and four members at large. The Board members are elected by a meeting of the general membership twice yearly and serve for a term of six months.

The Club membership normally exceeds 100 members. Student training accounts for approximately 90% of the total flying hours.

1. ELIGIBILITY:

a. All members of the Armed Forces.
b. Department of the Army Civilians (DAC).
c. Retired personnel of the Armed Forces.
d. Members of the Armed Forces Active Reserve.
e. Members of the State Department.
f. Department of Defense Civilians.
g. Invited Contractors.
h. Other civilians and personnel authorized foreign exchange privileges (accepted on a case-by-case basis, with the approval of CG, EUSA).

Note: Legitimate dependents of above listed personnel are eligible for membership.

2. FEES AND PROCEDURES:

a. A new member is required to pay a $25 initiation fee in order to join the Club. Due to a reciprocal agreement among service-connected clubs, providing a member has paid all bills and fees, he will receive a "letter of good standing" upon departure from Korea. This letter will enable him to join another service-connected club without payment of an additional initiation fee.

b. A deposit of $50 will be charged to all members and must accompany the application for membership. The deposit will be refunded on departure or termination.

c. Dues are $8 per month, payable on the first of each month with a ten-day period of grace.

d. The Club has seven aircraft: One L-16 Aeronca Champ and four Cessna 150's primarily for student training; one Cessna 180 and one L-5 Stinson for use on cross-country flying by private or higher rated pilots. The rates including gas and oil are as follows:

L-16	$ 6 per hour
Cessna 150	$ 8 per hour
Cessna 180	$10 per hour.

3. INSTRUCTION:

a. The cost per hour for an instructor in all Club aircraft is $5. For example, the cost of one hour dual instruction in a Cessna 150 would be $13. The flight instructor is paid directly by the member. All instruction fees and aircraft costs are payable upon the termination of the flight.

b. The Club is open seven days a week, 0800 hours to sunset, with instructors available. Local flights may be scheduled two weeks in advance. Cross-country flights may be scheduled up to three months in advance.

4. AIRCRAFT INFORMATION:

The Club has one full-time A&P mechanic and one mechanic assistant. All maintenance, gas and oil are the responsibility of the Club except on extended cross-country flights out of country.

2

5. JOINING THE EIGHTH ARMY FLYING CLUB AND REQUIREMENTS FOR A PRIVATE PILOT'S LICENSE:

a. A new member will complete an application form and pay the initiation fee of $25 plus the $50 deposit and the $8 dues at the time of the application. The membership card will be furnished after the Board of Governors approve the application for membership. As soon as a new member has paid the above mentioned fees, he may schedule his first flight, called the orientation flight.

b. Dues are not prorated according to the day a new member joins due to the fact that no dues are collected during the month in which the member departs.

c. Federal Aviation Administration (FAA) regulations specify that a minimum of 40 hours are necessary before applying for a private pilot license. However, there is no guarantee that a member will become a rated pilot in this minimum time. The average student usually has logged between 50 to 60 hours before going for his flight check. Of the minimum 40 hours, a student must have 20 hours of solo flight time to include a minimum of 10 hours solo cross-country time.

d. All instruction is given in phases of dual and solo periods. An individual usually makes his first solo flight between 8 and 15 hours.

e. An estimated cost of obtaining a private pilot's license in the Club is approximately $500 for the aircraft and instructor. This compares very favorably with the $800 to $1,000 cost of the same instruction from civilian sources. The time element depends upon such factors as number of hours flown per week, individual capacity to absorb instruction, weather conditions, and aircraft availability. Usually allow from three to six months to complete the program.

THIS IS YOUR INVITATION TO COME TO THE CLUB. INSPECT OUR NEW FACILITIES, AND START A NEW AND REWARDING HOBBY. SEE YOU AT THE CLUB HOUSE LOCATED ON K-16 AIRFIELD (SEOUL EAST). THERE IS A FREE US ARMY BUS BETWEEN YONGSAN TERMINAL AND K-16 ABOUT EVERY TWO HOURS DAILY.

1 Incl
Private Pilot Course Outline

ROBERT J. KRIWANEK
Colonel, MPC
President

PRIVATE PILOT COURSE OUTLINE

PHASE I	Orientation and basic maneuvers; straight and level, climbs, glides, turns, slow flight, stalls, ground reference maneuvers, simulated emergency situations. References: FAR's Part 1, 61, 91 and 430; Kershner's Student Pilot Manual; AC 00-6 Aviation Weather; AC61-23 Private Pilot's Handbook of Aeronautical Knowledge.
PHASE II	Pre-solo take-offs and landings including power-off full stall landings; power approaches; cross-wind take-offs and landings and proper patterns for all approaches.
PREREQUISITES for PHASE III	Class III medical and pre-solo written test passed. Radio telephone permit required for CONUS flights.
PHASE III	Three supervised solo periods in the traffic pattern.
PHASE IV	Three unsupervised solo periods to include take-offs and landings and review of basic airwork.
PREREQUISITES for PHASE V	Proper use of the Airman's Information Manual, compass errors, omninavigation orientation, short and soft field take-offs and landings (see Kershner's Manual), aeronautical chart and symbol familiarization, radio frequency utilization and computer and plotter use, cruising altitudes and FAR's.
PHASE V	Dual cross-country flying; pilotage, dead reckoning and omninavigation including traffic patterns, fuel consumption, figuring ETA's and inflight emergencies.
PHASE VI	Solo cross-country flying; 10 hours required, one trip to include a leg at least 100 miles from point of departure.
PREREQUISITES for PHASE VII	Private pilot written test passed 70%.
PHASE VII	Review and preparation for private check ride including a review of all private pilot maneuvers required by FAR 91.
PHASE VIII	PRIVATE PILOT CHECK RIDE.

Incl 1

기 안 용 지

분류기호 문서번호	미이 723 -	(전화번호)	전결규정 조 항 국장 전결사항
처리기간			
시행일자			
보존년한		국 장	
보조기관	북미 2과장	협조	조약과장
기안책임자	권 찬	북미 2과 (72. 2. 15)	
경유 수신 참조	교통부장관	발송	통제
제 목	SOFA 제 13조 해석에 관한 질의		

발송 No. 5028 1972. 2. 18 외무부

검열 1972. 2. 18

대 : 항운 1554 - 1897

1. 대호로 요청하신 Flying Club 의 한.미간 주둔군 지위협정 제 13조에 의한 특권및 대한민국 항공법의 규제대상 여부에 대한 회신입니다.

가. 당부에서는 아래의 이유로 Flying Club 이 한.미간 주둔군 지위협정 제 13조 규정의 적용을 받는 비세출자금 기관의 하나로 해석합니다.

(1) 동 클럽은 다른 비세출 자금 기관과같이 군 당국이 공인하고 규제하는 사교클럽(A Social Club)의 하나이며,

(2) 동 클럽의 회원은 다른 비세출 자금 기관과같이 합중국 군대의 구성원, 군속, 초청계약자및 그들의 가족들로 구성되어 있으며,

(3) 동 클럽이 소유하고있는 재산및 비행기는 미 정부의 소유로

정서 관인 발송

33

32

공용서식 1-2(갑) 1967. 4. 4. 승인 190mm×268mm(1급인쇄용지70g/m²) 조달청 (500,000매인쇄)

되어있으며, 비행기는 미 합중국 연방항공국 (FAA) 에 의해 인가 (licensed)를 받고 있음.

나. 동 클럽이 한.미간 주둔군 지위협정 제 13조의 적용을 받으나, 동 클럽의 항공기와 탑승원은 주둔군 지위협정 제 2 - 6조 에 규정된 시설과 구역밖의 대한민국의 영토내와 영공에서 대한민국의 항공법을 포함한 적용 될수 있는 관계법령의 적용을 받게 되는 것으로 해석합니다.

다. 동 클럽 항공기의 표지에 관하여는 한.미간 주둔군 지위협정 제 24조 제 2항에 따라 명확한 번호표 또는 이를 용이하게 식별할수 있는 개별적인 기호를 붙여야함으로, 현재 사용하고 있는 미국표지를 주한미군 소속의 표지로 변경하여야 한다고 사료 합니다.

2. 상기 1 다 항에 관련하여 미측과 현재 협의중이며, 타결되는대로 추후 통보 하겠읍니다. 끝.

33

외 무 부

미이 723 - (70 - 2324) 72. 2. 18.

수신 : 교통부장관

제목 : SOFA 제 13조 해석에 관한 질의

대 : 항운 1554 - 1897

1. 대호로 요청하신 Flying Club 의 한.미간 주둔군 지위협정 제 13조 에 의한 특전및 대한민국 항공법의 규제대상 여부에 대한 회신입니다.

가. 당 부 에서는 아래의 이유로 Flying Club 이 한.미간 주둔군 지위협정 제 13조 규정의 적용을 받는 비세출자금 기관의 하나로 해석합니다.

(1) 동 클럽은 다른 비세출 자금 기관과같이 군 당국이 공인하고 규제하는 사교클럽 (A Social Club) 의 하나이며,

(2) 동 클럽의 회원은 다른 비세출자금 기관과같이 합중국 군대의 구성원, 군속, 초청계약자 및 그들의 가족들로 구성되어 있으며,

(3) 동 클럽이 소유하고있는 재산및 비행기는 미 정부의 소유로 되어있으며, 비행기는 미 합중국 연방항공국 (FAA) 에 의해 인가 (license)를 받고있음.

34

나. 동 클럽이 한.미간 주둔군 지위협정 제 13조의 적용을 받으나, 동 클럽의 항공기와 탑승원은 주둔군 지위협정 제 2 - 6조에 규정된 시설과 구역밖의 대한민국의 영토내와 영공에서 대한민국의 항공법을 포함한 적용될수 있는 관계 법령의 적용을 받게되는 것으로 해석합니다.

다. 동 클럽 항공기의 표지에 관하여는 한.미간 주둔군 지위협정 제 24조 제 2항에 따라 명확한 번호표 또는 이를 용이하게 식별할수 있는 개별적인 기호를 붙여야함으로, 현재 사용하고 있는 미국표지를 주한미군 소속의 표지로 변경하여야 한다고 사료 합니다.

2. 상기 1. 다. 항에 관련하여 미측과 현재 협의중 이며, 타결되는 대로 추후 통보 하겠읍니다. 끝.

외 무 부 장 관

35

공 란

ARMY REGULATION
No. 28-95

HEADQUARTERS
DEPARTMENT OF THE ARMY
WASHINGTON, D.C., 15 October 1968

WELFARE, RECREATION, AND MORALE
ARMY FLYING CLUB PROGRAM

Section I. GENERAL

1. Purpose and mission. This regulation authorizes the establishment of Army Flying Clubs and sets forth basic policies and procedures under which these clubs will function. This program will be conducted solely as an off-duty, voluntary participation program in the interest of welfare, recreation, and morale.

2. Scope. These policies and procedures are applicable in continental United States and Alaska. Other oversea commanders will be guided by this regulation and policies established by commanders of unified commands. Where conflicts exist, the policies of the unified commander will govern.

Section II. BASIC OPERATIONAL PRINCIPLES

3. Establishment. *a.* Army Flying Clubs may be established at installation level and operated as sundry fund activities on a self-supporting basis under the provisions of AR 230-5. These funds are Government instrumentalities and are entitled to limited assistance as stipulated in AR 210-55 and AR 420-80, including hangaring and/or tying down of aircraft at installations when adequate facilities and space are available.

b. Clubs will be organized under a constitution and bylaws which provide for their operation and dissolution in accordance with this regulation and other applicable regulations.

c. Local policies and regulations may be issued to insure that clubs operate smoothly, efficiently, and properly, provided the policies are consistent with this regulation and other applicable regulations.

d. Flying clubs established as private associations under the provisions of paragraph 1-2c, AR 230-5, do not fall within the purview of this regulation.

4. Membership. Membership will be voluntary and composed predominately of military personnel. Membership may be extended to the following categories of personnel subject to such further

*This regulation supersedes AR 28-95, 2 July 1964, including Change 1; letter, AGPN(M) (1 Dec 64) 4 December 1964, subject: Army Flying Club Program; letter, AGMS-A(M) (24 Jan 67), 2 February 1967, subject: Administration and Operation of Army Flying Clubs; DA message 844742, 21 December 1967, and rescinds Reports Control Symbol CAB-1001.

TAGO 422A—October 340-468°—68

37

restrictions as may be prescribed by installation commanders:

a. Active membership will be extended to military personnel on active duty.

b. Associate membership may be extended to—

(1) Retired military personnel.

(2) Adult dependents (16 years or older) of active duty military personnel.

(3) Civilian employees of Department of Defense paid from appropriated or nonappropriated funds.

(4) Members of the Armed Forces Reserve Components.

(5) Allied military personnel stationed in CONUS under the foreign student exchange program for a period greater than 90 days. Participation by allied military personnel is contingent upon—

(*a*) Sufficient fluency in the English language to assure effective air-ground communications and safe operation of aircraft (para 6*b* (1)(*g*) and (2) are applicable).

(*b*) Favorable recommendation by installation and major Army commanders of application submitted by each individual concerned. Individuals will include in their applications a signed and witnessed statement, prepared by the local staff judge advocate, relieving the flying club concerned and the United States Government of any liability or responsibility in the event of accidental injury or death of the applicant while participating in flying club activities.

(*c*) Specific approval, in each case, by The Adjutant General, Department of the Army, and the foreign government concerned.

5. Flight participation. The following individuals are authorized as passengers aboard Army Flying Club planes:

a. Active and associate members as defined in paragraph 4.

b. Dependents of active and associate members when the club plane is piloted by the sponsor member.

c. Other passengers are not authorized, except for persons whose official duties require them to be passengers, such as FAA inspectors, and civilian instructors hired by the local flying club.

6. Responsibility. *a.* Major Army field commands and The Surgeon General will—

(1) Assure that, where feasible, clubs are established at locations where the maximum number of interested personnel may participate. For this purpose, the establishment of flying clubs on a regional basis to cover all posts, camps, and stations located within a designated area is authorized.

(2) Allocate airplanes made available by the Department of the Army in a manner designed to meet the above requirements.

(3) Exercise control over all phases of this program.

(4) Notify The Adjutant General, ATTN: AGMS, Department of the Army, when airplanes allocated pursuant to (2) above and club-owned aircraft become excess to major command requirements (exempt report, para 7-2*a*, AR 335-15).

(5) Notify The Adjutant General, ATTN: AGMS, Department of the Army, when airplanes owned by or on loan to a club are transferred between flying clubs within the major command, and of other disposition (exempt report, para 7-2*o*, AR 335-15).

b. Installation commanders assigned the responsibility for flying clubs will—

(1) Supervise operations and administration to insure—

(*a*) That flight records reflect the names of passengers and are retained for a minimum period of 12 months for review by appropriate officials.

(*b*) That a custodian and board of governors are elected or appointed from the active membership.

(*c*) That an officer who is a rated pilot is appointed as club advisor to assist the club board of governors and custodian.

(*d*) That effective air and ground safety programs are followed.

(*e*) That clubs operate in an economical, efficient, and businesslike manner and are solvent at all times.

(*f*) That a reasonable radius of operations from the home field is established for the various club-operated aircraft. In establishing such boundaries, consideration will be given to terrain, type of aircraft, cruising range, population density, and the ability of the club to finance major repairs in commercial facilities or to defray shipping and transportation costs back to parent

TAGO 122A

38

installation if aircraft is not to be repaired at point of breakdown.

(g) Appropriate operational and administrative procedures are established and followed to insure maximum safety of flight. Cross-country flight plans will be filed with FAA or a military flight facility. Local flight plans will be filed and monitored at the home installation until the aircraft is returned. The rules and regulations of the FAA should be supplemented if required, based on flying experience available within the club.

(2) Assure that all personnel who fly or maintain airplanes belonging to or on loan to the clubs are appropriately licensed by the FAA and that all flying clubs maintain an up-to-date roster of club pilots showing their proficiency and physical flight qualifications.

(3) Provide equitable opportunity for all eligible personnel to take part in flying club activities.

(4) Notify The Adjutant General, ATTN: AGMS, Department of the Army, of the establishment or dissolution of flying clubs within their command (exempt report, para 7-2o, AR 335-15).

7. Property. *a. Club-owned.*

(1) Acquisition through procurement, contributions and donations will be made in accordance with AR 230-5.

(2) Classification and accountability will be in accordance with AR 230-65.

(3) Disposition will be in accordance with AR 230-60 as authorized by The Adjutant General, ATTN: AGMS, Department of the Army, after such aircraft has been determined excess to all Army Flying Clubs.

b. Government-loaned.

(1) Aircraft determined to be excess to requirements of the established Army supply program will be made available to major commands on a nonreimbursable basis. Planes will be moved from their present location at no expense to the Government.

(2) At installation level, these airplanes will be reflected in TDA as prescribed in AR 310-49 and accounted for in accordance with procedures specified in AR 735-35, and will be loaned to established flying clubs as Government-owned portable equipment.

(3) Title to this property will remain with the Government, but airplanes will be licensed by the FAA.

(4) Disposition. Aircraft determined to be excess to The Adjutant General, ATTN: AGMS, Department of the Army will be turned in to the installation supply officer for processing in accordance with AR 755-1, or, if authorized in writing by the installation supply officer, may be turned in to the nearest property disposal officer.

c. Station property officers may request surplus aircraft from the appropriate General Services Administration Regional Office. Any aircraft received through this source will be accounted for in the same manner as aircraft loaned to flying clubs.

8. Supply and maintenance. *a.* After an aircraft is transferred to the installation supply officer for assignment to flying clubs, maintenance and repair will become the responsibility of the individual flying club. Repair parts may be obtained by purchase from commercial sources, or by purchase through a property disposal sales office, at no cost to the Government, in the same manner as authorized the general public, or by transfer from a property disposal officer as authorized by AR 755-21.

b. Communications, electronic navigation equipment, and their respective repair parts, determined to be excess to the Department of the Army supply program requirements may, upon approval of the installation commander, be transferred to flying clubs when considered necessary in the interest of safety. Such items will be furnished to the flying clubs on a reimbursable basis and Army accountability will be dropped at the time of transfer.

9. Petroleum products. Procedures for procurement of petroleum products for Army Flying Clubs will be in accordance with AR 210-58.

Section III. SPECIFIC OPERATIONAL PRINCIPLES

10. Federal Aviation Administration. All airplanes utilized by Army Flying Clubs and all personnel flying, maintaining, giving, or undergoing instructions will be appropriately certified by the FAA. Installation commanders are responsible to insure that Federal Aviation Regulations in parts 61- and 91- will be strictly adhered to by club members.

11. **Pilot/Operator Aircraft Accident Report, General Aviation Aircraft, RCS DOT-1001.** Accidents incident to flight involving fatality, serious injury and/or damage exceeding $300 will be reported to the National Transportation Safety Board in accordance with part 320, National Transportation Safety Board Regulations. One additional copy will be prepared and forwarded to The Adjutant General, ATTN: AGMS, Department of the Army, Washington, D.C. 20315.

12. **Insurance.** Insurance coverage of all aircraft owned or leased by Army Flying Clubs or Government aircraft on loan to Army Flying Clubs will be in accordance with AR 230-8.

13. **Administration.** Administration of Army Flying Club sundry funds will be in accordance with applicable provisions of AR 230-60 and AR 230-65.

The proponent agency of this regulation is The Adjutant General's Office. Users are invited to send comments and suggested improvements to The Adjutant General, ATTN: AGMS, Department of the Army, Washington, D.C. 20315.

By Order of the Secretary of the Army:

W. C. WESTMORELAND,
General, United States Army,
Chief of Staff.

Official:
KENNETH G. WICKHAM,
Major General, United States Army,
The Adjutant General.

Distribution:

To be distributed in accordance with DA Form 12-9 requirements for AR, Welfare, Recreation and Morale:

Active Army: C (Quan Rqr Block No. 58).
ARNG: D (Quan Rqr Block No. 59).
USAR: C (Quan Rqr Block No. 58).

U.S. GOVERNMENT PRINTING OFFICE:1970

공 란

공 란

공 란

공 란

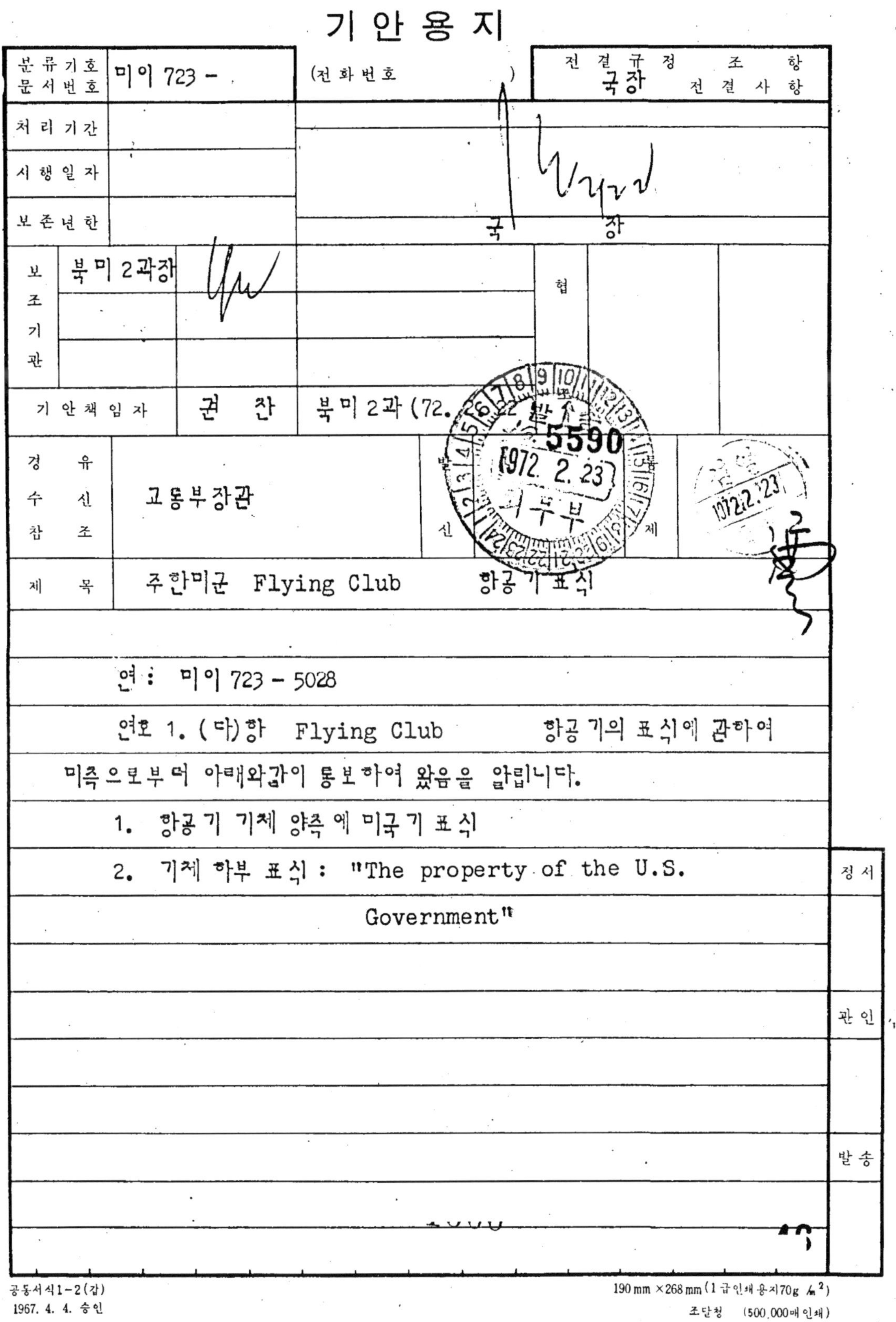

기 안 용 지

분류기호 문서번호	미이 723 -	(전화번호)	전결규정 조 항 국장 전결사항
처리기간			
시행일자			
보존년한		국 장	
보조기관	북미 2과장		협
기안책임자	권 찬	북미 2과 (72. 2. 22)	
경유 수신 참조	교통부장관	발신 1972. 2. 23 외무부 5590	1972. 2. 23
제목	주한미군 Flying Club 항공기 표식		

연 : 미이 723 - 5028

연호 1. (다)항 Flying Club 항공기의 표식에 관하여 미측으로부터 아래와같이 통보하여 왔음을 알립니다.

1. 항공기 기체 양측에 미국기 표식

2. 기체 하부 표식 : "The property of the U.S. Government"

정서 관인 발송

공동서식1-2(갑)
1967. 4. 4. 승인

190mm × 268mm (1급인쇄용지70g/m²)
조달청 (500,000매인쇄)

45

외 무 부

미이 723 - 72. 2. 23.

수신 : 교통부장관

제목 : 주한미군 Flying Club 항공기 표식

연 : 미이 723 - 5028

연호 1. (다)항 Flying Club 항공기의 표식에 관하여 미측으로부터 아래와같이 통보하여 왔음을 알립니다.

1. 항공기 기체 양측에 미국기 표식.

2. 기체 하부 표식 :

"The property of the U.S. Government." 끝.

외 무 부 장 관

46

공 란

공 란

공 란

공　　　　란

공 란

공 란

공 란

공 란

공 란

공 란

공 란

공 란

공 란

공 란

공 란

공　　　란

Friday, October 20, 1972 The Japan Times 3

Japan-U.S. Group Will Look Into Tank Issue

The Foreign Ministry announced Thursday that Japan and the United States had agreed to set up a subcommittee under the Joint Japan-U.S. Committee to study the question of heavy-duty U.S. military vehicles' passage on Japanese roads.

The subcommittee will deal with U.S. military vehicles, 2.5 meters or more in width, 12 meters or more in length, and 20 tons or more in weight, Foreign Ministry officials said.

The subcommittee will approve U.S. applications for passage of such vehicles on Japanese roads if the roads can withstand the load, they said.

Otherwise, the Japanese side will ask the U.S. to take necessary steps to ensure safe transportation, they added.

The subcommittee will consist of officials from the Construction and Foreign ministries and from the U.S. forces in Japan. It will start functioning early next week, they said.

As a provisionary step, officials of the joint Japan-U.S. committee Thursday approved the transport of large general cargo trucks from the U.S. Supply and Maintenance Activity at Sagamihara to Yokohama Port.

Meanwhile, chief Cabinet Secretary Susumu Nikaido quoted the U.S. side as saying it would be prepared to consider a Japanese request, if made, concerning scaling down and eventual closure of repair facilities for Vietnam-bound combat vehicles at the U.S. supply depot.

On Wednesday U.S. Embassy officials told reporters that the U.S. had no intention of reducing or stopping such activities.

3. 1973 년

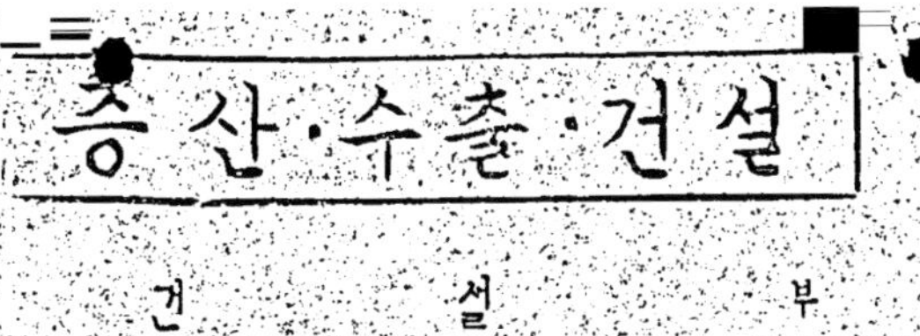

건 설 부

노정 431- 1935 23.3904 (70-4101) 1973. 6. 8.

수신 외무부장관

참조 구미국장

제목 미군용 차량 안전운행

한국도로공사 사장보고에 의하면 군간에 미군용 차량중에 고속도로상에서 과속주행 집단노견 정차등을 하는 사례가 빈번히 발생하고 있다는바 한미안전분과위원회(안전조사반)에 다음 사항이 준수되도록 조치하여 주시기 바랍니다.

다 음

1. 톨게이트 진출입시의 일단 멈춤
2. 집단 노견 정차
3. 규제속도위반. 끝.

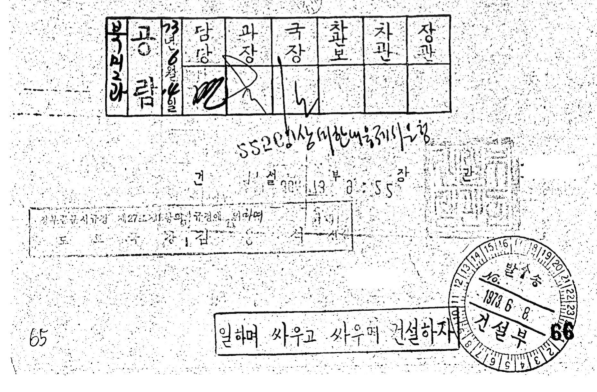

북미2과	공람	73년 6월 14일	담당	과장	국장	참관보	차관	장관
			(서명)	(서명)	(서명)			

SS2C에 대한 세출 요청

건 설 부 장 관

정부공문서규정 제27조제1항단서 규정에 의하여
도로국장 김 석

No. 발송 1973.6.8. 건설부

일하며 싸우고 싸우며 건설하자

65 66

고속도로 상의 미군차량 사고건수

1973. 5. 30. 현재

일 시	장 소	원 인	형 태	비 고
73. 1. 19.	경부 142.8km 하행선	조작미숙	추돌	트럭 (미장거미통신대 4H 1403 B 39)
73. 2. 1.	" 305.5km 상행선	과속	전복	
73. 2. 8.	" 97.4km 상행선	부당회전	추돌	3/4t A21 F31-B2
73. 3. 4.	" 131.6km 하행선	과속	도로외 추락	트레일타P 269,702 -128
73. 3. 22.	경인 10 km 상행선	조작미숙	시설물 충돌	트럭 B-79 (미8군)
73. 3. 30.	경부 299.7km 상행선	다이어마쓰	도로외 추락	3/4t, K-2 (대구)
73. 4. 3.	경부 330.5 km 하행선	다이어마쓰	추돌	승용차GNP -55 (미8군)
73. 4. 13.	" 139.5 km 상행선	부당정차	추돌	앰불란스
73. 5. 1.	경인 21 km 상행선	조작미숙	시설물 충돌	트럭
73. 5. 1.	경부 285.1 km 하행선	미상	도로외 추락	승용차
73. 5. 7.	경부 24.5km 하행선	과속 및 조향장치 고장	전복	
73. 5. 7.	" 7.8 km 상행선	과속	시설물 충돌	
73. 5. 7.	" 28.5km 하행선	과속	추돌	트럭
73. 5. 10.	" 230.6km 하행선	운행중 흡연	화재	트럭

66

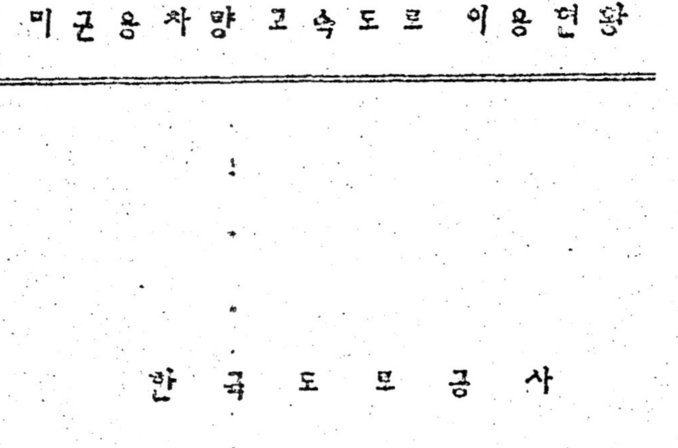

미군용차량 고속도로 이용현황

한 국 도 로 공 사

미군용차량 고속도로 이용 현황('73.1-'73.6)

구분		차종별 이용 차량대수								계
		1종	2종	3종	4종	5종	6종	7종	8종	
1월	서울-부산	4,761	4,550	513	1,931	3,556	5,911	660	2,197	24,079
	대전-전주	162	77	3	1	138	164	10	22	577
	신갈-새말	380	202	78	5	433	219	7	2	1,326
	서울-인천	2,934	2,219	632	1,142	3,528	4,186	458	1,387	16,486
	계	8,237	7,048	1,226	3,079	7,655	10,480	1,135	3,608	42,468
2월	서울-부산	4,151	4,092	512	1,879	3,466	5,368	656	1,789	21,913
	대전-전주	131	54	3	0	134	131	11	22	486
	신갈-새말	469	213	44	25	473	159	4	3	1,390
	서울-인천	2,947	2,478	875	1,152	3,331	3,961	480	1,220	16,444
	계	7,698	6,837	1,434	3,056	7,404	9,619	1,151	3,034	40,233
3월	서울-부산	4,981	4,759	619	2,016	3,864	5,903	708	2,206	25,056
	대전-전주	168	61	1	7	154	137	7	23	558
	신갈-새말	568	227	41	48	586	286	5	1	1,762

70

구 분		차종별 이용 차량대수								계
		1종	2종	3종	4종	5종	6종	7종	8종	
	서울-인천	3,303	2,741	718	1,251	3,656	4,737	615	1,407	18,428
	계	9,020	7,788	1,379	3,322	8,260	11,063	1,335	3,637	45,804
4월	서울-부산	5,060	4,751	506	2,043	4,085	6,180	651	2,407	25,683
	대전-전주	146	74	3	5	194	110	5	19	556
	신갈-새말	581	241	34	43	673	207	6	0	1,785
	서울-인천	3,071	2,375	692	1,125	3,170	4,297	512	1,335	16,577
	계	8,858	7,441	1,235	3,216	8,122	10,794	1,174	3,761	44,601
5월	서울-부산	4,954	4,990	532	2,254	4,570	5,964	655	2,663	26,582
	대전-전주	139	87	0	8	186	95	6	16	537
	신갈-새말	571	277	40	70	685	256	9	8	1,916
	서울-인천	2,792	2,304	613	1,023	2,824	4,146	504	1,046	15,252
	계	8,456	7,658	1,185	3,355	8,265	10,461	1,174	3,733	44,287

구분		차종별 이용 차량 대수								계
		1종	2종	3종	4종	5종	6종	7종	8종	
6월	서울-부산	4,499	4,816	553	1,915	4,200	5,976	744	2,228	24,931
	대전-전주	147	84	0	4	200	171	7	13	626
	신갈-새말	544	311	56	46	685	202	7	1	1,852
	서울-인천	2,594	2,069	666	898	2,425	3,389	434	896	13,371
	계	7,784	7,280	1,275	2,863	7,510	9,738	1,192	3,138	40,780
합계		50,053	44,052	7,734	18,891	47,216	62,155	7,161	20,911	258,173

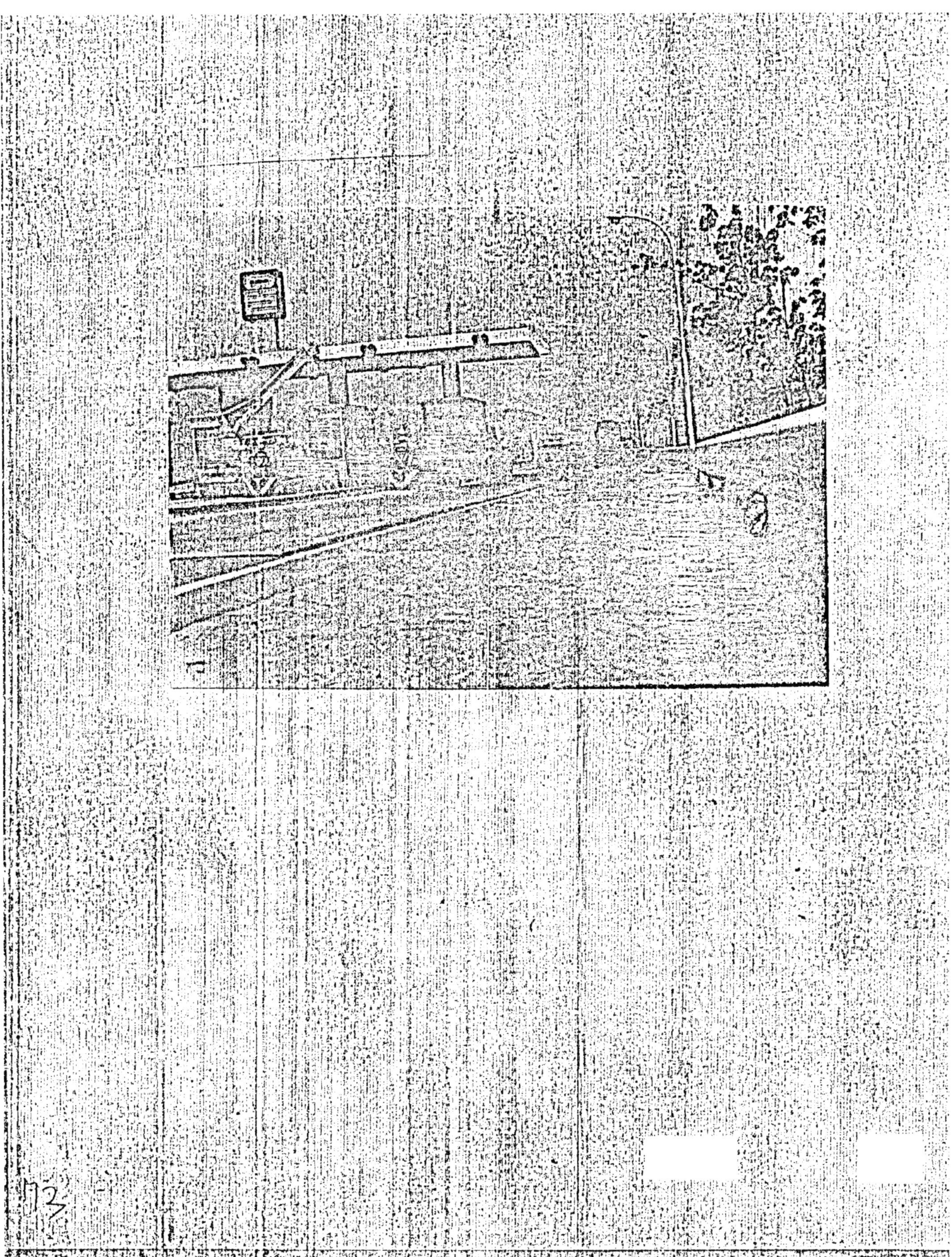

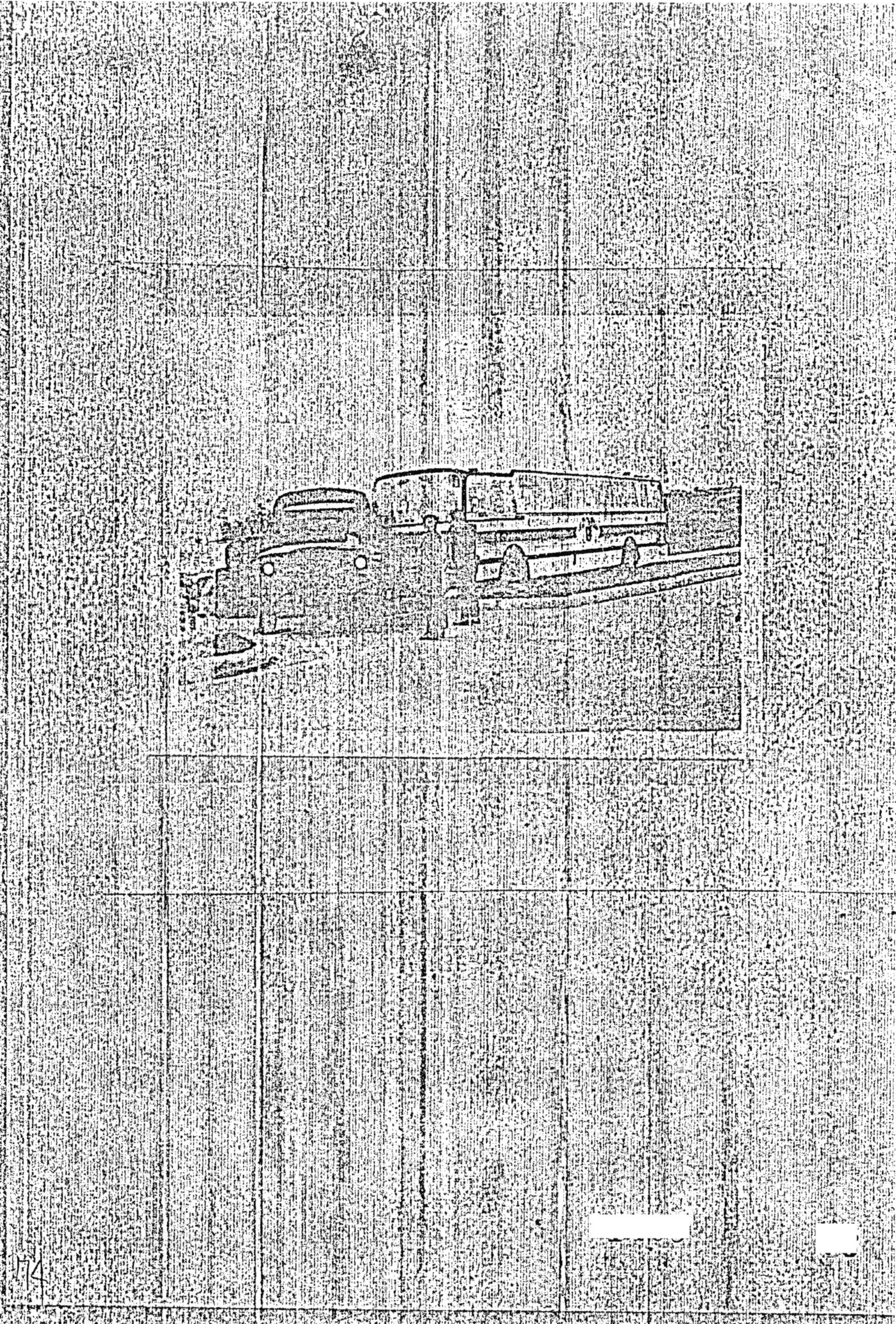

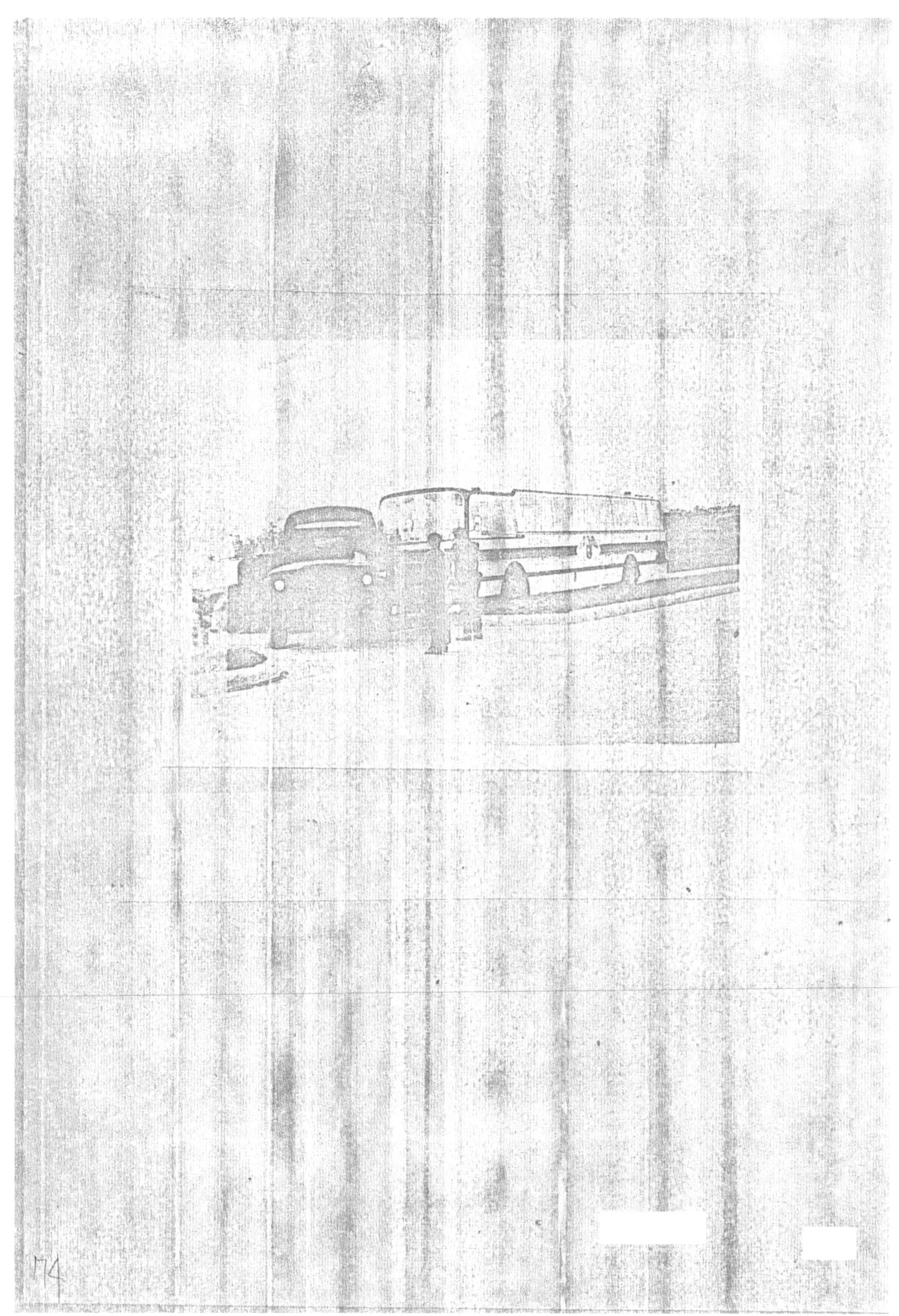

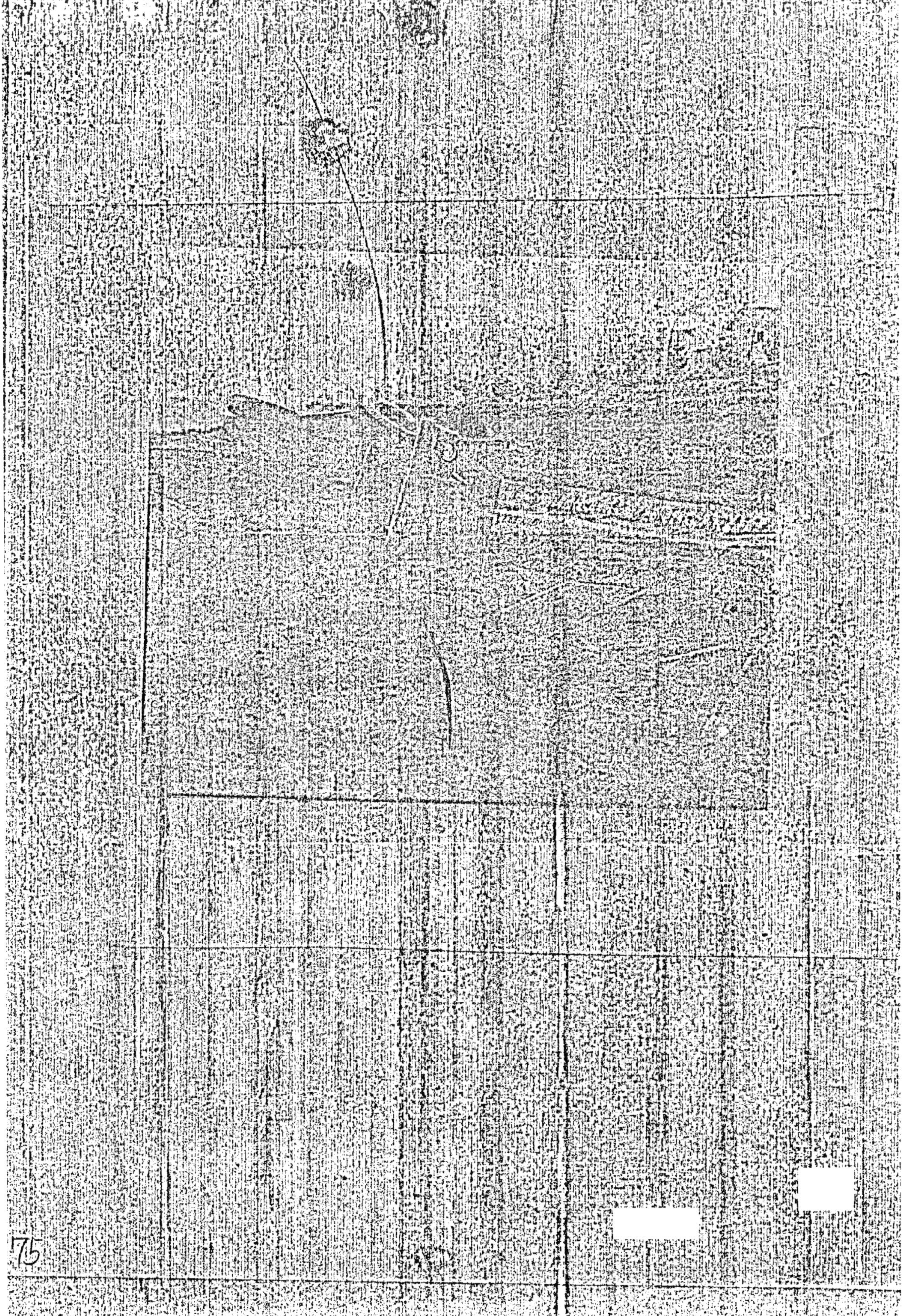

77

Parking on shoulder

5. 노견정차

178

Parking on shoulder

5. 노견정차

178

공 란

공 란

공 란

공 란

공 란

공 란

공 란

공 란

공 란

공 란

공 란

공　　란

공 란

공 란

공 란

한 국 도 로 공 사

영업안제 110 호 (23-3904) 1973. 7. 31.

수신 미8군사령관

제목 사고 발생 통보

73.7.28.14:40분경 서울-부산간 고속도로 서울기점 26.5키로 좌행선에서 38BDE DAIC-7 소속 64A 93868호 차량에 탑승한 미군 17명이 작업중인 당사 소속 작업원 조 동운에게 아무 이유도 없이 돌20여개를 던져서 부상을 입힌 사실을 통보하오니 앞으로 이러한 사례가 발생하지 않도록 조치하여 주시기 바라며, 부상자의 치료비는 의사의 진단에 따라 별도로 청구하겠읍니다. 끝.

사 장 박 기

94

KOREA HIGHWAY CORPORATION
Seoul, Korea

CPN-S 110 (Tel: 23-3904) 31 July 1973

SUBJECT: Report of Incident

Commander
Eighth United States Army
APO 96301

This report of incident is forwarded for your information and action.

At approximately 1440 hours, 28 July 1973, seventeen members of the US Army, riding on a motor vehicle, #64A 93868, 38BDE MAIC-7, threw some 20 rocks at CHO, Chong Yun, who is an employee of this corporation, while he was at work at the time, without any provocation from him, resulting in his sustaining injury. The incident occurred on the Seoul-Pusan Expressway, 26.5 kilometers South of Seoul. The vehicle was traveling south.

The victim's medical bill will be forwarded to you after he is examined by a medical doctor.

Sincerely,

OFFICIAL SEAL OF THE:

PRESIDENT, KOREA HIGHWAY CORPORATION
PAK, KI SOK

Translated by; Mr. KIM, Yong Hyok, Crim Inves, KGS-9, EAPM-I, 7 Aug 73

95

공 란

공 란

공 란

공 란

공 란

공 란

공 란

공 란

공 란

공 란

공 란

공 란

공 란

공 란

공 란

공 란

공 란

공 란

공　란

공 란

공 란

공 란

공 란

공　　　란

공 란

공 란

공 란

공 란

공 란

공　　　란

공 란

공　　란

공　　　란

공 란

공　　　란

공 란

공 란

공 란

공 란

공 란

공 란

외교문서 비밀해제: 주한미군지위협정(SOFA) 33
주한미군지위협정(SOFA) 재무 · 상무 · 교통 분과위원회 2

초판인쇄 2024년 03월 15일
초판발행 2024년 03월 15일

지은이 한국학술정보(주)
펴낸이 채종준
펴낸곳 한국학술정보(주)
주 소 경기도 파주시 회동길 230(문발동)
전 화 031-908-3181(대표)
팩 스 031-908-3189
홈페이지 http://ebook.kstudy.com
E-mail 출판사업부 publish@kstudy.com
등 록 제일산-115호(2000. 6. 19)

ISBN 979-11-7217-044-8 94340
979-11-7217-011-0 94340 (set)

책에 대한 더 나은 생각, 끊임없는 고민, 독자를 생각하는 마음으로 보다 좋은 책을 만들어갑니다.